DATE OF RETURN
UNLESS RECALLED BY LIBRARY

PLEASE TAKE GOOD CARE OF THIS BOOK

PAPAL MUSIC AND MUSICIANS IN
LATE MEDIEVAL AND RENAISSANCE ROME

Papal Music and Musicians in Late Medieval and Renaissance Rome

Edited by
RICHARD SHERR

CLARENDON PRESS · OXFORD
IN ASSOCIATION WITH
LIBRARY OF CONGRESS, WASHINGTON

This book has been printed digitally and produced in a standard specification
in order to ensure its continuing availability

OXFORD
UNIVERSITY PRESS

Great Clarendon Street, Oxford OX2 6DP

Oxford University Press is a department of the University of Oxford.
It furthers the University's objective of excellence in research, scholarship,
and education by publishing worldwide in

Oxford New York

Auckland Bangkok Buenos Aires Cape Town Chennai
Dar es Salaam Delhi Hong Kong Istanbul Karachi Kolkata
Kuala Lumpur Madrid Melbourne Mexico City Mumbai Nairobi
São Paulo Shanghai Taipei Tokyo Toronto

Oxford is a registered trade mark of Oxford University Press
in the UK and in certain other countries

Published in the United States
by Oxford University Press Inc., New York

ISBN 0-19-816417-3

Cover illustration:
Capella Sistina 4 fol. 3ᵛ. Reproduced by kind permission of Biblioteca Vaticana, Rome.

To the memory of Howard Mayer Brown

FOREWORD

By James H. Billington
Librarian of Congress

I N January of 1993 the Library of Congress opened an extraordinary exhibition of treasures from the Vatican Library. Entitled 'Rome Reborn: The Vatican Library and Renaissance Culture', the exhibition portrayed in stunning breadth the important contribution of the papacy to cultural and intellectual life in the Renaissance. More than 250 items—illuminated manuscripts, early printed books, musical scores, maps, and writings of the shapers of European history—testified to the active role of the papacy in the flowering of human creativity in all disciplines that occurred in this period.

Among the most striking items in the exhibition were the musical scores and texts. Beautifully illuminated chant manuscripts, early polyphonic masses and motets, engravings and documents depicting the daily lives of musicians, correspondence and treatises by early music theorists—all confirmed the importance and pervasiveness of music in the papal court and in the larger religious and secular community. This unprecedented assemblage of key musical documents of the Renaissance, surrounded by so many of the treasures of the period, called for a special convening of music scholars.

On 1–3 April 1993 the Library of Congress hosted a symposium, 'Music, Musicians, and Musical Culture in Renaissance Rome', to advance our understanding of the influence of the papacy in a seminal period of human history. Full credit for the planning of the symposium goes to Professor Richard Sherr of Smith College, Dr Norma Baker, the Library's Director of Development, and Dr James Pruett, former Chief of the Music Division of the Library. Together they assembled the most eminent musicologists and historians of the Renaissance era to present papers, and to share and synthesize ideas. The high level of scholarship represented at the symposium is preserved in this volume with the contributions of these distinguished scholars.

The Vatican Library and the Library of Congress have a special relationship that dates back to the 1920s and 1930s, when the Library of Congress, supported by a grant from the Carnegie Endowment for International Peace, sent teams of technical experts to assist in the modernization of the Vatican Library's technical operations. The loan of priceless treasures for 'Rome Reborn', which was seen by thousands of visitors and which still exists in electronic form on the Internet, was the Vatican Library's generous way of saying 'thank you'. This volume, which significantly extends our understanding of the influence of the papacy on world history, is another fruit of this special friendship and of the mutual respect of two great cultural institutions.

PREFACE

THIS volume had its genesis in the conference 'Music, Musicians, and Musical Culture in Renaissance Rome', held at the Library of Congress on 1–3 April 1993 in conjunction with the exhibition 'Rome Reborn: The Vatican Library and Renaissance Culture'. Under the general curatorship of Anthony Grafton, who edited the catalogue with the same title (1993), this exhibition of manuscript and printed treasures from the Vatican Library was the first of a series at the Library of Congress honouring great libraries of the world, and inaugurated the magnificent restoration of the Jefferson Building of the Library. Along with Norma Baker, Director of Development of the Library of Congress, I had the pleasure of co-curating the music section of the exhibition, and it was from discussions concerning that project that an idea of a conference on music in Renaissance Rome (meaning the period from the re-establishment of the papacy in the city in the late fourteenth century to the end of the sixteenth) emerged. Nineteen distinguished scholars participated in paper sessions and a round-table discussion held in the ornate Congressional Reading Room of the Jefferson Building; in addition the Capella Alamire, directed by Peter Urquhart, provided an excellent concert of mass movements from Vatican manuscripts performed from the original notation. One sad note was the absence of Howard Mayer Brown, whose untimely death had occurred shortly before the conference was to begin; the brief appreciation of Howard's life that opened the conference is included in this volume, which is dedicated to his memory.

The contents of this volume, however, does not follow the order of the conference programme, nor does it contain all the papers presented. For various reasons, some of the participants were unable to submit contributions; to fill this lacuna, I have added an essay myself and asked John Nádas, who chaired one of the conference sessions, to submit one as well (he responded with an article co-authored with Giuliano Di Bacco). I have divided the twelve contributions into three areas: Music for the Pope and his Chapel, the Papal Choir as Institution, and Studies of Individuals. The somewhat shorter contributions to the Round Table on the papal choir are interspersed with articles that had their origins in the papers read at the conference sessions. The order within each group is approximately chronological.

Although the conference title emphasized the city of Rome as a focus of discussion, most of the conference participants, and all the contributors to this volume, chose to concentrate on the papal court and its main musical institution, the choir of the papal chapel (this was also the focus of the music section of the exhibition). Hence the difference in titles between the Conference and this volume. The first essays deal with music for popes and for the papal chapel in the fourteenth to sixteenth centuries. It turns out, coincidentally, that all these authors ask in some way the same question: to what extent did the papal choir really perform the elaborate polyphony that has always been our major scholarly interest? What exactly was the repertory of the papal singers; in particular, what was it before it became codified (or ossified) in the seventeenth and eighteenth centuries? Margaret Bent offers a wide-ranging survey of motets written specifically for popes from the beginning of the fourteenth century to the beginning of the fifteenth (a period encompassing the Avignonese papacy and the Great Schism). Through careful analysis of texts and extant music, she proposes dates of composition and possible reasons for the production of these works. However, this music was not necessarily composed to be sung during the liturgy (presumably by the papal chapel); indeed Bent argues against the notion that motets in honour of popes were written to be performed at their coronations. And she points out that a complicated motet for John XXII (1316–34), whose bull *Docta Sanctorum* of 1324/5 notoriously bans the very type of polyphony represented by this piece, could hardly have pleased that pope or his musical advisers. Giuliano Di Bacco and John Nádas identify a large number of previously unknown singers employed in the papal choir in the era of the Great Schism (1378–1417), and provide new information about two important composers connected with the curia or cardinals resident in Rome (Antonio Zacara da Teramo and Johannes Ciconia). They also find polyphony related to the papacy in a number of little-known manuscripts. But while this, as they convincingly argue, points to the papal orbit (which in this period did not necessarily mean Rome) as an important musical centre that has been undervalued, it does not entirely follow that the music was performed by or written for the papal chapel, although some of it probably was. Alejandro Planchart agrees, reminding us that there were many good singers in the papal chapel of the early fifteenth century, but few who were composers. Considering one of these, he concludes that the music Du Fay could have composed specifically for the papal chapel probably consisted of examples of 'simple' substitute polyphony (Kyries and hymns), not complicated mass settings or motets. This somewhat negative outlook is taken up by Adalbert Roth, who places the beginning of the cultivation of elaborate polyphony in the end of the reign of Sixtus IV (1472–84) or even later.

Jeffrey Dean and Mitchell Brauner survey the repertory of the papal singers in the period of their greatest glory (the late fifteenth and the sixteenth centuries). In these years, there is much evidence of interest in contemporary large-scale settings of masses and motets in the manuscript collection of the *fondo* Cappella Sistina of the Vatican Library, accompanied by a steady stream of important composers (Weerbecke, Josquin, Arcadelt, Morales, and so on) as members of the papal choir. But as Dean and also Roth point out, the preservation of works in bound manuscripts is not necessarily an indication of their place in a continuous repertory. Indeed, the very act of the compilation of large choirbooks of polyphony may testify to the ephemeral nature of a repertory that was used up very quickly. However, Dean and Brauner argue that there are traces in papal chapel sources of a canon of specific works or of a tradition. For instance, Du Fay's hymn cycle of the 1430s was recopied with many contemporary additions into a manuscript of the 1490s; this can only point to an ongoing tradition of singing these hymns long after they were composed. Dean considers further in detail a curious polyphonic setting of 'Lumen ad Revelationem': the Vatican manuscript source is of the sixteenth century but its origins clearly lie in the early fifteenth. This he presents as an example of a true canonic work. Taking a slightly different view of the same question, Brauner identifies what he calls 'traditions'; that is categories of works rather than individual pieces that made up a continuous repertory, such as non-alternatim Magnificats, Lamentations, and certain types of mass settings.

The conclusion that can be drawn from these studies is a paradoxical one for modern scholars, namely that the music the papal choir valued most, that is, the music that became a long-standing part of the repertory, is the music we value least. Substitution polyphony for the offices (which the authors demonstrate to have been the core of the canon and tradition of the papal choir) never receives the sustained treatment that masses and motets do in scholarly discourse. Yet the masses and motets over which we enthuse were precisely the pieces that were considered expendable, constantly to be replaced. And overshadowing all these in terms of the sheer amount of time devoted to its performance was Gregorian chant, not, to be sure, the Gregorian chant of the tenth century, but that of the fifteenth and sixteenth. As Roth observes, chant was the 'daily bread' of the papal singers; in the fifteenth century, it was apparently considered to be more important than polyphony. Yet the study of the music and performance traditions of chant in this period has only now begun. Perhaps it is time that we stopped thinking that not finding an emphasis on the polyphony we admire produces, as Planchart puts it, a 'slightly melancholy picture', or engenders, as I put it, a 'negative outlook'. Obviously, the singers of the time thought differently.

The next contributions concern themselves with singers and musicians as individuals and as members of corporate entities. Pamela Starr explores the realm of the *per obitum* supplication, the legal means through which clerics began the process of devouring benefices left vacant by their recently deceased colleagues (sometimes even before they died). These provide useful information about the deceased and sometimes about the supplicant; Starr offers several case studies, one of them leading to the true identity of the composer Vincenet. My own contribution relates a chapter in the history of the corporate entity formed by the singers in the papal choir, the College of Singers, when, in a move dear to the secret hearts of all college faculties, they successfully outmanœuvred and contrived the removal of their hated appointed administrator, the *maestro di cappella*.

The final contributions concern individual composers and singers who were (or have been posited to have been) at some time members of the papal choir. James Haar investigates the masses of Josquin published in Petrucci's *Misse Josquin* of 1502 in an effort to determine which of them were preserved in Vatican manuscripts with readings so removed from Petrucci's as to be unrelated to the print, and therefore possibly close to Josquin himself (he was a member of the papal choir from 1489 to *c*.1495). He concludes that the Vatican versions may indeed 'speak to, or at least hint of, the composer's presence in the papal city'. Lewis Lockwood discusses an episode in the career of one of the most famous singers of his time, Antonio Collebaudi known as Bidon, who was enticed away from Ferrara to Rome in 1516 by Pope Leo X. As sometimes happens, this bold career move did not exactly work out as planned, and Lockwood presents two remarkable letters from the singer to Duke Alfonso I of Ferrara in which Bidon tries to wangle his way back into the duke's good graces. He failed; apparently, he grossly overestimated the ability of a musical virtuoso to manipulate the truly powerful, a lesson, as Lockwood observes, that is not out of place today.

Next, in what may be the most controversial of the essays, Louise Litterick looks at a composer who has long been thought to have been a member of the papal choir. Ninot le Petit has been identified with the Johannes Baltazar alias Petit who joined the choir in 1488 and died in 1502. This identification has resulted in a theory about the origins of the type of music in which Ninot excelled, the 'four-part arrangement' or new-style French chanson of the late fifteenth and early sixteenth centuries. Since Ninot/Baltazar was in Italy precisely at this time, it stands to reason that this quintessentially French popular form was in fact developed not in France but by French composers resident in Italy, specifically Rome. But what if Ninot is not Baltazar? Mustering evidence from biography, source studies, and musical style, Litterick argues that Ninot cannot have been the papal singer, that in fact he must be a French composer who remained in France in the period in which the new-style chanson was being created. If this is so, then we need a different theory about the origins of the new style.

Finally, Jessie Ann Owens looks at the most famous composer associated with the papal choir, Giovanni Pierluigi da Palestrina, and asks the question: how did Palestrina compose? Evaluating documentary evidence as well as corrections in the few extant Palestrina autographs, she concludes that he did not use a score while composing, even though scores were not a novelty in the late sixteenth century, and that he seems to have employed the lute as a vehicle for trying out works, or even for composing them. And with this discussion of a Roman musician who lived practically to the turn of the seventeenth century, the volume comes to a close.

R.S.

ACKNOWLEDGEMENTS

I SHOULD like to thank the members of the staff of the Library of Congress who were instrumental in organizing and supporting the Conference that was the progenitor of this volume, in particular Dr James H. Billington, Librarian of Congress, Norma Baker, Director of Development, and her assistant Jan Lauridsen, James Pruett, then Chief of the Music Division of the Library of Congress, and Michele Glymph, also of the Music Division. Thanks also to John Nádas, Richard Wexler, and James Pruett, who chaired the sessions at the conference, and to all who attended. A special thanks is owed to Bonnie J. Blackburn for her insightful editing.

CONTENTS

PART I. MUSIC FOR THE POPE AND HIS CHAPEL

LIST OF ILLUSTRATIONS

PLATES

(between pp. 132 and 133)

FIGURES

LIST OF TABLES

LIST OF MUSICAL EXAMPLES

LIST OF CONTRIBUTORS

Margaret Bent received her doctorate from Cambridge University and is Fellow of All Souls College, Oxford. Her extensive publications on major French, English, and Italian composers, repertories, manuscripts, and notational problems of the fourteenth and fifteenth centuries include *Dunstaple* and (with Andrew Hughes) the edition of *The Old Hall Manuscript*. She has also taught at Brandeis University and at Princeton University, and is a past President of the American Musicological Society.

Mitchell P. Brauner received his Ph.D. from Brandeis University and is Associate Professor of Music at the University of Wisconsin, Milwaukee. He has published articles on the repertory of the Sistine Chapel in the later sixteenth century and is preparing a monograph on the manuscripts copied by the papal scribe Johannes Parvus.

Jeffrey Dean received his Ph.D. from the University of Chicago with a dissertation on 'The Scribes of the Sistine Chapel, 1501–1527'; the Sistine Chapel sources provide a point of departure for most of his research. He has been a Fellow of the American Academy in Rome. He is currently a freelance editor, book designer, and typesetter in Manchester, England.

Giuliano Di Bacco received his Laurea from the University of Bologna in 1990, his Ph.D. in Musical Philology from the University of Pavia in 1996, and was a Fellow of the Villa I Tatti, Florence in 1996–7. He has published studies on Florentine music of the Middle Ages and on the transmission of Trecento music theory, and for a number of years has collaborated with John Nádas on a documentary history of the papal chapels during the Great Schism.

James Haar received his Ph.D. from Harvard University and is Professor of Music Emeritus at the University of North Carolina at Chapel Hill. His many publications on Renaissance topics include *Essays on Italian Poetry and Music* and (with Iain Fenlon) *The Italian Madrigal in the Early Sixteenth Century: Sources and Interpretation*. He is a past President of the American Musicological Society.

Louise Litterick received her Ph.D. from New York University and is Associate Professor of Music at Mt. Holyoke College. Her research has concentrated on the French chanson and its transmission in the fifteenth and sixteenth centuries, and she has also published on Brahms and Schubert.

Lewis Lockwood received his Ph.D. from Princeton University and is Fanny Peabody Professor of Music at Harvard University. He is the author of numerous studies of Renaissance music and musicians, including *The Counter-Reformation and the Masses of Vincenzo Ruffo* and *Music in Renaissance Ferrara, 1400–1505*. He is a past President of the American Musicological Society.

John Nádas received his Ph.D. from New York University and is Professor of Music at the University of North Carolina at Chapel Hill. He has published extensively on music and manuscripts in fourteenth-century Italy and was one of the co-editors of the facsimile of the Squarcialupi Codex. He is currently collaborating with Giuliano Di Bacco on a documentary history of the papal chapels during the Great Schism.

Jessie Ann Owens received her Ph.D. from Princeton University and is Professor of Music and former Dean of the College at Brandeis University. She has published on many aspects of Renaissance music and its reception. Her study of compositional process in Renaissance music—*Composers at Work: The Craft of Musical Composition 1450–1600*—was published by Oxford University Press in 1997. She is currently Vice-President of the American Musicological Society.

Alejandro Enrique Planchart received his Ph.D. from Harvard University and is Professor of Music at the University of California at Santa Barbara. His extensive list of publications includes *The Repertory of Tropes at Winchester* and studies of the life and works of Guillaume Du Fay. As the leader of various choral groups, he has made a number of recordings of Renaissance music.

Adalbert Roth received his doctorate from the University of Frankfurt where he studied with Helmut Hucke and Ludwig Finscher. He is the author of *Studien zum frühen Repertoire der päpstlichen Kapelle unter dem Pontifikat Sixtus' IV. (1471–1484): Die Chorbücher 14 und 51 des Fondo Capella Sistina der Biblioteca Apostolica Vaticana* and other studies on fifteenth-century topics.

Richard Sherr received his Ph.D. from Princeton University and is Professor of Music at Smith College. He is the author of *Papal Music Manuscripts in the Late Fifteenth and Early Sixteenth Centuries* and has published articles on a range of Renaissance topics.

Pamela F. Starr received her Ph.D. from Yale University and is Associate Professor of Music at the University of Nebraska. She has published studies on musicians in the papal chapel in the fifteenth century and is preparing a book on the history of the papal chapel from the Council of Constance to the pontificate of Julius II to be published by the Fondazione Palestrina. She has been a Fellow of the American Academy in Rome.

ABBREVIATIONS

ACP	Archivio Capitolare di Padova
ASMo	Archivio di Stato di Modena
ASP	Archivio di Stato di Padova
ASR	Archivio di Stato di Roma
AST	Archivio di Stato di Torino
ASV	Archivio Segreto Vaticano
AfMw	*Archiv für Musikwissenschaft*
BAV	Biblioteca Apostolica Vaticana
CG	Cappella Giulia
Census-Catalogue	*Census-Catalogue of Manuscript Sources of Polyphonic Music: 1400–1550*, 5 vols. (Renaissance Manuscript Studies 1; Stuttgart, 1979–88)
Collectanea I	*Collectanea I*, ed. Adalbert Roth (Capellae Apostolicae Sixtinaeque Collectanea Acta Monumenta, 3; Vatican City, 1994)
Collectanea II	*Collectanea II. Studien zur Geschichte der päpstlichen Kapelle. Tagungsbericht Heidelberg 1989*, ed. Bernhard Janz (Capellae Apostolicae Sixtinaeque Collectanea Acta Monumenta, 4; Vatican City, 1994)
CMM	Corpus mensurabilis musicae
CS	Cappella Sistina
CSM	Corpus scriptorum de musica
CW	Das Chorwerk
EM	*Early Music*
EMH	*Early Music History*
IE	Introitus et exitus
JAMS	*Journal of the American Musicological Society*
LADN	Lille, Archives Départementales du Nord
MD	*Musica Disciplina*
MMMA	Monumenta Monodica Medii Aevi
New Grove	*The New Grove Dictionary of Music and Musicians*, ed. Stanley Sadie, 20 vols. (London, 1980)
PMFC	Polyphonic Music of the Fourteenth Century
RL	Registra Lateranensia
RRMMA	Recent Researches in the Music of the Middle Ages and Early Renaissance
RS	Registra Supplicationum
RV	Registra Vaticana
TVNM	*Tijdschrift van de Vereniging voor Nederlandse Muziekgeschiedenis*

SIGLA OF MUSIC MANUSCRIPTS

Aosta	Aosta, Biblioteca del Seminario Maggiore, MS 15 (*olim* A[1] D19)
Apt	Apt, Cathédrale Ste-Anne, Bibliothèque du Chapitre, 16bis
Atri	Atri, Archivio Capitolare, Sala Innocenzo IV, Cartella A, no. 5
Barcelona 853c	Barcelona, Biblioteca de Catalunya (*olim* Central), MS 853c
Basle F.X.1–4	Basle, Öffentliche Bibliothek der Universität, MS F.X.1–4
Berlin 40091	Berlin, Staatsbibliothek zu Berlin—Preußischer Kulturbesitz, MS Mus. 40091 (*olim* Z 91)
Bologna 2216	Bologna, Biblioteca Universitaria, MS 2216
Bologna Q 1	Bologna, Civico Museo Bibliografico Musicale, MS Q 1
Bologna Q 15	Bologna, Civico Museo Bibliografico Musicale, MS Q 15
Bologna Q 17	Bologna, Civico Museo Bibliografico Musicale, MS Q 17
Brussels I/II	Brussels, Bibliothèque du Conservatoire, St-Gudule, fragm. I
Cambrai 6	Cambrai, Bibliothèque Municipale, MS 6
Cambrai 11	Cambrai, Bibliothèque Municipale, MS 11
Cambrai 29	Cambrai, Bibliothèque Municipale, MS 29
Cambrai 1328	Cambrai, Bibliothèque Municipale, MS B. 1328
Cambridge 1760	Cambridge, Magdalene College, Pepys Library, MS 1760
Casale Monferrato L	Casale Monferrato, Archivio e Biblioteca Capitolare, Duomo, MS L(B)
Casale Monferrato M	Casale Monferrato, Archivio e Biblioteca Capitolare, Duomo, MS M(D)
Chantilly	Chantilly, Musée Condé, MS 564 (*olim* 1047)
Cividale 101	Cividale del Friuli, Museo Archeologico Nazionale, MS CI
Copenhagen	Copenhagen, Det Kongelige Bibliotek, fragmentet 17
Cortona 1/2	Cortona, Archivio Storico del Comune, frammenti musicali 1 & 2
Dartmouth 2387	*See* Grottaferrata 197
Egidi	Currently untraceable, previously Montefiore dell'Aso, Biblioteca privata Francesco Egidi, framm. mus.
Florence 112bis	Florence, Biblioteca Nazionale Centrale, MS Magliabecchi XIX.112bis
Florence 2439	Florence, Biblioteca del Conservatorio di Musica 'Luigi Cherubini', MS Basevi 2439
Florence 2442	Florence, Biblioteca del Conservatorio di Musica 'Luigi Cherubini', MS Basevi 2442 ('Strozzi Chansonnier')
Florence II.I.232	Florence, Biblioteca Nazionale Centrale, MS II.I.232 (*olim* Magliabecchi XIX.58)
Florence Pal. 87	Florence, Biblioteca Medicea Laurenziana, Pal. 87 ('Squarcialupi Codex')
Florence SL 2211	Florence, Archivio di San Lorenzo, MS 2211

Foligno	Foligno, Archivio di Stato (*olim* Biblioteca Comunale), framm. mus.
Great St Bernard	Great St Bernard Pass, Bibliothèque de l'Hospice, MS Fragment 8
Grottaferrata 16	Grottaferrata, Biblioteca dell'Abbazia di S. Nilo, E.β.XVI (*olim* 374)
Grottaferrata 197	Grottaferrata, Biblioteca dell'Abbazia di S. Nilo, segn. provv. Kript. Lat. 224 (*olim* 197) and Dartmouth College, MS 002387 (*olim* US-SBam)
Grottaferrata s.s.	Grottaferrata, Biblioteca dell'Abbazia di S. Nilo, s.s.
Heilbronn X. 2	Heilbronn, Stadtarchiv, Musiksammlung, MS X. 2
Ivrea	Ivrea, Biblioteca Capitolare, MS 115
Jena 32	Jena, Universitätsbibliothek, MS 32
London 29987	London, British Library, Add. MS 29987
London 40011B	London, British Library, Add. MS 40011B ('Fountains fragment')
London 41667	London, British Library, Add. MS 41667 ('McVeagh fragment')
London Cotton Titus	London, British Library, Cotton Titus XXIV
Lucca A 8	Lucca, Seminario Arcivescovile, MS A 8
Mancini	Lucca, Archivio di Stato, 184 and Perugia, Biblioteca 'Augusta', MS 3065 ('Mancini Codex')
Melk 749	Melk, Stiftsbibliothek, MS 749
Merseburg	Domstift Merseberg, Archiv und Bibliothek, MS 13b
Modena 5.24	Modena, Biblioteca Estense e Universitaria, MS α.M.5.24 (ModA)
Modena α.M.1.2	Modena, Biblioteca Estense e Universitaria, MS α.M.1.2 (Lat. 457; *olim* VI.H)
Modena α.M.1.11	Modena, Biblioteca Estense e Universitaria, MS α.M.1.11 (Lat 454; *olim* V.H.11) (ModB)
Mons	Mons, Collection privée F. Leclercq
Montecassino 871	Montecassino, Biblioteca dell'Abbazia, MS 871 (*olim* 871N)
Munich 3223	Munich, Bayerische Staatsbibliothek, Ms. mus. 3223
Munich 14274	Munich, Bayerische Staatsbibliothek, Handschriften-Inkunabelabteilung, MS Latinus monacensis 14274 (*olim* Mus. 3232a; Cim. 352c) ('St Emmeram Codex')
Munich 29775/8	Munich, Bayerische Staatsbibliothek, 29775/8
Nuremberg 9	Nuremberg, Stadtbibliothek, fragm. lat. 9 & 9a
Old Hall	London, British Library, Add. MS 57950 (*olim* Old Hall, St Edmund's College)
Oxford 56	Oxford, Bodleian Library, MS Canon. Pat. lat. 56
Oxford 213	Oxford, Bodleian Library, MS Canonici Misc. 213
Padua A 1475	Padua, Biblioteca Universitaria, MS A 1475

Padua D 675	Padua, Biblioteca Universitaria, MS D 675
Padua D 684	Padua, Biblioteca Universitaria, MS D 684
Padua D 1225	Padua, Biblioteca Universitaria, MS D 1225
Paris 146	Paris, Bibliothèque Nationale de France, MS f. fr. 146 ('Roman de Fauvel')
Paris 568	Paris, Bibliothèque Nationale de France, MS f. it. 568
Paris 1597	Paris, Bibliothèque Nationale de France, MS f. fr. 1597
Paris 6771	Paris, Bibliothèque Nationale de France, MS nouv. acq. fr. 6771 ('Reina Codex')
Prague XI E 9	Prague, Universitní knihovna, MS XI E 9
Rochester 44	Rochester, Sibley Music Library, Fleischer Fragment 44
Rome Cas. 1671	Rome, Biblioteca Casanatense, MS 1671
Rome Cas. 2141–4	Rome, Biblioteca Casanatense, MSS 2141–4
Rome SC O.232	Rome, Biblioteca Musicale Governativa del Conservatorio di Musica Santa Cecilia, G.MSS.O.232 (*olim* Riv.B.I.I; 112)
Rome SG 59	Rome, San Giovanni in Laterano, Archivio musicale lateranense, Codice 59
St Gall 463	St Gall, Stiftsbibliothek, MS 463 ('Tschudi Liederbuch')
Siena 207	Siena, Archivio di Stato, frammenti di musiche, 207 (*olim* 326–327)
Strasburg	Strasburg, *olim* Bibliothèque de la ville, MS 222.C.22
Stuttgart 47	Stuttgart, Württembergische Landesbibliothek, MS Musica folio I 47
Trémoïlle	Paris, Bibliothèque Nationale de France, nouv. acq. fr. 23190. Previously Château de Serrant, Bibliothèque de la Duchesse de la Trémoïlle
Trent 87	Trent, Museo Provinciale d'Arte, Castello del Buon Consiglio, MS 87
Trent 89	Trent, Museo Provinciale d'Arte, Castello del Buon Consiglio, MS 89
Trent 90	Trent, Museo Provinciale d'Arte, Castello del Buon Consiglio, MS 90
Trent 92	Trent, Museo Provinciale d'Arte, Castello del Buon Consiglio, MS 92
Trent 93	Trent, Museo Provinciale d'Arte, Castello del Buon Consiglio, MS 93
Trent 1563	Trent, Biblioteca Comunale, MS 1563
Turin 2	Turin, Biblioteca Nazionale Universitaria, Codex T.III.2 ('Codex Boverio')
Uppsala 76a	Uppsala, Universitetsbiblioteket, MS Vokalmusik I Handskrift 76a
Uppsala 76b	Uppsala, Universitetsbiblioteket, MS Vokalmusik I Handskrift 76b

Utrecht 37 I	Utrecht, Bibliotheek der Rijksuniversiteit, MS 1846[1] (*olim* 6 E 37)
Vatican 10766	Vatican City, Biblioteca Apostolica Vaticana, MS Vaticani Latini 10766
Vatican CG XII.2	Vatican City, Biblioteca Apostolica Vaticana, MS Cappella Giulia XII.2
Vatican CG XII.3	Vatican City, Biblioteca Apostolica Vaticana, MS Cappella Giulia XII.3
Vatican CG XII.5	Vatican City, Biblioteca Apostolica Vaticana, MS Cappella Giulia XII.5
Vatican CG XII.6	Vatican City, Biblioteca Apostolica Vaticana, MS Cappella Giulia XII.6
Vatican CG XV.19	Vatican City, Biblioteca Apostolica Vaticana, MS Cappella Giulia XV.19
Vatican CS 15	Vatican City, Biblioteca Apostolica Vaticana, MS Cappella Sistina 15
Vatican CS 18	Vatican City, Biblioteca Apostolica Vaticana, MS Cappella Sistina 18
Vatican CS 21	Vatican City, Biblioteca Apostolica Vaticana, MS Cappella Sistina 21
Vatican CS 23	Vatican City, Biblioteca Apostolica Vaticana, MS Cappella Sistina 23
Vatican CS 35	Vatican City, Biblioteca Apostolica Vaticana, MS Cappella Sistina 35
Vatican CS 42	Vatican City, Biblioteca Apostolica Vaticana, MS Cappella Sistina 42
Vatican CS 71	Vatican City, Biblioteca Apostolica Vaticana, MS Cappella Sistina 71
Vatican CS 154	Vatican City, Biblioteca Apostolica Vaticana, MS Cappella Sistina 154
Vatican CS 163	Vatican City, Biblioteca Apostolica Vaticana, MS Cappella Sistina 163
Vatican CS 197	Vatican City, Biblioteca Apostolica Vaticana, MS Cappella Sistina 197
Vatican C VIII 234	Vatican City, Biblioteca Apostolica Vaticana, MS Chigi C VIII 234 ('Chigi Codex')
Vatican SMM 26	Vatican City, Biblioteca Apostolica Vaticana, MS Santa Maria Maggiore 26 (*olim* JJ.III.4)
Vatican SP B 80	Vatican City, Biblioteca Apostolica Vaticana, MS San Pietro B 80
Venice 145	Venice, Biblioteca Nazionale Marciana, MS Ital. Cl. IX.145 (Collocazione 7554)
Verona 759	Verona, Biblioteca Capitolare, MS DCCLIX

Vienna 11778	Vienna, Österreichische Nationalbibliothek, Handschriften- und Inkunabelsammlung, MS 11778 (*olim* Theol. 37; VIII.A.3)
Warsaw 52	Warsaw, Biblioteka Narodowa, III.8054 (*olim* Krasiński 52)
Warsaw 378	Now lost. Previously Warsaw, Biblioteka Narodowa, lat. F.I.378 (*olim* St Petersburg)
Wolkenstein A	Vienna, Österreichische Nationalbibliothek, MS 2777 ('Wolkenstein A')
Wolkenstein B	Innsbruck, Universitätsbibliothek, Ms. ohne Sign. ('Wolkenstein B')

Howard Mayer Brown
(1930–1993)

❦

JAMES HAAR

A T almost every scholarly conference I have attended I can recall saying, or hearing others say, 'has Howard arrived yet?'. And sooner or later he usually did show up, providing us a kind of signal that it was all right to go ahead. These are just the conferences I went to; there have been many others I didn't attend but Howard did, and whether he read a paper or not his presence was a sort of guarantee, both that the conference would be all right and that everyone would have a good time. His combination of seriousness of purpose with an inimitable wit, his cosmopolitan yet deeply American personality, somehow set the right tone for us all.

We all have memories of Howard Brown; my own go back a long way, to the time we were undergraduates together. I won't bore you with reminiscences, but I'm sure that anecdotes about Howard will continue to be told for a long time. For a great many of us his passing is a personal as well as a professional loss; each of us will miss him in our own way.

The professional loss is great. Howard worked with phenomenal energy, and showed no signs of slowing up; we might have expected to see and hear a lot more from him. The legacy is also great; if we think of the Renaissance fields he cultivated with great distinction—music in the theatre; instrumental music of every kind; the French chanson over a two-century span; ornamentation in theory and practice; the contrapuntal and tonal structure of Renaissance polyphony; problems of editing text and music; iconographic study, particularly in relation to performance practice; the rise of opera—we may begin to realize how much he has influenced our whole discipline.

If I were to go on for much longer I would start to hear Howard's voice, saying between sips of a martini something sly about bumbling perpetrators of fulsome praise. So I will stop; but it would not be right to begin this conference without a thought for someone we all very much wish were with us today, Howard Mayer Brown.

> Acoutrez vous d'habits de deuil:
> Josquin, Piersson, Brumel, Compère
> [et chaque commère et compère]:
> Et plorez grosses larmes d'œil;
> Perdu avez vostre bon père.

PART I

Music for the Pope and his Chapel

1

Early Papal Motets

❦

MARGARET BENT

THE fourteenth and fifteenth centuries were perhaps the most protracted period of instability the papacy has ever suffered. For much of the fourteenth century the papal residence was not in Rome but at Avignon. During the Great Schism from 1378 there were two popes, one in Avignon and one in Rome. Instead of ending the Schism, the election of a third pope at Pisa in 1409 ushered in a period of threefold division, since neither of the other popes was prepared to resign; but at least briefly it gave occasion for celebration and optimism. This threefold Schism lasted until the election of Martin V in 1417 at the Council of Constance. He and his successors gradually re-established the papal seat in Rome, though not without continuing schismatic rumblings. Not until later in the fifteenth century could there begin the golden period of building and patronage that led to the sumptuous architecture, sculpture, painting, and manuscript collections that now constitute the Vatican galleries and libraries. The famous series of music books for the newly stabilized choir of the Sistine Chapel also started in the late fifteenth century, but as Alejandro Planchart points out (see below, Ch. 3), the emphasis in the preceding centuries was on a team of singing clerks who brought multiple general skills to the curia, rather than on a choir as such, let alone a team of composer-singers, an image fostered by a line of composers from Du Fay onwards. Planchart deals with the standard repertory of the papal chapel in the period before and including Du Fay. Even then, occasional or ceremonial music written especially *for* popes or papal ceremonies seems to have been exceptional. Before Du Fay our knowledge of any such music written for popes is extremely sketchy and scattered. Moreover, very little time between about 1320 and 1420 was spent by any pope in Rome. The schismatic popes were of necessity itinerant; travelling courts or communities are much less likely to leave permanent monuments, whether architectural, artistic, or musical.

Various scholars have identified isolated polyphonic compositions between the early fourteenth century and the mid-fifteenth as being written for, or in honour of, popes. It is my purpose here to assemble this interesting and varied collection, which as a continuing repertory or even genre has received little notice. It is on the texts of such pieces that we depend for a papal association, which they signal with varying degrees of explicitness. In some cases, the text is reflected in aspects of the music, by choice of chant, or by some form of number or constructional symbolism; such evidence may support a papal association but is never the primary evidence for it. The number of motets for popes surviving before Du Fay is rather small, and two of them are incomplete and unperformable. The longer list given here includes pieces other than motets—ballades, Gloria tropes, and pieces of anomalous form—that appear to be written specifically in honour of popes, named or unnamed. To this list could be added pieces that deal directly with the Schism, praying for or celebrating its end; for an interim list of these pieces see the Appendix.

I have not gone further to include other music written by papal chaplains and familiars, and music generally from papal circles, though some of it is mentioned in passing. Such a list would quickly become unmanageable, potentially comprising the known works of all composers who at some time in their careers appear to have served in any papal chapel or household. These composers include Philippe de Vitry,[1] Matheus de Sancto Johanne,[2] Magister Franciscus, Haucourt (= Altacuria), Johannes Symonis (= Hasprois), Pelisson (= Johannes de Bosco),[3] Antonio Zacara da Teramo,[4] Matteo da Perugia, Humbertus de Salinis,[5] Nicolaus Zacarie,[6] Guillaume le Grant

[1] Although Vitry is not specifically documented in papal service, he has been securely tied, together with Petrarch, to cultural circles surrounding the court of Clement VI. See A. Coville, 'Philippe de Vitri: notes biographiques', *Romania*, 59 (1933), 520–47. Recent refinement of the context of Vitry's motet for Clement VI (*Petre clemens/Lugentium*) reinforces older claims linking him closely with papal circles in the 1340s. See Andrew Wathey, 'The Motets of Philippe de Vitry and the Fourteenth-Century Renaissance', *EMH* 12 (1993), 119–50, esp. 121, and Andrew Tomasello, *Music and Ritual at Papal Avignon 1309–1403* (Ann Arbor, 1983).

[2] Matheus was a papal chaplain 1382–6. See, *inter alia*, Ursula Günther, 'Matheus de Sancto Johanne', *New Grove*, xi. 820, and 'Zur Biographie einiger Komponisten der Ars subtilior', *AfMw* 21 (1964), 180–5, and Tomasello, *Music and Ritual*, 252–3. See also Andrew Wathey, 'The Peace of 1360–1369 and Anglo-French Musical Relations', *EMH* 9 (1990), 129–74.

[3] He served in the chapel of Clement VII.

[4] He was a singer and papal secretary in the Italian chapels of Boniface IX, Innocent VII, and Gregory XII; his presence in the chapel of Alexander V is indirectly inferred, but he is documented as *magister capelle* to John XXIII. See Agostino Ziino, ' "Magister Antonius dictus Zacharias de Teramo": alcuni date e molte ipotesi', *Rivista italiana di musicologia*, 14 (1979), 311–48; Nino Pirrotta, 'Zacarus Musicus', *Quadrivium*, 12 (1971), 153–75; John Nádas, 'Further Notes on Magister Antonius dictus Zacharias de Teramo', *Studi musicali*, 15 (1986), 167–82; 16 (1987), 175–6.

[5] New biographical material on this composer has been made available by John Nádas and Giuliano Di Bacco in advance of their publication. Also by their kindness, it is summarized in Robert Nosow, 'The Florid and Equal-Discantus Motet Styles of Fifteenth-Century Italy' (Ph.D. diss., University of North Carolina, Chapel Hill, 1992), 87–92. Salinis, of northern origin, had supplicated Boniface IX from the diocese of Braga in Portugal in 1403 for a benefice, and on 10 July 1409, three days after the election of Alexander V, he was

(= Guillaume le Macherier),[7] Nicolas Grenon, Pierre Fontaine, Guillaume Modiator (= Malbecque), Barthélemy Poignare, Gautier Libert, Jean Sohier (= Fedé), Arnold de Lantins, Johannes Brassart, and Guillaume Du Fay.[8] Names of chaplains and singers attached to papal and cardinalate chapels have now been splendidly augmented for the late fourteenth century by Giuliano Di Bacco and John Nádas, but with the striking exceptions of Ciconia and Zacara, few of the new names produced clearly identify composers of surviving works with chaplains listed for popes Gregory XI, Urban VI, or Clement VII.[9] Matteo da Perugia is documented in the service of a prelate later elected pope (Alexander V), but we lack evidence of his continuing service in the papal chapel. Humbertus de Salinis, on the other hand, is confirmed as a member of the papal chapel shortly after the election of the same pope, but no prior association is documented. Musicians could move freely between often rather short periods of papal employ and that of secular patrons, as the now well-documented case of Du Fay shows.[10] The Church Councils of Pisa, Constance, and Basle have frequently been cited as opportunities for recruiting and exchanges both of personnel and repertory; this was undoubtedly the case, and in this respect the Councils must have functioned like large present-day American professional meetings. The scattered remains of early papal pieces with ceremonial or political content reflect the itinerant condition of the chapel. Not until the papacy was securely re-established in Rome in the

already a papal familiar and singer, having amassed several Portuguese benefices in the intervening years. He is absent from the first complete chapel list for John XXIII, where Antonio Zacara is named *magister capelle*. He is not documented from this point. His Gloria 'Jubilacio' could well date not from Constance, as is usually assumed, but from the Council of Pisa, which at the time must have seemed like the end of the Schism. This piece is copied into early layers of Bologna Q 15 in company with other music by Zacara and Salinis that may have formed part of the repertory of the papal chapels in Pisa and Bologna between 1409 and 1414.

⁶ A papal singer in 1420–4 and 1434; it appears to be coincidental that the similarly named Antonio Zacara da Teramo was also a papal singer a generation earlier. Reaney's attempt to identify the two (*New Grove*) must now be set aside in view of the new clarification of Antonio's biography by Ziino and Nádas; see above, n. 4.

⁷ See Manfred Schuler, 'Zur Geschichte der Kapelle Papst Martins V', *AfMw* 25 (1968), 30–45 at 40, and Paula Higgins, 'Music and Musicians at the Sainte-Chapelle of the Bourges Palace, 1405–1415', in Angelo Pompilio *et al.* (eds.), *International Musicological Society, Report of the Fourteenth Congress, Bologna, 1987: Trasmissione e recezione delle forme di cultura musicale*, 3 vols. (Turin, 1990), iii. 689–701.

⁸ For most of these names see Alejandro Planchart in this volume, Tables 3.1 and 3.2, also Planchart, 'Guillaume Du Fay's Benefices and his Relationship to the Court of Burgundy', *EMH* 8 (1988), 117–71, and 'The Early Career of Guillaume Du Fay', *JAMS* 46 (1993), 341–68.

⁹ Giuliano Di Bacco and John Nádas, 'Verso uno "stile internazionale" della musica nelle cappelle papali e cardinalizie durante il Grande Scisma (1378–1417): il caso di Johannes Ciconia da Liège', *Collectanea I*, 7–74, and continuing work. Further names of papal chaplains were given in their paper delivered to the American Musicological Society Annual Meeting, 1994. Composers among these include Renzo da Pontecorvo (with Gregory XII), Nicolaus Ricci de Nucella Campli (with Boniface IX, Innocent VII, and Gregory XII), perhaps the 'Nucella' of the Strasburg MS, Ugolino of Orvieto (with Gregory XII), Guido de Lange (with Gregory XI and Clement VII), composer of a number of songs in the Chantilly MS, and perhaps Richardus de Bosonvilla (with Clement VII), who might be the 'Richart' of the Apt and Strasburg MSS.

¹⁰ For Du Fay's biography see Craig Wright, 'Dufay at Cambrai: Discoveries and Revisions', *JAMS* 28 (1975), 175–229; Planchart, 'Guillaume Du Fay's Benefices', and 'The Early Career'.

late fifteenth century, with adequate buildings and a stable establishment, can we point to a full and continuous series of associated polyphonic manuscripts.[11]

Most of the pre-Schism music tabulated in this chapter survives only in a single source, and some of it is fragmentary. When there is no network of concordances to define circulation, it is hard to estimate what is lost, beyond the uncontested assumption that the highest polyphonic skills must always have been an élite preserve and their practitioners few in number. The number of pieces with papal associations increases in the late fourteenth and early fifteenth centuries, that is, from the latter part of the Avignon papacy and the period during and immediately after the Schism. Arguments of varying strength have been advanced to associate manuscripts with itinerant papal courts in the early fifteenth century, but any such associations have to be argued from the contents and composers represented, not from a known papal provenance for the source itself. If a general thesis emerges from this survey, it is that the number of individual cases in which such pieces are not or cannot be inaugural is sufficient to dislodge the common presumption of first resort that they are more likely than not to be inaugural.

Avignon popes before the Schism

After the death of Clement V on 20 April 1314 it took the cardinals over two years to elect the Dominican Jacques Duèse, which they did on 7 August 1316 in Lyon, where he was crowned in September as John XXII. This delay is among the events darkly chronicled, alongside the misfortunes of the French royal house, in the apocalyptic interpolations to the *Roman de Fauvel* in Paris 146 and the parallel chronicle and narrative *dits* in the same volume.[12] The papal court had been often alienated from Rome and partly itinerant in the previous three centuries until established in Avignon by Clement in 1309, and retained there by John, beginning the period of so-called Babylonian captivity.

---

[11] Richard Sherr, 'Music and the Renaissance Papacy: The Papal Choir and the Fondo Capella Sistina', in Anthony Grafton (ed.), *Rome Reborn: The Vatican Library and Renaissance Culture* (Washington, DC, 1993), 199–223; pl. 147 shows the first list of singers for Eugene IV (1431) including Du Fay. For the state of the city of Rome and old St Peter's prior to the re-establishment of the papacy in Rome, see Anthony Grafton, 'The Ancient City Restored: Archaeology, Ecclesiastical History, and Egyptology', ibid. 87–123, and Christopher A. Reynolds, *Papal Patronage and the Music of St. Peter's, 1380–1513* (Berkeley, 1995).

[12] *Le Roman de Fauvel in the Edition of Mesire Chaillou de Pesstain: A Reproduction in Facsimile of the Complete Manuscript Paris, Bibliothèque Nationale, Fonds Français 146*. Introduction by Edward H. Roesner, François Avril, and Nancy Freeman Regalado (New York, 1990).

The first papal motet surviving from the fourteenth century appears to be *Per grama protho paret*. Duplum and tenor only are preserved in London 41667 (the McVeagh fragment).[13]

PEr grama protho paret onema[14] constancie romanorum quo claret iam decus ecclesie	Through the first letter is revealed the name of the Romans' constancy, whereby the glory of the Church now has lustre.
Tellus ovans satorem tollat sapiencie catholicorum florem genitum progenie	Let the cheering earth exalt the sower of wisdom, the flower born of Catholics' lineage.
Regi nato Maria placuit sic mittere largitione dya radium phox supere	It pleased the King born of Mary thus to send, by divine bounty, the ray of heavenly light.
Vere manet electus non a kari nomine omni bonoque tectus propinanti numine	Truly he remains the elect, not apart from the name of the dear one [i.e. John, the beloved Disciple], and covered with all good things by God's gift.
Summe vivens benignus Christo sic opifice pontificali dignus sublimatur apice.	Living with supreme good will, Christ thus being his maker, he is raised on high, worthy of the papal tiara.

Tenor: Valde honorandus est beatus Johannes
Blessed John is worthy to be honoured

Lacking its triplum, this motet is too fragmentary to be performed, and undoubtedly lacks textual clues to its original context; but the two surviving parts do permit some analysis of text and music. The motet has received little attention, though Besseler claimed, not very conclusively, that the illegible word at the top might be an ascription to Johannes de Muris.[15] The first line announces an acrostic, easily resolved as *Petrus*: 'through the first letter [of each stanza] is revealed the name of the Romans' constancy, whereby the glory of the church now has lustre'. The first two letters of the first stanza (*PE*) are required to give the name of the rock on which the Church is founded. The

[13] This motet has now been discussed and published (including a transcription of the music) by Daniel Leech-Wilkinson, 'The Emergence of *ars nova*', *Journal of Musicology*, 13 (1995), 285–317. For the translation of this and the following text I am indebted to Leofranc Holford-Strevens.

[14] *Onema = onoma*; not *enema = aenigma*; this corrects the misreading of Heinrich Besseler, 'Studien zur Musik des Mittelalters II: Die Motette from Franco von Köln bis Philipp von Vitry', *AfMw* 8 (1926), 218.

[15] Heinrich Besseler, 'Studien zur Musik des Mittelalters I: Neue Quellen des 14. und beginnenden 15. Jahrhunderts', *AfMw* 7 (1925), 196.

text goes on to refer to the beloved disciple, i.e. John, also named in the tenor, *Valde honorandus est beatus Johannes*, and to make further unmistakable papal references ('he is raised up on high, worthy of the papal tiara'). The conclusion is virtually inescapable that this must be for a pope named John. This can hardly be John XXIII, a century later, so it must be for John XXII, 1316–34. Nor did any other pope during this period have the Christian name John before election. Most motets are dated or placed on the basis of their texts, and this is no exception. Daniel Leech-Wilkinson discusses this motet as 'possibly celebrating the election of Pope John XXII and in that case dating from soon after 7 August 1316'.[16] John was crowned on 5 September 1316. There are no explicitly inaugural references in the text; the missing triplum might have helped. That it might have been written for John's coronation is neither supported nor discouraged by the text alone. However, placing it at the beginning of John XXII's reign makes it hard to reconcile with what we know about the rapid technical and notational developments in French music of that period.

Leech-Wilkinson has suggested the very early date of 1317, the occasion of the canonization of Louis of Toulouse (7 April, feast-day 19 August), for the motet *Flos ortus/Celsa cedrus/Quam magnus pontifex* in his honour, which he— credibly—attributes to Philippe de Vitry.[17] That motet requires the use of minim stems for its non-standard groupings and rests and for its nearly-isorhythmic hockets in the second section where the tenor appears in 2:1 diminution. On any spectrum of style-based chronology it would fall rather late; it has an 'advanced' pattern of overlapping *color* and *talea*—two *colores* spread over three and a half *taleae*, repeated in diminution. Leech-Wilkinson suggests an even earlier date—1316, the coronation of its dedicatee Pope John XXII—for *Per grama*, which likewise requires the use of minim stems for its non-standard groupings, rests, and hockets. Not only is its tenor isorhythmic, so is the motetus voice to a substantial degree, a feature understated by Leech-Wilkinson and hardly present yet in the motets of Machaut.[18] The encouragement for an early dating comes entirely from the texts. Whether they must or indeed could be quite as early as 1316 and 1317 is doubtful on musical

[16] Leech-Wilkinson, 'The Emergence of *ars nova*', 309.

[17] Louis was the second son of Charles II of Naples, became a Franciscan and bishop, and was canonized by his long-time associate Jacques de Duèse when the latter became Pope John XXII. He was the brother of Robert of Anjou, King of Naples (reigned 1309–43), honoured in another motet by Vitry: see below. *Flos/Celsa* is published in F. Ll. Harrison (ed.), *Motets of French Provenance* (PMFC 5; Monaco, 1965). For the dating, see Leech-Wilkinson, 'The Emergence', n. 45, and Karl Kügle, 'The Manuscript Ivrea, Biblioteca Capitolare 115: Studies in the Transmission and Composition of Ars Nova Polyphony' (Ph.D. diss., New York University, 1993), 144–5. See this dissertation also for an excellent discussion of 14th-c. motets and their chronology, in which, however, Kügle accepts Leech-Wilkinson's early dating of *Flos/Celsa* and related motets.

[18] Ursula Günther, 'The 14th-Century Motet and its Development', *MD* 12 (1958), 27–58. Ten Machaut motets have diminution in the second section, all with hockets. Only motet 15 is unipartite and completely isorhythmic.

grounds. This is precisely the time when musicians in Paris were adapting, assembling, and composing music for the massive enterprise that we know as the interpolated *Roman de Fauvel* of Paris 146, whose compilation Roesner has dated to 1317–18.[19] Its motets present for the first time some of the most advanced musical and notational usages then known, including the earliest appearance, by a long way, of mensurally transforming coloration, in *Garrit gallus*. Its composers were both pushing at the limits of what could be conceived in the state of the notational art, and introducing innovations, both in musical structure and in the specification of details. But there are no diminution sections, no overlapping *color* and *talea*, no significant isorhythmic recurrences in the upper parts, and almost no minim stems—indeed, none is necessary to deal with the rhythmic vocabulary of *Fauvel*, and there are no rhythmic groups below the level of the semibreve that require the use of minim stems or rests. That is because all groups of semibreves (even in the two pieces with some stems) fall within the conventions for performance of unstemmed semibreves (i.e. of any values below the breve). Their conventional interpretation is confirmed in all cases where later concordances are more explicitly notated with stems, and conforms to the standard groupings set out in treatises (the so-called *Ars nova* itself, and Anonymous III).[20] Between them, these theorists provide for up to three minims per semibreve in imperfect and perfect time—what was later called major prolation, though without requiring stems when standard combinations were to be interpreted conventionally. Groups of five semibreves (mostly unstemmed) occur only in *Quare fremuerunt*, conspicuously placed on fo. 1ʳ of *Fauvel*, and *O Philippe* (on King Philip V, r. 1316–22), one of the most modern motets and perhaps a king-pin in the planning of the collection. The *Fauvel* motets use two to five semibreves per breve of imperfect time, usually unstemmed, that is, major and minor semibreves and minims, in standard groupings, and with no minim rests or hockets.

Per grama protho paret makes use of the same groupings of two to five semibreves as the *Fauvel* motets, all in the standard patterns. It also uses stems, not because those particular groupings needed them, being standard, but because by the time it was notated other options were possible, necessitating the general introduction of stems. However, there are two factors that mark the construction and notation of this motet as being more advanced than anything in *Fauvel*. *Per grama protho paret* must always have had stems because it

---

[19] See *Le Roman de Fauvel*, Introduction, 49.

[20] Philippe de Vitry, *Ars nova*, ed. G. Reaney, A. Gilles, J. Maillard (CSM 8; American Institute of Musicology, 1964), which also includes a re-edition of Coussemaker, *Scriptorum de musica medii aevi*, iii, Anonymous III. See Sarah Fuller, 'A Phantom Treatise of the Fourteenth Century? The *Ars Nova*', *Journal of Musicology*, 4 (1986), 23–50.

also uses minim hockets, which cannot be notated without paired minim rests and single minims, something not possible in the notation of *Fauvel* nor called for in its repertory. Nor are there, in *Fauvel*, fully developed isorhythm or *color–talea* overlaps of the kind established later. *Per grama protho paret* has extensive isorhythmic recurrences in the surviving upper part over a cunningly overlapped *color* and *talea* in the tenor, another feature present in *Flos ortus/Celsa cedrus*, but not in *Fauvel*, and found in only a few of Machaut's motets two or more decades later.[21] There is no reason to think that the compilers of *Fauvel* were being deliberately archaic in matters of notation and rhythm. Composers including Philippe de Vitry were clearly reaching out for every possible technical means of enrichment for their enterprise. Once tasted, it would have been inconceivable for them to retreat from the powerful rhythmic variety permitted when minim stems came to signal departures from the standard formulae that governed unstemmed groups.

The attribution of *Flos ortus/Celsa cedrus* to Vitry is highly plausible on many grounds, including the separate survival of its texts in the tradition now documented by Andrew Wathey.[22] But the motets of Vitry it most resembles have usually been dated in the 1330s and are present only in the much later Ivrea manuscript,[23] not in *Fauvel*. An earlier dating of these other motets along with *Flos ortus/Celsa cedrus* would then require us to believe that Vitry and his collaborators, involved centrally in the *Fauvel* project, cultivated at the same time two distinct rhythmic/notational styles and technical levels; this in turn would remove most of the technical and notational advances by which some chronological sorting of fourteenth-century motets has seemed possible. These motets must surely be after *Fauvel*, at least in the 1320s or later, rather than the 1310s. No *Fauvel* motets are in Ivrea, which has always suggested some chronological separation of repertory. I have challenged the currently accepted *termini ante quos* for the three Marigny motets in *Fauvel* on the grounds that their integration into narrative allegory makes them more than merely documentary: all three motets could have been written after all the events that they present in series.[24] In this case, 1317–18 should be taken as a *terminus post quem*, not an absolute compilation date for the interpolated *Fauvel*; its compilation and new compositions could have extended as late as 1322. But even at the most conservative estimate, the most advanced music in *Fauvel* must be

---

[21] Seven Machaut motets have overlapping *color* and *talea* (nos. 4, 7, 9, 22, 19, 3, 14). See Günther, 'The 14th-Century Motet', 30. *Per grama protho paret* has three tenor *colores* of 15 notes each, a total of 45 notes, also patterned as 5 *taleae* of 9 notes each. Each *talea* is 12 longs, making a total of 60 longs.

[22] Wathey, 'The Motets of Philippe de Vitry'.

[23] Kügle now dates Ivrea in the 1380s and 1390s ('The Manuscript Ivrea', 130–3).

[24] 'Fauvel and Marigny: Which Came First?', in Margaret Bent and Andrew Wathey (eds.), *Fauvel Studies: Allegory, Chronicle, Music, and Image in Paris, Bibliothèque Nationale, MS français 146* (Oxford, 1997).

later than the precocious dating of these two technically advanced motets, whose overlapping of *color* and *talea*, use of partial upper-part isorhythm, and minim hockets have been considered as later traits, and also suggest a link between the two motets. If Vitry wrote one of them (and his authorship of *Flos ortus/Celsa cedrus* now seems highly likely), he could also have written the other (*Per grama*).

It is precisely its technical features that draw attention to another puzzle about *Per grama protho paret*, perhaps one of the earliest compositions to use minim hockets and minim rests, and therefore to need to sign minims with stems. The famous bull *Docta sanctorum patrum* (1324/5) of the austere and elderly Dominican Pope John XXII complains that disciples of the new school, concerned with measuring out breves in new notes, prefer to fashion (*fingere*) their own music rather than sing the old songs; that ecclesiastical chants are sung by the moderns in semibreves and minims, and that everything is struck through (punctured? *percutiuntur*) by little notes. For they cut across (*intersecant*) the melodies with hockets, they make them slippery with discants, they even stuff the tripla and moteti with vernacular [texts].[25]

Per grama protho paret is, then, hardly a manifesto piece written to the austere prescriptions of a Cranmer or a Council of Trent. Could it even have been this piece that prompted the strikingly technical condemnations that John was persuaded to sign?[26] Or was the motet written after the bull, either in negligence or nescience of the approved style guidelines? John or his musical advisers could hardly have been pleased by something that so plainly flouted his directive, unless the story, and his position, is much more convoluted than we have thought it to be. However, the bull seems not to condemn these stylistic features as evil in themselves, but to proscribe them in liturgical observance, together with other features (such as secular texts in motets). If this were to provide an oblique hint against the performance of these motets in a liturgical context, we might have another reason to dissociate them from papal coronation ceremonies, a point that will recur in the course of this paper. A date closer to 1330 would be more musically convincing, especially if either or both motets are to be considered candidates for the authorship of Vitry. The resolution of the crisis with Louis of Bavaria and the submission to John in 1330 of Nicholas V (Pietro Rainolducci, antipope 1328–30) could have afforded an

---

[25] On the bull, see Helmut Hucke, 'Das Dekret "Docta Sanctorum Patrum" Papst Johannes' XXII.', *MD* 38 (1984), 119–31, and Valentino Donella, 'La Costituzione "Docta Sanctorum Patrum" di Giovanni XXII (1324–25): una persistente attualità', *Rivista internazionale di musica sacra*, 4 (1983), 353–77. The reference to hockets does not yet need to be the minim hockets cultivated in ars nova motets from about 1330 onwards; it could well refer to the hocket technique established in 13th-c. theory and practice.

[26] For the observation that the musical part suggests a different author from the rest of the bull, see Hucke, 'Das Dekret', 122.

occasion for reaffirming John's authority. The ideological victory implicit in mentions of old Rome and the papal tiara lends weight to such a late dating. Another context for *Per grama* could be as late as 1333, when a successful case was made to the still very active Pope John XXII to authorize a crusade; the delegation was led by Pierre Roger, the future Pope Clement VI and a colleague of Vitry (see below).[27] Vitry was involved in crusade politics through his patron Louis of Bourbon, whose political relationships with Robert of Anjou, King of Naples, were close enough in the mid-1330s to have provided the occasion for Vitry's composition of the motet in honour of Robert, *O canenda/Rex quem*, on a tenor for St Louis (the French King Louis IX), and with full isorhythm, diminution, and minim hockets. Robert's name appears as an acrostic in the duplum,[28] as does that of 'Petrus' in *Per grama*. The same Vitry–Bourbon–Anjou link might also have occasioned the composition at the same period of *Flos ortus/Celsa cedrus* for the king's saintly brother, Louis of Toulouse. It seems to me not impossible that Vitry could be the composer of all three motets.

Beside the strictures of *Docta sanctorum patrum* may also be set the musician motet *Musicalis scientia/Scientie laudabilis*, which complains about those who divide up single notes with rests (*dividunt simplicia faciendo suspiria*),[29] the anonymous *In virtute/Decens carmen/Clamor meus*, perhaps by Vitry, which inveighs against incoherent texts,[30] and the Old Hall motet *Are post libamina* by 'Mayshuet' (Matheus de Sancto Johanne),[31] which complains about hypocritical and vainglorious singers who multiply small notes (*notulas multiplicant*) and sing to please magnates rather than to please God.

John XXII was followed by the likewise ascetic Cistercian Benedict XII, pope from 20 December 1334 to 25 April 1342. Perhaps not surprisingly, no polyphonic music has yet come to light that can be associated with his reign. The surprise is rather that there should be any kind of motet, particularly one like *Per grama protho paret*, for his predecessor, who has been associated

---

[27] For information on the crusade-related Bourbon–Anjou connections in the 1330s I am much indebted to Andrew Wathey (private communication of material in a paper delivered at the AMS annual meeting, New York, 1995), who proposed a mid-1330s date for *O canenda/Rex quem* on grounds quite independent of the stylistic ones included here.

[28] Kügle suggests the period 1319–24, when Robert was in the North ('The Manuscript Ivrea', 145), but Wathey's most recent suggestion makes a northern constraint unnecessary.

[29] In Paris, Bibliothèque Nationale de France, MS Coll. de Picardie, 67. Harrison (ed.), *Motets of French Provenance*.

[30] Attributed to Vitry by Daniel Leech-Wilkinson, 'The Emergence'. The motet is published in Harrison (ed.), *Motets of French Provenance*, and a translation of the text by David Howlett is included with the recording by the Orlando Consort on CD-SAR 49.

[31] See above, n. 2. The motet is in Andrew Hughes and Margaret Bent (eds.), *The Old Hall Manuscript*, 3 vols. (CMM 46; American Institute of Musicology, 1969–73), no. 146.

explicitly with opposition to precisely the musical features of the motet in his honour. But things were soon to change.

Cardinal Pierre Roger, Archbishop of Rouen, and previously chancellor to Philip VI, was elected Pope on 7 May 1342, partly in reaction against Benedict's austere rule. As Clement VI he held the most brilliant court in Europe; it was he who did most to establish the luxurious image of the Avignon papacy. He exercised notable patronage of all the arts, cultivating contacts with the leading intellectuals of his day, including Petrarch. Among non-musical works dedicated to Clement are several by Johannes de Muris, including an astronomical calendar from the fifth year of Clement's pontificate, a set of prophetic prognostications referring to planetary conjunctions in 1357 and 1365, and a treatise in collaboration with Firmin de Belleval on the reform of the Julian calendar in 1344 –5.[32]

Two musical tributes addressed to Clement VI survive: the motet *Petre clemens/Lugentium/Non est inventus* by Vitry, and a motetus text troping a Gloria, 'Clemens deus artifex tota clementia', no. 42 in Ivrea, the unique source for both compositions. Vitry was an associate of Pierre Roger through his notarial service in the French royal chancery; from 18 July 1343 he was one of the domestic chaplains of the pope (*capellani commensales papae*), as distinct from the less intimate *capellani capelle*.[33] In addition to the Gloria, a Kyrie troped 'Rex angelorum' has a further motetus trope, starting 'Clemens pater', which may be a companion piece to the Gloria 'Clemens deus artifex', although it has no specific language that would allow associations outside the Kyrie.[34] The composition of both Gloria and Kyrie as bitextual motets is unusual; their common technique and opening word further encourage a pairing.

[32] See *New Grove*, s.v. Jehan des Murs, and Lawrence Gushee, 'New Sources for the Biography of Johannes de Muris', *JAMS* 22 (1969), 3–26.

[33] Tomasello, *Music and Ritual*, ch. 4.

[34] The Gloria and Kyrie are published respectively as nos. 22 and 2 in Hanna Stäblein-Harder (ed.), *Fourteenth-Century Mass Music in France* (CMM 29; American Institute of Musicology, 1962). The Kyrie is in both Apt and Ivrea: [Apt 1 = Iv 68] Kyrie motetus trope:

Clemens pater, conditor syderum
mundi rector datorque munerum
verax deus destructor scelerum,
eleyson. Kyrie eleyson.

Rex pie celi potens virtutibus
tremor factus cunctis demonibus
qui ruerunt ab altis sedibus,
eleyson. Christe eleyson.

Jesu Christe, nostra redemptio
fili Dei vera dilectio
a quo cuncta manat perfectio,
eleyson. Christe eleyson.

Sacrosancte amborum spiritus
qui vocaris semper paraclitus
placans omnis languentium gemitus,
eleyson. Kyrie eleyson.

Sacrum flamen superna bonitas
ignis ardens li[que] caritas
una manens in tribus deitas,
eleyson.

This Kyrie is the opening piece in the Apt manuscript, which also contains (as no. 38, no. 12 in the edition) a more normally troped Kyrie *Summe clementissime rex eterne glorie* eleyson.

Clemens deus artifex
tota clementia
actuque specie
mirabilis essentia
carens carie   5
spurcitia
dux venie
patriarcharum
missus pro iustitia
pastor ecclesie   10
conservator fidei sanctie
triumphator pro victoria.
extirpandi hostis tormenta varia
crucem mysterii previa
o que spiritus incendia   15
o redemptor, o rex pie
splendor eterne glorie
fac fidelium virtutem
resistere contra vitia
ut mederi nullus valeat   20
iam infectum fecis sanie
et dimittat ius profanum
venenosum et insanum
errorem ad fidelia
perennis dona gratie   25
constanter indefectivia
Amen

The merciful creator God, all clemency, in deed and in appearance, marvellous in essence, lacking decay and filth, commander of mercy sent for the justice of the patriarchs, shepherd of the church, preserver of the holy faith, triumpher for the victory of wiping out various devices of the enemy with the cross of mystery going before.

O what fires of the spirit! O redeemer, O merciful king, splendour of eternal glory, cause the virtue of the faithful to hold out against vices, so that none may heal one already infected by the filth of dregs, and let him discard profane law, a poisonous and insane error, for the faithful gifts of eternal grace, constantly never-failing.

The most interesting of the tributes to Clement is Philippe de Vitry's motet *Petre clemens/Lugentium*, for which Andrew Wathey has found a new text source in a collection of Clement's sermons copied in Avignon in the late 1340s. It is therefore the earliest of the text-only copies of Vitry motet texts, made during the lifetimes of both Clement and Vitry.[35] No texts survive separately for any fourteenth-century composer other than Vitry, and the anonymous texts belong only to those compositions that at least some modern scholars have suspected to be possibly his work. The motet texts in the sermon volume are immediately preceded by a longer verse celebration of Clement's rule beginning *Aperi labia mea*. They are followed by a tenor incipit, *Non est inventus similis illi*, absent from the musical sources of the motet, and by a brief colophon, added in a different but contemporary hand, which attributes the

[35] See Diana Wood, *Clement VI: The Pontificate and Ideas of an Avignon Pope* (Cambridge, 1989), and Wathey, 'The Motets of Philippe de Vitry', including text and translation by David Howlett.

texts clearly to Vitry and supplies a date for their composition: 'Magister Philippus de Vitrejo in laudem Pape Clementis vj^{ti} anno suo primo circa natalem domini' (i.e. around Christmas 1342; taking the confines of the feast literally this could be narrowed to 24 December 1342–5 January 1343). There are two sermon cycles: the first includes sermons of Pierre Roger as Archbishop of Rouen preached in Avignon in the 1330s; the second consists exclusively of sermons by Clement dating from immediately before his coronation and from the early years of his pontificate. Most are associated with special occasions and special themes. The most important of these are for April 1343 and April 1346, and refer to part of his campaign against Louis of Bavaria, the pretender to the Imperial crown. There are bulls against Louis, and there is Clement's often-quoted reply of 27 January 1343 to the embassy of Roman citizens, discussed below.

The motet texts have often been assumed to be for Clement's coronation, or just generally laudatory. There is nothing specifically inaugural in them, and with this new loosening of the—anyway weak—basis for assuming that motets are more likely to be inaugural than not, a primary function as propaganda to promote papal diplomacy can now be contemplated. At Christmas 1342 a Roman delegation came to Avignon to petition for the return of the papacy to Rome. Clement's reply included the famous expression 'ubi papa ibi Roma'. He supported his refusal not only with practical reasons arising from the Anglo-French wars but also with doctrinal considerations. He upheld the independence of the papacy from the bishopric of Rome, and the universal rather than the local character of papal power. In the words of the text: *Petrus primus petrum non deseris, vices eius quia recta geris* (You first Peter [pope] do not abandon the rock [*petrus*, St Peter—i.e. of the church] because you guide it rightly in his stead). We might find here, also, an allusion to the rocky fortress of Avignon as a suitable seat for Peter's successor.

Petre clemens is Vitry's longest and probably latest surviving motet, with 251 perfect breves of major prolation. Its rhythmic vocabulary differs from the earlier motets in availing itself of the new and wider notational range. If this motet seems less compactly structured than his earlier works, or indeed than the two precocious motets discussed above, that could simply mean that it has not yet yielded up its formal secrets. Karl Kügle and Manuel Pedro Ferreira have found structural patterns in text and music that they relate to the 'sixthness' of Clement, and to gematrial puns on his name: Clemens = 67; Clemens is the 67th word in the motetus.[36] But there are also other

---

[36] Both gave papers dealing with this motet at a conference in Princeton in Oct. 1989: 'The Gothic Motet: Politics, Words and Music in the Fourteenth Century'. See Kügle, 'The Manuscript Ivrea', ch. 3. The triplum and motetus are arranged in alternating periods of breves, grouped respectively 12 + 3 + 3 | 9 + 3 + 3, and 15 + 3 | 12 + 3.

compelling numerical structures, of 7 × 33-breve *taleae* (preceded by 14 breves and followed by 6), and other motets use multiple sets of numbers.

The tenor of the motet remained unlabelled and unidentified until Wathey's recent discovery, which provided a verbal tag from which Alice Clark identified *Non est inventus similis illi* as the verse of the Gradual *Ecce sacerdos magnus* for the Common of One Confessor. Finding this Gradual used for the fourth-century pope Silvester, she argues a connection with Constantine's tolerance of Christianity and the establishment of papal authority at that time.[37] Joanna Melville made an independent identification, showing that the long single-*color* tenor of this motet in fact appears to be a confection of several chants, all selected for their close suitability to the subject.[38] Her identifications presume a somewhat flexible relationship between the tenor and its chants, though not an unparalleled one, and gaps in identification remain. Nevertheless, this promising suggestion merits extension beyond the *Liber Usualis*, to which her search was limited. The chants are *Memento Domine David* (the Introit for a Confessor Bishop, from Ps. 132), *Non est inventus similis illi* (the tag found in a text manuscript, from the Gradual *Ecce sacerdos magnus*, also from the Mass for a Confessor Bishop), *Tu es Petrus* (Vespers antiphon for SS Peter and Paul), and the hymn *Iste Confessor Domini* (second vespers for the Common of a Confessor Bishop). Why, we might ask, is the tag given in the text manuscript not the chant of the opening of the tenor (*Memento Domine*)? It *is*, however, the text of the chant at the point where the first isorhythmic *talea* starts.

On the basis of the new evidence placing *Petre clemens* several months into the new pope's reign and thus dissociating it from his coronation, Wathey argues that a single monofunctional association between motets and narrowly defined state purposes, royal and papal coronations in particular, no longer appears justifiable in all cases. Official festivity was indeed one, but not necessarily the only, performance context. This fits perfectly with later evidence for multiple use of occasional pieces, and may ease the dilemma outlined above for earlier ones. Many of the occasional motets in Bologna Q 15 were clearly written in honour of dedicatees or occasions. In some cases they might have been inaugural, in others they clearly cannot have been. Some of these motets were recopied long after the deaths of their dedicatees without verbal change. I have discussed elsewhere the case of Ciconia's motet *Venecie mundi splendor/Michael qui Stena domus*, which is often alleged to celebrate the installation in 1400 of Doge Michele Steno, whose name opens the second cantus part. Ciconia's affiliation with

---

[37] Alice V. Clark, 'Concordare cum Materia: The Tenor in the Fourteenth-Century Motet' (Ph.D. diss., Princeton University, 1996), ch. 5.

[38] Joanna Melville, 'A Study in Coherence in Four Motets by Philippe de Vitry' (MA thesis, University of Wales, Bangor, 1994), i. 62, ii. exx. 23, 49.

Carrara circles at that time makes that association rather unlikely, and shifts attention rather to the period after the fall of Carrara Padua to Venice in 1405, and specifically to the submission in January 1406 of the Paduan Signoria to Venetian rule in a ceremony in Piazza San Marco, when the oration by Ciconia's patron Zabarella might well have been complemented by this motet.[39]

Pope Gregory XI (1370–8) was Pierre Roger de Beaufort, a nephew of Clement VI. The Chantilly motet *Pictagore per dogmata/O terra sancta, suplica/Rosa vernans caritatis* must have been written for him. Ursula Günther places it early in 1375, certainly between 1374 and September 1376, when Gregory left Avignon in order to take up residence in Rome.[40] The text is a plea to recapture the Holy Land, used here as a metaphor for the recapture of Rome.[41] There is play on the name Rosiers, Roger, for the untraced tenor *Rosa vernans caritatis* refers to the Roger arms, identical for Clement VI and Gregory XI, which bear six roses. Gregory's other paternal uncle Hugues had refused the papal tiara in 1362.

The Great Schism

Throughout the Avignon period, attempts were made to secure a return of the papacy to Rome. Urban V was in Italy 1367–70, and the first to re-establish the *sedes romana*, even temporarily. Gregory XI was in Rome with seventeen cardinals early in 1376, and remained there until his death in March 1378. Under pressure to choose an Italian, these same cardinals elected the Neapolitan canonist Bartolomeo Prignano, who was enthroned as Urban VI at Easter (18 April). Urban behaved with an authoritarianism that alienated the cardinals, whose life-style he tried to simplify and whose wish to return to Avignon he quelled. Violent outbursts and impolitic and abusive behaviour created difficulties that eclipsed the firmness of purpose and austerity that had helped his candidacy. Repelled by Urban's behaviour, the French cardinals defected under the leadership of Robert of Geneva, whom they elected pope at a new conclave in Fondi on 20 September 1378, thus opening the Schism. Taking the name of Clement VII, Robert remained in Italy at first, moving to Avignon in May 1379, where he died 16 September 1394.

Clement's election is celebrated, and Urban condemned as Antichrist, in the texts of a motet discovered by Martin Steinmann and Wulf Arlt

---

[39] See Johannes Ciconia, *Works*, ed. Margaret Bent and Anne Hallmark (PMFC 24; Monaco, 1985), p. xii.

[40] Ursula Günther (ed.), *The Motets of the Manuscripts Chantilly, Musée Condé, 564 (olim 1047) and Modena, Biblioteca Estense, α.M.5.24 (olim lat. 568)* (CMM 39; American Institute of Musicology, 1965).

[41] Tomasello, *Music and Ritual*, points to the parallel ancestries of the Roman people and of Gregory XI. He is Mars, Clement VI his uncle was Phoebus. Ursula Günther believes the unnamed planet of seven is Saturn, before his fall, whom she identifies as Gregory; Tomasello disagrees.

in two independent fragments (but still incomplete) in Basle, *Gaudeat et exultet/Papam querentes*.[42] This is the only known motet that refers so explicitly to two factions in the Schism. In anticipation of their promised study of this highly intriguing piece, which is awaited with great interest, I refrain from further comment here.

The musical culture of the Avignon chapel is as well attested as its other artistic expressions. John, Duke (subsequently king) of Aragon instructed his agents in 1379 to seek good singers in Avignon for his chapel. They were to be young, unmarried, preferably able to play an instrument, and not to have been (as was Matheus de Sancto Johanne) in the service of the Duke of Anjou. They were to bring a book of *cant de la missa notat e un libre* (containing many) *motets e rondels e ballades e virelays*.[43] This becomes particularly suggestive in the light of the repertory of the Chantilly manuscript, which contains no masses but exactly 100 songs, as well as thirteen motets. Recent studies by Reinhard Strohm and John Nádas combine to eliminate Avignon itself and to advance Visconti circles in Pavia as a likely place of origin for that manuscript and as the centre from which French music of the so-called *ars subtilior* may have been disseminated in Italy.[44]

Clement VII's court continued and extended the sumptuous style established by Clement VI. The three compositions directly associated with him are all in Chantilly, two French ballades and one in Latin. He is the only one of our musically celebrated popes for whom no motets survive; but it is too rash to extrapolate a decline in popularity of motet composition from the particular case of the Chantilly manuscript or from the particular ethos of his court. Moreover, we must not lose sight of the fact that many motets of this period were hardly less secular than ballades. They may have had symbolic tenors drawn from chant, and as such fallen under the general restrictions on ecclesiastical chant of John XXII earlier in the century; but their newly composed texts were no less enthusiastically packed with classical allusions and sophistries.

Mayhuet de Joan's three-stanza ballade *Inclite flos orti Gebenensis* refers in its opening line to Robert of Geneva's origin, and the tenor is labelled: Tenor 'pro papa Clemente' [VII].[45] Matheus de Sancto Johanne received a canonry from Clement in 1378, while he was serving in the chapel of Louis I, Duke of Anjou. He was one of the private chaplains of the pope in Avignon from 1382

[42] Reported in Lorenz Welker, *Musik am Oberrhein im späten Mittelalter: Die Handschrift Strasbourg, olim Bibliothèque de la ville, C.22* (Habilitationsschrift, Basle, 1993), 77, 101.

[43] Tomasello, *Music and Ritual*, 40.

[44] Reinhard Strohm, 'Filippotto da Caserta, ovvero i francesi in Lombardia', in Fabrizio Della Seta and Franco Piperno (eds.), *In cantu et in sermone: A Nino Pirrotta nel suo 80° compleanno* (Florence, 1989), 65–74, and John Nádas and Agostino Ziino (eds.), *The Lucca Codex (Codice Mancini). Introductory Study and Facsimile Edition* (Ars Nova, 1; Lucca, 1990).

[45] Modena 5.24, fo. 15, Chantilly, fo. 41.

until at least 1386. Because of the references in this text to Spanish acceptance of his papacy, it has been thought that this piece must date from later in his reign. Castille recognized Clement in 1382, Aragon in 1387, Navarre not until 1390.[46] However, Giuliano Di Bacco and John Nádas now believe that *Inclite flos* could have been written during Clement's residence in Naples between September 1378 and May 1379, especially since Matheus was probably in Italy during those months, and he had previously served Clement. Early Spanish support for Clement was evidently undergirded by many more factors than the later confirmations suggest.[47]

Magister Egidius' ballade *Courtois et sages* affirms the validity of the election and names Clemens in an acrostic. *Par les bons Gedeons*, a ballade by Filippotto da Caserta, has the refrain line *le souverayn pape qui s'appelle Clement*.[48] In the recently discovered Turin manuscript (Turin 2), which has connections with the Pisan popes Alexander V and John XXIII, this same ballade appears with the variant *antipape* in this line![49]

Popes named Clement of course invite punning salutations, and we must take care not to see them where they are not, for example, in the invocation 'O clemens' in the *Salve regina*. But another troped Gloria from the older Padua fragments cannot be excluded as a Clementine composition. The Gloria 'Clementie pax' presents Clement as the first word of a trope that expands and further tropes the Gloria trope 'Spiritus et alme'. Clement VII died in 1394; F. Alberto Gallo and Kurt von Fischer recognize this as being a Gloria for a late fourteenth-century Marian Mass.[50] The text mentions Esther, who also appears in the motet for John XXIII (see below), as she does in several other English and French compositions during the Hundred Years War. This is not included in the Appendix, the reference being too unspecific.

Abandoned in Rome by the cardinals who left for Fondi, Urban VI created twenty-five new cardinals, one of whom was the Valois Philippe d'Alençon, of whom more below. Although the papal entourage in Italy had to moderate considerably the luxurious style to which it had become accustomed in Avignon, even on a reduced scale the retinues of pope and cardinals included foreign musicians who had been in Avignon, thus starting a two-century

---

[46] Tomasello, *Music and Ritual*, 41.

[47] See Di Bacco and Nádas, below, Ch. 2. They very kindly communicated this point to me privately.

[48] Published in Willi Apel (ed.), *French Secular Compositions of the Fourteenth Century* (CMM 53; American Institute of Musicology, 1970), i. 21 and 82.

[49] See Agostino Ziino (ed.), *Il Codice T. III.2 (The Codex T.III.2), Torino, Biblioteca Nazionale Universitaria, Studio introduttivo ed edizione in facsimile a cura di Agostino Ziino (Introductory Study and Facsimile Edition by Agostino Ziino)* (Ars Nova, 3; Lucca, 1994), fo. 5ᵛ.

[50] Ed. F. Alberto Gallo and Kurt von Fischer, *Italian Sacred Music* (PMFC 12; Monaco, 1976), no. 9, p. 30. It is in Padua, Biblioteca Universitaria, MS 1475, from the older complex of Paduan fragments that also includes the Sanctus St Omer and the *Ite missa est* of the Machaut mass.

tradition of northerners in Italy.[51] There is also a reverse direction: the musicians who had been in Rome but then returned to Avignon with Clement VII may have had some reciprocal influence.

One of the most puzzling of papal motet survivals is another fragmentary work, *Alme pater*, of which triplum and tenor only (of originally four parts) are preserved in the English paper Fountains manuscript of around 1400, one of the earliest documents of void notation.[52] Roger Bowers has proposed a convincing solution to the historical events dealt with in the motet.[53]

Alme pater, pastor vere	Kindly father, true shepherd of all Christ-
christicolarum omnium,	worshippers, for you for a long time the minds of
per te diu doluere	all our people have lamented.
mentes nostrorum omnium.	
....	
.... misera trucibus	You, captured, alas have suffered such miserable
sustulisti tam perversa	improprieties from brutal hands.
heu, captivatus,[54] manibus	
......	
.... neepolitani nobiles	The Neapolitan nobles, indeed whom you highly
quos diligebas tamen	esteemed, were alas no gentlemen.
heu, non fuerunt nobiles.	
Ulcissi tuum munere	With [due] reward, avenge your fate upon their
egena illorum atria.	beggarly halls! Your ungrateful native land had
repleverat innumere	rewarded them inordinately.
ingrata tua patria.	
Dudum profusis lacrimis	A little while ago our faces were anointed with
nostre sunt uncte facies,	copious tears because, while you were restraining
quod te dum malos comprimis	wicked men, the cruel blade threatens you.
atrox obcedit acies	
Intra suos vidit muros,	Within her walls, Luceria (every day to be praised
omni cantanda feria.	in song) has seen you for a long time to suffer
casus diu pati duros	harsh, lamentable mischances.
te flebiles luceria.	

[51] Di Bacco and Nádas, 'Verso uno "stile internazionale"'. On the subject of northerners in Italy, see also Reinhard Strohm, 'Filippotto da Caserta'.

[52] London, British Library, Add. MS 40011B. Published in facsimile in Margaret Bent (ed.), *The Fountains Fragments* (Musical Sources, 26; Clarabricken, 1987). The provenance of the Fountains manuscript remains uncertain. The host MS is an account book of Fountains abbey of the 1440s, but the music is mostly based on Sarum chants from the lowlands.

[53] Roger Bowers, 'Fixed Points in the Chronology of English Fourteenth-Century Polyphony', *Music and Letters*, 71 (1990), 313–35, esp. 317–20. He extends the similar conclusion of Peter M. Lefferts, reached independently; *The Motet in England in the Fourteenth Century* (Ann Arbor, 1986), 184, 348–9. The translation is by Bowers.

[54] An irregular abbreviation. I had originally read it as *captivarum*, which led me down a different but related path of investigation into the captivity of Queen Joanna.

What is such a text doing in an English manuscript? The motet may be English or French in origin, but neither side had much enthusiasm for Urban. The English were at least nominally on the side of the Roman pope at this time. The pope addressed must be Urban VI (1378–89), the events his misfortunes at the siege of Nocera (also called *Luceria christianorum*). Before his election the Neapolitan Urban had been Archbishop of Bari and vice-chancellor of the papal household. He was recognized by English church and government against Clement VII as the Schism developed in 1378–9. To the anger of Urban, Queen Joanna I of Naples sided with Clement. With Urban's help, Charles of Durazzo deposed and murdered Joanna in 1381, but as king of Naples (Charles III) he failed to show gratitude to Urban, who then took up residence in 1384 at the castle of Nocera, where he was besieged (i.e. *captivatus*) and subjected to many indignities between March and July 1385.

Roger Bowers gives a masterly account of the competing claims and loyalties that led not only to the composition of this piece (perhaps by an Englishman, and probably in 1385). He also suggests how it may have come to be copied in a later English source, pointing out that few Englishmen had reason to favour Urban, especially as he imprisoned and tortured the English Cardinal Adam Easton during the siege, a cardinal Reinhard Strohm thinks may be responsible for the motet text.[55] Bowers identifies John of Gaunt as one of few English well disposed towards Urban; he recognized his counter-claim to the Castilian throne in 1381 and supported his military campaign of 1386. Bowers observes that after Urban's death in 1389 the motet can hardly have remained long in any live repertory, and offers parallel events in 1405–7 as a possible occasion for the motet's revival and recopying, the 1380s being too early a dating for the Fountains manuscript. There are, however, instances, from *Fauvel* to Ciconia, of the later copying of pieces no longer topical, for reasons ranging from satire to musical interest, which should caution against over-literal assumptions about the topical life of such compositions.

The motet has six stanzas—for Urban VI? As well as being an early example of void notation, the tenor uses coloration in the unusual reversed sense to provide perfect notes, the basic void notes being imperfect.[56] With some irregularities, it appears to have been isorhythmic in all voices.

---

[55] Reinhard Strohm, *The Rise of European Music 1380–1500* (Cambridge, 1993), 16–17; see the rest of his Introduction for more comments on this repertory.

[56] Also found in *Alpha vibrans* and *O amicus*. For the latter see Margaret Bent with David Howlett, '*Subtiliter alternare*: The Yoxford Motet *O amicus/Precursoris*', in Peter M. Lefferts and Brian Seirup (eds.), *Studies in Medieval Music: Festschrift for Ernest Sanders* (New York, 1990) = *Current Musicology*, 45–7 (1990), 43–84.

The Pisan Antipopes

We move now to the events surrounding the Council of Pisa. The Veneto abandoned the Venetian pope Angelo Correr, Gregory XII, in favour of Pietro Filargo of Candia (Venetian Crete), who was elected Pope Alexander V (26 June, crowned 7 July 1409). The ranks of those who were to be his supporters were augmented in the preceding few years by deserters from Rome, impatient at Gregory's nonfeasance. Briefly thought to have ended the Schism, this third papacy was of necessity itinerant, but based mainly in Bologna.

Two compositions, neither of them conventional motets, allude to Alexander, and one motet survives for his successor John XXIII. The two pieces for the first Pisan pope are by two front-rank composers, neither of them directly documented in his service, Ciconia and Zacara.

Several possibilities have been put forward for the addressee and subject of Ciconia's *O Petre Christi discipule*.[57]

O Petre, Christi discipule,
prime pastor ecclesie,
funde preces quotidie
pro Petro nostro presule.

Peter, Christ's disciple, thou first shepherd of the Church, pour forth thy prayers daily for our bishop Peter.

O princeps apostolice,
turbe Cephas dominice,
pastorem nostrum dirige,
quem omni malo protege.

O prince of the apostles, Cephas, rock for the Lord's multitude, guide our shepherd and protect him from every evil.

Da sit in cunctis providus,
corpus et mentem candidus,
omni virtute splendidus,
in bono semper fervidus.

Grant that he be foresighted in all things, fair in body and mind, resplendent in all virtue, ever eager in what is good.

O Christe, ductor ovium,
perenne presta gaudium;
pastorem, clerum, populum
salva per omne seculum.

O Christ, thou leader of the sheep, grant eternal joy; save thy shepherd, clergy and people for ever and ever.

There are two ways of reading this text. The more obvious one is that both the first two verses address St Peter, initially as Christ's disciple and then first pope, second as prince of the Apostles, both invocations requesting St Peter's support for the new prelate Peter. In the Ciconia edition I adopted this weaker reading, seeing St Peter invoked by Ciconia for the new bishop of Padua, Pietro Marcello. But the most recent consensus is that it must, after all, be for

---

[57] Translation by Leofranc Holford-Strevens.

a pope. Now that we have secure evidence that Ciconia was not in Avignon but in Rome, we can set aside Suzanne Clercx's hypothesis that it might be for the antipope Benedict XIII (Pedro di Luna), in Avignon, 1394. Giuliano Di Bacco and John Nádas have proposed the interesting and persuasive hypothesis that it was written for Alexander V. Pope Peter is Pietro Filargo, and 'Pastorem nostrum . . . Corpus et mentem candidus' is a pun on Filargo's origin in Candia (Crete). Ciconia's attachment to Zabarella is almost sufficient reason in itself to assume Ciconia was at the Council of Pisa in 1409, but he may have come into contact with Filargo before then. The Roman link now provides additional reasons to assume his presence at Pisa.

But the text could also be taken as three levels of invocation, as Di Bacco and Nádas have proposed, first addressing the new Pope Pietro [Filargo] who watches over another Pietro, then St Peter (*cephas*) who protects the new pope; then finally addressing Christ the leader of all, setting out three levels *pastorem, clerum, populum*. The addressee must be Peter and/or a pope, and the subject for whom intercession is made a pope and/or a bishop. But if there are indeed three layers, which bishop is the third Peter? Di Bacco and Nádas suggest that the other Petrus for whom prayers are sought might be Pietro Marcello, appointed bishop of Padua earlier in 1409 and confirmed by Alexander V.[58] This makes good sense in the context of Ciconia's Paduan connections throughout the first decade. He wrote a full-dress motet for the Paduan bishop, probably for his enthronement, *Petrum Marcellum venetum/O petre antistes*, in September 1409, an occasion notable for humanist oratory and for which there was ample time to prepare. But despite Ciconia's specifically Paduan allegiance, could the two-part piece equally well be addressed to the new Pisan pope in the name not of Marcello but of Pietro Emiliani, appointed to the see of Vicenza by Alexander as one of the earliest appointments after his election, on 12 August 1409? Emiliani seems to have been a patron of polyphonic music, and his attachment and gratitude to Filargo were still expressed in his will twenty years later.[59]

One puzzling feature of the piece is that it is not an Italian motet, of the type increasingly associated with ceremonial dignity in the Veneto, where Ciconia was now based under the patronage of Zabarella. It has two equal low-cleffed voices, a single text, and no tenor, and is unique to Bologna Q 15. But after

---

[58] Di Bacco and Nádas, 'Verso uno "stile internazionale" ', 33 n. 63. For the motet and its text see Ciconia, *Works*, ed. Bent and Hallmark.

[59] I have given preliminary information on Emiliani in 'Humanists and Music, Music and Humanities', in Raffaele Pozzi (ed.), *Tendenze e metodi nella ricerca musicologica. Atti del Convegno internazionale (Latina 27–29 Settembre 1990)* (Florence, 1995), 29–38, and 'Pietro Emiliani's Chaplain Bartolomeo Rossi da Carpi and the Lamentations of Johannes de Quadris in Vicenza', *Saggiatore musicale*, 2 (1995), 5–16. See also Dieter Girgensohn, 'Il testamento di Pietro Miani ('Emilianus') vescovo di Vicenza (†1433)', *Archivio veneto*, ser. 5, vol. 132 (1989), 5–60.

Ciconia had already written several Veneto motets, why would he revert to a unique texture and form for *O Petre Christi*? David Fallows has discussed equal-voice compositions of this period.[60] There are two by Ciconia, both in Bologna Q 15. One is clearly a ballata contrafact, as *O beatum incendium*, of *Aler m'en veus*. *O Petre Christi* shows none of the symptoms of contrafaction. A new addition to this two-equal-voice repertory is also provided by the new Turin fragments (Turin 2), the ballata *Dime, Fortuna, poi che tu parlasti*.[61] Both its manuscript neighbours and its musical and vivid autobiographical text style strongly suggest Zacara as the composer. It includes the words 'Se Alessandro a Roma gito fosse, Fortuna, al tuo despecto uscia de fosse'. This seems to express the speaker's frustration at Fortune that Alexander V had not returned to Rome, that is that the Pisan election had not worked, and that the dependent speaker was thereby deprived of going to Rome with him. If they are both addressed to Alexander during his lifetime, they must date from the same nine-month period.

Alexander's short papacy was followed by that of John XXIII (the Neapolitan Baldassare Cossa, elected 17 May 1410). Before his election, he had been archbishop and papal legate in Bologna, a prime mover in the Council of Pisa, and one of those who helped get Alexander V elected. Together with Louis II of Anjou, he had led the successful siege and military campaign against Rome on behalf of Alexander V, laying siege and finally taking the city in January 1410. When he was deposed and condemned by the Council of Constance, he was accused of having poisoned Alexander and his physician, and of all kinds of fraud and sexual misdemeanours.

Antonio Zacara da Teramo had been a singer and secretary in Rome under popes Boniface IX, Innocent VII, and Gregory XII from early in 1391 to at least 1407;[62] his presence in Rome therefore overlapped with Ciconia's. Di Bacco and Nádas have now pushed Zacara's Roman residence back to at least 5 January 1390, when he was paid for the writing, notation, and illumination of an antiphonal for the hospital of Santo Spirito, in a document that also reveals his patronymic: *Magister Antonius Berardi Andree de Teramo alias dictus vulgariter Zacchara*.[63] Zacara's presence as *magister capelle* of John XXIII in Bologna in 1412–13 (after which he disappears)[64] shows that he had trans-

---

[60] David Fallows, 'Two Equal Voices: A French Song Repertory with Music for Two More Works of Oswald von Wolkenstein', *EMH* 7 (1987), 227–41.

[61] Ziino, *Il Codice T. III.2.*   [62] Ziino, 'Magister Antonius', and Nádas, 'Further Notes'.

[63] Di Bacco and Nádas, 'Verso uno "stile internazionale" ', 27, drawing on the 1390 document published in Anna Esposito, ' "Magistro Zaccara" e l'antifonario dell'Ospedale di S. Spirito in Sassia', in Paolo Cherubini, Anna Esposito, *et al.*, 'Il costo del libro', in Massimo Miglio *et al.* (eds.), *Scrittura, biblioteche e stampa a Roma nel Quattrocento, Atti del 2. seminario* (Littera Antiqua, 3; Vatican City, 1983), 334–42, 446–9.

[64] Nádas, 'Further Notes', 178–9. See also Di Bacco and Nádas, 'Verso uno "stile internazionale"', 28, for the narrowing of Zacara's death date to between May 1413 and Sept. 1416.

ferred to the Pisan faction at some stage. Indeed, an earlier association with Alexander V is attested by the new text in the Turin fragments. However, his continued activity as *scriptor litterarum apostolicarum* show that he was in Rome up to the eve of Gregory XII's departure in June 1407. Here, if not before, he must have come into contact with Pietro Emiliani, who had served Gregory as clerk of the papal Camera from March of that year, and then as vice-chamberlain. Emiliani followed Gregory to Viterbo and Siena that summer, but left Gregory's retinue in October 1407 and was present in Pisa as a sup-porter and beneficiary of Filargo.[65] Zacara could have done the same, or he could have left Gregory with other defectors in July 1408 to gather in Pisa in preparation for the Council.[66] The presence of Zacara's work in the Cividale fragments has been taken to imply that he may have been there for the abortive Council of Cividale called by Gregory XII from June to September 1409 when, deserted by most of his cardinals, he had fled with his remaining ret-inue. But there is no evidence that Zacara remained with Gregory after 1407 or that he accompanied him to Cividale; the presence of his and Filippotto's music in the Cividale fragments does not necessitate their physical presence there.

No motet survives for the new pope by Humbertus de Salinis or Matteo da Perugia, both known to be composer-singers in his retinue. Pietro Filargo must be suspected of strong musical persuasions and tastes, from the very fact of having at least two notable composers in his retinue. It has been suggested that the first stage of Modena 5.24 may have been prepared for him by Matteo; the manuscript contains three essays by Ciconia in styles very differ-ent from each other, and each apparently unique in his output—*Sus un fontayne*, *Le ray au soleil*, and *Quod jactatur*.[67] But Modena 5.24 preserves neither *O Petre Christi* nor *Dime Fortuna*, which are only in Bologna Q 15 and Turin 2 respectively.

Reinhard Strohm proposed that Pavia rather than Avignon was the main centre of cultivation of the French *ars subtilior*, and suggested that Filippotto and Antonello da Caserta, Ciconia, Matteo da Perugia, and Senleches may have been guests or clients of Giangaleazzo Visconti (ruled 1385–1402).[68] More recently, Anne Stone has pointed out that Filargo is known from later evidence to have had a house in Pavia, and convincingly suggests a possible

---

[65] Girgensohn, 'Il testamento', 19.   [66] Nádas, 'Further Notes', 169.

[67] See Reinhard Strohm, 'Magister Egardus and Other Italo-Flemish Contacts', *L'Ars nova italiana del Trecento*, 6 (1992), 41–68; 59 for the suggestion that Modena 5.24 originated in Filargo's circle, and that the pieces listed by Bartolomeo and Corradus may have been written for his coronation. See, for further develop-ment of this hypothesis, Anne Stone, 'Writing Rhythm in Late Medieval Italy: Notation and Musical Style in the Manuscript Modena, Biblioteca Estense, Alpha.M.5.24' (Ph.D. diss., Harvard University, 1994).

[68] Strohm, 'Filippotto da Caserta', 65–74.

genesis for the manuscript Modena 5.24 in his circle.[69] Matteo da Perugia had served in Filargo's chapel when he was archbishop of Milan, and Salinis was confirmed as a member promptly after the election. In the case of this conciliar election of a third pope, there was not an existing chapel for him to inherit, except in so far as deserters from Gregory were available in Pisa. Bologna Q 15 also presents the Paduan work of Ciconia, including the two motets for his patron Francesco Zabarella, who along with Jean Gerson and Du Fay's patron Pierre d'Ailly were noted supporters of music in addition to being the prime legal, theological, and tactical movers in attempts to end first twofold and then threefold Schism at the councils respectively of Pisa and Constance.

Matteo da Perugia is presumed to have followed his patron from Milan to Pisa and remained with him after his election as pope. His continuing service is not documented, but may be implied by his absence from Milan cathedral between 1407 and 1414.[70] Humbertus de Salinis appears as a papal familiar and singer on 10 July 1409, three days after Alexander's coronation.[71] Boniface IX awarded his first papal benefice (as a deacon) on 29 May 1403 in a document indicating that he was at the time in Braga. This need not mean that he was Portuguese by birth; indeed his use of old texts known in the north and a motet for the Liégeois St Lambert strongly suggest that he like so many other singers in receipt of high patronage came from northern Europe. If he was too young to be a priest in 1403, there is one work which may be out of line chronologically. This is the ballade *En ce gracieus temps* (Chantilly) for Thomasse le Blanc, the mother of Olivier du Guesclin. She died in 1406, but Gilbert Reaney says it could date from Olivier's lifetime, before 1397. The earlier date now looks less likely. Three Salinis motets are grouped together in Florence SL 2211 (late 1410s); in the first layer of Bologna Q 15 they are scattered. His Good Friday motet, *Jesu salvator*, heads the original form of Oxford 213;[72] it can perhaps also be read as a salutation of new begininings through Church councils. We know he was at Pisa; for Constance we have no evidence.

One other work by Ciconia is associated with this period and these events. Unlike the simultaneous tropes of the two Clementine Glorias, Ciconia's Gloria 'Suscipe Trinitas' is troped in the more normal manner, with alternating sections, in three-part harmony for the text of the Gloria of the Mass, and two-part sections for the added trope, otherwise unknown. The verses of the trope

[69] Stone, 'Writing Rhythm in Late Medieval Italy', 15, 44–51.

[70] Brad Maiani, 'Notes on Matteo da Perugia: Adapting the Ambrosian Liturgy in Polyphony for the Pisan Council', *Studi musicali*, 24 (1995), 3–28, esp. 4–7.

[71] See Nosow, 'The Florid and Equal-Discantus Motet'.

[72] See Graeme MacDonald Boone, 'Dufay's Early Chansons: Chronology and Style in the Manuscript Oxford, Bodleian Library, Canonici Misc. 213' (Ph.D. diss., Harvard University, 1987), 29–31, and David Fallows (ed.), *Oxford, Bodleian Library MS. Canon. Misc. 213* (Late Medieval and Early Renaissance Music in Facsimile, 1; Chicago and London, 1995).

are addressed to the Trinity, to Mary, and to St Peter, the first pope and 'heavenly keeper of the keys'. The trinitarian references have contributed to the suggestion that the trope must date from the period of threefold Schism between the election of a third pope in 1409 and Ciconia's death in 1412.[73] Reinhard Strohm suggests that it may have followed the election of John XXIII in 1410, 'whose support exceeded that of the other schismatic popes'.[74] But for a new proposal, see the contribution of Di Bacco and Nádas to this volume (Ch. 2).

Salinis's troped Gloria 'Jubilacio' celebrates the end of the Schism, and has usually been dated to the election of a single pope, Martin V, in 1417. However, Salinis is no longer listed as a papal chaplain in 1413, when Zacara is named as *magister capelle* for John XXIII, and there is no evidence of his activity after that. It now seems more likely that the Gloria trope dates not from Constance (1417), but from Pisa (1409), when the election of Salinis's patron as Alexander V could well have been celebrated as ending the Schism. Until the discovery of Florence SL 2211, all Salinis's mass music and motets were unique to Bologna Q 15, except the Gloria 'Jubilacio', which also appears in Venice 145. His mass music is transmitted together with Zacara's in Bologna Q 15; we surely have here remnants of the repertory of Pisa–Bologna from the years 1409–14 as well as additions from Constance.

The motet *Argi vices/Cum Philemon*, unique to the later Aosta manuscript, is explicitly for John XXIII, possibly for his election in May 1410, but perhaps for the start of the Council of Constance, and at any rate before 1414, when he was discredited.[75] The composer is named in the text simply as Nicola[us], the poet as Guillermus. Previous scholars considered both Nicolaus Zacarie and Nicolas Grenon as candidates for identification with this composer, but in the absence of evidence of their connection with John's chapel, their candidacy has weakened. It has to be stated, however, that evidence for Nicolaus Frangens de Leodio, currently assumed by some to be the composer, is no more secure. Certainly the use of the verb 'frangit' in triplum line 41 is insufficient: it is the clouds that are being broken through, and to attach this

---

[73] Ciconia, *Works*, ed. Bent and Hallmark, p. xi.   [74] Strohm, *The Rise of European Music*, 17.

[75] The motet has been published most recently by von Fischer and Gallo in PMFC 13. The editors reject attributions to Nicolaus Zacarie and Grenon and favour Nicolaus Frangens de Leodio (commentary, p. 285). The motet is discussed at length by Marian Cobin, 'The Aosta Manuscript: A Central Source of Early Fifteenth-Century Sacred Music' (Ph.D. diss., New York University, 1978), with translation. Robert Nosow has pulled together this composer's biography and itinerary, 'The Florid and Equal-Discantus Motet'. Von Fischer rightly adds it to the list of Italian motets I published in 'The Fourteenth-Century Italian Motet', *L'Ars nova italiana del Trecento*, 6 (Certaldo, [1992]), 85–125. He thus vindicates Guillaume de Van's claims for the piece, which I had overlooked because of its later transmission and because of an uncertain cut-off date for precedents for Ciconia. However, his 'Bemerkungen zur Trecento-Motette: Überlegungen zu einem Aufsatz von Margaret Bent', in *Die Motette: Beiträge zu ihrer Gattungsgeschichte* (Neue Studien zur Musikwissenschaft, 5; Mainz, 1991), 19–28, contributes little else to what is frankly a restatement of my thesis.

epithet to the composer involves special pleading of an unacceptable kind.[76] If he is to have written *Argi vices*, we have to assume a change of papal allegiance for which there is no evidence other than the wish to attribute the motet to him. This theory makes him move to Bologna shortly after (putatively) leaving Gregory. He went to Cividale, moved to Treviso on 15 September 1411,[77] then returned to Cividale 1414–18, where he died in 1433 after a time in Chioggia, 1419–21. His presence in Cividale, again, after the time when *Argi vices* must have been written, severely weakens the case for attributing it to him. In all, it must be concluded that a single Christian name, Nicholas, is much too fragile a basis for the attribution of this motet to any Nicholas not known to have been in John's chapel and not known to have been a musician, and the identity of the composer had better revert to unknown status.[78] The texts have many points of interest and are packed with classical and biblical allusions, deserving of extended study.

The Council of Constance

The powerful Roman Colonna family had provided several fourteenth-century cardinals, but Martin V was its only pope. He had been a supporter of the Malatestas, for whom Du Fay wrote at least three pieces, of which the ballade *Resveilles vous* celebrates the wedding on 18 July 1423 of Carlo Malatesta, the brother of Cleophe and Pandolfo, to the pope's niece, Vittoria Colonna, in a grand ceremony at Rimini. This not only cements the close bonds between Du Fay's patron families at this time, but provides a natural link for Du Fay's transition from Malatesta to papal patronage in the 1420s.[79] Hugo de Lantins, another Malatesta client, may have composed the rondeau *Mirar non posso* for the same occasion; it refers to the Colonna family.

We have seen that the Chantilly manuscript represents a high point for celebratory pieces in Latin and French that include but are not confined to motets. The composition of ceremonial and topical ballatas and madrigals in Italy also reached its height around 1400, as represented in the repertory of the

---

[76] A Nicolaus Simonis de Frangees de Leodio started his career in Avignon with Clement VII in 1380, though he is not identified as a singer. He was a mansionary at Cividale (Pierluigi Petrobelli, 'La musica nelle cattedrali e nella città', *Storia della cultura veneta*, 5 vols. (Vicenza, 1976–), ii, pt. 2, 467) in 1407; he joined the chapel of Gregory XII in May 1409 at Rimini and remained with him until March 1410, by which time Gregory had withdrawn south to Gaeta. This is summarized in Robert Nosow, 'The Florid and Equal-Discantus Motet', 84.

[77] Giovanni D'Alessi, *La Cappella musicale del duomo di Treviso* (Treviso, 1954), 36–7.

[78] Reinhard Strohm also draws attention to the motet's Italian features (*The Rise of European Music*, 116–18) and seeks to reinstate an attribution to Nicolaus Zacarie, who first appears in the chapel of Martin V. He does this in the context of a magisterial survey of musical repertory and patronage of the conciliar period.

[79] Schuler, 'Zur Geschichte der Kapelle Papst Martins V'.

Modena and Lucca codices. This tradition is continued from the 1420s by the new generation of composers after Constance. Many of these vernacular pieces are for occasions connected closely to papal concerns or even driven by papal politics. Lantins's *Tra quante regione*, like Du Fay's motet *Vasilissa ergo gaude*, celebrates the wedding (or at least the nuptial journey) of Cleophe Malatesta to the despot Theodore Palaiologos of Mystra; she departed on 20 August 1420. This wedding was part of a post-Constance campaign to heal the rift between the eastern and western churches by marrying Italian princesses to Byzantine rulers. Du Fay's unique vernacular motet *Apostolo glorioso* was for Cleophe's brother Pandolfo Malatesta as bishop of Patras, an appointment with a similarly ecumenical (or even territorial) intent. It is rather striking that we have no pieces from Du Fay's pen that are overtly dedicated to Martin, in whose chapel he served from 1428, while we do have pieces by him for Eugene IV from his periods of service with that pope (until 1433, and 1435–7 in Florence). However, Alejandro Planchart has shown that Du Fay had already left Constance at the time of Martin's election, and was in Cambrai from at least late 1417 to early 1420, so he could not yet have been a papal singer.[80]

Nicolaus Zacarie's vernacular ballata *Già per gran nobeltà*, another two-voice piece, but not, this time, for equal voices, may date from 1420 when this composer first appears in Martin V's chapel;[81] it immediately precedes Du Fay's Malatesta–Colonna ballade *Resveilles vous* in Oxford 213. It is certainly a better piece than Zacarie's presumably later motet for St Barbara written (by internal signature) in Tarento, and strongly indebted to Ciconia's *O felix templum*. Despite the coincidences of name and cogent arguments on behalf of the various candidates, I do not think he can be the composer Nicolaus of the motet *Argi vices* for Pope John XXIII, discussed above.

The motet *Clarus ortu/Gloriosa mater* for Martin V has been treated as anonymous because the author's name is cut off in its unique source: ... *composuit*. Robert Nosow persuasively reads 'Fr[ater] Antonius de Civitato' by analogy with the attribution to this composer elsewhere in the same manuscript.[82]

CANTUS I

Clarus ortu, clarior opere	Illustrious in birth, more illustrious in
clarissimus regnans in ethere	achievement, most illustrious ruling in
digna laudum dignus suscipere	heaven, worthy to undertake things
Georgius Capadox genere	worthy of praise, George, Cappadocian

[80] Planchart, 'The Early Career', 361.   [81] Schuler, 'Zur Geschichte'.

[82] Oxford 213, fos. 117ᵛ–118ʳ, published in Charles van den Borren (ed.), *Polyphonia Sacra* (Burnham, 1928), no. 23. Nosow, 'The Florid and Equal-Discantus Motet', 73–6. The comparable inscription is on fo. 8ᵛ. The text has been emended by David Howlett and Leofranc Holford-Strevens; the translation following is by David Howlett.

tribunatum solitus agere 5
Palestinam festinat subdere
miserando Lydditas solvere
truculentem draconem cedere
mesto regi filiam reddere
pro mercede thesaurum spernere 10
nudam fide turbam induere
debis binis regem instruere
ecclesiam mente diligere
sacerdotum decus attollere
officio Dei persistere 15
de misello compungi paupere
Christianos lugens deficere
hos tormentis istos in carcere
Dacianum videns succumbere
caput offert cruenti dextere 20
ut sit carnis excussus onere
beatorum letetur munere.
Felix Roma cujus in aggere
Georgius dignatur tollere
felix nomen quod felix federe 25
cardinalis levita prospere
gloriatur inceptum gerere
velum gaudens aureum jungere
generose martyr amplectere
vota nostra sursum erigere. 30

by race, accustomed to fulfil the
tribune's office, hastens to subdue
Palestine, to free the wretched men of
Lydda, slay the fierce dragon, restore
the sad king his daughter, refuse a
treasure for his reward, clothe the
naked crowd in faith, instruct the king
in twice two things: to love the church
with his mind, to exalt the honour of
the clergy, to hold fast to God's
service, to take pity on the unhappy
poor man; be wearied with weeping for
Christians, some under torture, others
in prison; seeing the Dacian succumb,
he offers his head to the right hand of
the bloodstained one that freed thus of
the burden of the flesh he may rejoice
in the rank of the blessed.

Happy Rome on whose hill George
deigns to exalt his happy name that,
happy in the covenant, the cardinal
deacon auspiciously glories to carry on
what he has begun, rejoicing to join
the golden veil; noble martyr, embrace
the upraising of our prayers.

CANTUS II

Gloriosa mater ecclesia
orbem sacris alens uberibus
pretiosa ducens primordia
ex unici Christi visceribus
desponsari non amat pluribus 5
sed tueri rite vicaria
uno gaudet de stirpe regia
et Romanis imperatoribus
cuius amor
absterget lacrymam neque luctus
    erit neque clamor. 10

Glorious mother church, feeding the
world with thy holy breasts, drawing the
precious beginnings from the entrails of
Christ the unique, does not have to be
betrothed to man, but properly to
preserve the successions rejoices in one
of royal stock and the Roman emperors,
whose love shall wipe away tears, nor
shall there be weeping or crying.

De Columna fit Odo primitus
tunc futurus basis justitie
Georgius titulum meritus
cardinalis levita gratie.
Nunc Martinus lucerna glorie 15

Oddo Colonna, who would then be the
basis of justice, first became George,
having earned his title of grace, a
cardinal deacon. Now he is Martin the
lamp of glory, possessing the papal

dignitate papali preditus
vita bonis malis interitus
ad jus ejus status pastorie
    redigendus
hic tibi precipue sit pura mente
    colendus   20

Verus pastor ut deus colitur
dum residet nixus in specula
lex Moysi per eum regitur
archa Noe Petrina vicula
turris David vas implens vascula   25
lapis Jacob oleo tingitur
vite mortalis divus efficitur
cuncta claudens sub ejus regula majestatis
facit ut pateant celesti regna beatis.

dignity, life to the good, death to the
bad. The state of the pastorship must
be restored to its right; let this above
all be honoured by thee with pure
mind.

The true shepherd is worshipped as a
god while he dwells leaning on the
watchpost; the law of Moses is
governed by him, Noah's ark, Peter's
skiff, the tower of David, the vessel
filling smaller vessels; Jacob's stone is
oiled; a mortal is made divine,
enclosing all things under the rule of
his majesty, and causes the celestial to
be opened to the blessed.

The tenor is *Justus non conturbabitur*, an obsolete Gradual from the old office proper to St Stephen, celebrated as pope and martyr on 2 August.[83] The motet texts honour the Colonna family, especially its members who were church dignitaries, and above all Martin V, who before his election was Cardinal-Deacon at the church of S. Giorgio in Velabro in Rome, otherwise known as *Sancti Georgii ad Velum aureum*, and is thus referred to in both texts. Martin's strong connection with Rome (and even with the Roman emperors) is stressed: Cantus I refers to the eighth-century elevation of the church within the walls of Rome as the seat of the cardinalate,[84] and Cantus II expresses hopes for a return of papal law (*lex moyse*), stresses Old Testament antecedents, and may also underlie the choice of tenor. A parallel is implied between St George's rescue of Christians from persecution at the hands of Dacian in Cantus I, and the position of Martin V at the end of the Schism. Nosow suggests performance on St George's Day after Martin's eventual entry into Rome in September 1420, i.e. 23 April 1421.[85]

Musically, it has a long single *color* (like *Petre clemens*), but divided into two sections (like St Martin's cloak?). The tenor for the second division has a ↄ

---

[83] *Le Codex 121 de la Bibliothèque d'Einsiedeln* (Paléographie musicale, 1st ser., 4; Solesmes, 1894), 284, and *Antiphonarium Tonale Missarum. XIᵉ siècle. Codex H. 159 de la Bibliothèque de l'École de Médicine* (Paléographie musicale, 1st ser., 7 (Tournai, 1901)), 179.

[84] Nosow, 'The Florid and Equal-Discantus Motet', 74.

[85] Nosow's persuasive account of this motet ('The Florid and Equal-Discantus Motet Styles') enables us to set aside Manfred Schuler's suggestion ('Die Musik in Konstanz während des Konzils 1414–1418', *Acta musicologica*, 38 (1966), 161–2) that it was for Martin's nephew Prospero Colonna, who was likewise Cardinal-Deacon at S. Giorgio in Velabro, from 8 November 1430. It seems altogether right to recognize this as yet another papal motet with political and propaganda import, composed not for the papal coronation itself but early in the new pope's reign.

signature, implying four new minims in the time of three preceding. Each section has three *taleae*. There is a 𝄴 twelve-breve introitus, with canonic imitation at two breves' distance, strict until the last two. This is the first known motet composed for Rome in the fifteenth century, celebrating the return of Martin V to his titular church as the sole legitimate pontiff.

Johannes Brassart is recorded as a singer with Eugene IV (elected 3 March) on 5 March and 24 April 1431, and remained until November. He was succentor at St Jean l'Évangeliste, Liège, from 1422 to 1431 and celebrated his first Mass there in 1426, and from 1428 he also held a post at the Cathedral of St Lambert in Liège. He was admitted in his own right to the Council of Basle in 1433, was *rector capelle* to the Emperor Sigismund from 1434, and remained in imperial service until at least 1443.[86] Two of his motets may refer to Martin V.

The texts of *Magne deus potencie/Genus regale esperie* are problematic. They have been privately judged by no less a Latinist than Leofranc Holford-Strevens to be 'almost incomprehensible, with very little grammatical coherence, almost as bad as [the fourteenth-century motet] *Apta caro*'.[87] The texts are not given here, and must await further study. Ambros suggested that the motet was for a pope, but without venturing to say which one.[88] Brassart was a member of the papal choir in 1431, which has led several scholars to believe that *Magne deus* was written for the election of Eugene IV.[89] Brassart's two motets *Ave maria gracia plena/O maria gracia plena* (also in Trent 87, fo. 51ᵛ) and *Magne deus potencie/Genus regale esperie* (*unicum*) are both present in the *original* layer of Bologna Q 15, which must have a terminal date hardly later than 1425.[90] For this reason I reject the possibility that it could be for Eugene's coronation. If *Magne deus* is for a pope, it cannot be for one later than Martin V, although there is not even a *columna* in the text to encourage that association.

---

[86] *O rex Fridrice* is for the accession of Frederick III in 1440. The last document referring to him is dated 7 Feb. 1445 (Keith Mixter, *New Grove*).

[87] Private communication.

[88] August Wilhelm Ambros, *Geschichte der Musik* (2nd edn., Leipzig, 1881).

[89] e.g. David Fallows, *Dufay* (London, 1982), 264. Laurenz Lütteken, *Guillaume Dufay und die iso-rhythmische Motette: Gattungstradition und Werkcharacter an der Schwelle zur Neuzeit* (Schriften zur Musikwissenschaft aus Münster, 4; Hamburg, 1993), now rejects a dedication to Eugene IV (I agree, but for different reasons), as he rules out his own earlier suggestion that it could be for Amadeus V of Savoy, which is much too late to fit the motet's early transmission (286–7). The best summary of interpretations of this motet is given in Jon Michael Allsen, 'Style and Intertextuality in the Isorhythmic Motet 1400–1440' (Ph.D. diss., University of Wisconsin-Madison 1992), 430–2. Allsen concludes partly on the basis of stylistic affinity that this motet belongs with a group from the early and middle 1420s; I agree.

[90] The text erasures at the beginning of this motet seem to have been made solely to clarify the underlay and do not change the text itself. As Lütteken points out (*Guillaume Dufay*, 286), the common reading *decus* results from a misreading of this erasure.

Brassart did, however, spend time at the curia of Martin V.[91] On 16 May 1424 he was given permission to leave Liège to visit the Roman curia, and was paid his salary for the entire year before departing.[92] 1425 was a Jubilee year and Rome was thronged with pilgrims. He reappears in the Liège archives in 1426 when, now as *dominus*, he celebrates his first Mass. We cannot yet tell if this was an isolated connection with the curia or if the visit had musical antecedents or consequents. Brassart's papal visit could also have permitted the transmission of this or other works to Bologna Q 15, as well as opening the possibility that they acknowledge favours granted by Martin to Brassart or that they are supplicatory motets written by Brassart for Martin.

Musically, *Magne deus* resembles other motets from papal circles in the 1420s, including *Clarus ortu* (discussed above), *Ad honorem* by Grenon, and *Apostolo glorioso* by Du Fay. There is no list of Martin's singers immediately prior to his death; but those confirmed by Eugene in a standard supplication on 5 March 1431, just two days after his election, surely include many of Martin's chaplains. Brassart is one of the fourteen singers listed; there is a strong probability that he had some previous connection with Martin's chapel.[93]

This tentative dating of *Magne deus* prompts a closer look at another motet by Brassart, *Te dignitas presularis*. The single text of this motet quotes at the end an entire antiphon for St Martin (*Martinus adhuc*):[94]

Te dignitas presularis	Thee the priestly dignity,
strenuitas militaris	military valour, and the charity of faith
et fidei caritas	make an apt shepherd, a most diligent
habilem reddunt pastorem	guardian, of the Lord's flock.
solertissimum tutorem	
ovilis Dominici	
decor nam si corporalis	For if you had corporal beauty,
tamen vita liberalis	yet you had generous life; whom
quem sanctorum paritas	equality with the saints has ennobled,
adornavit qua dilectus	where the beloved Jesus is, and chosen
Ihesu et mundo electus	by the world, glorious, duly magnificent.
clarens rite magnificus.	

[91] Keith Mixter, 'Johannes Brassart: A Biographical and Bibliographical Study', *MD* 18 (1964), 40. Several recent discussions of the date of *Magne deus* neglect this contact, but the case is fully and judiciously set out by Allsen, 'Style and Intertextuality', 430–2.

[92] 'Item xvi maii Jo. brassar de ludo pro gratia sibi facta per capitulum qui Ivit versus curiam Romanum . .'; ibid. 40.

[93] Note the different case of Matteo da Perugia, who was a personal chaplain to Filargo and remained with him on his election as Pope Alexander V.

[94] Both motets are published in Johannes Brassart, *Opera omnia*, ed. Keith Mixter, ii (CMM 35; American Institute of Musicology, 1971). For the antiphon, see Hesbert, *Corpus antiphonalium officii*, iii (Rome, 1968), no. 3712. and *Antiphonale Sarisburiense*, ed. W. H. Frere (London, 1901–24), pl. 594. The translation is by David Howlett.

O Martine exaudi nos qui dignus	O Martin, hear our prayer who art
audire Ihesum digne promere Martinus	worthy to hear Jesus, worthy to take
adhuc cathecuminus hac me veste	forth, Martin while still a catechumen
contexit.	clothed me with this garment.

Oddo Colonna was elected on St Martin's Day, 11 November 1417, and took the name Martin. Given the other connections between Brassart and this pope, although they still lack archival anchorage apart from the 1424 visit, it seems very likely that this text to St Martin also addresses Pope Martin as the earthly type of the saint (*ovili dominici decor/solertissimum tutorem*: glory of the flock of God, one and only protector). It may also represent a petition for protection by the composer to his employer, present or future: cover me with your cloak (St Martin).[95]

Nosow places this motet on St Martin's Day 1430, presumably because Brassart is assumed not to have been free to join the papal chapel until about this time.[96] The possibility must remain open that after his 1425 visit Brassart retained contacts, and a musical relationship, with Martin; we have stated that *Magne deus* must be from the first half of the decade.[97] The fermata chords on *O Martine*, the treble-dominated style, and the single text are among stylistic features that make a dating around 1430 quite comfortable for this motet, as also for *Excelsa civitas Vincencia* of 1433.[98]

Te dignitas presularis (also in Trent 87, fos. 77ᵛ–78ʳ) is one of three motets by Brassart copied into Bologna Q 15 at the second stage of compilation in the early 1430s. The others are *O flos fragrans* (also in Oxford 213, Trent 87), and *Gratulemur Christicole* (*unicum*). *Summus secretarius* (also in Oxford 213) is added on a second-layer opening but at the third stage (1434 onwards), which also includes mass settings by Brassart. It is likely that these latest works were collected and added by the Vicenza delegation to the Council of Basle, *c.*1434. Brassart's motet *Summus secretarius* was thought to be for an unknown papal secretary, but Robert Nosow has recently confirmed that we need look no further for a candidate than the Holy Ghost; this removes it from the list of topical or potentially datable pieces.[99] We can now tentatively add *Clarus ortu* and *Te dignitas presularis* to the list of motets composed for a pope but not for his coronation, possibly also *Magne deus potencie/Genus regale esperie*.

---

[95] A similar petition is embodied in the John the Baptist motet *O amicus/Precursor precursoris*. See Bent and Howlett, 'Subtiliter alternare'.

[96] Nosow, 'The Florid and Equal-Discantus Motet', 116.

[97] *Pace* Lütteken, *Guillaume Dufay*, 286, 91.

[98] For the dating of *Excelsa* not in 1409 but in 1433, see Margaret Bent, 'A Contemporary Perception of Early Fifteenth-Century Style: Bologna Q15 as a Document of Scribal Editorial Initiative', *MD* 41 (1987), 183–201.

[99] Nosow, 'The Florid and Equal-Discantus Motet'.

Martin V died on 20 February 1431; Eugene IV (the Venetian Gabriele Condulmer) was elected on 3 March and crowned on 11 March. Promptly after his election he reinstated the members of Martin V's chapel (on 5 March), including Du Fay. He antagonized the Colonnas by seeking to undo the territorial web set up by Martin for his nephews. His antagonism towards both the Colonnas and the Malatestas, two of Du Fay's patron families, led to some discomfort and a rapid exodus of the singers he had retained, despite efforts soon after his election to secure benefices for them. He also at the same time encouraged attention to both the fabric and the musical traditions of cathedrals.

Du Fay's grand and solemn motet *Ecclesie militantis* has invited many datings. Haberl proposed a date of 1436, when Florence, Venice, and Francesco Sforza formed a league against the Visconti, Milan, and Genoa.[100] A further temptation to consider this date is provided by a bull of Eugene IV (24 November 1436) starting 'Militantis ecclesie', relating to the reformed congregation of S. Giustina and naming to office the Archbishop of Milan, the bishops of Castello and Rimini, and the Abbot of Montecassino.[101] *Ecclesie militantis* is the only datable work by Du Fay that falls within the repertory cultivated by the Bologna Q 15 scribe but was not included in that manuscript. It survives uniquely, and in an anomalous layout, in Trent 87, probably copied in the late 1430s. A dating of the motet in 1436 would have helped to point to about that time as the terminal date of work on the manuscript and a more mundane reason for its exclusion. But the church militant is too common a formulation to impose such an interpretation; and Julie Cumming, who gives the best recent summary of the debate about the motet's dating, has pointed to uses of 'ecclesia militans' in other conciliar documents from Constance and Basle,[102] describing Eugene's stand as a declaration of war. The Church Militant was clearly in the air. The elegiac couplets of the Contratenor confirm the militant spirit:

> Bella canunt gentes: querimur, Pater optime, tempus.
>
> The nations sing of war; we bewail, o best father, the time.

An even later date, 1439, has been suggested by David Crawford.[103] Besseler and de Van have won wider acceptance for their identification of the

[100] Fr. X. Haberl, *Wilhelm Du Fay* (Bausteine für Musikgeschichte, 1; Leipzig, 1885), 88.

[101] Tommaso Leccisotti, 'La Congregazione benedettina di S. Giustina e la riforma della chiesa al secolo XV', *Deputazione Romana di Storia Patria Archivo*, 67 (1944), 461.

[102] Julie Emelyn Cumming, 'Concord out of Discord: Occasional Motets of the Early Quattrocento' (Ph.D. diss., University of California, Berkeley, 1987), ch. 10. For the manuscript format, see Welker, *Musik am Oberrhein*, 78–80.

[103] David Crawford, 'Guillaume Dufay, Hellenism, and Humanism', in Carmelo P. Comberiati and Matthew C. Steel (eds.), *Music from the Middle Ages through the Twentieth Century: Essays in Honor of Gwynn S. McPeek* (New York, 1988), 81–93. Cumming elegantly refutes his case ('Concord out of Discord', ch. 10).

piece as a coronation motet for Eugene IV in 1431.[104] Hamm's doubt, on mensural grounds, about a dating as early as 1431 for this piece assumes added interest in the context of the piece's absence from Bologna Q 15.[105] Alejandro Planchart has suggested that the motet might have been excluded from Bologna Q 15 because it would have 'appeared to many as a cruel joke, particularly in the years 1434–8. Eugene's moment of glory went by very quickly and, in fact, were it not for Philip the Good, he would probably be reckoned today as an antipope.'[106] The survival of the piece in the 'conciliar' Trent source makes good sense in the context of the diplomatic positions taken in relation to the Council of Basle between 1431 and 1433. The Council had been called by Martin V shortly before his death and it got off to a slow start. Eugene tried to dissolve it and failed to do so. It was not until 1433 that he officially supported it and, once he was himself persuaded of its value, applied pressure on bishops for their support. Stanza 3 refers to the pope's election, but in the past tense, and in sombre rather than celebratory mood. But the mention of the election with use of his previous name Gabriel [Condulmer] would tend to place it early in his reign.

Julie Cumming's argument is amplified with a musical analysis of the warring elements combined in this extraordinary work, and accepts this motet as a political statement and propaganda on behalf of Eugene, likewise early in the new pope's reign, likewise recognizing both his new and his papal name, but more concerned with the immediate (and in some ways parallel) political problems that the new pope had to address in the first year of his pontificate. *Ecclesie militantis* therefore presumably dates from sometime after Eugene's election but before Du Fay's departure from Rome for Savoy in August 1433; he rejoined the papal chapel in Florence in 1435. Because of the prominent mention at the beginning of 'Rome seat of the Church Militant' it is presumably before Eugene was driven from Rome on 4 June 1434, not to return until 1443, unless it can be argued that the affirmation of Rome would be made precisely because of Eugene's exile.

Few if any of the motets here reviewed have any claim to be ceremonial coronation pieces. *Supremum est mortalibus* celebrates the meeting of Eugene and King Sigismund in Rome before Sigismund's imperial coronation, and is not a motet for the coronation itself. We should perhaps entertain the idea of

---

[104] Among those who have more recently affirmed this dating are David Fallows, *Dufay*, 112, and Lütteken, *Guillaume Dufay*, 286, where he also speculates how Dufay could have composed *Ecclesie militantis* in only a week by starting before the pope had chosen his new name.

[105] Charles Hamm, *A Chronology of the Works of Guillaume Dufay, Based on a Study of Mensural Practice* (Princeton, 1964), 67–70.

[106] Private communication of 28 Sept. 1980.

their use as edifying and politically charged chamber music in private and semi-private contexts.

There is surprisingly little recycling, contrafaction, or even neutralizing of occasional motets at this period. An isolated case is *Stirps mocinigo*, where Bologna 2216 substitutes 'N' for this doge's name. Rather the reverse: the manuscript Bologna Q 15 gives us a unique example of repertory renewal within the detectable history of a single book. Many pieces, including for example textually neutral Magnificats, were jettisoned; at the same time, occasional motets for long-dead patrons were recopied up to twenty years after their and Ciconia's death without textual change but often with musical modification. In some cases the circumstances of the commission and first performance can be inferred or guessed. But why were they recopied? There is strong evidence for the use of that manuscript for domestic performance for Pietro Emiliani, bishop of Vicenza, by his own familiars and by visiting musical canons of Vicenza and Padua cathedrals, depending on where he and they were at the time. This merely confirms what we thought happened anyway, but the evidence for it in Emiliani's case is particularly suggestive and multistranded. Feragut's motet *Excelsa civitas Vincencia* was written close to the time of the election of Francesco Malipiero in 1433, and the text even makes it possible that it was in this case inaugural, but for Malipiero, not Emiliani; the scribe reassigned it to Emiliani (bishop 1409–33) after the latter's death, helping to cement the view that the collection stands very close to the household familiars of the music-loving bishop.

With the other political and commemorative motets of Du Fay we enter well-trodden ground and more certain anchorage, a good point at which to end this survey. It has perhaps provided a framework and incentive for further discussion of connections and *topoi* that establish papal motets as a sub-genre, albeit of a tradition fragile at first in identity and in preservation. Dating considerations presented here suggest that we should be cautious in applying the default assumption that a commemorative motet is likely to be inaugural. That leaves open the question on whose initiative or commission such pieces were written, and may shift more of the responsibility from formal papal commission to individual initiative by composers, whether already within the curia or as supplicants from outside.

The crusades form an abiding theme, and aspects of the motet texts reflect the shift from the particular crusade politics of the 1340s that provide the context for Vitry's *Petre clemens* to those of a century later. Military elements are increasingly common in papal discourse in the fifteenth century, with more emphasis on reconciliation with or recovery of the eastern church, crusades against the Turks, and eventually the fall of Constantinople in 1453. Indeed, connections with the crusades and their papal component have often been pointed out in discussions of the complex of *l'homme armé* compositions. In the fourteenth century there is naturally a stronger emphasis on the recovery of Rome, the historical Holy See. The secular alliances and military support that were needed before the papacy could be securely re-established in Rome mean that imagery of and allusions to the Church militant were never far away, culminating in Du Fay's *Ecclesie militantis/Sanctorum arbitrio/Bella canunt gentes*.

Appendix: Music for Popes John XXII to Eugene IV

Composition	Composer	Pope	Source(s)
Motets			
Per grama protho paret (Du)/Valde honorandus est beatus Johannes	Anon.	John XXII	London 41667, fo. 26r (no. 1)
Petre clemens/Lugentium/Non est inventus	Vitry	Clement VI	Ivrea, fos. 37v–38r
Gloria 'Clemens deus artifex'	Anon.	Clement VI	Ivrea, fos. 27v–28r
Pictagore per dogmata/O terra sancta/Rosa vernans	Anon.	Gregory XI, 1375	Chantilly, fos. 63v–64r
Alme pater (Tr/T)	Anon.	Urban VI, 1385?	London 40011B, fo. 14v
O Petre Christi discipuli	Ciconia	Alexander V?	Bologna Q 15, fos. 259v–260r (I)
Argi vices Poliphemus/Cum Philemon rebus paucis	Nicolas/Guillermus	John XXIII	Aosta, fos. 4v–7r
Gaudet et exultet/... Papam querentes	Anon.	Clemens VII and Urban VI	Basle, Univ.-Bibl., Musikfragmente I–II
Gloria 'Suscipe trinitas'	Ciconia	Schism	Warsaw 378, fos. 25v–27r, Padua D 675, fo. 2v; Grottaferrata 197, fos. 9v–10v; Grottaferrata s.s., fo. 2v
Benedicta viscera/Ave mater/Ora pro nobis	Velut	Schism; Virgin birth	Oxford 213, fos. 102v–103r
Eya dulcis/Vale placens	Tapissier	prayer to Virgin for end of Schism	Oxford 213, fos. 139v–140r
Venite adoremus/Salve sancta	Carmen	Schism; God and Trinity	Bologna Q 15, fos. 224v–225r, 311v–312r (I); Oxford 213, fos. 138v–139r

Composition	Composer	Pope	Source(s)
... de qua cordis/Trinitatem	Anon.	1409–15, threefold Schism?	Cambridge, Mass., Houghton Library, fMS Typ 122
Gloria 'Jubilatio'	Salinis	end of Schism	Bologna Q 15, fos. 62v–64r (I); Venice 145, fos. 15v–19r
Clarus ortu/Gloriosa mater ecclesia/ Justus non conturbatitur*	Antonio de Cividale?	Martin V, 1420?	Oxford 213, fos. 117v–118r
Te dignitas presularis*	Brassart	Martin V	Bologna Q 15, fos. 266v–267r (II); Trent 87, fos. 77v–78v
Magne deus/Genus regale	Brassart	Martin V?	Bologna Q 15, fos. 253v–254r (I)
Balsamus et munda cera*	Du Fay	Eugene IV, 7 Apr. 1431	Bologna Q 15, fos. 191v–192r (III)
Ecclesie militantis/Sanctorum arbitrio/ Bella canunt gentes*	Du Fay	Eugene IV, 1431–3?	Trent 87 (1), fos. 85v–86r and 95v–96r
Supremum est mortalibus*	Du Fay	Eugene IV and Sigismund, 21 May 1433	Bologna Q 15, fos. 190v–191r (III); Bologna 2216, fo. 28v; Trent 92, fos. 32v–34r; Munich 14274, fos. 107v–109v; Modena α.X.1.11, fos. 66v–67r; Copenhagen, 17
Nuper rosarum flores	Du Fay	Eugene IV; Florence, 25 March 1436	Modena α.X.1.11, fos. 67v–68v; Trent 92, fos. 21v–23r

Latin ballades and vernacular pieces

Title	Composer	Notes	Sources
Inclite flos orti Gebennensis*	Mayhuet de Joan	tenor 'pro papa Clemente' [VII]	Modena 5.24, fo. 15ʳ; Chantilly, fo. 41ʳ
Courtois et sages*	Magister Egidius	Clement VII (acrostic); validity of election	Modena 5.24, fo. 35ʳ; Paris 6771, fo. 54ʳ
Par les bons gedeons*	Filippotto da Caserta	'le souverayn pape qui s'appelle Clement' [VII]	Modena 5.24, fo. 31ʳ; Chantilly, fo. 45ᵛ; Turin 2, fo. 5ᵛ ('antipape')
Veri almi pastoris	Conradus de Pistoia	for a pope?	Modena 5.24, fo. 36ᵛ
Dime, Fortuna, poi che tu parlasti (ballata)	A. Zacara?	'Se Alessandro a Roma gito fosse' [Alexander V]	Turin 2, fo. 2ʳ
Arte psalentes*	Bartolomeus de Bononia	musical collegium singing for a true shepherd, supreme pontiff [Alexander V or John XXIII?]	Modena 5.24, fos. 37ᵛ–38ʳ
Mirar non posso	H. de Lantins	Colonna: Vittoria or Martin V?	Oxford 213, fo. 26ʳ
Gia per gran nobeltà (ballata)*	N. Zacara	Martin V, 1420?	Oxford 213, fo. 125ᵛ
Sanctus ('papale')	Du Fay		Trent 92, fos. 213ᵛ–215ʳ; Trent 90, fos. 277ʳ–279ᵛ; Trent 93, fos. 350–352ᵛ; Bologna Q 15 (III), fos. 134ᵛ–135ʳ
Agnus 'Custos et pastor ovium'	Du Fay		Trent 92, fos. 208ᵛ–210ʳ

* Recorded by the Orlando Consort on 'Popes & Antipopes'; MET CD 1008 on CD-SAR 49.

2

The Papal Chapels and Italian Sources of Polyphony during the Great Schism

❦

GIULIANO DI BACCO and JOHN NÁDAS

To Kurt von Fischer
on his eighty-fifth birthday

I T is our aim in the present essay to develop the documentation and ideas first presented in a study of the late fourteenth-century papacy that focused essentially on the administrative history of the papal chapels and, in particular, the early careers of the composers Johannes Ciconia and Antonio Zacara da Teramo.[1] Here we wish to explore the implications of the documentary evidence even further, assessing in more detail the consequences of the presence of the papal chapels in Italy in the early years of the Great Schism (1378–1417): the creation of a musical repertory and its circulation in manuscript sources of the period. In investigating the development and major routes of dissemination of musical repertories in Italy at the end of the fourteenth century, our archival research has yielded new evidence of an important cultural centre in central Italy, specifically the seat of papal government. A systematic examination of the surviving historical documentation in the Vatican Archives covering these years has allowed us to record the presence of a great number of native and foreign musicians in Rome in the service of papal and cardinalate chapels, some of whom then had occasion to pursue their musical careers outside the papal See. It is in this context that we now wish to attempt to associate, to a greater and lesser extent, a number of musical sources with late Trecento Rome and the travels of the papal curia in the early years of the Quattrocento.

[1] Giuliano Di Bacco and John Nádas, 'Verso uno "stile internazionale" della musica nelle capelle papali e cardinalizie durante il Grande Scisma (1378–1417): il caso di Johannes Ciconia da Liège', in *Collectanea I*, 7–74; preparatory materials for the latter and present articles were offered in two papers (John Nádas and Giuliano Di Bacco, 'Towards an International Style in the Period of the Great Schism: Musicians in Papal and Cardinalate Households', and eid., 'Italian Sources of the Early Quattrocento') read at the 1992 and 1994 Meetings of the American Musicological Society (Pittsburgh and Minneapolis), respectively. The research and writing of these studies as well as the present essay are credited equally to each author.

Although Pope Urban V had attempted to return to Rome during the late 1360s, the move proved far too uncertain and ended in failure. It was with Gregory XI a decade later that the papacy transferred definitively to Italy, despite the election of a contender who returned to Avignon.[2] The re-establishment of a Roman papacy in 1377 with its entire administrative structure and the whole of the curial entourage, including not only papal singers but also the *capellani capelle* of curial cardinals, signals the first continued presence of northern musicians in Italy in the period between the death of Guillaume de Machaut and the early career of Guillaume Du Fay.[3] A full listing of singers, including not only musicians who travelled to Rome with Gregory XI and his cardinals but also those known to be in Italy in the entourage of Urban VI and Clement VII in the period surrounding the start of the Schism, has been given elsewhere.[4]

---

[2] Pope Gregory XI (Pierre Roger de Beaufort), elected at Avignon on 30 Dec. 1370, entered Rome the week before Christmas 1376. He could have restored Rome as the traditional papal See, after about seventy years of residence *super flumina Babylonie*, and after the failed attempt by his predecessor Urban V, who had been in Italy between Apr. 1367 and Sept. 1370. But Gregory died prematurely, on 27 Mar. 1378, without having had enough time to establish favourable conditions in this regard. His cardinals, under pressure from Roman noblemen and citizenry, on 8 Apr. elected as the new pope Bartolomeno Prignano, archbishop of Bari (not a Frenchman but a Neapolitan, and, most significantly, not a cardinal), who took the name of Urban VI. By the end of June, the thirteen French cardinals contested the newly elected pope and abandoned Rome, travelling south to Anagni. Shortly thereafter the entire Sacred College reached Fondi, and there with the support of the local ruler, Onorato Caetani, and Queen Johanna of Naples, they elected Clement VII (Robert of Geneva) as the 'legitimate successor' of Gregory XI. On that day, 20 Sept. 1378, the Great Schism can be said to have begun, and two days later Urban proceeded to create his own Sacred College: twenty-nine new cardinals, most of them Italians. Our general historical references for the period are taken from (but checked when necessary against our own documents) the *Histoire de l'Église depuis les origines jusqu'à nos jours*, ed. F. Delaruelle, P. Ourliac, and E.-R. Labande, xiv/1: *L'Église au temps du Grand Schisme et de la crise conciliaire* (Paris, 1962); Ferdinand Gregorovius, *History of the City of Rome in the Middle Ages*, 7 vols., trans. from the 4th German edn. by Annie Hamilton (London, 1900).

[3] One of the goals of Di Bacco and Nádas, 'Verso uno "stile internazionale"', was to demonstrate the existence and consistency of cardinalate chapels and to underscore the role that these played at the largest structural level of the papal curia. Consideration of such chapels was a necessary step, given the ever increasing attention paid to the study of cardinals' families; for our period, see Bernard Guillemain, *La Cour pontificale d'Avignon (1309–1376): Étude d'une société* (Bibliothèque des Écoles Françaises d'Athènes et de Rome, 201; Paris, 1962); Norman P. Zacour, 'Papal Regulation of Cardinals' Households in the Fourteenth Century', *Speculum*, 50 (1975), 434–55; Anne-Lise Courtel, 'Les Clientèles des cardinaux limousins en 1378', *Mélanges de l'École Française de Rome. Moyen Age–Temps Modernes*, 89 (1977), 889–944; Bernard Guillemain, 'Cardinaux et société curiale aux origines de la double élection de 1378', in *Genèse et débuts du grand schisme d'occident, 1362–1394*, Proceedings of the Conference held in Avignon, 1978, ed. Jean Favier (Colloques Internationaux du Centre National de la Recherche Scientifique, 586; Paris, 1980), 19–30. See also the following relevant studies on the households of some of the most influential cardinals at the beginning of the Schism: Jacques Verger, 'L'Entourage du cardinal Pierre de Monteruc (1356–1385)', *Mélanges de l'École Française de Rome. Moyen Age–Temps Modernes*, 85 (1973), 515–46; Anne-Lise Rey-Courtel, 'L'Entourage d'Anglic Grimoard, Cardinal d'Albano (1366–1388)', in *Genèse et débuts*, 59–64; Margaret Harvey, 'The Household of Cardinal Langham', *Journal of Ecclesiastical History*, 47 (1996), 18–44.

[4] See Di Bacco and Nádas, 'Verso uno "stile internazionale"', 37–46, App. 1 and 2, respectively, for papal singers (from Oct. 1376 under Gregory XI, and later under the two schismatic popes) and for the chaplains of Clement VII's cardinals. For both tables the ending date is May 1379, when Clement left Naples by boat for Marseille. He and his curia then arrived at Avignon on 20 June.

Certainly what is surprising is the pronounced strength of that musical presence: during the period October 1376–May 1379 we have documented thirteen singers in Gregory's chapel, four in Urban VI's chapel, and seventeen in Clement VII's chapel. During the same period, we can account for forty-two singers in cardinals' chapels, some of whom transferred to one of the papal chapels after arriving in Italy.[5] Many of these singers had already enjoyed long, distinguished careers as musicians at the Avignonese court. At least three in Gregory's entourage—Egidius de Lens, Henricus de Latinia, and Johannes Volkardi—probably remained with Urban VI after Clement VII's election; but surely many more could be so counted had not the loss of Vatican documents from this period been so great.[6] A number of musicians in Clement's chapel in Italy continued to serve him upon his return to Avignon, and some also went on to other important cultural centres such as the courts of Aragon and Burgundy. Clement VII was elected and crowned at Fondi and he remained in and around Naples for the following eight months before setting sail for Avignon. As a direct consequence of that situation, there is a distinct possibility that at least some of the musical compositions praising Clement and lauding his papacy could have been written in Italy during these months, but not, as far as we know, by composers directly serving the papal curia at this time: for example, Filippotto da Caserta's French-texted ballade, *Par les bons Gedeons*.[7]

---

[5] We were able to find documents for the personnel of the chapels of twelve of the cardinals in Italy at the start of the Schism: three were 'senior' cardinals created by Urban V (Guillelmus de Agrifolio, Petrus Corsini, and Petrus de Stagno); the others had been appointed by Gregory XI in 1371 (Guillelmus Noelleti, Johannes de Croso, Petrus Flandrini, and Petrus de Vernhio) and in 1375, before leaving for Italy, Geraldus de Podio, Hugo de Montelegum, Johannes de Grangia, Petrus de Luna, and Petrus de Sortenaco. The information has been gleaned in large measure from the cardinals' *rotuli supplicationum*, petitions to the popes presented on behalf of those serving in their entourage, and in general these documents give us a rather 'synchronous' picture of the makeup of those chapels. In reality this picture could change, either because documentation is lacking for so many members of the Sacred College, or because the personnel in the chapels could be incompletely represented in the surviving *rotuli*. Nevertheless, it must be noted that, even if without the entire documentation at hand, some chapels appear to have been quite small, while others were rather large: for example, we note eight chaplains listed for the younger but already highly influential Cardinal Petrus de Luna (the future Avignonese pope Benedict XIII) in comparison with the two to four chaplains in most of the others; even more significant is the fact that in six of those cardinalate chapels the mention of the qualification of *tenor capelle* is a signal that the chaplains undoubtedly performed polyphonic repertory as well as monophony.

[6] The pontificates of Clement VII and his successor Benedict XIII are the best documented of the period even if at present incomplete: we have both cameral (mainly the *Introitus et exitus* series) and chancery holdings (the supplications presented to the pope and the documents, partly in response, issued by him as 'letters'). For the Italian side, documents of this sort for Urban VI are almost entirely lacking (the only substantial data have been found in a fragmentary state or in miscellaneous registers, and are sometimes revealed after the fact, by documents from adversarial or later obediences); for his successors, from Boniface IX to the Council of Constance, we are left with less than two hundred volumes of papal letters and a single, incomplete register of supplications. In this regard, Gregory XI fared no better, for all his supplication volumes are gone. The fundamental reference tool for a study of archival documentation at the Vatican, is Leonard A. Boyle, *A Survey of the Vatican Archives and of its Medieval Holdings* (Subsidia Medievalia, 1; Toronto, 1972).

[7] Sources: Modena 5.24, fo. 31ʳ ('Phylipoctus de Caserta'), Chantilly, fo. 45ᵛ, and Turin 2, fo. 5ᵛ. Edition of the text by Samuel N. Rosenberg in Willi Apel, *French Secular Compositions of the Fourteenth Century* (CMM

On the Italian side, the sudden creation of such a vigorous cultural environment in Rome attracted not only foreigners but also many musicians native to central Italy, thus considerably extending the papal chapel's musical influence. Beginning with the 1390s we can document an increasing interest on the part of local musicians in becoming professional singers. To give an idea of the richness of the situation, we present the totality of papal chapel membership in Italy for the duration of the Schism, emphasizing in italic the central Italian cities of origin in the names of the chaplains (see the Appendix). It must be stressed that these singers, far from being the isolated, odd examples of local musicians, lost at the periphery to the mainstream of musical traditions, were in every sense professionals attracted to the institution that would count as the fourth major cultural centre of the peninsula, after those dominating studies up to now: Florence,[8] the Veneto,[9] and Milan/Pavia.[10] The papal curia, of

53; American Institute of Musicology, 1970), i, pp. lxiv–lxv (from Modena 5.24): 'Ire, devision et partialité . . . sunt cause de la sisme'; 'Le monde est jus mis, se Dieux par sum avis | Ne le remet en vie de vray sentiment | Par le souverayn pape qui s'apelle Clement'; see also Gordon Greene (ed.), *French Secular Music* (PMFC 19; Monaco, 1982), 70–3. Reinhard Strohm, 'Filippotto da Caserta, ovvero i francesi in Lombardia', in Fabrizio Della Seta and Franco Piperno (eds.), *In cantu et in sermone: A Nino Pirrotta nel suo 80° compleanno* (Florence, 1989), 65–74, has argued that Filippotto was active at Pavia but was originally from Caserta. The text in Turin 2, a manuscript clearly related to the Pisan obedience, carries a telling variation in the refrain, citing Pope Clement, obviously at some distance, as 'antipape' rather than 'pape' of the other sources (Agostino Ziino (ed.), *Il Codice T. III.2 (The Codex T.III.2), Torino, Biblioteca Nazionale Universitaria, Studio introduttivo ed edizione in facsimile a cura di Agostino Ziino (Introductory Study and Facsimile Edition by Agostino Ziino)* (Ars Nova, 3; Lucca, 1994), 55). Another work that may have been composed soon after Clement VII's coronation, although possibly at Avignon immediately upon his return from Italy, is the Latin-texted ballade *Inclite flos orti Gebenensis* by Matheus de Sancto Johanne: Modena 5.24, fo. 15ʳ and Chantilly, fo. 41ʳ ('Mayhuet de Joan', with the rubric 'Tenor, pro papa Clemente'). Matheus had served Clement before the start of the Schism, and he was to be one of his singing chaplains from 1382 to 1387. He may have reached Rome in the first year of the Schism, although he is reported as a familiar of Louis I, duke of Anjou, in Nov. 1378. Matheus could be a superb example of contacts between the Continent and England: since at least 1366 he may be the Matheus de Sancto Johanne who served as a singer for Enguerrand de Coucy, accompanying him during his years in England. There, Matheus would have met the musicians in King Edward III's chapel, and those in the chapel of his son, the Black Prince (namely, Nicolas Hungerford and Simon Clement, cited in the contemporary motet *Sub Arturo plebs*). Contrary to previous interpretations, the clear allusions of French and Spanish loyalty to Clement's obedience in the text of Matheus' ballade are supported right from the start of the Schism by the documentary evidence.

[8] The major scholars of Italian late medieval polyphony were first attracted to the great number of sources originating in Florence and the richness of documentation for the composers in that cultural milieu. This is not the place to attempt to give full credit to the voluminous bibliography on Trecento Florence; we need only cite the most important scholars—Wolf, Becherini, Pirrotta, Li Gotti, von Fischer, D'Accone, and Reaney—whose works are easily found listed in the recent publication of the Squarcialupi facsimile/study: F. Alberto Gallo (ed.), *Il codice Squarcialupi* (Lucca and Florence, 1993).

[9] After *c*.1955, with the publication of *Les Colloques de Wégimont II, 1955: L'Ars nova. Recueil d'études sur la musique du XIVᵉ siècle* (Paris, 1959), Kurt von Fischer's *Studien zur italienischen Musik des Trecento und frühen Quattrocento* (Publikationen der Schweizerischen musikforschenden Gesellschaft, 2/5; Berne, 1956), and the discovery of a corpus of Paduan musical fragments (summarized in Giulio Cattin, 'Ricerche sulla musica a S. Giustina di Padova all'inizio del Quattrocento (I): Il copista Rolando da Casale. Nuovi frammenti musicali nell'Archivio di Stato', *Annales musicologiques*, 7 (1978), 17–41, and Franco Facchin, 'Una nuova fonte musicale trecentesca nell'Archivio di Stato di Padova', in Giulio Cattin and Antonio Lovato (eds.), *Contributi per la storia della musica sacra a Padova* (Fonti e ricerche di storia ecclesiastica padovana, 24; Padua, 1993), 115–39), stimulated the study of yet another musical area centred in the city of Padua and on the activity of the composer Johannes Ciconia, the highlights of which were Suzanne Clercx's *Johannes Ciconia: Un musicien liègeois et son*

course, in contrast to the other centres, was not to be a geographically fixed point of attraction, but instead moved about quite freely with its chapel of musicians: in 1378–9, with the start of the Schism, two papal chapels co-existed between Rome and Naples, and in the years before and after the Council of Pisa (1409) the Roman papal curia travelled a good deal as well, at first mostly within central Italy and then later extensively throughout northern and central Italy. This increased movement of personnel and the distinctive musical/cultural tastes associated with the four centres served to bring about an 'internationalization' of musical styles and repertories within the Italian peninsula itself. It is not an overstatement to claim that in the decades sur-rounding the year 1400 we may point to the heretofore unrecognized creation of a new musical world in and around Rome, in which it should be possible to witness the absorption of imported repertories that at once contrast and go hand in hand with what we know to have taken place at the other centres.

From the earliest years of the Schism and in the following decades Italian singers were attracted to the papal curia from areas more or less proximate to the Holy City, and there they mixed with French and Flemish musicians bound through their native dioceses to the Roman obedience:[11] some Italians came from cities quite close, such as Rieti (Antonius Martini) and Frosinone (Paulus Jacobi);[12] a distinct group came from the Abruzzo: Antonius Nanni Marsicani and two singers from Aquila (an Antonius and a Jacobus Johannis), all compatriots of the famous composer/singer Antonio Zacara da Teramo; another circumscribed group hailed from the south of Rome—Johannes Pulce de Gaeta, Paulus de Aversa, Johannellus de Alderisio, Franciscus de Amodeis de Posilipo, and Cobellus Maioris—testimony to the natural Urbanist sympa-thy of the Neapolitan territories long disputed between the allies of the Avignonese and Roman popes. Other singers emanated from more distant

temps (vers 1335–1411), 2 vols. (Classe des Beaux-Arts, Mémoires, ser. 2, vol. 10, fasc. 1a/1b; Brussels, 1960) and the the edition of his works by Margaret Bent and Anne Hallmark, *The Works of Johannes Ciconia* (PMFC 24; Monaco, 1985).

[10] Much more recently Ursula Günther ('Zur Biographie einiger Komponisten der Ars subtilior', *AfMw* 21 (1964), 172–99; 'Problems of Dating in Ars nova and Ars subtilior', *L'Ars nova italiana del Trecento*, 4 (1978), 289–301; 'Unusual Phenomena in the Transmission of Late Fourteenth-Century Polyphonic Music', *MD* 38 (1984), 87–118), Reinhard Strohm (*Music in Late Medieval Bruges* (Oxford, 1985); 'Filippotto da Caserta'; 'Magister Egardus and Other Italo-Flemish Contacts', *L'Ars nova italiana del Trecento*, 6 (1992), 41–68), Nádas and Ziino (*The Lucca Codex (Codice Mancini). Introductory Study and Facsimile Edition* (Ars Nova, 1; Lucca, 1990)), and Anne Stone ('Writing Rhythm in Late Medieval Italy: Notation and Musical Style in the Manuscript Modena Alpha.M.5.24' (Ph.D. diss., Harvard University, 1994)) have shed light on yet another centre, the court of the Visconti at Milan/Pavia, significant for its role in welcoming and disseminating music associated with the *ars subtilior* style.

[11] On the Italianization of the Roman curia, see Denys Hay, *The Church in Italy in the Fifteenth Century* (Cambridge, 1977), ch. 3, esp. p. 41.

[12] See the Appendix for the different spellings of the toponym, which can be identified either with Frosinone or perhaps with a smaller town 90 km. east called Frosolone.

cities, reflecting the extent of Roman papal control and attraction: moving to the north-east we have Angelus Gregorii de Spoleto, Nicolaus Ricii de Nucella Campli (diocese of Nocera Umbra, not far from Assisi),[13] Angelus de Macerata,[14] and Samperinus de Pensauro (Pesaro).[15] Particularly noteworthy in this regard for the pontificate of Gregory XII and his long residence in the Veneto are the central Italian singer-composers Laurentius (Rentius) Nicolai de Cartono de Pontecurvo[16] and Ugolinus de Urbeveteri, for whom we have

[13] Nicolaus Ricii, papal singer from 1401 (ASV, RL 87, fo. 245^{r-v}) to 1410 (for Gregory XII: ASV, RL 133, fos. 50^v–51^v), is probably the composer of a work carrying the ascription 'Nucella' in Strasburg (*De bon parole*, no. 149). In fact, he is known by this alias in documents from 1402–3 in a register of St Peter's (BAV, Archivio del Capitolo di San Pietro, Censualia 3) as well as in a document of 1413 in which he is qualified as a papal *scriptor* and *familiaris* of Gregory XII (ASV, RV 338, fo. 157^{r-v}).

[14] Abbot of St Benedict of Gualdo, near Nocera Umbra, he is documented as *magister capelle* in Aug. 1397 (Archivio del Vicariato di Roma, S. Maria in Trastevere, Pergamena XXXIII) and Feb. 1400 (in a unique and precious fragment of cameral records published by Richard Sherr, 'Notes on Some Papal Documents in Paris', *Studi musicali*, 12 (1983), 5–16).

[15] He was the *magister capelle* of Urban VI by 2 Mar. 1382 (ASV, Arm. XXXI, vol. 36, fo. 22^r). We are aware that the *magister capelle* was a position that was half administrative and half musical, as already suspected by Nino Pirrotta, 'Music and Cultural Tendencies in 15th-Century Italy', *JAMS* 19 (1966), 127–61 (Italian edn., 'Musica e orientamenti culturali nell'Italia del Quattrocento', in *Musica tra medioevo e rinascimento* (Turin, 1984), 213–49 at 217–20), where he cites G. Despy, 'Notes sur les offices de la curie d'Avignon: les fonctions du "magister capelle pape"', *Bulletin de l'Institut historique belge de Rome*, 28 (1953), 21–30, who claimed that the position was altogether non-musical. Elsewhere (Di Bacco and Nádas, 'Verso uno "stile internazionale"', 10 n. 7) we have shown that a good number of *magistri* rose up from the ranks of the singers (supporting Andrew Tomasello, *Music and Ritual at Papal Avignon, 1309–1403* (Ann Arbor, 1983), ch. 3, esp. 94–100), but the lack of full documentation for the Italian chapels of the Schism is such that it is not always possible to distinguish between *magistri* who were administrators and musicians (or, above all, musicians), except in the case of Antonio Zacara, *magister* in the spring of 1413 (see below, n. 51). We are cautious then in not excluding individuals who may have been musicians, at the same time cognizant of the uncertainty that attaches to most cases in this regard: the *magistri capelle* have therefore been included in the overall picture presented in the Appendix.

[16] The following document of Mar. 1410 provides the complete name and an unpublished biographical sketch of the composer: 'Gregorius etc. Dilecto filio Laurencio Nicolai de Cartono de Pontecurvo . . . Salutem. . . . Cum itaque postmodum canonicatus et prebenda ecclesie sancte Marie Civitatis Austrie Aquilegensis diocesis quos iniquitatis filius Odoricus de Glemona [= Gemona?] olim ipsius ecclesie canonicus obtinebat ex eo vacaverint et vacent ad presens, . . . tibi qui capelanus et cantor in capella nostra existis . . . canonicatum et prebendam predictos . . . conferimus. Non obstant[e quod] . . . duo altaria sine cura in dicta ecclesia obtines et nos dudum tibi de prepositura sancte Marie de Atino Soranensis diocesis . . . per alias nostras litteras mandavimus provideri; [seu quod] tibi de uno vel duobus beneficio vel beneficiis . . . ad collationem . . . Episcopi et dilectorum filiorum Capituli Aquinati, ac Abbatis et Conventus Montis Casinii ordinis sancti Benedicti, quod nullius diocesis existit, communiter vel divisim pertinente seu pertinentibus, . . . gratiose concessimus provideri . . . Datum Gaiete, III idus marcii, anno IV' (ASV, RL 133, fos. 3^v–4^v). Although 'Pontecorvo' could possibly also refer to a bridge and quarter of Padua, and notwithstanding his benefice conferred at Cividale in this document, the fact that Rentius held several earlier benefices in the diocese of Sora (Naples), Aquino and Montecassino (the latter two *sub expectatione*), suggests a provenance in the city of Pontecorvo, near Frosinone. In general, it is our impression that toponymic surnames are almost always used with reference to cities, and it is remarkable that two 14th-c. bishops of the said diocese of Aquino are named Antonius de Pontecurvo (elected in 1360) and Johannes de Pontecurvo (his successor, elected in 1375); see Konrad Eubel, *Hierarchia Catholica medii aevii sive summorum pontificum, S.R.E. cardinalium, ecclesiarum antistitum series ab anno 1198 usque ad annum 1431 perducta* (2nd edn., Münster and Regensburg, 1913), 100. 'Cartono', probably a place name qualifier, has still not been identified; perhaps it refers to the name of his father, Nicolaus de Cartono, and deserves further investigation.

discovered some new documents.[17] Moreover, the composers Filippotto and Antonello da Caserta come again to mind as musicians from central Italy who, however, were apparently most active at the court of the Visconti in Milan/Pavia.[18]

Chief among the musicians to emerge on the Roman scene during this period are the central Italian composer Antonio Zacara da Teramo, a papal singer and scribe, and Johannes Ciconia from Liège, a musician in the family of one of the most influential cardinals in Rome—both of them present in the Holy City at the end of the century.[19] The notion of the possibility of reinterpreting the manuscript evidence during the final decades of the Trecento—in terms of both repertory and circulation—originated precisely in the new documentation for the career of Ciconia, a key figure of the period in the transition from the late medieval Ars nova to the dominance on Italian soil of composers from the Low Countries during the Quattrocento.

Summarizing briefly the elements that were presented in our earlier publication on this topic, we should like here to add new information and set out in some detail the basis of how the Roman phase of Ciconia's career informs

[17] On 13 May 1413 Ugolinus de Urbeveteri is documented as a singer for Gregory XII: '[Rimini] Die xiii maii, honorabiles viri dompnus Ugolinus de Urbeveteri, rector parrochialis ecclesie sancte Marie de Carpineta et dompnus Jacobus, rector plebis sancti Martini in Rubicone, Cesenatensis diocesis, presbiteri, domini nostri pape cantores . . . abiuraverunt scisma . . .' (ASV, Arm. XXXIV, 4, fo. 90ᵛ). He is swearing allegiance to Gregory, together with the priest Jacobus who probably is the same Jacobus Masii de Frullivio documented as his musical colleague in 1417 at Florence Cathedral (Frank A. D'Accone, 'Music and Musicians at Santa Maria del Fiore in the Early Quattrocento', in *Scritti in onore di Luigi Ronga* (Milan and Naples, 1973), 99–126 at 120–1). Polyphonic songs by Ugolinus, author of the *Declaratio musice discipline* (ed. Albert Seay in CSM 7; Rome, 1959–62), are to be found in Rome, Biblioteca Casanatense MS 2151 (see Albert Seay, 'Ugolino of Orvieto, Theorist and Composer', *MD* 9 (1955), 111–66) and in Florence SL 2211 (Frank D'Accone, 'Una nuova fonte dell'Ars Nova italiana: il codice di S. Lorenzo 2211', *Studi musicali*, 13 (1984), 3–31; John Nádas, 'Manuscript San Lorenzo 2211: Some Further Observations', *L'Ars nova italiana del Trecento*, 6 (1992), 145–68).

[18] Filippotto's years at the Visconti court have been studied most recently by Strohm, 'Filippotto da Caserta'; Antonello served the same family, but seems to have worked exclusively for Giangaleazzo at Pavia (Nádas and Ziino, *The Lucca Codex*, 38–40).

[19] We would also include here the more transitory figures of the Polish composer Nicolaus de Radom and the Netherlander Magister Egardus. It has been strongly suggested that Radom probably went to Rome during the great Jubilee Year of 1390; see Henri Musielak, 'W poszukiwaniu materiałów do biografii Mikołaja z Radomia', *Muzyka*, 18 (1973), 82–9; Miroslaw Perz, 'Il carattere internazionale delle opere di Mikolaj Radomski', *MD* 41 (1987), 153–9; id., 'Polish Contributions to the Problem of Polyphonic Repertories in the 14th and 15th Centuries', in *Atti del XIV Congresso della Società Internazionale di Musicologia (Bologna 1987)*, i: *Round Tables* (Turin, 1990), 175–81. The extant Vatican documents for him, although not specifying his presence in Rome, nevertheless are striking in their number and frequency during the Jubilee Year: ASV, RL 4, fos. 167ʳ–168ʳ, 273ᵛ–274ᵛ, and 275ᵛ–276ʳ. Although no Roman documentation has yet come to light for a Magister Egardus, clearly a musician, he has tentatively been identified by Strohm on the basis of Bruges documents with a papal scriptor Eckardus, who should be the same person as the *succentor* of St Donatian's in Bruges in 1370–1, Johannes Ecghaerd, who also held a chaplaincy in Dixmuide near Veurne (Strohm, 'Magister Egardus', citing Marguerite Gastout (ed.), *Suppliques et lettres d'Urbain VI (1378–1389) et de Boniface IX (cinq premières années: 1389–1394)* (Analecta Vaticano-Belgica, 29: Documents relatifs au Grand Schisme, vii; Rome, 1976), Part II, doc. no. 884, pp. 638–9). Due to some inconsistencies and contradictions in the Vatican documents, we believe that this particular identity is still open to investigation.

our hypotheses for interpreting the evidence of the musical sources.[20] The composer Johannes Ciconia was at first confused by his first great biographer, Suzanne Clercx, with his father, due to the identity of their names.[21] The possible error was first suggested by Heinrich Besseler in 1955, and more strongly in 1976 by David Fallows:[22] the Johannes Ciconia who was born *c*.1335 and who was a familiar of cardinal Albornoz in the 1360s, travelling with him to Italy, could not have composed the surviving music attributed to a Ciconia unless at a quite advanced age, to judge from the style of the works and the likely dates of the manuscripts in which they are found. The incongruence of this fundamental fact led Fallows first to a passage in a Liègoise chronicle stating that the descendant of a noble family, 'une fille mal provee', had produced 'pleuseurs enfans natureis de Saignor Johan de Chywongne, canonne de Saint-Johan', and secondly to a Paduan document of 1405 in which the musician is said to be the son of a 'quondam Johannis de civitate Leodii'.[23] The composer, who has always been associated with a Paduan career, can be identified as a 'duodenus' documented in 1385 at St-Jean in Liège, presumably born in the years 1360–70. Clercx vigorously refuted this hypothesis, furthermore identifying the father of the canon/composer as the fur-trader Johannes Ciconia documented up to the 1350s, but this did not resolve the principal questions regarding the chronology and style of the surviving music.[24]

In accepting the thesis of 'Ciconia padre e figlio', still to be explained is the composer's musical education and his apprenticeship as a musician, for at the start of his Paduan years Ciconia already reveals a solid musical preparation and, above all, a remarkably deep knowledge of Italian genres and styles of the Trecento. If, therefore, the biography of the composer diverges from that of the father, where may we imagine that his musical career developed during the last decade of the fourteenth century? A partial answer was presented in the study of the Lucca Codex by Nádas and Ziino, who in 1990 recognized important elements that helped to place Ciconia, if only briefly, at the Visconti court in Pavia.[25] In 1991, during the course of our systematic examination of

[20] For more complete information, see Di Bacco and Nádas, 'Verso uno "stile internazionale"', esp. 13–17, 24–7.

[21] Her monumental work was collected in the book-length study, *Johannes Ciconia*.

[22] Heinrich Besseler, 'Hat Matheus de Perusio Epoche gemacht?', *Musikforschung*, 8 (1955), 19–23; David Fallows, 'Ciconia padre e figlio', *Rivista italiana di musicologia*, 11 (1976), 171–7.

[23] The chronicle is *Le Miroir des nobles d'Hesbaye* of J. de Hemricourt, cited first by Clercx, *Johannes Ciconia*, i. 40. The 1405 Paduan document is ACP, Diversorum, 13, fo. 94ʳ, transcribed in Clercx, i. 46.

[24] See Clercx, 'Ancora su Johannes Ciconia (1335–1411)', *Nuova rivista musicale italiana*, 11 (1977), 573–90 and her *New Grove* entry of 1980 (worklist by David Fallows). The new view of Ciconia's biography is accepted in Ciconia, *Works*, ed. Bent and Hallmark, and Anne Hallmark, 'Gratiosus, Ciconia, and Other Musicians at Padua Cathedral: Some Footnotes to Present Knowledge', *L'Ars nova italiana del Trecento*, 6 (1992), 69–84. Hallmark's dissertation is forthcoming and will include the complete documentation of Ciconia's Paduan years.

[25] Nádas and Ziino, *The Lucca Codex*, 41–5.

the Vatican Archive for documentation on papal chapels during the period of the Great Schism, we had the good fortune to find a letter from Pope Boniface IX, dated 27 April 1391, presenting the following relevant information:[26] a *clericus* by the name of Johannes Ciconia, the illegitimate son of a priest, served as *clericus capelle* of cardinal Philippe d'Alençon (who had travelled to northern Europe as a papal legate);[27] Ciconia, who had already obtained a papal dispensation for his illegitimacy (*de defectus natalium de presbitero natus*), as well as a *gratia expectativa* (at the church of the Holy Cross in Liège), now was granted the possibility of pursuing an ecclesiastical career, the right to hold benefices even in churches in which his father is beneficed, and allowed never to have to mention again his state of illegitimacy. A document from the following July, moreover, makes clear that *clericus* Ciconia did indeed follow the cardinal from Liège back to Rome, where he is present as a witness to a document drawn up at the titular church of the cardinal, S. Maria in Trastevere.[28] We suggest that this cleric Johannes Ciconia can be identified with the musician later residing in Padua,[29] and in fact he probably owed his first contacts with Padua to his Roman patron, Cardinal d'Alençon, at the papal curia.[30]

Ciconia's Paduan career can be filled in as follows with the addition of a number of new documents that have surfaced recently.[31] The first appearance

[26] The document is ASV, RL 14, fo. 141ʳ⁻ᵛ. A complete transcription is to be found in Di Bacco and Nádas, 'Verso uno "stile internazionale"', 13–14; the document had been calendared by Marguerite Gastout, *Suppliques et lettres*, Part II, doc. no. 430, pp. 418–19, but it remained unnoticed by music historians.

[27] Philippe d'Alençon was one of the most extraordinary members of the college of cardinals in Rome, given his noble parentage (he was a son of Charles II of Valois, and thus a cousin of King Charles V of France), and for the fact that he was one of two French cardinals who crossed over to the Roman obedience (a real gem for Urban's aspirations to be considered the one true pope). For his biography and further bibliography, see Di Bacco and Nádas, 'Verso uno "stile internazionale"', 17–20; and for members of his household, 20–4 and 47–62.

[28] BAV, MS lat. 8051, 'Chartularium S. Mariæ Transtiberim MDCCLXXIIII', vol. I, fos. 62ʳ–63ʳ; this is an 18th-c. copy of a lost original. A transcription is available in Di Bacco and Nádas, 'Verso uno "stile internazionale"', 25. It is worthwhile mentioning that another fellow cleric from Liège, Johannes Bellini, is also cited in this document as a witness, and both he and Ciconia are members of Philippe's household.

[29] In summary, we believe him to be the *duodenus* of St-Jean of Liège in 1385 and one of the illegitimate sons of the canon of the same name in that collegiate church. His move to Italy was doubtless due to his desire to pursue an ecclesiastical career, for which, by the norms of his day, he acquired the proper papal dispensation with the help of an influential cardinal, Philippe d'Alençon, papal legate in his own country.

[30] From 1381 to 1387 Philippe d'Alençon was the administrator of the Patriarchate of Aquileia, and in that position he supported Francesco Carrara in contesting Venetian expansionist policies. To reward and protect Philippe when he was struggling and had to flee Friuli, Francesco invited him to stay in Padua, where he resided just outside the city at Monselice. Philippe was also for a short period abbot *in commendam* of Santa Giustina in Padua; for details, see Di Bacco and Nádas, 'Verso uno "stile internazionale"', 19–20.

[31] Our recent examination of the documentation at the Paduan State Archives (ASP, in June 1995), searching precisely for local documents attesting to Philippe's residence, also revealed new Ciconia documents, a number in a notarial register just recently restored: we wish to thank Dott. Anna Vomiero for her kind help. Anne Hallmark has since very generously allowed us to see the appendices of her forthcoming dissertation ('Johannes Ciconia in Padua', Princeton University), and she includes documents that have not yet appeared in published studies, among them some of the ones listed below and others that supply details for Ciconia's beneficial career and his duties at the cathedral.

of Ciconia in the Veneto can be pushed back to 11 July 1401, the day of his appointment as holder (*collatio*) of a *beneficium clericalis* (i.e. reserved for clerics) in the church of S. Biagio di Roncalea (today Roncaglia): the benefice is granted to Ciconia by the archpriest of the cathedral, Francesco Zabarella, and most importantly the *clericus* Ciconia is said to be the son of a Johannes Ciconia, almost certainly the *canonicus* documented in Liège during the same period. Three days later Ciconia is also granted a chaplaincy in the cathedral.[32] The other benefices granted to Ciconia are well known from Clercx's research and are now confirmed and corroborated by Anne Hallmark: by 21 June 1404 he is a canon at S. Fidenzio in Meliadino;[33] by 8 June 1405 he has a *canonicalis beneficium* at S. Lorenzo in Conselve;[34] from 1406 he was rector of the hospital (*hospitali sive ecclesie*) of S. Pietro in Valdastico (diocese of Padua, district of Vicenza); and finally in 1409 he resigns a benefice in the church of S. Giovanni de Ospedaletto (Este).[35] As for Ciconia's professional career as a musician, we can simply note that he was *cantor et custos* of Padua Cathedral, beginning at least in April 1403, and he was recognized as having held this post until his death, between 10 June and 12 July 1412.[36] But it is worthwhile adding here that on 3 March 1402 the Chapter granted Ciconia a *beneficium mansionarie* valued at 100 gold *denari*;[37] up to that day he held a benefice (*beneficium et cap-*

---

[32] These two documents, found in the notarial volume just recently restored, have not been noted before; here follows a brief summary of their contents: 'Collatio clericalis beneficii S. Blaxii de Ronchalea facta . . . [in margin:] Magistri Johanni Cyconie filii Johannis ('Zigogne' crossed out) Ciconie clerici de civitate Leodiensi per dominum Archipresbiterum . . . 1401, indic. IX, die XI iulii' (ASP, Notarile 142, Notaio Petrus Bonus, fo. 292ʳ); 'Collatio beneficii . . . Capelanie ecclesie maioris Paduane quod obtinebat presbiter Blaxius de Iadra, vacante per . . . predicti presbiteri Blaxii . . . facta magistri Johanni Cyconie . . ., per dominum Archipresbiterum predictum. Eisdem millesimo, anno, indic., die jovis 14 mensis iulii, Padue [in the house of the Archpriest]' (ibid., fo. 292ᵛ). Prior to the discovery of these two documents, Ciconia was known to have taken possession of the benefice at San Biagio on 30 July 1401 (Clercx, *Johannes Ciconia*, 39: ASP, Notarile 286, Notaio Albertini, fos. 112ᵛ–113ʳ). The canon Johannes Ciconia is certainly present at Liège in Nov. 1401; see Léon Lahaye, *Inventaire analytique des Chartes de la Collégiale de Saint-Jean l'Évangéliste à Liège* (Brussels, 1921), i. 293–4.

[33] New document found by Hallmark: ACP, Canipa 1, fo. 105ᵛ. See also Clercx, *Johannes Ciconia*, 47.

[34] ACP, Diversorum 13, fo. 57ᵛ (Clercx, *Johannes Ciconia*, 47); from a newly discovered notarial document issued on the same day we are able to confirm this, and can add that the benefice was granted 'per mortem Johannis de Briadi' (ASP, Notarile 342, Notaio Antonio Rossi, fo. 46ʳ).

[35] From ASP, Notarile 286, Notaio Albertini, fo. 122ʳ, and ACP, Diversorum 14, fo. 12ᵛ; both of these benefices were known by Clercx, *Johannes Ciconia*, 47.

[36] It is Hallmark who has verified the continuity of this position, starting with the first document: ASP, Notarile 40, Notaio Nicolini, fos. 304ᵛ–305ʳ (cf. Clercx, *Johannes Ciconia*, 40). On 27 Apr. 1403 Ciconia is called 'musicus et custos', but the qualification of 'musicus' appears to be an error that derives from the word 'fisicus' written first by the notary (ibid., fos. 284ʳ–285ʳ: cf. Clercx, 40). Ciconia's death is to be placed between the date of the last document in which he is evidently alive (ACP, Diversorum, 14, fo. 133ʳ; see Hallmark, 'Gratiosus, Ciconia', 82) and those of the two citing his death (ACP, Diversorum, 14, fo. 136ᵛ; both are in Clercx, 49). Chapter expenses are documented 'pro funerali magistri Johannis Cichonie in die obitus sui' in ACP, Canipa 2, fo. 27ʳ, cited in Clercx, *Johannes Ciconia*, 49.

[37] 'Et similiter promiserunt facere ('dominum' crossed out) magistro Johanni Ciconie de beneficiis(?) [illegible] ad summam denariorum centum auri. [in margin:] Pro ('presbitero' crossed out) magistro Johanne Ciconia'. On the same day: 'Electione Magistri Johannis Cigonie ad beneficium mansionarie [vacantem] per

pellania sacerdotalis) in the Paduan cathedral which had to be resigned upon receiving the benefice (as well as the office) of *mansionarius*.[38] The final issue to take up regarding Ciconia's Paduan career concerns his possible rise to the rank of *presbiter* and whether he ever truly became a canon of the cathedral. From the documents we now have, notwithstanding the fact that both qualifications appear sporadically here and there, we may have to conclude that the answer is in the negative.[39] This state of affairs may depend on the difficulties of a Ciconia who as *clericus capelle* of Philippe d'Alençon, but branded as one with a *defectus natalium*, might have expected to attain a certain number of benefices; he indeed acquired benefices, but not of a status sufficiently high to permit a more substantial ecclesiastical career.[40]

The new Roman documents associated with cardinal Philippe d'Alençon appear thus to fill precisely the void that scholars of the period imagined, and the hypothesis that Ciconia had lived in Italy—at Rome—is convincing from

mortem presbiteri Francisci de Sancto Petro in ecclesie Paduane. Et comissio fratri presbiteri Baptiste mansionario et domino Gulliclmo de Laude custode . . . presentandi dictum electum et immediate . . . in ecclesia . . . MCCCCII indictione Xa, die veneris tercio marcii Padue. In ('camera episcopali' crossed out) sacristia maioris ecclesie Paduane' (ASP, Notarile 142, Notaio Petrus Bonus, fo. 300ʳ⁻ᵛ).

[38] 'Vacante beneficio et capellania sacerdotali in ecclesia Paduane per acceptationem Magistri Johannis Cigonie ad mansionariam vacantem in eadem per mortem presbiteri Francisci de Sancto Petro. Predicti beneficii domini Archipresbiter, canonici et capitulum volentibus providere . . . de codem beneficio . . . Anthonio de Malamoche ibidem presente . . . investivit. [in margin:] Collatio beneficiorum capellaniarum vacantibus . . . primo beneficii capellanie Magistri Johannis Cigonie vacante per receptionem mansionarie a Johanni facta, a presbitero Anthonio predicto et beneficii dicti Anthonii facta presbitero Nicholao' (ASP, Notarile 142, Notaio Petrus Bonus, fo. 304ʳ; benefice issued in Mar. 1402).

[39] Hallmark has cited more than one case in which the qualification of *presbiter* given to Ciconia in chapter lists is then cancelled; see the documents cited by Bent and Hallmark in Ciconia, *Works*, p. ix (the first of the series is included by Hallmark in the appendix to her dissertation and is dated 1404: ACP, Canipa 1, fo. 106ʳ). More complex is the question whether Ciconia ever became a canon of the cathedral, as is given in some documents cited by Clercx and Hallmark, and to which we may now add a new series: ASP, Notarile 41, fos. 205ʳ⁻206ʳ, 208ʳ⁻ᵛ, 214ᵛ and Notarile 44, fos. 13ᵛ, 73ᵛ⁻74ʳ, 75ʳ⁻ᵛ, 76ʳ, 81ᵛ⁻82ʳ, 85ʳ⁻86ʳ, 89ʳ, 95ᵛ⁻96ʳ (both registers of the notary Nicolini). All the documents containing this qualification date from the last two years of Ciconia's life (the first is 5 Aug. 1410), and so it is possible that at the end of his career he was able finally to take on one of the highest ecclesiastical duties in the city. But given that his name with the qualification of canon always appears within a list of canons, and that from the earliest payments as *custos* he is listed within the same pay accounts as are the cathedral canons, the possibility remains that such a designation refers more to the site of his professional activity (the chapter) than to a specific rank and beneficial right, for which no direct beneficial or administrative documentation has ever been found. The following document may serve to reveal the inherent problem: on 9 Feb. 1411 a number of people are present for the drawing up of a document, among them Ciconia: 'omnes canonici ecclesie Paduane seu habentes vocem in capitulo, ac constituentes et representantes totum et integrum capitulum et in quibus residebat et residet ad presens totius capituli auctoritas, vis et potestas' (ASP, Notarile 41, Notaio Nicolini, fo. 110ʳ⁻ᵛ; cf. Clercx, 49). So it is possible that Ciconia was responsible for (and called upon, by virtue of his decade of service) the representation of the chapter in legal matters, although he remained only a *custos* right up to his death (ASP, Notarile 41, Notaio Nicolini, fos. 240ᵛ⁻241ʳ, where his office is given to Luca di Lendinara; cf. Clercx, 49).

[40] See Di Bacco and Nádas, 'Verso uno "stile internazionale"', 34–6. However, let us emphasize the fact that, by virtue of the papal dispensation in 1390, Ciconia was allowed in the future to omit mention of his illegitimacy of birth; this alone, we believe, absolves one from having to find a Paduan document that might mention this element and thus provide a direct connection with Boniface's letter—that is, the one element that would finally eliminate all doubt as to the identity of Philippe's familiar with the composer.

a number of standpoints, both biographical and musical. But even if the purely biographical information gleaned from these documents were not considered to be sufficient to prove the identity, as is the case in many other instances of composers' careers, a consideration of a wider range of documentary data adds to our conviction that the identity is almost certain.[41] First and foremost, the important status of our Liègoise clerk in Philippe's family merits particular attention: he is qualified as a *clericus capelle*, a position in the chapel that often was taken by young musicians. We state this with all due caution, since the term was also used to indicate, pure and simple, assistants for liturgical rites, yet in the many cases of documented chapels staffed by singers, we have found that the *clerici* often rose through the ranks to become *capellani capelle*.[42] With d'Alençon, there is no question that a number of singers served him: Guillelmus (Wilhelmus) de Hildernisse, Johannes Sapiens, Angelus de Macerata, and Guillelmus Clari.[43] Thus we can seriously consider the Johannes Ciconia in his chapel as having had a connection with the musical functions of the chapel.

Finally, there is the dating of his compositions and the manuscript sources that carry his works; some of these will be discussed later in this essay, but suffice it to say for now that they appear substantially to support the hypothesis that Ciconia remained in Rome for an extended period of time in the 1390s, perhaps until the death of his curial patron and even slightly beyond. It is true that most of his securely datable works are from his Paduan years, but at least a few, we would suggest, were composed during a period of Roman residence and must have entered the manuscript tradition quite early on, in Rome and its environs during the 1390s and early years of the Quattrocento. In general, a Roman residence during the 1390s would have permitted Ciconia more fully to absorb Italian culture (literary as well as musical), of

[41] The known documents from Liège containing various persons named Ciconia found by Clercx and Hallmark cast some doubt perhaps on the father having died by 1405, as stated in the Paduan document cited above, n. 23; the problem lies in the realization that there are indeed many Ciconias in Liège during the period of the Schism, and we agree with Hallmark in having for the moment to consider a group of 'unknown Johannes Ciconia'; among them we may now add perhaps another male member of the extended family, found by Alejandro Planchart in a document from 1418 in which a Johannes Ciconia and a Renerus de Betincourt are in litigation over a canonicate and prebend at St-Jean in Liège: RS 109, fo. 7ʳ). This Johannes could even be a son of the 'uncle' Guillaume Ciconia who resided in the chapter house normally occupied by the Ciconia 'family' (for the various Ciconias and the associated problems with their identities, see Clercx, *passim*, and cf. Di Bacco and Nádas, 'Verso uno "stile internazionale"', 32–3 n. 62; the entire documentation is forthcoming and newly studied in Hallmark's dissertation.

[42] We have elsewhere shown that a number of singers were earlier qualified and paid as *clerici capelle* in both papal and cardinalate chapels of the period: Di Bacco and Nádas, 'Verso uno "stile internazionale"', 9 n. 5.

[43] For these singers, see ibid. 23 and the *personalia* in app. 3. All four were—or were about to become—members of Pope Boniface's chapel: Hildernisse and Sapiens as *cantores*, Angelus as *magister*, and Clari again as *clericus capelle* (see also the Appendix).

which he is clearly in command during his Paduan years, and it would allow us to account for works otherwise unclear in terms of dating and provenance. Notable among these is the motet *O virum omnimoda/O lux et decus/O beate Nicholae*, one of the most puzzling of Ciconia's works; now we are in a position to associate its composition with the presence at the Roman curia of two ecclesiastics, the influential *auditor apostolicus* Richardus de Sylvestris and the papal *scriptor* Jacobus Cubellus. The latter succeeded the former in 1393 as Bishop of Trani (in Puglia), an event that coincided with the celebration of the third centenary of the death of the patron saint of the city, S. Nicola Pellegrino; the new bishop and S. Nicola are indeed the subjects of the motet's texts. This is a compelling element in favour of Ciconia's prolonged residence in Rome, to which we shall presently add a new hypothesis for the dating of another important work, his troped Gloria 'Suscipe Trinitas'.[44] Ultimately, a period of Roman residence would also help explain the reciprocal influence between Ciconia and Antonio Zacara, seen in particular in the Mass pair Gloria/Credo nos. 3–4 (in Ciconia's complete works) influenced by Zacara's Gloria 'Micinella' and Credo 'Cursor',[45] and in similar contrapuntal and declamatory techniques heard in a number of their songs.[46]

As early as January of 1390 'Magister Antonius Berardi Andree de Teramo alias dictus vulgariter Zacchara' evidently enjoyed a remarkable reputation in Rome as a musician and as a copyist and illuminator of liturgical manuscripts.[47] He may have sung in the papal chapel as early as Urban VI's

[44] The first to associate the work with the centenary of the death of the saint (1094–1394) was Margaret Bent (Ciconia, *Works*, 222, edition on 81–4), but a definitive association was possible only after the realization of Ciconia's Roman residence. For the documentation on the death of Richardus de Sylvestris *in curia* in 1393 and the installation of the new bishop of Trani, see Di Bacco and Nádas, 'Verso uno "stile internazionale"', 31–2.

[45] See Ciconia, *Works*, 13–24, and F. Alberto Gallo and Kurt von Fischer (eds.), *Italian Sacred and Ceremonial Music* (PMFC 13; Monaco, 1987), 3–7 (the latter also in Gilbert Reaney (ed.), *Early Fifteenth Century Music*, vi (CMM 11; American Institute of Musicology, Stuttgart, 1977); see also Di Bacco and Nádas, 'Verso uno "stile internazionale"', 28–30.

[46] See, for example, Ciconia's *La fiamma del to amor* and Zacara's *Ferito già d'un amoroso dardo*; David Fallows has also recently suggested attributing a few of Ciconia's songs to the composer's Roman years: the ballatas *Chi vole amar* and *Poy che morir* (see his notes to the CD 'Johannes Ciconia' by the French ensemble Alla Francesca & Alta (Opus 111, OPS 30-101).

[47] This wonderfully revealing document was first published by Anna Esposito, '"Magistro Zaccara" e l'antifonario dell'Ospedale di S. Spirito in Sassia', in Paolo Cherubini, Anna Esposito, *et al.*, 'Il costo del libro', in Massimo Miglio *et al.* (eds.), *Scrittura, biblioteche e stampa a Roma nel Quattrocento, Atti del 2. seminario* (Littera Antiqua, 3; Vatican City, 1983), 334–42, 446–9. This is the document that gives us the most complete form of the composer's name; it is a Jan. 1390 contract with the Hospital of Santo Spirito in Sassia, a stone's throw from the Vatican, by which Antonio 'optimo, perito et famoso camtore' will prepare for the Hospital 'uno bono antiphonario magno, notato et scripto optima littera, pro uso et necessitate ecclesie dicti hospitalis et pro divinis officiis reverenter et honorabiliter celebrandis' and also have musical responsibilities 'nec non etiam pro honore, decoro et utilitate ac doctrina et arte musica docenda fratribus, oblatis et iuvenibus clericis morantibus in dicta ecclesia ad divina officia celebranda . . . et ad docendam musicam'. In return he is to receive the value of one hundred gold florins, but instead of cash ('cum ad presens non habeant pecunias manuales nec res mobiles unde possint dare et solvere dicto Magistro Antonio dictos centum florenos auri pro suo salario') he is to receive a house, 'quedam domus dicti hospitalis terriena et solerata sita in Urbe in regione Pontis in strata Recta in

pontificate, and in 1391 he was appointed by Boniface IX as a scribe of papal letters (*scriptor litterarum apostolicarum*). He served in both capacities throughout the reigns of Boniface IX and his successors, not leaving Rome until he followed Gregory XII north in 1407.[48] Beyond the papal documents, we have suggested elsewhere that a number of Zacara's compositions must have been written during his Roman years, associated with one of the most powerful families in the Trastevere and Ponte quarters of the city, the Miccinelli.[49] His Gloria 'Micinella' and Credo 'Cursor', the mass pair that served as a model for the Ciconia pair mentioned above, may be associated with the churches of S. Maria de Monte (also known as S. Maria de' Miccinelli) and S. Angelo de Monte Giordano (also known as S. Angelo de' Miccinelli), the latter given officially in perpetuity to the papal *cursores* (messengers) later in the fifteenth century.[50] Zacara's final years witnessed the peregrinations of Gregory XII's curia through Umbria and Tuscany, and the composer may even have gone as far as Cividale, where Pope Gregory XII held his competing council in June–September 1409, before he switched allegiance to the Pisan obedience. He is next documented as serving in John XXIII's Bolognese chapel from early 1412 until May of 1413, at which time he disappears from the records; a probable autobiographical piece from the period of Pisan obedience is his ballata *Dime, Fortuna* (anonymously transmitted in Turin 2) in which he laments the

parrochia ecclesie Sancte Marie de Monte, iuxta res ipsius ecclesie Sancte Marie de Monte, iuxta res Cecchi Iannis Gibelli de regione Pontis', that is, across the Tiber; see also Di Bacco and Nádas, 'Verso uno "stile internazionale" ', 27.

[48] The papal letter of appointment is dated 1 Feb. 1391 and is in ASV, RL 12, fo. 246[r–v]; it was published by Agostino Ziino, ' "Magister Antonius dictus Zacharias de Teramo": alcune date e molte ipotesi', *Rivista italiana di musicologia*, 14 (1979), 311–48, esp. 311–12, and previously published by F. Savini in his *Septem dioecesis aprutinensis* (Rome, 1912), 467. Due to the immense loss of papal registers from this period, the only other document to have survived that documents Zacara's position as a singer in the papal chapel is from Feb. 1400, a fragment of a book of the *mandati camerali* of the eleventh year of the pontificate of Boniface IX, now MS L166 no. 6 of the Archives Nationales of Paris; see Sherr, 'Notes on Some Papal Documents'. Parchment letters prepared by the *scriptor* Zacara are to be found copied in the (paper) series ASV, *Registra Vaticana*; those cited by Ziino are not, therefore, the original parchment documents sent abroad, of which we have found but a single example with the help of Patrick N. R. Zutshi's *Original Papal Letters in England (1305–1415)* (Vatican City, 1990), no. 400, p. 203. Thus, if one wishes to see an autograph of Zacara's, though unfortunately not a musical one, it is available in a papal letter, London, Public Record Office, SC7/41/7. In any case, the list of letters signed by Zacara as established by Ziino constitutes the proof of his continued presence and employment in curia, at least as a *scriptor*, up to June 1407.

[49] For details see Di Bacco and Nádas, 'Verso uno "stile internazionale" ', 28–9.

[50] The fact that the Miccinelli were definitely a Roman family is tantalizingly confirmed by a 'Missa Miccinella', in BAV, Reg. lat. 352, fos. 27[r]–28[v], a small collection of miscellaneous orations, notes on historical antiquities of Rome, and medical prescriptions (we thank Agostino Ziino for having noted the existence of the volume). The last copyist of the manuscript is probably the person who also copied the 'Messa Miccinella', a certain Stephanus Baroncello (de Baroncellis), who often names himself, provides a coat of arms, and also specifies that he is of 'genere romanus' [*sic*]; the manuscript, therefore, appears to be genuinely Roman and may have been copied in the first few decades of the Quattrocento. The 'Messa Miccinella' consists only of a Latin/Italian text of various elements of the Ordinary and Proper of a Marian Mass; there is nothing, however, here that might allow us to connect it directly with the works of Zacara.

failed return of the papacy to Rome.[51] Zacara may then have returned to
Rome anyway, or to his native Teramo; newly discovered Roman documents
establish his death sometime between May 1413 and September of 1416.[52]

On the basis of our suggestion of Rome as the initial area of compositional
activity not only of Zacara but also of Ciconia, we wish to claim that at least
some of their works must have initially entered the written tradition in the
Roman papal orbit during the 1390s and early 1400s—that is, as part of the
repertory of the papal chapels.[53] We may begin a close look at sources we wish
to associate with late Trecento Rome by first citing the fourth item in Table
2.1, a single parchment bifolio at Foligno containing three polyphonic Glorias
almost certainly copied in Italy before the end of the Trecento. The bifolio was
used as the external cover of a volume that we believe can be identified as a
1524 print housed at the Foligno library and containing the works of the
eleventh-century theologian Theophilactus.[54] The volume previously

---

[51] The last recorded presence of Zacara in John XXIII's chapel is an entry in the *Introitus et Exitus* books from
20 May 1413: Florence, Biblioteca Nazionale Centrale, MS Magl. XIX.81, fo. 136ᵛ. On the interpretation of
Dime, Fortuna as a work referring to Alexander V, see Ziino, *Il codice T.III.2*, 47–9.

[52] In a will dated 1416, the universal heir of Zacara names his procurators: 'Lellus Blaxii Petri sutor nepos ac
heres universalis quondam Magistri Anthonii Berardi Andree dicti alias Zaccharii dudum cantoris et scriptoris
Romane Curie et Sedis apostolice ac avunculi dicti Lelli eius nepotis et heredis prefati dudum de civitate Terami
sita in provincia Aprutinensi et nunc morans in Urbe et in Regionem Pontis eiusdem Lelli bona? propter libera
et spontanea voluntate . . . hac presenti die fecit creavit constituit et ordinavit suos veros et legitimos procura-
tores factores . . . videlicet venerabiles et providos viros dompnum Gervasium germanum fratrem dicti Lelli ac
sacerdotem et rectorem ecclesie Sancti Benedicti site in quodam castro vulgariter nuncupato Contraguerra sito
in diocesi civitatis predicte; necnon et fratrem Andream Priorem ecclesie Sancti Heunufrii site in comitatu quod
vulgariter dicitur Campi diocesis et civitatis prefate . . . presentes . . .'. From this long document we learn that
in Teramo Zacara owned 'domos terras et territoria ac vineas et possessiones' and precisely 'quandam domus
trium et pro parte soleratis cum orto . . . in loco quo vulgariter dicitur Sestieri? Sancti Anthonii iuxta muros dicte
civitatis'. 'Item . . . certas terras . . . nucium et aliarum diversarum arborum fructium sitas in territorio civitatis
predicte extra portam Sancti Anthonii in loco qui vulgariter dicitur Logniano'. 'Item etiam certas quedam terras
et territoria pro parte incultas et pro parte vineatas ipsius quondam magistri Anthonii sitas in territorio civitatis
predicte extra dictam portam S. Antonii in loco qui dicitur Pezalogna (Pezalegna? Perzalegna?)' and other real
estate (Rome, Archivio di Stato, Collegio dei Notai Capitolini, vol. 1163, fos. 611ᵛ–615ʳ; the notary of this
document is Magaloctus de Magalocti notario 'de Regio Columpna'. (We are indebted to Margaret Harvey, who
mentioned this document to us, pointing out that it concerned a papal singer.) We may date Zacara's death more
precisely on the basis of other documents regarding the house in Rome. A document signalled in a summary of
instrumenta pertaining to the church of S. Agostino (Rome, Archivio di Stato, Agostiniani in S. Agostino, reg.
34, fos. 87ᵛ–88ʳ), which also includes the 1390 contract for the antiphoner studied by Esposito, was found by
us as an original parchment roll in Rome, Archivio Generale degli Agostiniani, C.6 n. 22–3, dated 17 and 20
Sept. 1416: cited in a complex legal context we find 'quondam Magistri Antonii, artis musice cantoris et scriptoris olim sacri palatii apostolici, alias vulgariter Zacchari'.

[53] Although the discovery of an earlier Roman phase of Ciconia's career is relatively recent, this is not the
case with Zacara, and it is surprising that up to now no one has considered the written dissemination of his
works in conjunction with his long presence in the Roman curia.

[54] Foligno was first studied by Nino Pirrotta, 'Church Polyphony apropos of a New Fragment at Foligno',
in Harold Powers (ed.), *Studies in Music History: Essays for Oliver Strunk* (Princeton, 1968), 113–26 (including
photographs of the leaves); for the Italian reprint with a 'post scriptum' see his 'Polifonia da chiesa: a proposito
di un frammento a Foligno', in *Musica tra medioevo e rinascimento* (Turin, 1984), 115–29. Most recently, Janet
Palumbo has carefully analysed the disposition of the mass movements in the fragment: 'The Foligno Fragment:

TABLE 2.1. A preliminary assessment of selected musical sources from the period of the Great Schism (1378–1417)

I. *Sources that may be associated with contacts made by foreign and native musicians in Rome during the early decades of the Great Schism*

Atri
Cortona 1/2
Egidi
Foligno
Frosinone, Archivio di Stato, framm. musicale senza segnatura
Grottaferrata 197 + Dartmouth
Guardiagrele, Chiesa di Santa Maria Maggiore, Codici 1 & 2 (now lost)
Rome, Archivio di Stato, Fondo Agostiniani in S. Agostino, busta 34 (polyphony cited in the 1431–2 inventory of the library)
Rome, Archivio Storico del Vicariato, Fondo S. Maria in Trastevere, Arm. I, Cell. A, n. 3, ord. IV (now lost)
BAV, Urb. lat. 1419
Warsaw 378

II. *Sources whose contents may be associated with the repertory of the papal chapels during their travels, 1407–14*

Bologna Q 1
Cividale del Friuli, Museo Archeologico Nazionale, Codici 63 & 98 + Udine, Archivio di Stato, framm. 22 (*olim* Arch. Not. Antico, busta 773)
Cividale del Friuli, Museo Archeologico Nazionale, Codice 79
Florence SL 2211
Florence Pal. 87
Grottaferrata s.s.
London 29987
Munich 3223
Siena 207
Strasburg
Trent 1563
Turin 2

A Reassessment of Three Polyphonic Glorias, ca. 1400', *JAMS* 40 (1987), 169–209. The latest account of the source is by Pier Giuseppe Arcangeli, 'Digressioni infra-musicologiche. Tre ipotesi medioevali', *Esercizi. Musica e spettacolo*, 11 (1992), 5–9. The fragment was transferred from the city library to the State Archives in the 1960s: during our visit to Foligno in 1994 we were able to examine some copies of Theophilactus' *Enarrationes in Evangelia* (as first reported by Pirrotta, the bifolio carries the modern indication 'Theophilact. in E.' on the folded portion that corresponds to the spine of the host volume); one of these copies—Biblioteca Comunale, shelf mark B2.VI.9—now lacks a cover, and its small format and 478-page size match perfectly the dimensions and fold-lines of the music bifolio. Moreover, the general appearance given by the reuse of the musical bifolio is similar to that of other volumes in the same original library collection, the library of the monastery of S. Bartolomeo in Foligno. We are grateful to Dott. Lidia Silveri for her invaluable assistance during our stay in Foligno.

belonged to the library of the monastery of S. Bartolomeo in Foligno, which surely must be the place where the original music manuscript was dismembered and used as binding material. A brief inventory of the fragmentary source is given in Table 2.2.

TABLE 2.2. Inventory of Foligno

A^{r–v}	Anon., Gloria (3³: C1 complete, C2 to 'Patrem omnipotens', T to 'ad dexteram Patris') London Cotton Titus, 3v, 2ʳ, 3ʳ (in score); Grottaferrata 197, 1ᵛ–2ʳ (fragm.)
Bʳ	Anon., Gloria ([3³]: C missing, CT from 'peccata mundi', T from 'tu solus sanctus')
Bᵛ	Anon., Gloria ([3³]: C1 complete, C2 to 'tibi propter', T missing)

What is most remarkable is the inclusion, by an Italian scribe, of a much earlier Gloria setting that originated as part of the English fourteenth-century repertory notated in score; this first of the Gloria settings in Foligno concords with a fragmentary copy in London, British Library, Cotton Titus XXIV that doubtless is the oldest and closest to the original.[55] Details of the translation process, particularly as regards the misinterpretation of English trochaic semibreve pairs and the English swallowtail in French notational practice, have been discussed by Palumbo and others; the important point to make here is that the Gloria is decidedly English in style and origin. The translation into Continental part-notation, moreover, led the scribe to mark clearly the divisional breaks in the music at the end of syntactic units of the Gloria text, as given in his presumably English exemplar: these vertical lines may appear as rests of some sort and are ornamented with red ink, but they plainly are meant to exclude a 'mensural' interpretation.

This is an English practice, as far as we can tell, visible as well in an English *Kyrie* preserved in score notation in a notationally related source, Pisa, Biblioteca Cateriniana, MS 176, where such divisions are rendered as short, double strokes per staff of score notation, again without strict mensural meaning. Some modern editors of the Foligno English Gloria, however, have inter-

---

[55] This Gloria was first edited by Günther, 'Quelques remarques sur des feuillets recemment decouverts à Grottaferrata', *L'Ars nova italiana del Trecento*, 3 (1970), 315–97 at 354–9, and by F. Alberto Gallo and Kurt von Fischer in *Italian Sacred Music* (PMFC 12; Monaco, 1976), 13–16. The first scholar to identify its English origins and the concordance in the London manuscript as the earliest version was Ernest Sanders in his edition with Peter Lefferts, *English Music for Mass and Office* (I) (PMFC 16; Monaco, 1983), 75–7, as pointed out by Palumbo (see above), Gallo and von Fischer, *Italian Sacred and Ceremonial Music*, 295, and William Summers, 'Fourteenth-Century English Music: A Review of Three Recent Publications', *Journal of Musicology*, 8 (1990), 120–1. Summers provides a facsimile of the London manuscript fragment in pls. 58–61 of his *English Fourteenth-Century Polyphony: Facsimile Edition of Sources Notated in Score* (Tutzing, 1983). On English 14th-c. notation, see also Margaret Bent, 'A Preliminary Assessment of the Independence of English Trecento Notations', *L'Ars nova italiana del Trecento*, 4 (1978), 65–82.

preted them as rests.[56] We suggest that English mass music must have first been brought to Italy with the French papal and cardinalate chapels of Pope Gregory XI, or with the Flemish musicians who subsequently joined the Roman chapels (cf. Appendix), not to mention direct contacts with English musicians during this period. This is the moment to restate that the English presence in Italy at the start of the Schism was not inconsiderable, if for no other reason than the fact that England followed the Roman obedience from the beginning. Two highly influential English cardinals travelled to Italy— Simon Langham, previously Archbishop of Canterbury, and Adam Easton— and both employed a great number of English clerics in their households.[57]

But still another remarkable thing about the Foligno fragment and its English Gloria is that the latter is found in Grottaferrata 197, a key source for us, first studied by Oliver Strunk and Ursula Günther in the late 1960s. The leaves that comprise it had then recently been found in the binding of a book in a private Roman collection and were removed and restored at the Abbazia Greca di S. Nilo at Grottaferrata.[58] An inventory of its contents is given in

[56] Facsimile in Summers, *English Fourteenth-Century Polyphony*, pls. 209–10. As described by Reinhard Strohm, 'Ein englischer Ordinariumssatz des 14. Jahrhunderts in Italien', *Musikforschung*, 18 (1965), 178–81, the host volume containing the single 14th-c. leaf is a missal, one of a pair in the Biblioteca Cateriniana in Pisa (MSS 176 and 177). Although a connection with St Vincent Ferrer may be posited on the basis of an internal note in MS 177 ('ad usum fratri philippi carpa filius dicti conventus per venerabilem patrem ludovicum de ter- amo' (1485)), such a connection is not as clear for MS 176.

[57] For the most recent study of English clerics in the papal chapels, see Harvey, 'The Household of Cardinal Langham', *Journal of Ecclesiastical History*, 47 (1996), 18–44, and Andrew Wathey, 'The Peace of 1360–1369 and Anglo-French Musical Relations', *EMH* 9 (1990), 129–74. The versions we now have in Foligno and Grottaferrata 197 represent the copying of the Gloria within the cosmopolitan ambience of the Roman curia at the start of the Schism; the English work, together with the other French or Italian Glorias, was copied by a non-English scribe. It is perhaps in the context, too, of the late Trecento Roman chapels that we may place the citation of a now-lost(?) copy of the English motet, *Sub Arturo plebs*, in a 1431 inventory of the Augustinian library in Rome (listed in Table 2.1): Rome, Archivio di Stato, Agostiniani in S. Agostino, reg. 34, fo. 147ʳ: 'Libri Cantus' . . . 'Liber quidam can- tus figurati in papiro, cuius principium *I Contratenor fons cythariçantium*, finis vero *et ascendit*'.

[58] Oliver Strunk, 'Church Polyphony apropos of a New Fragment at Grottaferrata', *L'Ars nova italiana del Trecento*, 3 (1970), 305–13; Günther, 'Quelques remarques' (with eight facsimile reproductions and six tran- scriptions). To the thirteen leaves known to Günther, another may be added, once belonging to Prof. Denis Stevens and now in the Dartmouth Library, MS 002387, which we indicate as Dartmouth; the new single leaf was first announced by Margaret Bent in her review of PMFC 12 (*JAMS* 32 (1979), 575), and cited in Gallo and von Fischer, *Italian Sacred and Ceremonial Music*, 261, as well as by Greene, *French Secular Music* (PMFC 18), 159, and studied most recently by William Summers, 'Medieval Polyphonic Music in the Dartmouth College Library: An Introductory Study of Ms. 002387', in Bernd Edelmann and Manfred Hermann Schmid (eds.), *Alte im Neuen, Festschrift Theodor Göllner zum 65. Geburtstag* (Tutzing, 1995), 113–30. On the basis of offset musical and verbal texts present on the extant leaves, it is now possible to say that at least two other leaves must have been in the binding of the host volume when it was taken apart to recover the music source (the fol- lowing groups of leaves must have been in contact with each other in the binding: 11ᵛ⁻ʳ/1ʳ⁻ᵛ/9ᵛ⁻ʳ; 8ᵛ⁻ʳ/2ʳ⁻ᵛ/3ʳ⁻ᵛ; Dartmouthᵛ⁻ʳ/4ʳ⁻ᵛ; 13ᵛ⁻ʳ/7ᵛ⁻ʳ/12ᵛ⁻ʳ/lost folio?; lost folio?/5ʳ⁻ᵛ/6ʳ⁻ᵛ; the offsetting of verbal and musical texts on these folios has helped in reconstructing the original structure of the source, and in general we are confirming the succession of works as already given by Günther. Her conclusion that the source originated in the Veneto (probably S. Giustina in Padua) has generally been accepted in more recent studies, or at least not questioned. The book containing the musical leaves belonged in the early 1960s to the Liguori family in Rome; it can no longer be traced. We thank Padre Marco, Librarian of the Monastery at Grottaferrata, and Dr Parenti, his assis- tant, for their help during our study of the source.

TABLE 2.3. Inventory of Grottaferrata 197 and Dartmouth (D)

Fo.	Scribe	Composition
1ʳ	I	Magnificat (plainchant; *Antiphonale Romanum*, 8th tone)
1ᵛ–2ʳ	I	Anon., Gloria Foligno, Aʳ⁻ᵛ (fragm.); London Cotton Titus, 3ᵛ, 2ʳ, 3ʳ (in score)
2ᵛ–3ᵛ	I	Anon., Gloria 'Qui sonitu melodie' Apt, 5ᵛ–7ʳ; Budapest 297, 1ʳ; Cambrai 1328, 3ᵛ–4ʳ; Ivrea, 36ᵛ–37ʳ; Munich 29775/8, Aʳ⁻ᵛ; Nuremberg 9, 2ᵛ–3ᵛ (fragm.); Padua A 684, 2ʳ; Rochester 44, 1ᵛ–2ʳ; Strasburg, 40ᵛ–41ʳ
3ᵛ–Dʳ	IV	[Filippotto da Caserta], *En atendant soufrir m'estuet* Chantilly, 33ᵛ ('Jo. Galiot'); Modena 5.24, 20ʳ ('Magister Filipoctus'); Paris 6771, 84ᵛ
Dᵛ–4ʳ	I	[Magister Egardus], Gloria Modena 5.24, 21ᵛ–22ʳ ('Egardus'); Padua D 1225, a (=1) verso; Warsaw 52, 204ᵛ–205ʳ ('Opus Egardi')
4ᵛ	I/Ia?	[Antonio Zacara], Gloria 'Micinella' Atri, recto; Bologna 2216, 4ᵛ; Bologna Q 1, recto; Bologna Q 15, 16ᵛ–17ʳ ('Z. Micinella' *a 4*)
5ʳ	II?	[Prunet/Perneth/Bonbarde], Credo Apt, 29ᵛ–32ʳ ('Bonbarde'); Barcelona 853c, 8ʳ⁻ᵛ; Brussels II, r–v; Cortona 2, 2ʳ; Padua A 684, 3ᵛ ('Perneth'); Strasburg, 3ᵛ–6ᵛ ('Prunet')
5ᵛ–6ʳ	III	*Marce, Marcum imitaris* Egidi, 2ʳ
6ᵛ	I	[Antonio Zacara], Credo Bologna Q 15, 88ᵛ–90ʳ ('Zacar'); Modena 5.24, 24ᵛ–26ʳ ('Zaccharias'); Padua D 1225, 2ᵛ ('M. Antonius'); Turin 2, 9ʳ; Warsaw 378, 6ᵛ–9ʳ
7ʳ	(Blank–Ruled)	
7ᵛ–8ᵛ	IV	[Antonio Zacara], Credo Siena 207, 1ʳ; Trent 1563, r–v; Turin 2, 9ᵛ–10ʳ; Warsaw 52, 193ᵛ–195ʳ ('Opus Zacharie'); Warsaw 378, 2ᵛ–4ʳ ('Slowye szacharie mneysche')
9ʳ	(Blank–Ruled)	
9ᵛ–10ᵛ	IV	[Johannes Ciconia], Gloria 'Suscipe Trinitas' Grottaferrata s.s., 2ᵛ; Oxford 56 (front pastedown, verso); Padua D 675, 1ʳ⁻ᵛ ('M. Jo. Ciconia'); Warsaw 378, 25ᵛ–27ʳ
11ʳ	(Blank–Ruled)	
11ᵛ	V	[Johannes Ciconia], Credo Bologna Q 15, 4ᵛ–6ʳ ('Jo. Ciconie')
12ʳ	V	Anon., Credo
12ᵛ–13ʳ	VI	[Johannes Vaillant], *Par maintes foy* Brussels I, 1ᵛ + Mons, recto; Cambrai 1328, 20ʳ; Chantilly, 59ᵛ–60ʳ; Mancini, LXXIVᵛ–LXXVʳ; Munich 14274, 27ᵛ–28ʳ (contrafact); Strasburg, 65ᵛ–66ʳ (contrafact); Wolkenstein A, 19ᵛ–20ʳ (contrafact); Wolkenstein B, 22ᵛ–23ʳ (contrafact)
13ᵛ	(Blank–Ruled)	

Table 2.3; on the basis of a fresh re-examination of the fragments we also include a reconstruction of the original gatherings as shown in Fig. 2.1.[59]

The surviving leaves of Grottaferrata 197 appear to come from two adjacent sexterns containing essentially a collection of mass movements. These were originally planned by a first scribe to be a set of four Glorias (the first of which, as in the group in Foligno, is the English work) positioned within the first of the gatherings, followed by a section of Credos, the beginning of which he marked by inserting Zacara's Credo on fo. 6ᵛ. We would submit that Ciconia's troped Gloria 'Suscipe Trinitas' and his Credo that follows, on fos. 9ᵛ–11ʳ, were deliberately copied together (for generic reasons, seemingly out of place) as a mass pair, with the importance of the Gloria movement further highlighted through an elaborately embellished opening capital letter.[60] To this corpus was added an opening monophonic Magnificat, an anonymous Credo (one part of which is on fo. 12ʳ), a Veneto motet at the gathering join, *Marce Marcum imitaris*, and secular works that served to fill in other unused space.[61]

There are compositions in Grottaferrata 197 that would certainly suggest a Roman origin or—for those we consider part of the 'international repertory'— a Roman provenance: chief among them are Zacara's Gloria 'Micinella', and perhaps his two Credo movements as well, and additionally the widely disseminated anonymous Gloria 'Qui sonitu melodie' and the Credo by Perneth/Bombarde, works that must have been brought to Rome in the years surrounding the start of the Schism and then circulated to other musical centres on the peninsula.[62] Certainly there are several compositions here that

---

[59] Identifying the relative position of the leaves was made possible by the musical continuity of the works as well as the watermark evidence, disposition of voice-parts, and in some cases the identification of the mould sides of the paper. We note, for example, that a number of rectos were left intentionally blank in the original planning process, with most compositions begun on a full opening. The order of succession of fos. 5 and 6, as given by Günther, has been reversed.

[60] See PMFC 24, nos. 7 and 10. Although several other Credo movements have been suggested as closely matching the style of this troped Gloria, we stand by Günther's suggestions that the movements were musically as well as scribally paired, particularly with regard to the short repeated-note units in the two-voice sections and the syncopated passages in the three-voice sections. Due to substantial trimming of the folio, only a very small part of the embellished capital letter 'E' remains on fo. 9ᵛ.

[61] *Marce Marcum imitaris* is dedicated to Marco Cornaro, elected doge of Venice in 1365 and successor to Francesco Dandolo, for whom another motet had been written, published in 1968 by F. Alberto Gallo, 'Da un codice italiano di mottetti del primo Trecento', *Quadrivium*, 9 (1968), 25–36; see Günther, 'Quelques remarques', 334. The works copied at gathering joins are quite often additions to the original repertorial plans set into motion by the first scribes of a collection; this is particularly true in the event that two gatherings are destined to contain two diverse types of works, as appears to be the case with the two sexterns of Grottaferrata 197.

[62] Besides the works already mentioned for their relevance in relation to Ciconia and Zacara in Rome, Kurt von Fischer has argued on stylistic grounds for Zacara composing a number of his mass movements in Rome, before he moved north; see his 'Bemerkungen zur Überlieferung und zum Stil der geistlichen Werke des Antonius dictus Zacharias de Teramo', *MD* 41 (1987), 161–82. For the two internationally famous works that made their way to the Holy City—the Gloria 'Qui sonitu melodie' and Perneth's Credo, nos. 3 and 7 in the inventory—arguments have already successfully been made by Günther, Kügle, Strohm, and the editors of the modern editions concerning their earlier notational status in the Grottaferrata 197 redactions as compared with concordances in other sources of the Quattrocento; see Günther, 'Quelques remarques', 322–6 and 332–4;

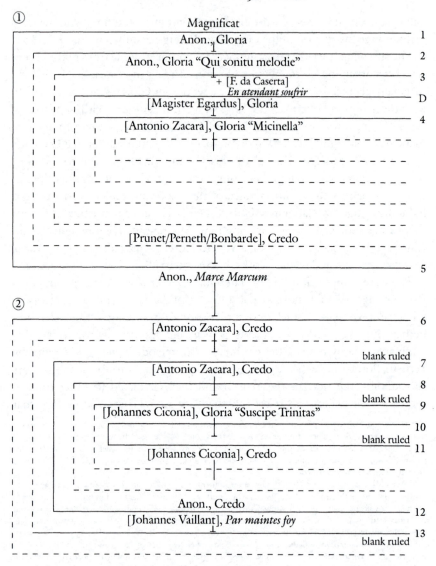

Fig. 2.1. Gathering structure of Grottaferrata 197

Kügle, 'The Manuscript Ivrea', 325–41, and id., 'Codex Ivrea, Bibl. cap. 115: A French Source "Made in Italy"', *Revista de Musicología*, 13 (1990), 527–61; Strohm, *The Rise*, 25–35, and Giulio Cattin and Francesco Facchin, *French Sacred Music* (PMFC 23A/B; Monaco, 1989), nos. 27 and 51. Particularly strong is the excellent musical and formal analysis offered by Strohm, above, highlighting the Perneth Credo as a superb representative of the repertory of the Avignonese papal chapel prior to the Schism. On the 'international style' as a concept in the music of this period, see the following: Reinhard Strohm, 'Vom Internationalen Stil zur Ars Nova? Probleme einer Analogie', *MD* 41 (1987), 5–13, and id., 'Centre and Periphery: Mainstream and Provincial Music', in Tess Knighton and David Fallows (eds.), *Companion to Medieval and Renaissance Music* (New York, 1992), 55–9.

have caused scholars to regard the collection as a Veneto source, copied during the first or second decades of the Quattrocento. Paramount in that judgement is the presence of the motet celebrating a Venetian doge of the 1360s and the works by Zacara, Ciconia, and Egardus largely familiar through north Italian sources.[63] But now with the revised biography of Ciconia in mind, and the subordinate position that the Venetian motet occupies within the original plan of this collection, it may be possible to consider Grottaferrata 197 as having originated outside of the Veneto and much closer to—if not, in fact, in—the orbit of the Roman popes.

TABLE 2.4. Inventory of Egidi

1ʳ [Antonio Zacara], *Cacciando per gustar/Ay cinci ay toppi* ([3³]: T only, fragm.)
    Modena 5.24, 16ᵛ–17ʳ ('Mag[iste]r Z[acharias]'); Florence Pal. 87, 176ᵛ–177ʳ ('M. Zacherias chantor domini nostri pape'); Strasburg, no. 7 (contrafact: *Salve Mater Jesu Christi*)

1ᵛ Anon., *Leonarde pater inclite* ([3²]: only C1, fragm.)

2ʳ Anon., *Marce Marcum imitaris* ([3²]: only C2, fragm.)
    Grottaferrata 197, 5ᵛ–6ʳ

2ᵛ Anon., *Florencia mundi speculum[/Parce pater pietatis]* ([3²]: only C1, fragm.)
    Florence SL 2211, 69ʳ (only C2, palimpsest)

Further support for the possible insertion of *Marce Marcum* into a central Italian source comes from the single concordance of the motet in the Egidi fragment (see Pls. 1–4 and the inventory in Table 2.4), which also contains a *caccia* by Zacara, *Cacciando per gustar/Ay cinci ay toppi*, with clear central Italian linguistic traits (see Pl. 2.1):[64]

> (Tenor)
> – Ay cinci, ay top[pi, ai bretti,
> ai ferri, ai rame rotto]! –
> – [A] l'acora, a le fusa;
> a la merçaria menuta, Madona! –
> – Chi ha de [la rasina? –
> – Chi ha frescie o zagane vecchie?] –

---

[63] Cf. the inventory of Grottaferrata 197. It could well be that the Gloria by Egardus in this manuscript represents the work of a composer serving in a papal—or cardinalate—chapel at the end of the Trecento. Strohm has identified the composer attributions to Egardus or Magister Egardus (Modena 5.24 and Padua A 1475 and Padua D 1225, Utrecht 37 I) with a succentor at St Donatian's in Bruges during the 1370s; moreover, he has claimed the composer is one and the same as a papal scribe, Johannes Eckart, suggesting that he was one of the Flemings who had joined the chapel of Boniface IX in the 1380s or 1390s (*Music in Late Medieval Bruges*, 112; 'Magister Egardus', 44–5). See also above, n. 19.

[64] Antonio Zacara da Teramo, *Cacciando per gustar*, Egidi, fo. 1ʳ. Text lacking in Egidi has been placed in square brackets here and is taken from the edition by Giuseppe Corsi, *Poesie musicali del Trecento* (Bologna, 1970), 313 (vv. 47–78). Our edition of the text adds punctuation and accents; note that 'a' as a form of the verb 'avere' is given in modern spelling as 'ha'.

– Sals, sals,

Salsa verde mostarda! –

– Chi ha de l'ova, chi ha de la sem[mola? –

– E so fiechi ques]si? –

– A l'oglo, a l'oglo! –

– Cy, cy sta', che scy scortegato.

Voglione sey soldi. –

– An[na!, va' for, che te scortiche. –

– Non ne vo'. –

– Co]mo li day? Voyne dare doy? –

– A l'algi a l'alg[i!

Chi le vo' le bon cepolle?] –

– Avanti, avanti, chi se vole ciarmare. –

– [Chi vol secar li piectene?

Chi vòl aconc]iar li pectini da capo? –

–Al dente, al dente,

chi ha male dente   ha male parente,

[e chi ha 'l mal vecino   ha 'l mal matino.] –

– Chi vol conçar caldare,

cen[trare   e capisteri,

e comparare   trespidi e] copergie? –

– A l'açito, a l'acito, como lo tossico.

Chi vòl cernere? –

– Sì, [maduonna, sì, sallo su. –

Chi altro, chi farina compra, vende

chi dorme, caccia, stuta e chi accende.]

We thank Prof. Luca Serianni of the Department of Italian Philology of the University 'La Sapienza' of Rome for having analysed in some detail the linguistic features of Zacara's *caccia*.[65] The conclusion is that the text of the *caccia* as it appears in Egidi is 'centro-meridionale', belonging to a linguistically defined geographic area bordered at the top by an imaginary line drawn from Rome to Ancona, and at the bottom including the southern portion of the

[65] Private communication of Jan. 1996. In general, these features were first reported by Prof. Francesco Egidi in his short article of 1925 ('Un frammento di codice musicale del secolo XIV', in *Nozze Bonmartini–Tracagni XIX Novembre MCMXXV* (Rome, 1925)), which also reproduced two of the pages of the bifolio. More recently the existence of the fragment was announced by Kurt von Fischer, 'Neue Quellen zur Musik des 13., 14. und 15. Jahrhunderts', *Acta musicologica*, 36 (1964), 85. In the 1950s Prof. Egidi gave Kurt von Fischer two black-and-white negatives of the source (unfortunately quite blurred and of poor quality), since deposited at the Musicological Institute in Zurich, a copy from which Margaret Bent very kindly allowed us to first study the fragment. Most recently, Kurt von Fischer has had the film duplicated for us, and we should like to thank both scholars for their invaluable help. The whereabouts of the fragment are not known at present. The four folios of the fragment reproduced here are computer-enhanced images produced at the Department of Computer Science, University of North Carolina in Chapel Hill, with the help of Graham Gash, whom we thank warmly for his expertise.

peninsula, but excluding the Salento region (south of Naples) and south-central Calabria as well as the city of Rome itself (especially notable are the readings 'cinci' and 'acito'). On the other hand, the versions in Modena 5.24 and in Florence Pal. 87 are progressively more Tuscanized.[66]

The evidence of the verbal text of Zacara's *caccia* might be compelling in itself, but to it can be added the fact that Egidi also contains portions of two motets that can be associated with events within the papal curias in central Italy in the early years of the Schism. Cantus I of *Leonarde pater inclite* reveals a piece written to honour Leonardo de Rossi da Giffonio, leader of the Franciscan order, upon his appointment as cardinal by Clement VII in December 1378 (see Pl. 2):[67]

> [Le]onarde, pater inclite,
> Minorum ductor ordinis,
> cuius [. . .]ndit effigiem
> omnium virtutum predite,
> cultor beati numinis
> verus [. . .]maginem,
> corde magnificus [. . .]
> morum norma legifera
> princeps vere salvificus.
> Sacram geris in pectore
> sophiam celesti munere
> cunctis astris [. . .
> . . .] prudencie,
> mi, pater benignissime,
> [pa]te[t] regalis presidencie.

On that occasion, he was in fact also confirmed (or reinstated) as General of the Order, a dignity of which he had been deprived earlier that year by Urban VI. The event must have encompassed some sort of double election for Leonardo, articulated by two political gestures on the part of Clement: bestowal of the Purple cloak for having opposed the Roman pope (and also to thank Queen Johanna for her support) and the Brown vestments (the Franciscan habit) to represent Clement's aspirations of control over the entire administration of the Church.[68]

---

[66] There are some 'mixed' elements in the Egidi version of the *caccia* reported by Prof. Serianni that do not allow for a perfectly black-and-white situation in terms of geographical localization. On the whole, however, it is felt that the text still clearly reflects a central Italian rather than Tuscan or Veneto tradition.

[67] Anon., *Leonarde pater inclite* (Motet, Cantus I), from Egidi, fo. 1ᵛ. Our edition of the text adds capital letters and punctuation. Text in square brackets is tentative; lost text (due to trimming) is represented by ellipses enclosed in square brackets.

[68] Leonardo was elected General of the Order in Toulouse in 1373 and governed the Franciscans until the outbreak of the Schism. In the fall of 1378, however, he refused Urban VI's offer to join the cardinalate and

The other motet voice in Egidi, *Florentia mundi speculum*, is a Cantus I part which, together with the second Cantus in Florence SL 2211, *Parce pater pietatis*, likewise seems to address a striking moment in the history of the Franciscan Order, of some years later and on the Urbanist side (see Pl. 4).[69] In early 1387 Urban VI nominated Enrico Alfieri to be General of the Order, and he was elected to the position at a general council held in Florence at the church of Santa Croce on 25 May of that year.[70] The surviving portion of this fragment, then, contains motets that appear to span some decades of the late Trecento, among them only one that originated in the Veneto, and another most likely at Naples. The third motet may be associated with an event in Florence, but one that is tied ultimately to the Roman papal curia none the less.[71] The bifolio also includes Zacara's *caccia*, but the likely position of the fragment as the second bifolio within a gathering of five in the original music

moved to the Clementine camp. On 16 Dec. Clement VII appointed him as cardinal priest of S. Sisto. The lavish banquet and festivities attending this event are documented by the *Chronicum siculum incertis auctoris ab anno 340 ad annum 1396*, ed. Jo. de Blasiis (Naples, 1887), 34, 124. The election must have been highly supported by Queen Johanna and Count Onorato of Fondi. On Leonardo's career, see C. Schmitt, 'La Position du card.' Leonard de Giffoni OFM dans le conflict du Grand Schisme d'Occident', *Archivium franciscanum historicum*, 50 (1957), 273–331; 51 (1958), 25–72, 410–72, esp. 285–7. Previous suggestions that the motet could date from the years 1373–9 may be considering a period too wide in its coverage, for although it may be possible to take the 1373 election as the likely occasion celebrated by the work, the very incompleteness of the piece seems to allow for a second Cantus part whose text would probably speak of 'Cardinal' Leonardo. If the work does reflect Leonardo's first election as General of the Order in Toulouse, then we would speculate that the most likely way it would have arrived in Italy is with Gregory XI's curia.

[69] The discovery that the two disparate voice parts in fact belong to one motet is Margaret Bent's ('The Fourteenth-Century Italian Motet', *L'Ars nova italiana del Trecento*, 6 (Certaldo, 1992), 85–125 at 106–8, with an edition on 114–19). See also Gallo and von Fischer, *Italian Sacred and Ceremonial Music*, 246–8.

[70] The history of the Order is treated by Raphael M. Huber, *A Documented History of the Franciscan Order: From the Birth of St. Francis to the Division of the Order under Leo X, 1182–1517* (Milwaukee, Wis., 1944), 288–90; see also the entry 'Enrico Alfieri' in the *Dizionario biografico degli italiani*, ii (1960), 268–9. Our new reading of *Parce pater* (from an enhancement of an ultraviolet photograph of the folio in Florence SL 2211) differs at several important points and permits us to posit a papal connection and suggest the 1387 election of Alfieri as a likely occasion bringing together the city of Florence, the Franciscans, and one of the reigning popes: 'Parce pater pietatis tolle donum caritatis quod tibi Florentia [. . .] claritatis. Dum manna(?) benignitatis [. . .]sa conditoris dono apostolice decoris tenes [. . .]igilum fulgentem [. . .] collegium [. . .]foris pacis pastor grati moris [. . .] celestem bravium intuere ergo et devoto qui tibi tam fecit no[. . .] Hymatis februus populum prehendo(?) [. . . . . .]resie clementia.' The text of Cantus I in Egidi reads as follows: 'Florentia mundi speculum luc[. . .] di[. . .]s radi[um] per cuncta mundi climata exempla docens seculum. Virtutis dando gladium contra terrena stigmata. Non mirum si flos dixeris dum tui odoris fragrancia celi sideris reficis [. . .] estiteris annorum tua clementia quando in mundo proficis plaude decus [. . .] ta[. . .] signa pietatis. In minorum collegio diffundens alte deitatis famam sequens dignitatis cum sacro ministerio.'

[71] In early 1387 Urban VI, then residing in Lucca, nominated Alfieri to the highest leadership position in the Franciscan Order. It seems possible to us that this may have been the event that occasioned the composition of the motet, perhaps the work of a composer in Urban's chapel, and the motet then became part of the papal chapel's musical repertory. Even if the piece were to have been written in or near Florence close to the actual date of election, 25 May 1387, we suppose that it would have been brought back to Rome and its environs by the pope's musicians. Urban had much to gain from the composition of the motet, for it was great publicity for him and his power to continue to exert control in the area where he once had been deeply wounded: when Leonardo, General of the Order, refused appointment to the cardinalate in 1378. This too was a delicate moment for relations between Urban and Florence, unsteady in its support of the Roman obedience, and the honour bestowed upon the city would no doubt have been quite deliberate and politically motivated on the pope's part.

manuscript from which it was taken would place the *caccia* on the first recto, followed by the three motets. We believe that the outstanding musical artifice of the *caccia*'s opening canon between the top voices would have suggested its similarity to the opening of *Marce Marcum* in particular (see Pl. 3), sparking its inclusion in this collection.[72] Although it could be argued that we may be witnessing the importation of works included in a Veneto source, the last piece of evidence to suggest that the reverse is true in fact is the geographical location of the host volume. This is an element that was noted for Foligno, above, and assumes even more importance in the present case. In the case of Egidi, our recent findings allow us to state that it served as the cover for a volume of notarial acts of the city of Macerata, an archive and a series of documents that have been shown by other scholars to have made exclusive use of parchment manuscripts from central-east Italy in the course of restoration and maintenance during the sixteenth century. Indeed, Macerata was one of the great administrative centres for the Papal States, and one may easily consider Rome and its environs as the most accessible source for such manuscript material.[73]

Our recent conclusion that Ciconia's motet, *O virum omnimoda*, was composed in Rome in 1393–4 for the installation of the new bishop of Trani is also relevant to the identification of Egidi as a central Italian source with papal connections.[74] Ciconia's motet shares many features with what has been described as Italian motet style; indeed, the striking use of imitation and sequence as well as the harmonic language in this work might suggest a re-examination of the exclusive Veneto provenance of such compositions. It seems possible, at least, that older Veneto motets such as *Marce Marcum* had been brought to Rome

---

[72] On the similarities between *caccia* and Italian motet styles, see Margaret Bent, 'The Fourteenth-Century Italian Motet', 104. The inclusion of Zacara's *caccia* in Modena 5.24 was argued on the same grounds; see Nádas and Ziino, *The Lucca Codex*, 45.

[73] Archivio di Stato di Macerata, Fondo Notarile di Macerata, modern numbered vol. 517, Notary Roberto de Robertis, containing documents from 1551 to 1554 (originally numbered 28 and 33; see facsimile above). This case is not unlike that of the Lucca Codex leaves; see Nádas and Ziino, *The Lucca Codex*, 16–19. In the years 1905–10 the archivist Salvatore Faraone, assisted by Prof. Ludovico Zdekauer, removed all the parchment leaves from the bindings of notarial registers in that archive. The holdings of this material, the 'fondo tabulario diplomatico', came to be known by local historians for its imposing size and substance as a focus of systematic research; the most extensive studies have been of Beneventan script and are useful to us in not only demonstrating that the parchment codices were reused in the years 1530–70 by order of papal bulls on the conservation of notarial acts, but also that the dismembered leaves were taken from manuscripts produced in the area comprising the actual regions of the Marches and the Abruzzo and kept in this area that reveals itself to have been far richer culturally than the present patrimony might lead one to think. For details see Pio Cartechini, 'La Miscellanea Notarile dell'Archivio di Stato di Macerata', in *Atti del III Convegno di Studi Maceratesi, Camerino 26 Novembre 1967* (Macerata, 1968), 3–22; Attilio De Luca, 'Frammenti di codici in beneventana nelle Marche', in *Miscellanea in memoria di Giorgio Cencetti* (Turin, 1973), 101–40. De Luca, in particular, believes that there was an especially vigorous commerce in the reuse of old manuscripts, given the richness of the region (104–10). The bifolio which served as the cover for notarial volume 517 was given to Prof. Egidi in the 1920s by Zdekauer, as Egidi himself tells us, because of its contents: the archivist knew that the *caccia* text in particular would appeal to a literary scholar whose interests in vernacular writings of the region were known.

[74] See above, p. 56 and n. 44.

in the late Trecento, and that Ciconia was as much influenced by those works as he was by repertory that was specifically created at the papal curia or had been brought to Rome from France, the Low Countries, and England. That is, in the past we have waited for Ciconia to get to Padua before the principal features of his motet style matured and matched related works from that area; now we are tempted to suggest that that style developed in a parallel fashion in Ciconia's first essays in the genre, starting in Rome in the 1390s.

To return to the Grottaferrata collection, there is yet one work that must be discussed. Perhaps the most critical piece in the manuscript is Ciconia's troped Gloria 'Suscipe Trinitas', for which we now wish to devote some discussion to its proposed Roman provenance and a date within the last decade of the Trecento. The Latin trope text and a translation read as follows:[75]

(Gloria in excelsis Deo . . . bonae voluntatis.)

Suscipe, Trinitas, hoc pacis jubilum	Accept, o Trinity, this jubilus of peace
horrendi scismatis remove nubilum	and remove the cloud of schism,
a superadditis gregi fidelium, ut fiat	which has been imposed on thy flock, so
unicum.	that it may be one.

(Laudamus te . . . glorificamus te.)

Extra signum unitatis non te laudat devius,	He that leaves the (true) path, outside the sign of unity, doth not praise thee,
cum abusu racionis justus fiat impius;	since the righteous man becomes unholy by abuse of reason:
dum adorat, benedicit, est sibi contrarius.	while he worships and blesses thee, he contradicts himself.

(Gratias agimus . . . Pater omnipotens.)

Opere claruit atque miraculis invicta veritas,	By word and miracle thy unconquerable truth shone forth;
sed tua dextera errata dirigas ut fiat equitas.	but with thy right hand guide what is gone astray that justice may be done.

(Domine fili . . . Filius Patris.)

Summe Pater, Agne Jesu, Spiritus, vivifica.	Father most High, Jesu the Lamb, Spirit, give life;
Sume preces, flecte mentes, carnalibus obvia,	accept our prayers, bend our minds, oppose those carnal ones
qui favore racionis negant a se posita.	who with the aid of reason deny their own premisses.

[75] Although we presented a translation at the AMS Meeting of 1994 quite close to the one given here, we should like to thank Leofranc Holford-Strevens for his stimulating help in significantly improving it; we print here, in fact, his translation as it appears in the 1995 Orlando Consort's CD 'Popes and Antipopes: Music for the Courts of Avignon and Rome', Metronome 1008.

(Qui tollis . . . deprecationem nostram.)

Virgo Mater advocata, omni lapso subveni;	Virgin Mother, our advocate, come to the aid of all that are fallen;
Tempus instat quo inserta ventris instes fructui	the time is at hand for thee to trust thyself in and
sponsa pro hac lacessita reducenda cultui.	plead with the fruit of thy womb to restore this injured bride to her proper worship.

(Qui sedes . . . Jesu Christe.)

Claviger etheree interveni sedule.	Heavenly doorkeeper intercede constantly;
Pax tibi sit unice cosmice ecclesie.	the peace of a united universal church be unto thee.

It has been thought, and appears to be commonly accepted, that the opening invocation to the Trinity, by itself, in the context of a plea to end the Schism must place the work in the years of threefold Schism—that is, after participants at the Council of Pisa in 1409 elected a third contender to the papacy.[76] What we wish to point out, however, on the basis of a number of contemporary witnesses to be discussed shortly, is the fact that the prayer to the Trinity here is to be taken, first, as an assertion of faith and, secondly, as a plea to the ever present figure of unity as the symbolic goal to attain during the entire period of Schism. More to the point: the Trinity as a symbol of eternal unity could be—and indeed was—invoked as a common literary topos on a good number of occasions during all phases of the period of Schism, whether it be twofold or threefold, and this element alone cannot be used fruitfully to further date a text; the more crucial criteria, it seems to us, reside in specific passages in the rest of the texts of such Schism pieces. In addition, we also believe that the Trinity certainly could not easily be equated with the very division that was tearing the church apart, and it seems that any such ready association of the threefold Schism with the Holy Trinity probably would have been considered heretical!

What leads us, then, to Ciconia's Roman years is that there is really nothing in the text of this work that alludes to the threefold Schism of Pisa and beyond, and there is certainly no mention made of the new pope, Alexander V—or even John XXIII, if we wish to consider yet another election one year later.[77] On the

[76] Ciconia, *Works*, ed. Bent and Hallmark, no. 7, pp. 36–43; the text was edited and translated by Michael J. Connolly (202–3).

[77] This last is suggested by Strohm, who placed the work within the post-Pisan conciliarism that must have attended the election of John XXIII in May 1410 (see *The Rise*, 17). Humbertus de Salinis's Gloria 'Jubilatio', another troped Gloria written with the ending of the Schism in mind, does in fact make clear reference to a newly elected pope who will bring the Schism to an end; we believe the pope to be Alexander V at Pisa on the basis of papal documents that place Humbertus precisely at Pisa in 1409 (especially a letter from Alexander V to Salinis, dated Pisa, 10 July 1409 (ASV, RL 138, fos. 105ʳ–106ʳ): 'dilecto filio Humberto de Salinis canonico Bracharensi, familiari nostro . . . in capella nostra cantor existis'; see also Strohm, *The Rise*, 100); the commonly accepted context for the work has been the Council of Constance; see Reaney, *Early Fifteenth-Century Music*,

other hand, knowledge that the composer's patron, Cardinal Philippe d'Alençon, had indeed played an active role in trying to bring the Schism to an end during the 1390s suggested that we look there for, if not a single occasion, at least the intellectual-theological climate that would have given rise to this text. We have found in significant passages of the text suggestive allusion to two important focal points surrounding efforts to end the Schism from the Roman and Avignon sides, both possible contexts within which to place the Gloria 'Suscipe Trinitas': the Jubilee Year of 1390 and efforts in 1395 to force Benedict XIII's abdication.

From the very start of the Great Schism in 1378–9, contemporaries sought immediately to find a solution to end it. The thirty long years that passed before Christendom, with the support of intense theological machinations, could find a way to call a general council not led by papal authority and the strength to depose the standing rival claimants to the papacy, were witness to repeated attempts at multiple solutions. The first call for a general council (the possible resolution that came to be called the *via concilii*) in fact dates from the summer of 1378; it was made by Italian cardinals hoping quickly to demonstrate Urban VI's legitimacy, but the implementation of conciliar action was only first fully realized at Pisa in 1409.

Among attempts to end the Schism from the Roman side, we may point to Urban VI's actions in the late 1380s deliberately planned to help end the Schism. It is clear that Urban, in a famous bull of 1385, intended to appeal to the very fundamental teachings of Christianity, and to this end he demanded of all who would be true Christians a profession of faith in God and the basic belief in the dogma of the Holy Trinity.[78] His most famous call to all Christians came in the March 1389 proclamation of the following year as a Jubilee Year, a grand unifying gesture meant to attract all Christendom to

---

pp. vii, ix, and xxv, and Ziino, *Il Codice T.III.2*, 50. The most significant passages of the trope are the following: 'Gloria, jubilatio | uni Deo et simplici, | vero Christi vicario, | nostro summo pontifici. | . . . Gratias tibi ferimus | quia, excluso scismate, | sacro dedisti pneumate | verum papam quem credimus. | Patris sedens ad dexteram, | solus sanctus et dominus, | regesque sponsam dexteram, | papam nostrum quem colimus.' Although Salinis's papal documents reveal him to be heavily beneficed in Portugal (Braga and Lisbon), the French diocese by far most represented by clerics using the surname 'de Salinis' is that of Besançon (Bisuntinensis). One other work whose text is a prayer for the end of the Schism and quite likely written at the Council of Pisa is the anonymous two-voice piece *Le temps verra tan toust apres* in Turin 2, fos. 24ᵛ–25ʳ. It appears to be the work of an Italian composer, in a convoluted mixture of French and Italian, briefly recounting the main events of the Schism leading up to a conclave that fills all who arrive 'per terre e per mare' with the hope of a solution (for a facsimile and transcription of the text, see Ziino, *Il Codice T.III.2*, 124–5, 184–5).

[78] Urban VI's bull 'Ad propagationem catholice fidei', promulgated on 1 Aug. 1385 (published, among other places, in the *Bullarium privilegiorum ac diplomatum romanorum pontificum amplissima collectio* (Rome, 1740); repr. as *Magnum bullarium romanum* (Graz, 1964), iii. 372–4). The bull, addressing 'hereticis, schismaticis, alisque a sacrosancta apostolica romana et universali ecclesia quomodolibet deviantibus, et ad eiusdem ecclesie unitatem, obedientiam, et reverentiam redeuntibus formam possessionis fidei praestandam praescribit', makes clear its insistence on faith as the ultimate healing power.

Rome.[79] Intimately tied to the call for the Holy Year was another gesture on Urban's part, the institution of a new feast-day—the Visitation of the Blessed Virgin Mary—and by so doing he was explicitly asking the Blessed Virgin to intercede directly in protecting the Church from the devastating effects of the Schism.[80] Due to Urban's untimely death in October 1389, the bull of proclamation was in fact issued shortly thereafter by his successor, Boniface IX.[81]

It is in this light that the first stanza of Ciconia's trope text could be read as a prayer to the Holy Trinity to accept the shouts of 'jubilation' of 1390 (echoing, after all, the well-known phrase from the Canon of the Mass: 'Suscipe Sancta Trinitas'), and asking that the cloud of schism imposed upon God's flock be removed and the faithful restored to unity and 'peace'. The most important festivity of 1390 thus assumes pride of place in the text. The following three stanzas (the second, third, and fourth) seek in their theological legalese an end to the Schism in Christian dogma, referring to the ill-reasoned papal sanctioning of the break, and in general criticizing all who would try to resolve the Schism 'through reason'. The conclusion it would have listeners draw is that to praise God, but at the same time to accept more than one pope, is not to praise him at all. Placed in a relatively subordinate position as the fifth stanza is the petition to Mary to intercede on behalf of all concerned in restoring Church unity; but perhaps the usual prayer to Mary acquired an even more

[79] The events leading to the proclamation of 1390 as a Jubilee Year are reported fully by Jaroslav Polc, *De origine festi visitationis B.M.V.* (Corona Lateranensis, 9A; Rome, 1967), 78–82. It is noteworthy that in his urgency Urban was forcing a Jubilee Year in 1390, changing the normal interval of fifty years first set by Boniface VIII in 1300. Of course, the jubilee was to be a financial boon for the Roman papacy, drawing thousands to the Holy City from all over Europe for the promised indulgences—and benefices—as rewards, all designed to legitimize Urban as the only true vicar of Christ on earth.

[80] See Polc, *De origine festi*, and Ruben Weltsch, *Archbishop John of Jenstein (1348–1400): Papalism, Humanism and Reform in Pre-Hussite Prague* (The Hague and Paris, 1968), for excellent studies of how the feast was instituted. It was initiated as a local feast in Prague in 1385 by its archbishop Johannes Jenstein then caught up in fervent Marian worship. In 1386 Jenstein asked Urban that the feast be instituted for all of Christendom, giving rise to three years of discussion at the Roman curia, culminating in an intense *processus* in spring of 1389 (summarized by an associate of Jenstein at the Roman curia in notes that survive in MS I.F.777 of the Wrocław University Library; see Polc, *De origine festi*, 48–78, and Weltsch, *Archbishop John of Jenstein*, 87–91; our thanks to Margaret Harvey for pointing us to that manuscript source and sending us relevant photocopies from it). Its conclusion clearly allowed Urban to proclaim the feast as an attempt to have the Mother of God intercede on the Church's behalf for an end to the Schism, declaring 2 July as the feast-day and putting into place the music and text for the new Office. The music was written by one of the papal chaplains, Henricus de Latinia, and the text originally offered by Jenstein himself was revised by one of the four cardinals charged with examining the feast, the English cardinal Adam Easton (one of his colleagues in this affair was none other than Philippe d'Alençon). See Andrew Hughes, *Late Medieval Liturgical Offices: Resources for Electronic Research* (Toronto, 1994), for a thorough study of texts for the feast; an older edition of Easton's Office is available in Dreves, *Liturgische Reimofficien des Mittelalters* (Analecta Hymnica, 4), 89–94.

[81] Boniface's bull 'Superni benignitas' is dated 9 Nov. 1389, the day of his coronation as pope; see the *Magnum bullarium romanum*, 378–9. Although properly remembering Urban VI as the founder of the feast, no mention is made of an association between the new feast and solutions sought for the Schism. Clearly, for Boniface there was a hierarchy in the sense of festivities for 1390—first the Jubilee Year, the rewards of which he would reap directly, and secondly the institution of the Marian feast, which had been largely the work of his predecessor and for which Boniface as cardinal had not played a particularly significant role.

solemn meaning in the context of the institution of the new Feast of the Visitation, because her name in the musical setting is set in high relief above all others through the use of long-held sonorities. One thus encounters here a weighing of the two significant celebrations within the same year: the Jubilee is strongest, politically as well as in its public manifestation; the Feast of the Visitation lends the Marian theme a particular emphasis in its new context. The final stanza calls for aid from St Peter as the first pope.[82]

Equally attractive, if perhaps not more so in some regards, as a source for the interpretation of our troped Gloria is the context of French attempts at ending the Schism in the mid-1390s, efforts with roots in the rigorous theological reasoning aired during the earliest years of the Schism. As early as September of 1378, prelates and theologians met at the University of Paris to find a conciliar way to a solution. It is with the works of two German scholars on the faculty at Paris that the writings take on a decidedly reasoned approach: the tracts of Heinrich Heynbusch von Langenstein and Konrad von Gelnhausen from 1379 and the early 1380s were to form the very manifestos of the conciliar movement, their ideas being quickly taken up by others, chief among them Pierre d'Ailly and Jean Gerson, chancellors of the university, and Simon of Cramaud, all leading theologians who were to prove formidable voices later at the Councils of Pisa and Constance.[83] In particular, Langenstein's *Epistola pacis* and Gelnhausen's *Epistola brevis* and *Epistola concordiae* of 1379–80 draw on historical arguments to demonstrate that even in less grave situations Christendom had had recourse to the convocation of councils to resolve disputes.[84] One of the citations most invoked in supporting this resolve is, significantly, the opening chapter of the decretals of Gregory IX, cited as 'De

---

[82] The musical setting of this Gloria is of interest in other respects. It has not passed unnoticed that the style is rather archaic for Ciconia, containing awkward counterpoint in spots, and in general lacking the vigorous mix of sequence and imitation that we have come to associate with him. No doubt, the usual, strict relegation of the trope text to duos, and mass text to the full trios, can be viewed as a desire to make the occasional text stand out—effectively delivering a message that had to be clearly understood.

[83] C. M. D. Crowder, *Unity, Heresy, and Reform, 1378–1460: The Conciliar Response to the Great Schism* (New York, 1977); R. N. Swanson, *Universities, Academics and the Great Schism* (Cambridge Studies in Medieval Life and Thought, 12; Cambridge, 1979); Howard Kaminsky, *Simon de Cramaud and the Great Schism* (New Brunswick, NJ, 1983); and Giuseppe Alberigo, *Chiesa conciliare: identità e significato del conciliarismo* (Testi e ricerche di scienze religiose, 19; Brescia, 1981). In addition, we have found particularly insightful for an understanding of the roles played by French nobility and the University of Paris, Kaminsky, 'The Politics of France's Subtraction of Obedience from Pope Benedict XIII, 27 July, 1398', *Proceedings of the American Philosophical Society*, 115 (1971), 366–97, and Malcolm L. De Weese, 'A Study of Decision-Making in France During the Reign of Charles VI (The Rejection of the Avignon Papacy 1395)' (Ph.D. diss., University of Washington, 1973). Strohm, *The Rise*, 17–18, also cites the writings of Langenstein and Gelnhausen as significant for understanding the context of conciliar theories at the later councils, but he does not bring their ideas to bear on contemporary events of the 1380s and 1390s.

[84] The treatises are published in F. Bliemetzrieder, *Literarische Polemik zu Beginn des großen abendländischen Schismas* (Vienna, 1909), 111–40, and James Kerr Cameron, 'Henry of Langenstein: A Letter on Behalf of a Council of Peace', in Matthew Spinka (ed.), *Advocates of Reform: From Wyclif to Erasmus* (Philadelphia, 1963), 106–39.

summa trinitate'.[85] In so doing, they legitimized very early on the role to be played by the University of Paris and its master theologians. Not to be shown as unco-operative, in 1393 Clement VII instituted a Mass for the end of the Schism that came to be well known by his followers throughout the Continent, originally called the 'Missa pro pace et unitate ecclesie'.[86] Another theologian writing slightly later still refers to the principles of Gregory IX's decretal and the surrounding contemporary debate in discussing the pairing of the unity of the three entities of the Holy Trinity with the necessary reunification of the three bodies of Christianity, 'populi, animi et prelati'.[87]

By the mid-1390s, however, the University as a key player in debates was joined in its efforts by the royal princes of France—the dukes of Burgundy, Berry, and Orléans—to push for the second of the three solutions being aired: the *via cessionis*, or mutual abdication by the two reigning pontiffs. It is at this stage that our French cardinal Philippe d'Alençon, although in the Roman camp, also began to campaign vigorously for such a solution. What must be kept in mind, however, was that the events of 1394–5 served to turn attention exclusively towards the Avignon papacy, to the exclusion of Rome: the stimulus came with the death of Clement in 1394 and the almost immediate election of a successor, Pedro de Luna as Pope Benedict XIII, in October of that year. In the flurry of correspondence among the Avignon pope, the University of Paris, the dukes, Philippe d'Alençon, and the court of Aragon, both the resolve of the new pope not to respond and the French wish to push for forced abdication were made evident.[88] The climactic moment came with the call for a council of prelates and theologians of France held at the royal palace in Paris

[85] The decretals (papal letters on questions of canonic rights) collected by Gregory IX are one of the major such compilations of issues by preceding pontiffs (here Gregory specifically selected writings that extend back to the pontificate of Innocent III): edition by A. Friedberg in *Corpus Iuris Canonici, pars secunda, Decretalium Collectiones; Decretalium Gregorii pape IX [et al.]* (Leipzig, 1879; repr. Graz, 1955). The 'Titulus I: de summa Trinitate et fide catholica' is in cols. 5–7. See also G. Fransen, *Les Décrétales et les collections de décrétales* (Tournhout, 1972), 15, 25.

[86] The Mass was first studied by S. Salaville, 'L'Origine avignonnaise de la messe "ad tollendum schisma"', *L'Année théologique*, 3 (1942), 117–22. More recently it has received attention from Robert Amiet, 'La Messe pour l'unité des chrétiens', *Revue des sciences religieuses*, 28 (1954), 1–35; a reworking and slight expansion of this article by the author has appeared as 'La Messe "pro unitate ecclesiae"', *Ephemerides liturgicae*, 76 (1962), 296–334. The word 'pax' is used ubiquitously in all these efforts as representing the goal of ending the Schism.

[87] 'Circa quod considero quod haec unio, sive connexio debet constare ex tribus: Ex populi uniformitate, ex animi unanimitate, ex praelati singularitate . . . vicari[i] Jesu Christi', from the 'Effectus propositionis factae per dominum abbatem S. Michaelis coram rege Aragoniae, quando fuit missus ibi per regem pro facto unionis Ecclesie' published in E. Martène and E. Durand (eds.), *Thesaurus novus Anecdotorum*, ii (Paris, 1717), cols. 1165–72, from a manuscript source dated 1398.

[88] The correspondence is available in Caesar Egassius Bulaeus [César Du Boulay], *Historia Universitatis Parisiensis, collegiorum plus quam triginta fundationes, statuta, privilegia, reformationes. . . aliarum universitatum erectiones. . . aliaque id genus ex autographis desumpta manuscriptis codicibus et membranis*, 4 vols. (Paris, 1668; repr. 1966), 687–851. See also Heinrich Denifle, *Chartularium Universitatis Parisiensis*, 4 vols. (Paris, 1894; repr. Brussels, 1964), iii (1350–1394), 630–1, doc. no. 1689, letter from Philippe d'Alençon to the University of Paris dated 8 July 1394 (= Bulaeus, 705–6).

in the first two weeks of 1395, the result of which was the strong insistence that Benedict XIII step down. A delegation led by the French dukes went to Avignon to settle the matter, or so it was thought. Instead Benedict was discovered to have reversed himself on the oath taken by all cardinals at the conclave of 1394—when each promised, in case he became pope, to pursue all possible avenues to end the Schism, including the *via cessionis*—and protracted negotiations only produced convoluted and forced arguments from the pope as to why still a third solution to end the Schism would be best.[89] It is at that moment, in late 1395 and early 1396, that the spotlight of forced abdication was turned almost entirely on the Avignon pope, as it was generally felt that Boniface IX had accepted the *via cessionis*; moreover, Benedict's actions only proved that, should a church council have had to decide then and there, clearly Boniface stood a good chance of being legitimized as the only true pope.[90]

It is in this light that the Gloria trope may also be read with a sense of associating it with these current events. The invocation of the Trinity remains an article of faith, as in our previous reading. What changes, however, is the pointed attack on a particular pontiff in stanzas two to four, in which Benedict XIII's general refusal to co-operate is made manifest in his arguments to the contrary ('abusu rationis') and in the suggestive play on his name ('dum adorat, benedicit, est sibi contrarius'), for an unholy pope, it is suggested, cannot truly bless anyone. That such wordplay is not forced upon the text by us, and that contemporaries would have been open to it in this context, is made evident in a letter to Benedict from the University of Paris, dated 23 October 1394:

Ecce Pater Beatissime, nunc salutem Ecclesiae! nunc pacem et concordiam, nunc innumerabilium malorum exterminium, Ecclesiam citra finem omnem per tot iam Schismatis annos istantium in dextra vestra portatis. Si qua es spes remedii, si qua expectatio ex vobis est, oculi omnium in te sperant Domine, omnia a te expectant effecta benedictionis. Aperi ergo nunc manum tuam, imple omne animal benedictione. Sed qua benedictione? illa de qua est scriptum in Psalmo 'Benedicat tibi Dominus ex Sion, et videas bona Ierusalem omnibus diebus vitae tuae'. *O vos vere Benedictum, Pater Beatissime, si nos benedixistis ista benedictione.* O vos feliciter natum! O fortunatos parentes qui vos ad tam egregium et memoriale opus ediderit![91]

---

[89] Benedict's insistence on the *via iusticiae*, by which the rival pontiffs would meet and decide the matter only between themselves, was categorically rejected by all other parties. See Kaminsky, *Simon de Cramaud*, 137–45.

[90] A rare and welcomed examination of the Roman curia's response is to be seen in Margaret Harvey's *Solutions to the Schism* (Sankt Ottilien, 1983), chs. 3 and 4, esp. 87–96. By late 1396, however, the French began serious discussions with the English on this topic, and for the first time since the start of the Schism the English were willing to enter on the playing field and demand of their papacy in Rome to take action in the scenario of mutual abdication. In fact a joint delegation of French and English intellectuals set out to visit the two pontiffs in 1397; they met their greatest resistance in Avignon, but less so in their Roman sojourn in September (arriving scarcely a month after the death of Philippe).

[91] Emphasis in italics is ours. See Bulaeus, *Historia universitatis parisiensis*, iv. 713–15.

Stanza four in particular can be read as alluding to Benedict's then famous denial of the oath taken at the conclave ('qui favore rationis negant a se posita').[92]

These two possibilities for interpreting the Gloria 'Suscipe Trinitas' have been strong factors in arguing for a date between 1390 and the death of Philippe d'Alençon in 1397, and, consequently, for the Roman phase in Ciconia's career when he would have been close to the major players in these dramatic efforts to end the Schism.

We should like to return now to a final element in Grottaferrata 197 that bears directly on the manuscript's relative position chronologically within the corpus of sources to have survived from the Great Schism, believing that this may aid in the conviction that the fragment is indeed an early source belonging to Zacara's and Ciconia's Roman years. We are referring specifically to those passages in the Cantus part of Zacara's Credo no. 23 in which the simultaneous use of black and red notation on a single stave signals the splitting of the one voice-part into two (so-called 'divisi' notation) with the attendant momentary absence of the lower parts.[93] To be noted as well is the flexibility in the length of divisi passages: the impression of changing textures is one of momentary and casual effect rather than of structural articulation (as seen in Ex. 2.1, the composer sometimes sets single words and short phrases in this manner).

A remarkable feature of Zacara's Credo in Grottaferrata 197 is that it is the only version among concordant sources to present the opening passage ('Patrem omnipotentem') with red notes; the top of the folio was severely trimmed, and the visible notes do not correspond to the pitches of the single part given by other sources (see Ex. 2.2). It seems to us that the only solution is to read those notes as part of an opening divisi passage in which we now can see only the lower of two parts, ending on a *d'* (probably to be sung in unison with the other split voice). In fact, the notation of such passages in

---

[92] On this point, see Kaminsky, *Simon de Cramaud*, 143–5, and De Weese, 'A Study of Decision-Making', ch. 5, 103–32. In this case, the plea to Mary in stanza 5 may assume a more generalized invocation, although it should be pointed out that Marian devotion must have been deeply felt by Philippe d'Alençon, given his continued residence at Santa Maria in Trastevere throughout his cardinalate career, and reflected as well in the Marian iconography of his tombstone, which goes well beyond the topical significance of his death on the eve of the Feast of the Assumption, 14–15 Aug. 1397 (see Di Bacco and Nádas, 'Verso uno "stile internazionale"', 20).

[93] Gallo and von Fischer, *Italian Sacred and Ceremonial Music*, no. 23, 136–45; see also Reancy, *Early Fifteenth-Century Music*, iv. 103–17; Miroslaw Perz (ed.), *Sources of Polyphony up to c. 1500: Facsimiles* (Antiquitates Musicae in Polonia, 13; Graz and Warsaw, 1973), 78–81, 106–9; id., *Sources of Polyphony up to c. 1500: Transcriptions* (Antiquitates Musicae in Polonia, 14; Graz and Warsaw, 1976), 61–71, 311–21, and Günther, 'Quelques remarques', 379–82 (partial transcription). The striking textural change may be found in the following passages (in reference to the PMFC edition): bars 21–34, 58–60, 86–8, 99–114, 125–9, 141–4, 178–200, 235–8, 267–70, 291–9 (consultation of fos. 7ᵛ–8ᵛ in Grottaferrata 197 is necessary, however, in order to understand precisely how this notation is used).

Ex. 2.1. Zacara, Credo (PMFC 13, no. 23), Cantus, bb. 84–8, 99–103: two divisi passages (red notation in Grottaferrata 197, fo. 7ᵛ; black void notation in Turin 2, fo. 9ᵛ)

Grottaferrata 197 leaves tacitly understood a crucial factor: the singers would have known that each of these special passages begins and ends with a unison, as can be seen spelt out with careful use of mixed full/void notes in Turin 2, fo. 9ᵛ (Ex. 2.1).[94] Also to be noted is the fact that red notation in these passages could be used by Zacara for its mensural significance as well as a visual signal for textural change, cleverly complicating the way these voice-parts appear in the manuscript, especially if they cross: this is the case with the passage at 'vitam venturi seculi' in Grottaferrata 197 (see Ex. 2.3); in the later of the two Polish versions of this passage (Warsaw 52) we see that the red notation is used only to distinguish the split voices, losing the mensural finesse of the opening imitative gesture.[95] In this context, the reading in Grottaferrata 197 appears to hold a more authoritative position in the written tradition. As we have already seen in the case of Turin 2, black/void combination may have later been used precisely to avoid such notational confusion: this holds true as well for the concordance in Trent 1563, in which this passage also lacks its original

Ex. 2.2. Zacara, Credo (PMFC 13, no. 23), Cantus, opening divisi passage reconstructed from Turin 2, fo. 9ᵛ (black notation) and Grottaferrata 197, fo. 7ᵛ (red notation)

---

[94] Ziino, *Il codice T.III.2*, p. 154. Another similar notational redaction of a Zacara work is the Credo fragment in Cividale MS 98, fo. 2ᵛ (Gallo and von Fischer, *Italian Sacred and Ceremonial Music*, PMFC 13, no. A6), which makes use of black void and full notes in divisi passages but also employs them in overlapping combination to denote unisons (both semibreves and breves).

[95] Perz, vol. 13, p. 80, 6th stave.

Ex. 2.3. Zacara, Credo (PMFC 13, no. 23), Cantus, bb. 291–9 (Grottaferrata 197, fo. 8ʳ)

mensural sophistication, even though the scribe was using black, void, and red coloration throughout the rest of the work.[96]

It is all the more remarkable, then, to find the notation of this Grottaferrata 197 Credo in a nearly identical reading in Warsaw 378, and, further, to recognize this particular notational trait in a number of Zacara's and Nicolaus de Radom's works in that Polish source (an inventory is given in Table 2.5). This is a collection containing mostly mass music, which can be attributed exclusively to Ciconia, Zacara, or Radom. As Charles Brewer has convincingly argued, all the anonymous works can also be reasonably attributed to one or the other of these composers, and this encourages the conclusion, much more so than could the documentary evidence alone, that Radom did effectively go to Rome for a period of time in the 1390s and most likely kept Polish–Roman musical contacts alive for some time thereafter.[97]

Before Warsaw 378 perished in the last World War, the Polish scholar Maria Szczepańska marked the red notes with dots on the only existing set of photographs. The anonymous Gloria on fos. 14ᵛ–15ʳ, for example, is very similar in style to Zacara's Credo no. 23 just discussed, but it does display a number of variations in 'divisi' technique. Here we find fifth and octave beginnings and ends of the divisi passages, split voices are used for just two major sections of

[96] Margaret Bent, 'New Sacred Polyphonic Fragments of the Early Quattrocento', *Studi musicali*, 9 (1980), 175–9.

[97] Charles Brewer, 'The Introduction of the "Ars Nova" into East Central Europe: A Study of Late Medieval Polish Sources' (Ph.D. diss., City University of New York, 1984), 276–9, 303–9 (NB. all references to Nicola Zacara should be to Antonio Zacara). His analysis of the two Polish sources has helped convince us that Warsaw 378 is not only the earlier of the two, but that it could easily date from the early years of the 15th c., containing a collection of Roman mass music, most likely brought to Poland at various times during decades surrounding the year 1400, and related works by Radom. See Perz, *Sources of Polyphony up to c. 1500: Facsimiles*, for a reproduction of the photographs of the lost source. More recently, Perz has restudied the source, although the considerably later dating of c.1440 remains: 'The Structure of the Lost Manuscript from the National Library in Warsaw, No. 378 (WarN 378)', in Albert Clement and Eric Jas (eds.), *From Ciconia to Sweelinck: Donum Natalicium Willem Elders* (Chloe: Beihefte zum Daphnis, 21; Amsterdam, 1995), 1–11.

TABLE 2.5. Inventory of Warsaw 378

1ʳ–2ʳ	Anon., Credo
2ᵛ–4ʳ	Antonio Zacara, Credo (*'divisi' notation*) Grottaferrata 197, 7ᵛ–8ᵛ; Siena 207, 1ʳ; Trent 1563, r–v; Turin 2, 9ᵛ–10ʳ; Warsaw 52, 193ᵛ–195ʳ
4ᵛ–6ʳ	Nicolaus de Radom, Credo (*'divisi' notation*)
6ᵛ–9ʳ	[Antonio Zacara], Credo Bologna Q 15, 88ᵛ–90ʳ ('Zacar'); Grottaferrata 197, 6ᵛ; Modena 5.24, 24ᵛ–26ʳ ('Zaccharias'); Padua D 1225, 2ᵛ ('M. Antonius'); Turin 2, 9ʳ
9ᵛ–11ʳ	[Johannes Ciconia], Credo Warsaw 52, 202ᵛ–204ʳ
11ᵛ–12ʳ	Blank
12ᵛ–14ʳ	[Antonio Zacara], Gloria ['Ad ogni vento'] Bologna Q 15, 154ᵛ–156ʳ; Melk 749, r–v; Warsaw 52, 196ʳ, 198ʳ–200ʳ
14ᵛ–15ᵛ	Anon., Gloria (*'divisi' notation*)
15ᵛ–16ʳ	[Johannes Ciconia], Gloria Bologna Q 15, 95ᵛ–96ʳ; Warsaw 52, 196ᵛ–197ʳ
16ᵛ–17ᵛ	[Antonio Zacara], Gloria ['Anglicana'] Bologna Q 15, 156ᵛ–157ʳ
18ʳ–19ʳ	[Antonio Zacara], Gloria 'Laus, honor' Bologna Q 15, 86ᵛ–88ʳ; Munich 3223, 37ᵛ–38ᵛ; Old Hall, 28ᵛ (without trope); Padua D 1225, 2ʳ; Siena 207, 1ᵛ
19ᵛ–20ʳ	Anon., Gloria
20ᵛ–21ᵛ	Anon., Gloria 'Bone Ihesu Criste'
22ʳ	Blank
22ᵛ–23ʳ	Nicolaus de Radom, Gloria (*'divisi' notation*)
23ᵛ–24ʳ	[Nicolaus de Radom], Gloria Warsaw 52, 200ᵛ–201ʳ
24ᵛ–25ʳ(?)	[Johannes Ciconia], Gloria Bologna Q 15, 161ᵛ–162ʳ; Oxford 213, 103ᵛ–104ʳ; Warsaw 52, 192ᵛ–193ʳ
25ᵛ–27ʳ	[Johannes Ciconia], Gloria 'Suscipe Trinitas' Grottaferrata 197, 9ᵛ–10ᵛ; Grottaferrata s.s., 2ᵛ; Oxford 56 (front pastedown, verso); Padua D 675, 1ʳ⁻ᵛ ('M. Jo. Ciconia')
27ᵛ–29ʳ	Anon., *Cracovia civitas* Warsaw 52, 173ʳ–174ʳ
29ᵛ	Anon., *Omnes sancti et electi*

the movement, and the opening divisi passage ('Et in terra pax hominibus') has been given an alternative setting at the end of the work, with imitation between the two top parts. Folios 22ᵛ–23ʳ of Warsaw 378 contain a Gloria by Nicolaus de Radom that also exhibits some innovative uses of a style of divisi writing he had probably witnessed during his stay in Rome in the 1390s. It too has a divisi Cantus, including some very short passages in the style Zacara used to adorn special portions of the text, but the piece begins, in fact, with divisi writing for the Tenor and Contratenor parts!

Our examination of divisi technique in this repertory suggests the need for further investigation of textural contrast in early fifteenth-century Italian music. Divisi passages in polyphonic mass movements are almost exclusively to be found in the works of Antonio Zacara, and composers in his circle. It would appear to be a technique or style that could have been invented by him, or at least adapted from improvised performance practices and a similar but simpler two-voice notated style in some earlier and contemporary Italian sources.[98] In its earliest notational manifestation, divisi singing appears to have been more improvisational, less prescriptive, in some of its attributes. Its notational development, as seen in slightly later concordant sources, shows more control of its elements: fully realized passages in either red or void notes, to include notated unisons at beginnings and ends of passages. This interest in contrasting textures in a piece of polyphony—reduction from full forces to two equal upper parts (perhaps to be sung by two soloists)—is a style trait that was sometimes misunderstood at the time, and to a certain extent then coexists with and gives way to the development of what we have come to know as 'unus–chorus' textural alternation in later sources.[99]

[98] Earlier, simpler works that may have been models for the notation of two voice-parts on a single stave, using black and red notes, include Berlin, Staatsbibliothek — Preußischer Kulturbesitz, Ms. mus. 40563 (RISM B iv/3, 327) and Cividale, Codice 57 (RISM B iv/4, 747). See in particular Reinhard Strohm, 'Neue Quellen zur liturgischen Mehrstimmigkeit des Mittelalters in Italien', *Rivista italiana di musicologia*, 1 (1966), 77–87, where he describes two relevant sources: Bologna, Biblioteca Universitaria, MS 2866, with a *Benedicamus* setting almost identical in Venice, Biblioteca Nazionale Marciana, Z.lat. 160 (= 1781). Red coloration for divisi writing continued to be used through the period of the Council of Constance: cf. the Strasburg version of the 'Zeltenpferd' Gloria (bars 1–15), demonstrating a divisi passage that does not survive in the concordant manuscript London 29987 (not a corrupt two-voice version, as reported in Gallo and von Fischer, *Italian Sacred and Ceremonial Music*, 295). In the context of the dissemination of divisi writing, it is worthwhile noting that the 'Zeltenpferd' Gloria quotes the 'Amen' of Zacara's Gloria 'Micinella'; see Lorenz Welker, *Musik am Oberrhein im späten Mittelalter: Die Handschrift Strasbourg, olim Bibliothèque de la Ville, C. 22* (Habilitationsschrift, Basle, 1993), i. 140–7.

[99] One intriguing result of this development is that we have been left with a few mass movements with apparent exchanges of Cantus parts in their later written versions—for example, the first six bars of the Cantus in Zacara's three-part Gloria 'Micinella' in Grottaferrata 197, Atri, and Bologna Q 1 (all papal-related sources from this period) follow Bologna Q 15's Cantus I, but thereafter they follow Q 15's Cantus II. This in itself, we believe, could be a signal that an earlier version using divisi writing with the crossing of split parts was later separated into two independent Cantus voices; but rather than following the 'color' of the notated parts, their relative height in pitch served as the indicator.

We close this essay with an examination of the final source to be considered, one that serves well to reinforce the point we have made concerning the dissemination of repertories out from Rome and central Italy to the rest of the Italian peninsula: new fragments in Cortona's Archivio Storico del Comune (Cortona 2; see Pls. 5–8 and Table 2.6 for an inventory of their contents). The very recent discovery of two new leaves, here referred to as Cortona 2, first came to the attention of Anthony Cummings several years ago; and it is through the generosity of Alice Clark at Princeton University that we came to know about them in 1994. The two parchment leaves have already been removed from the covers of their host volume, a sixteenth-century city estates register, and have now been examined and studied in their entirety for the first time (in their restored but still quite precarious, worm-eaten state).[100] The fragments evidently derive from two different bifolios of the same manuscript, the first of which was mutilated in the sixteenth century (see Fig. 2.2). Folio 2 fared much better in this sense, cut so as to leave the area of text and music relatively intact and giving us a truer sense of the dimensions of the original source.

TABLE 2.6. Inventory of Cortona 2

1ʳ	(a)	Anon., *Deo gracias conclamemus* (motet Duplum, 1¹)
		Munich 3223, recto
	(b)	Anon., Gloria ([3³?]
		Anon., *Dame a qui bon an doner* (virelai, 3¹)
1ᵛ	(c)	Anon., Credo (Cantus)
		London 29987, 83ᵛ–85ʳ
	(d)	Anon., Sanctus (Cantus?)
2ʳ		[Prunet/Perneth/Bonbarde], Credo (CT/T fragm.)
		Apt, 29ᵛ–32ʳ ('Bonbarde'); Barcelona 853c, 8ʳ⁻ᵛ; Brussels II, r–v; Grottaferrata 197, 5ʳ; Padua A 684, 3ᵛ ('Perneth'); Strasburg, 3ᵛ–7ʳ ('Prunet')
2ᵛ		Anon., Gloria (3³)

---

[100] The volume, consisting of 234 pages, carries the number T.4 in the 19th-c. series titled 'Descrizioni de' beni della canonica', and on fo. 1ʳ we read the following rubric: 'El presente libro, coperto di coio pavonazzo, ligato et capitolato di numero di carte . . ., intitolato notificatione di tereni di Selva Piana e del comune di detta cita di Cortona, fatto et ordinato el mese di giugno de l'anno 1520'. The volume lists the rental of communal properties in that area up through 1549. We wish to thank Bruno Gialluca, the archivist, for having made the fragment available to us during a number of visits, during which time we were also able to photograph the leaves. The dimensions of the two fragmentary leaves are as follows: fo. 1, 321 × 238 mm.; fo. 2, 259 × 319 mm. The total size of the original leaves was probably only slightly larger than that of fo. 2. The full writing space is visible on fo. 2, which has eleven staves on its recto side, and twelve (with the addition of an extra one) on its verso.

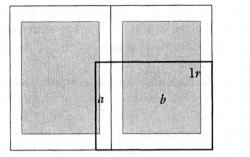
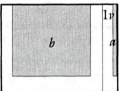

Fig. 2.2. The first of two parchment leaves of Cortona 2

The international scope of the contents is readily apparent, even from the few works that so far have been identified, and it is this point above all that we wish to discuss here. The Credo by Perneth on fo. 2ʳ is the movement we have already seen in Grottaferrata 197, as well as in papal-chapels related sources Apt and Strasburg. To give an idea of how little remains of text and music on fo. 1ʳ (a) (see Pl. 5 on the left), but enough to have permitted the identification of the Duplum of an isorhythmic motet found also in the Italian source Munich 3223, we give the full text below with italics showing the portion visible on the Cortona leaf.[101]

> Deo gracias conclamemus
> omnes hic iam consodales,
> nam ipse *egit ut es*semus
> dulcis Christi commensales,
>
> partecipante*s huius misse*
> *de* sacro beneficio,
> gratulantes interfuisse
> iam huic sacrificio.
>
> Ergo ad propria revertentes,
> summum deum veneremur
> ut ad celestia transeuntes
> sine fine collocemur.
>
> Amen.

Notable, too, is the one voice of a Credo movement on fo. 1ᵛ (c) (see Pl. 6), which concords with an addition to the Florentine songbook, London 29987. This Credo was added to the Tuscan collection sometime during the second

---

[101] Modern edn. by Gallo and von Fischer, *Italian Sacred and Ceremonial Music*, 254, 290. See RISM B iv/3, 359–60.

decade of the Quattrocento by the same scribe responsible for copying all of Florence SL 2211, so central to our knowledge of musical repertories in Tuscany *c.*1410–20, and in which context we now also understand the inclusion of Zacara's songs in Florence Pal. 87.[102]

In the early 1970s another Cortona fragment, Cortona 1, was discovered by Federico Ghisi, who described the contents of the visible side of a single parchment folio glued to another account book in the same city archive.[103] But only recently has the first composition on that folio been correctly identified by Reinhard Strohm as the Triplum of the anonymous motet *Almifonis melos/Rosa sine culpe spina*, and the work on the bottom three staves as the widely disseminated rondeau *Amis tout dous* by Pierre de Molins (see the inventory in Table 2.7).[104] In 1976, when Agostino Ziino was able to see the other side of the newly restored leaf then recently lifted from the leather cover, he was able to report a single motet voice, whose text begins 'Plausu querulo' (a text honouring Thomas Becket of Canterbury), with its possible Tenor, but otherwise unidentified and unknown.[105] The recent rediscovery of Cortona 1, which suprisingly had been left together with its host volume at the Florentine

TABLE 2.7. Inventory of Cortona 1

recto	Anon., *Plausu querulo* (motet Duplum?; mostly offset onto leather cover)
	Trémoïlle, index
	Anon., *Veni sancte spiritus* (motet Duplum?)
verso	Anon., *Almifonis melos/Rosa sine culpe spina* (motet Triplum, [3³])
	Ivrea, 11ᵛ–12ʳ; Trémoïlle, index
	Pierre de Molins, *Amis tout dous* (rondeau, 3³ 'Molinus')
	Grottaferrata 16, 1ʳ; Ivrea, 2ᵛ–3ʳ; Paris 568, 3ᵛ–4ʳ; Prague, 251ʳ; Strasburg, 24ʳ and 79ᵛ;
	Trémoïlle, index; Prodenzani, *Liber Saporecti*, sonnet 32 ('El molin de Paris')

[102] On Florence SL 2211, see D'Accone, 'Una nuova fonte dell'ars nova italiana'; John Nádas, 'The Transmission of Trecento Secular Polyphony: Manuscript Production and Scribal Practices in Italy at the End of the Middle Ages' (Ph.D. diss., New York University, 1985), 459–86; and id., 'Manuscript San Lorenzo 2211'. The importation of new repertory to Florence after the Council of Pisa can be seen not only in sources such as Paris 568 and Florence SL 2211, but also in the inclusion of Zacara's Italian songs in Florence Pal. 87 as the result of an extended residence in Florence by Pope John XXIII and his curia (see Nádas, 'Further Notes on Magister Antonius dictus Zacharias de Teramo', 177–81).

[103] Federico Ghisi, 'Inno lauda polifonica all'Assunta ritrovato nell'Archivio Comunale di Cortona', *Quadrivium*, 15 (1974), 105–11 (includes a facsimile of Cortona 1, verso side only). Ghisi identified the fragment as a single parchment leaf serving as reinforcement for the cover of a 'Libro dell'Inventario della Chiesa e Sagrestia della Collegiata di Santa Maria Nova di Cortona—1624'.

[104] Strohm, 'Magister Egardus', 51.

[105] Agostino Ziino, 'Precisazioni su un frammento di musica francese trecentesca conservato nell'Archivio Comunale di Cortona', in I. Deug-su and E. Menestò (eds.), *Università e beni culturali: il contributo degli studi medievali e umanistici* (Florence, 1981), 351–8 (including faint reproductions of the recto side of the leaf—both the leaf itself and the leather cover containing so much of the offset music, text, and staves).

laboratory where it was restored in the 1970s, allowed us to return it to its home in the Cortona archive from which it came and to more closely examine the Becket motet.

Although still very much tentative, a fresh reading of the text (aided by the offset words on the leather cover; see Pl. 9) reveals passages that clearly celebrate Thomas on an appropriate day to worship him (presumably the day of his martyrdom, 29 December, although possibly referring to the feast of his translation as well, on 7 July): 'Plausu querulo clangat ovans hodie Cantuarie merorem, miscens organo luctum, mistice, cum leticia cordis, operans more Thome, laudans preconia cleri vero pugillus, festa cuius annua colitur, cum tripudio lugens.' The text goes on, as do so many texts honouring Thomas, to describe the circumstances of his horrible death and the knowledge that his blood continues to stain the Holy Church ('Syon filia tam devota, nota per cuncta mundi climata, hodie rosea facies Abel almo orrende rubricatur sanguine'), ending with the pronouncement of the four virtues of his martyrdom: 'in tam titulo in propatulo palam patet previa, quatriplex sibi redditur auriola'. It is possible that the reference to Thomas's four virtues could have happily coincided with the fourth jubilee of his martyrdom in 1370, an event that was especially celebrated in Avignon at the papal curia.[106] It is also well to keep in mind that Thomas Becket was much admired by theologians of the Schism who cited him on numerous occasions as someone who had martyred himself in helping to heal the much earlier schism of the 1160s.[107]

We soon realized that the two sets of fragments, Cortona 1 and 2, appeared to derive from a common source, an observation based not only on a careful codicological comparison of the fragments, but also on the reasonable assumption that sixteenth- and seventeenth-century archivists in Cortona would have had at their disposal but one old parchment source of polyphonic music of this sort to use as binding reinforcement. As a result, we must combine the contents of the two sets of fragments in considering the nature of the original collection's repertory; the results serve to reinforce the impression we have of a sizable body of disparate sacred works brought to Italy *c*.1400. We

---

[106] See Raymonde Foreville, *Le Jubilé de Saint Thomas Becket: du XIIIe au XVe siècle (1220–1470)* (Paris, 1958); id., 'L'Idée de Jubilé, chez les théologiens et les canonistes (XIIᶜ–XIIIᶜ s.) avant l'institution du Jubilé romain (1300)', in *Thomas Becket dans la tradition historique et hagiographique* (London, 1981), essay no. XIV. When Simon Langham accepted Urban V's appointment to the cardinalate and resigned his archbishopric at Canterbury in 1368 without express permission of the king of England, relations between Canterbury and the king remained strained for many years, resulting in rather feeble celebrations at Canterbury itself on the occasion of the fourth jubilee in 1370; at Avignon, on the other hand, Cardinal Langham saw to it that Thomas was properly honoured with great pomp and festivities on the feast of his translation (Foreville, *Le Jubilé*, 40–5).

[107] I. S. Robinson, *The Papacy 1073–1198* (Cambridge, 1990), 167–8, 280–1. Thomas Becket is cited in Prague MS I.F.777, fos. 121ᵛ–122ʳ, a source mentioned earlier in the context of Archbishop Jenstein of Poland, and he is again invoked at the Paris Council of Feb. 1395 (Bulaeus, *Historia universitatis parisiensis*, iv. 738).

are grateful to Peter Lefferts for having pointed out to us a most significant concordance for *Plausu querulo*. This Duplum text was included on the index page of a Burgundian source, Trémoïlle, in the column of motets copied by the year 1376.[108] The striking thing about the compositions in Cortona 1 and 2, as noted in their inventories, above, is that such a high percentage concord with Trémoïlle. Of course, other sources from our period also document the far-reaching dissemination of a central French tradition, among them Ivrea and, especially, the bifolio Paris, Bibliothèque Nationale de France, n. a. l. 2444, of which the total contents—five motets—are included in Trémoïlle.[109] It seems to us that the Cortona fragments are a fine new example of the collection of ultramontane polyphonic music in central Italy, repertories that must have first been brought to Italy by musicians in papal and cardinalate chapels.

There are of course a number of other musical manuscripts that deserve future study in the light of the issues raised in this essay. For our present purposes, the sources we list in Table 2.1 are grouped into two main categories reflecting the major chronological and geographical phases of the Schism, although we recognize the categories themselves as being far from mutually exclusive. Following the particular mix of native and foreign repertories of the papal chapels in Rome during the earlier decades, we note that the later pontificates played a particularly important role at the various northern church councils and through continued contacts with distant musical centres, and this has been generally recognized by modern scholarship. Our primary criteria for selecting musical sources for inclusion in Table 2.1 have been the identification of relevant composers and their works (often based on close readings of their texts) and the significant histories of the sources themselves, shown to have been in the possession of cities and institutions associated with the papal chapels and their travels. But the contents of many collections of the period no doubt resulted from a series of complex interchanges and superimpositions of repertories, and thus other sources, perhaps even those closely connected with non-papal musical centres on the peninsula, could be called upon to contribute to the picture offered here but do not easily fit within the more rigid parameters imposed upon the two groupings we have established.

---

[108] Private communication, Sept. 1994. For studies and facsimiles of the index, see E. Droz and G. Thibault, 'Un chansonnier de Philippe le Bon', *Revue de musicologie*, 7 (1926), 1–8; Craig Wright, *Music at the Court of Burgundy 1364–1419* (Henryville, Ottawa, and Binnengen, 1979), 138, 147–58; Margaret Bent, 'A Note on the Dating of the Trémoïlle Manuscript', in Brian Gillingham and Paul Merkley (eds.), *Beyond the Moon: Festschrift Luther Dittmer* (Ottawa, 1990), 217–42.

[109] See RISM B iv/2, 199–200. The total number of five motets includes the citation of *Zolomina/Nazarea* as a catchword on fo. 49ᵛ; we thank Andrew Wathey for this information.

At the present stage of investigation, we have been most interested in those elements that allow us to consider extant sources within the cultural ambience of central Italy. It is enough to say that against the backdrop of the musically vigorous Italian papal chapels of the Great Schism, the Cortona fragments, Grottaferrata 197, and the evidence of other sources we could only touch upon here serve to illuminate the widespread dissemination of musical styles and repertories throughout Italy in the decades just before and after the year 1400. In particular, these sources cast their strongest light on a hitherto obscured musical crossroads on the Italian peninsula, one that is only now coming into clearer focus in the range of its activities, in the identification of its key figures, and in the complex aspects of its long-lasting influence: the orbit of the Roman popes.[110]

[110] After completing the present article, the authors became aware of the recent manuscript discoveries of Paolo Peretti ('Fonti inedite di polifonia mensurale dei secoli XIV e XV negli archivi di stato di Ascoli Piceno e Macerata', *Quaderni musicali marchigiani*, 3 [1996], 85–124), newly found late-medieval music fragments which lend further support to our analysis of the Central-Italian source picture. Based on our experience in searching for and finding the host volume of the Egidi fragment in Macerata (cf. p. 69, n. 73), our suspicion that other music manuscript leaves might continue to be found as binding materials in notarial holdings there—in other than the city's notarial registers, already thoroughly checked by Faraone and Zdekauer—was indeed quickly realized. More precisely, one of the new fragments was found by Peretti in a previously independent archive transferred from the city of Recanati and now housed in the state archives of Macerata.

Of the three fragments found by Peretti, those from notarial volumes of Recanati and Montefortino (the latter now in the state archives of the nearby city of Ascoli) contain relevant polyphonic compositions from the period *c.* 1400: motets (including an isorhythmic work and a number of settings of Marian texts), French rondeaux (one of which was widely disseminated throughout Europe), and Mass movements (comprising troped and untroped Glorias, Credos, Sanctus, and Agnus Dei settings). Of great interest are pronounced Italian notational features found in these two fragments, especially the consistent use of dots of division, one-pitch ligatures, oblique-stemmed semibreves, and even a brief cadential passage in 'divisi' notation. Also noteworthy are two extra fragmentary attributions that read ' . . . de Eugubio,' referring to the city of Gubbio in Umbria; the toponym, in hypothetical conflation with a 'Dompnus Antonius . . .' appearing in a preceding work, is taken by Peretti as an indication of a composer whose full name would be Antonius de Eugubio. This, however, is somewhat improbable for codicological reasons, leaving open the possibility that 'Antonius' could refer to one of two known composers of the period: Antonio Zacara da Teramo or Antonio da Cividale.

Although the new leaves and the Egidi fragment appear to have originated in distinctly separate musical manuscripts (as far as one may judge from the few and insufficiently clear photographs and evidence available), Peretti—failing to consider the Egidi source altogether—does not draw a contextual connection among them, preferring to see the new sources almost entirely as products of a local musical culture. For us, instead, the mixture of internationally known works with possibly local sacred compositions (those attributed to ' . . . de Eugubio') and other works surely created by professional church musicians points to the papal court of Rome and its far-reaching area of influence—both culturally and administratively—in Central Italy.

Appendix: A Provisional List of Papal Singers of Roman and Pisan Obedience, 1378–1415

Note. In this table we include available information on the provenance of the singers (we include everyone qualified as a *capellanus capelle, clericus capelle*, and *magister capelle*; see Di Bacco and Nádas, 'Verso uno "stile internazionale"', 9–10). The indication 'from' is to be understood as a reference to the diocese of origin, not necessarily to a city. When the documents lack such precise information, we have inferred a provenance from benefices held by the musician (marked with a '?'). We are grateful to Alejandro Planchart, who very kindly shared with us his work on Vatican documents of Martin V's and Eugene IV's pontificates, helping to clarify some identities and biographies; in some cases, later documents contain references to activities of personnel in the chapels of the schismatic popes.

Papal singers	Roman Obedience				Pisan Obedience	
	Urban VI	Boniface IX	Innocent VII	Gregory XII	Alexander V	John XXIII
Angelus de *Macerata*, Marche; abbot of the monastery of St Benedict of *Gualdo*, Umbria						
Angelus Gregorii de *Spoleto*, Umbria		•				•
Antonius de *Aquila*, Abruzzo		•				
Antonius Martini de *Reate* (Rieti), in northern Lazio		•				
Antonius Nanni *Marsicani* (Marsica), Abruzzo		•				
Antonius Berardi dictus Zacharias (Zacchara) de Teramo, Abruzzo [a]	?	•	+	+	+	•
Cicchus [b]	?	•				
Cobellus *Maioris* (Maiori?), near Amalfi		•				
Cristianus Grave, from Thérouanne		•				
Daniel de Aken, from Cambrai			•	•		
Egidius de Lens (dictus de Leyns), from Liège	?	•				•

Eligius de Bray, from Thérouanne

Franciscus Cervarie

Franciscus de Amodeo de *Positipo* (Posillipo), Naples

Franciscus Gousserat [c]

Gabriel de Belonis (Belonibus) de *Mediolano* (Milan) [d]

Guido de Busco, from Rouen

Guillelmus Bladeti, from Nîmes? [e]

Guillelmus Clari [f]

Guillelmus Guillelmi (Wilhelmus Wilhelmi) Nicolai de Hildernisse, from Liège

Guillelmus Stephani, from Marseille

Henricus Desiderii (Dezier) de Latinia (Latunna), from Liège

Henricus (dictus) Tulpin (Turpini)

Herasmus, perhaps from *Gaeta*, near Naples [g]

Humbertus de Salinis, from France (Besançon) or Portugal (Braga)?

Jacobus Brunelli, from Arras?

Jacobus de Romendin, from Liège [h]

Jacobus Johannis de *Aquila*, Abruzzo

Jacobus [identical with Jacobus Masii de *Frullivio*, i.e. Forlì?] [i]

Johannellus de Alderisio dictus Bramericus (de Bramericho) de *Neapoli* (Naples) [j]

Papal singers	Roman Obedience				Pisan Obedience	
	Urban VI	Boniface IX	Innocent VII	Gregory XII	Alexander V	John XXIII
Johannes Blondeel, from Tournai?	?					
Johannes Bordon (Johannes Frederich alias Bordon, Bourdon, Bridon)						
Johannes Bruandi						•
Johannes Brunet						•
Johannes Bunman						•
Johannes (de) Ortega de Nebula		•				
Johannes de *Papia* (Pavia)		•				•
Johannes de Semeriaco (Semeries) alias Jonatas de Valaing…ᵏ						
Johannes Jacobi						
Johannes dictus Sapiens (Le Sage), from Liège?		•				•
Johannes Pelerini, from Luçonˡ		•			?	
Johannes Tribulaer		•				•
Johannes Pulce de *Gaieta* (Gaeta), near Naples		?			?	
Johannes Volkardi (Volcardi, Volquardi, Volkaerdi) ᵐ	•					
Julianus de Spyrolis de *Janua* (Genoa)					•	
Laurentius Nicolai de Cartono de *Pontecurvo* (Pontecorvo, between Rome and Naples)		•	•	•		
Matheus de Mozate					•	
Matheus Hanelle, from Thérouanne						+

Matheus Thorote alias Bruyant (Briant, Bruyandus, Abruyandus), from Cambrai?

Michael de Wettere, from Tournai

Michael (de) Goye

Nicolaus Leschenchius (Leschenchier)

Nicolaus Huge[n]

Nicolaus olim Symonis de Frangees de Leodio (Liège)

Nicolaus Ricii de *Nucella Campli*, Abruzzo

Paulus de *Aversa*, north of Naples

Paulus Jacobi de *Frosoloma* (Frosolone or Frosinone), both north of Naples

Petrus Johannis de Mirabello, from Liège?[o]

Petrus Lair, from Le Mans

Petrus Pont

Petrus Rusello, perhaps from *Aversa*, north of Naples

Henricus Sandewins[p]

Ruoella[q]

Samperinus de *Pensauro* (Pesaro)[r]

Stephanus Channelle

Symon de Mirabiliis de *Mediolano*

Thomas de Namurco, from Liège

Ugolinus Francisci de *Urbeveteri* (Orvieto)

Vincentius de Campotorto

Walterus de Male (Maele), from Cambrai

- • Singer whose presence in a particular chapel is clearly documented
- + Singer not documented in a particular chapel, but whose presence can be determined by context
- ? Singer whose presence is merely speculative and derives from external circumstances
- a In Innocent VII's and Gregory XII's pontificates his presence in the curia is documented by his activity as *scriptor* of papal letters (cf. Ziino, 'Magister Antonius', 319–20). For his presence in Alexander V's chapel, see his recently discovered song *Dime fortuna* in Turin 2. Given his notoriety as a 'famoso camtore' in the 1390 document of S. Spirito in Sassia, there is a distinct possibility that he became a papal singer during Urban VI's pontificate.
- b Still unidentified; the only other detail available for him is that he was a *presbiter* in 1400.
- c He was appointed as a papal singer at Constance (*sede vacante*) in June 1417 'de obedientia olim Gregorii veniens': this cannot be taken as conclusive evidence of previous employment in Gregory XII's curia—although probable—either as a singer or in some other capacity.
- d Singer for Urban VI and Innocent VII. He is not listed among Boniface's singers in Feb. 1400.
- e Papal singer at the very beginning of Boniface's pontificate and probably to be identified with Urban V's singer in Rome in Dec. 1370.
- f Papal singer who died at the very beginning of Boniface's pontificate; cited as a past familiar of Urban VI.
- g Still unidentified.
- h Romendin is documented as a singer for Gregory XII, from the very beginning of the pontificate through 1408. It is uncertain when he joined the Pisan obedience, but he is with John XXIII starting in Sept. 1414, at the latest.
- i A singer Jacobus had a benefice in the diocese of Cesena when he joined Gregory XII's chapel with Ugolino of Orvieto. The latter is documented in 1417, appointed as *cantor* at Florence Cathedral together with Jacobus Masii de Frullivio (see D'Accone, 'Music and Musicians at Santa Maria del Fiore', 120–1).
- j Johannellus is documented as a singer in 1400 and between 1408 and 1410.
- k Papal singer at the very beginning of John XXIII's pontificate.
- l Pelerini is first qualified as a singer in a document issued on John XXIII's day of coronation.
- m Volkardi was a papal singer before the Schism. Clement deprived him of benefices when he joined the Urbanist side: he was the first *magister capelle* of the Roman obedience. It is uncertain if he continued to serve under Boniface IX.
- n Huge is documented as a singer for Innocent VII and Gregory XII through 1408. Before his death in 1413 he served John XXIII, but it is uncertain when he joined the Pisan obedience.
- o Singer in Boniface's chapel and 'per plura tempora tunc facta fuit . . . cantor domini nostri pape.' Therefore he may have served Petrus Tomacelli in his cardinalate chapel.
- p Later documents also cite a Robertus Sandewins, perhaps a brother, who sang for Martin V.
- q This unidentified singer may be either Gregory XII's lesser known singer, Petrus Rusello, or more likely Toussanus de Ruella, later a singer in Martin V's and Eugene IV's chapels and still alive in 1451.
- r Later bishop of Vieste, Puglia (we are grateful to Pio Cenci OFM for this information).

3

Music for the Papal Chapel in the Early Fifteenth Century

❦

ALEJANDRO ENRIQUE PLANCHART

A common view of the papal choir in the late Middle Ages and the early Renaissance is that it represented, as did for example the chapel of the dukes of Burgundy, one of the most important centres of musical composition of its time, an institution that was dominated by composers and out of which came an important repertory of works. Such a view is misleading and applies, if it applies at all, to a narrow period covering the few decades that go from the end of the fifteenth century to the middle of the sixteenth. The recent work of John Nádas and Giuliano Di Bacco on the papal chapels at the time of the Schism shows that such a view is largely untenable for the end of the fourteenth century despite the presence and activity of Antonio Zacara da Teramo, in the chapel of several popes,[1] and the same is confirmed by Pamela Starr's work on the pontificates of Nicolas V, Pius II, and Calixtus III.[2] Jean Lionnet's investigation of the papal chapel at the end of the sixteenth century shows an ingrown and largely stagnant institution, particularly in terms of the repertory it sang, not to speak of the absence of major figures in its ranks.[3] It is interesting also to read later accounts of visitors such as Burney and even Berlioz, for they confirm the picture of the institution painted by Lionnet.[4]

---

[1] Giuliano Di Bacco and John Nádas, 'Verso uno "stile internazionale" della musica nelle cappelle papali e cardinalizie durante il Grande Scisma (1378–1417): il caso di Johannes Ciconia da Liège', in *Collectanea I*, 7–74. See also above, Ch. 2.

[2] Pamela Starr, 'Music and Music Patronage at the Papal Court, 1447–1464' (Ph.D. diss., Yale University, 1987).

[3] Jean Lionnet, 'Una svolta nella storia del collegio dei cantori pontifici: il decreto del 22 giugno 1665 contro Orazio Benevolo, origine e conseguenze', *Nuova rivista musicale italiana*, 17 (1983), 72–103; id., 'Performance Practice in the Papal Chapel during the 17th Century', *EM* 15 (1987), 3–15.

[4] Charles Burney, *The Present State of Music in France and Italy*, in P. A. Scholes (ed.), *Dr. Burney's Musical Tours of Europe*, vol. 1: *An Eighteenth-Century Musical Tour in France and Italy* (London, 1959), 230–4; Hector Berlioz, *Memoirs of Hector Berlioz from 1803 to 1865*, trans. Rachel Holmes and Eleanor Holmes, rev. Ernest Newman (New York, 1966), 154–60.

To some extent the slightly melancholy picture that emerges from these accounts, that of an institution that time had passed by, is something of a boon for us, for it was also an institution that in its backwards-looking tradition did not discard the sources and records of its own century of glory, as had been the case with Cambrai Cathedral and other northern churches in the wake of the Council of Trent,[5] or as was the case in Rome itself during the unquestionably innovative pontificate of Nicholas III (1277–80), when dozens of Roman liturgical books written in the traditional Roman neumes instead of the new Franciscan *nota quadrata*, including most likely numerous sources for the Old Roman rite and its chant, were fed to a bonfire.[6]

This is not to say that the popes were not intent on having a good choir, but rather that their primary interest was, most of the time, to have good singers who could perform plainsong and figural music—although plainsong was the norm at least until the end of the fifteenth century—and that being a good performer is not the same thing as being an important and prolific composer. The typical career of a papal singer until the middle of the fifteenth century and probably beyond is represented not by a man such as Guillaume Du Fay, but by Gilles Flannel, called Lenfant, Mathieu Hanelle, and Jehan de la Croix, called Monamy. Such singers in earlier centuries would have spent their entire lives as part of the itinerant 'floating bottom' that supported the music of most of the northern churches, the *clerks de matines* at Notre-Dame de Paris, the *petits vicaires* at Notre-Dame de Cambrai, or the unemployed and slightly disreputable *magistri organi* of the Parisian left bank. Now, thanks to the expansion of the possibilities for ecclesiastical preferment for non-nobles in the late fourteenth and early fifteenth century, they found an avenue towards social and financial advancement through employment in the curia. Some of them, like Flannel, served in the papal chapel for a very long time and were apparently highly valued by their patrons, but once their curial years were over and they had obtained a number of benefices that allowed them to live comfortably, they went to one or another of the churches where they held a substantial prebend, often one in their native land, though Johannes Ciconia and Pierre Grosseteste are exceptions.[7] We often view their lives in their cathedral towns as some sort of 'retirement', for we regard them largely as musicians, but reading the chapter acts of Cambrai or Laon, it is patently clear that such was

[5] This view of Cambrai may need modification in the light of the plundering of the city in the years 1579–84 at the hands of the French forces under the Baron d'Inchy. The cathedral had kept its liturgical traditions intact throughout the period of the Council, but the records of the fabric show the complete cessation of all the endowed ceremonies in those years and a new beginning in the years after 1586.

[6] Bruno Stäblein and Margareta Landwehr-Melnicki, *Die Gesänge des altrömischen Graduale Vat. lat. 5319* (MMMA 2; Kassel, 1970), *77–*78.

[7] Ciconia, although a native of Liège, ended his days in Padua, though not as a canon. Pierre Grosseteste, originally from Tournai, died as a canon of Besançon; see Starr, 'Music and Music Patronage', 182–3.

not the case. They had different duties, be they administrative or pastoral, and these were complex and manifold, although they were apparently largely unconnected with music, at least in terms of the performance of polyphony. In the case of the three musicians mentioned above, Flannel, De la Croix, and Hanelle, all of whom had been *magistri cappellae* of the papal chapel,[8] we have not only extensive information about their life after they left Rome, but also detailed inventories of their possessions at the time of death.[9] Their work at Cambrai only very occasionally involved them with the musical establishment of the cathedral, and at death not a single sheet of music was to be found in their estate. This contrasts not only with what we know of Du Fay's music collection,[10] but with estates of clerics for whom we have no record of musical activity, such as the physician of Benedict XIII, Arnoul de Halle, who at his death in 1417 left an immense collection of musical instruments, including eight harps, and Gregoire Nicolai, a secretary of the duke of Burgundy and his proctor in Rome for a number of years, who at his death owned thirteen parchment fascicles of plainsong masses copied by Simon Mellet.[11]

Nevertheless, the research of Nádas and Di Bacco, as well as that of Andrew Tomasello,[12] points to considerable musical activity not only at Avignon but on the Urbanist side of the Schism. Interestingly enough, many of the cardinals had chapel choirs capable of singing polyphony, as one assumes from the presence of *tenoristae* among their *familiares*,[13] but it is far from clear what kinds of sacred polyphony these chapels sang. The surviving sources place far greater emphasis on secular music, and from the output of composers who were members of some of these chapels, such as Johannes Ciconia, Simon de Haspre, or even Antonio Zacara da Teramo and Matteo da Perugia, it is plausible to think that the liturgy was performed largely in plainsong, with only very occasional polyphony, and that polyphony was largely part of the secular activities of these *familiares* in their role as members of a court.

A temporary change in this situation may have been brought about by two essentially unrelated circumstances: the convening of the Council of

[8] As an exception to the usual pattern, where the *magister cappellae* of the papal chapel was a high prelate, between at least 1423 and 1436 the *magistri cappellae* were singers of the chapel. This is shown in a number of entries in Vatican documents, e.g. ASV, RS 172, fo. 7ʳ (1423) and IE 400, fo. 80ᵛ (1436). During these years it is clear that the first singer listed in the mandates of payment is the *magister cappellae*.

[9] LADN, 4G 1337 [Flannel], 4G 1364 [Hanelle], 4G 1413 [De la Croix].

[10] See Craig Wright, 'Dufay at Cambrai: Discoveries and Revisions', *JAMS* 28 (1975), 218.

[11] LADN, 4G 1039 [Nicolai], unnumbered last folio of the executors' account: 'Item ont este trouvez xiii cahiers de velin contenant plusieurs messes pour mettre avecq celles du pareil volume escriptes de la main de messire Simon Melle corisiez', and 4G 1360 [De Halle], fo. 18ʳ. Both documents are cited in Jules Houdoy, *Histoire artistique de la cathédrale de Cambrai, ancienne église métropolitaine Notre-Dame* (Paris, 1880), 259 and 265, but the citations are inaccurate.

[12] Andrew Tomasello, *Music and Ritual at Papal Avignon (1309–1403)* (Ann Arbor, 1983).

[13] See Di Bacco and Nádas, 'Verso uno stile internazionale', 31–9, and also Alejandro Enrique Planchart, 'Guillaume Du Fay's Benefices and his Relationship to the Court of Burgundy', *EMH* 8 (1988), 117–71, esp. 128.

Constance in 1417, where a number of lordly *familiae* from different parts of Europe and representing different traditions were brought together, most likely kindling a spirit of competition and emulation, and the fact that until shortly before Pope John XXIII's arrival at Constance his chapel had among its members one of the most important composers of the time, Antonio Zacara da Teramo, whose works were known as far afield as Poland, and who is the only non-English composer whose music appears in the Old Hall manuscript.[14] Antonio, who was at that time nearing the end of his career, had written a number of settings of the ordinary of the mass and given them names that associated them either with Roman families, such as the Micinelli,[15] or with some categories of the clerical bureaucracy, such as the *cursores*. It is probably no coincidence that the two settings most clearly identified with Roman and by extension papal ceremony, the Gloria 'Micinella' and the Credo 'Cursor', appear in Bologna Q 15 in a context indicating that they were performed by the chapel of John XXIII and by its successor, the conciliar chapel, in Constance.

The manuscript context for these two movements is a composite mass where the Kyrie, Sanctus, and Agnus are the work of Guillaume Du Fay. These pieces traditionally have been regarded as among Du Fay's earliest works because the Sanctus and Agnus Dei are related to a setting of the Sanctus by Richard de Loqueville, *magister puerorum* at Cambrai during Du Fay's last years as a chorister there and presumably one of his music teachers. I have proposed that Du Fay was in Constance from 1415 to 1417, where he may have sung with the Council chapel, and that the composite mass in Bologna Q 15 probably reflects the tradition of Constance.[16]

If Du Fay was a member of the conciliar chapel, he, like many others at the time, stayed for only a short period.[17] By November of 1418 he was back at Cambrai, where he remained probably until Easter of 1420.[18] After he left Constance, however, and until the time he joined the papal chapel in late

---

[14] See John Nádas, 'Further Notes on Magister Antonius Dictus Zacharias de Teramo', *Studi musicali*, 15 (1986), 167–82.

[15] Di Bacco and Nádas, 'Verso uno stile internazionale', 28–30.

[16] See Alejandro Enrique Planchart, 'The Early Career of Guillaume Du Fay', *JAMS* 46 (1993), 357–9.

[17] The mandates of the *camera apostolica* in ASR, Fondo Camerale I, Conti della depositeria generale, Registro 824, go from June 1418 to May 1421. They record the monthly salary of the singers and have two *lacunae*, one the failure to record the mandates for Feb. and Mar. 1419, and the other the loss of twenty-five leaves (fos. 63–97) going from Aug. 1419 to Feb. 1420. From these, and from the incomplete record of inductions into the chapel in the *liber officialis*, ASR, Fondo Camerale I, Registro 1711, covering relatively well the period from Dec. 1417 to July 1418, we can determine the membership of the chapel of Martin V with some precision month by month.

[18] LADN, 7G 2918, fo. 18ʳ, showing him at Cambrai on 17 Nov. 1418, and 7G 2925, fo. 6ʳ, showing him there on Ash Wednesday of 1420.

1428,[19] a number of composers did serve in the chapel. These are listed in Table 3.1. Before proceeding any further I must explain the exclusion of Johannes Vincenet. To this day there is some question whether the papal singer Vincenet was a composer, although he is certainly not the singer at the court of Aragon later in the century.[20] But the papal singer (June 1426–June 1429) was a priest from Toul and not a married man like his Aragonese namesake, and simply cannot be the composer of any of the works attributed to a Vincenet in the sources, all of which are much too late. (On this Vincenet, see below, Ch. 7.)

TABLE 3.1. Composers in the papal chapel: 1418–1428

Composer[a]	Dates of service
Pierre Fontaine	April 1420 to May 1422
	January 1423 to November 1428
Nicolas Grenon	June 1425 to November 1427
Guillaume le Macherier	October 1418 to July 1421[b]
Barthélemy Poignare[c]	June 1425 to November 1427 as chorister
Nicola Pietro Zaccaria	June 1420 to November 1422
	September 1423 to July 1424

[a] Excluding Johannes Vincenet or Vincenot(Jan. 1426 to June 1429).
[b] Oct. 1418 is the date of his induction recorded in the *Liber officialis*; the first mandate of payment for him is Apr. 1419.
[c] See also Table 3.2.

Barthélemy Poignare is known for just a single work, a short Gloria *Ave regina caelorum*, found on fos. 51ᵛ–52ʳ of Trent 87, and an early example of a fully polytextual mass movement, where the plainsong cantus firmus is elaborately paraphrased. The work is given in Ex. 3.1. It must date from his stay in the papal chapel, for like Hanelle and Flannel, he did not remain an active musician after leaving the chapel. Born in 1408 near Arras,[21] he was one of the choirboys or *iuvenes cantores* who came with Grenon or with Flannel to the papal chapel in 1425, and was the only one of that group to remain as an adult

[19] There is no record of Du Fay's induction into the chapel in the *liber officialis*. His first salary is for Jan. 1429 (paid 20 Dec. 1428), but in a *littera de fructibus* sent on his behalf by Benedetto Guidalotti to the chapters of Laon and Saint-Géry on 14 Apr. 1429, he is described as having been a member of the chapel for 'about six months' (BAV, Diversa Cameralia 11, fos. 257ᵛ–258ʳ), so that he must have joined the chapel shortly after his ejection from Bologna in Aug. 1428. His is not the only instance of a gap between induction and first payment; see e.g. the case of Guillaume Le Macherier in Table 3.1, where both records survive.

[20] See e.g. Tom Ward, 'Johannes Vincenet', *New Grove*, i. 781–2, and Vincenet, *The Collected Works*, ed. Bertran E. Davis (RRMMA 9–10; Madison, 1978), pp. vii–ix.

[21] See Karl August Fink, *Repertorium Germanicum*, iv (Berlin, 1958), col. 191.

Ex. 3.1. Bartholomeus Poignare, Gloria (Trent 87, fos. 51ᵛ–52ʳ)

Ex. 3.1. *cont.*

Ex. 3.1. *cont.*

lus al - tis - si - mus Ie - su   Chri-ste. Cum San-cto spi - ri - tu   in glo - ri - a De -

Chri - - - - - - stum   ex -

i Pa - tris.   A - men.

o - - - - - - - ra.

singer. He was in Martin's chapel until July of 1430, and then went north, but returned upon the election of Eugene IV, staying from March 1431 to September 1433. By 1437 he had become a resident canon in Arras, and there is no evidence that he continued his musical career. He was apparently a friend of Du Fay, whom he visited on number of occasions in the 1440s.[22] The Gloria at times has the melodic grace of someone who has been hearing some of the music of Grenon and the young Du Fay, but its good moments are connected by thinly worked out counterpoint that does not rise above decent craftsmanship.

Poignare was a member of the papal chapel longer than any of the other composers listed in Table 3.1 except Pierre Fontaine. Not a single sacred work by him is known, so it is likely that he contributed nothing to the papal repertory. We still know so little about the career of Guillaume le Macherier that it is impossible to give anything like a chronology of his works. Before joining the papal chapel he had served in the Sainte-Chapelle at Bourges and then as a

---

[22] LADN, 4G 7446 (Bread & Wine, 1446–7), fo. [6ʳ]: Poignare, a canon of Arras, receives bread on 12 Sept. 1446 and on St Francis's Day. The second time he is at the house of Du Fay. Several other such visits are recorded at Cambrai during the 1440s.

chaplain of King Sigismund,[23] and it was as a chaplain of the king that he came to Constance in 1418.[24] The only work of his that has a date, a Credo in Oxford 213 dated 1426, was written long after he had left the papal chapel.

Grenon's position in the chapel was exceptional. He came in at the time when Martin V decided to add choristers to the papal chapel, and was clearly the master of the choristers, probably recruiting some of them, although evidence from Bolognese city records also indicates that Gilles Flannel and Toussaint de la Rouelle also recruited a number of choristers.[25] Grenon was paid separately from the other adult members of the chapel and together with the choristers for his entire tenure, and when he left Rome all the choristers except for Poignare left at the same time.[26] In any event there is not a single surviving work by Grenon that could possibly have been written for the papal chapel.

Although the presence of choristers automatically makes one think that the chapel did cultivate polyphonic music to a considerable extent, it should be clear by now that whatever polyphony was sung at the chapel of Martin V before 1428 was not written by members of the chapel, or at least that such a repertory has not survived. The temptation is very strong therefore to suggest that the papal liturgy of the early fifteenth century consisted largely of plain-song to even greater an extent than in a place like Cambrai Cathedral or churches such as Saint-Géry de Cambrai, Saint-Pierre de Lille, Sint Donaas in Bruges, or Sint Goedele in Brussels.[27]

The situation does not seem to change appreciably after Du Fay's entry into the papal chapel in 1428. Composers in the papal chapel from that year until the end of the reign of Eugene IV are listed in Table 3.2. The overlapping member, Poignare, has already been discussed. Of the others, several need not detain us. Arnold de Lantins spent the last ten months of his life as a papal singer and it is unlikely that he wrote much for the chapel. Gautier Liebert spent only nine months in the chapel and we have no sacred music by him.

---

[23] See Paula Higgins, 'Music and Musicians at the Sainte-Chapelle of the Bourges Palace, 1405–1415', in Angelo Pompilio *et al.* (eds.), *International Musicological Society, Report of the Fourteenth Congress, Bologna, 1987: Trasmissione e recezione delle forme di cultura musicale*, 3 vols. (Turin, 1990), iii. 689–701, and Planchart, 'The Early Career', 354.

[24] ASV, RS 107, fo. 81ʳ⁻ᵛ.   [25] See Planchart, 'Guillaume Du Fay's Benefices', 127.

[26] ASV, RS 219, fo. 55ʳ, 1 Dec. 1427. The choristers leaving with Grenon are Étienne de Heldedronque, Jean Rongh, Pierre Chareton, Guibert Nettelet, and Johannes Wyet, all of whom came from the dioceses of Cambrai and Tournai.

[27] The recent work of Barbara Haggh, 'Itinerancy to Residency: Professional Careers and Performance Practices in 15th Century Sacred Music', *EM* 17 (1989), 359–67 and Reinhard Strohm, *The Rise of European Music* (Cambridge, 1993), 170–83, suggest that the liturgy of these churches would look considerably more like that of Rome in terms of the proportion between chant and polyphony if we took account only of the *missae in choro* and not the privately endowed services in the side chapels. At Cambrai this appears to change in the late 1440s, since the copying of polyphonic books in pairs began in 1449 (Wright, 'Dufay at Cambrai', 225–6).

TABLE 3.2. Composers in the papal chapel: 1428–1447

Composer	Reigning pope	Dates of service
Johannes Brassart	Martin V	August 1430–March 1431
	Eugene IV	March–August 1431[a]
Guillaume Du Fay	Martin V	October 1428–March 1431[b]
	Eugene IV	March 1431–August 1433
		June 1435–May 1437
Arnold de Lantins	Eugene IV	September 1431–June 1432
Gautier Libert	Martin V	January–September 1429
Guillaume Modiator, called de Malbecque	Martin V	August–October 1427
	Eugene IV	October 1431–March 1433
		January 1434–October 1436
		January 1437–March 1438
Jean Sohier, called Fedé	Eugene IV	November 1443–July 1445
Barthélemy Poignare	Eugene IV	March 1431–September 1433

[a] Brassart could have joined the chapel as early as Aug. 1430 and certainly by Mar. 1431. His last documented payment is for Aug. 1431, but he may still have been in the chapel in Sept.

[b] First paid in Dec. 1428, but a letter of Benedetto Guidalotti to the chapter of Laon and St-Géry de Cambrai, dated 14 Apr. 1429 (ASV, Diversa Cameralia 11, fos. 257ᵛ–258ʳ) states Du Fay had been a papal singer 'for about six months'.

Guillaume Modiator, despite his relatively long tenure as a papal singer, has left not a single sacred work, and the same applies to Jehan Sohier.[28] Furthermore, as one can see from Table 3.2, there was a relatively long period, from the withdrawal of Du Fay to the arrival of Sohier, when there were no composers in the papal chapel, a situation that also obtains for long years under the successors of Eugene IV.

Two composers remain in Table 3.2 from whom we actually have some music that may have been written for the papal chapel or at least used extensively by it: Johannes Brassart and Guillaume Du Fay.

At this point it may be well to make a short excursus concerning the kinds of music that we may expect to be part of the papal chapel repertory before 1450. Apart from the occasional ceremonial motet, of which there are several

[28] It is possible that both Modiator and Sohier wrote music for their churches after retiring from the papal chapel, particularly since Modiator became dean of Saint-Vincent de Soignies and was in contact with Du Fay, whose receiver he was for the parish church of Wattebraine until his death in 1465, and with Binchois, for whose will he served as executor.

examples by Du Fay and Brassart, we should expect these works to be liturgical music in the strictest sense of the term, something that at this time probably excluded festal cantus-firmus masses, then cultivated exclusively by English composers, and even such plenary masses as Du Fay's *Missa Sancti Jacobi* or Lantins's *Missa Verbum incarnatum*. Instead, we should look for isolated movements of the ordinary of the mass that could be used on a number of occasions, and perhaps plainsong settings, precisely the kinds of pieces that we encounter in the one earlier source that may reflect a papal repertory, namely Apt.[29] In this respect I believe that the papal chapel (and the conciliar chapels, for that matter) was appreciably different in terms of the repertory it cultivated than the private chapels of secular princes, such as the dukes of Burgundy, where the liturgy was also seen as a manifestation of princely magnificence. This consideration seems not to enter into the papal chapel until the last quarter of the fifteenth century.

Du Fay and Brassart have left us a remarkable amount of liturgical music other than festal masses and ceremonial motets, but in the case of Brassart, his stay in the chapel was of short duration, and his later career took place in an organization such as the chapel of the Council of Basle, where the kinds of music that were sung were probably very similar to those of the papal chapel. It is thus quite possible that his cycle of introits, for example, which are liturgical music *par excellence*, could have been written for the conciliar chapel, where he had a much longer tenure than in the papal chapel.[30]

This brings us to Guillaume Du Fay. By the time he joined the papal chapel in 1428 he was well regarded as a composer. He had composed works that were sung at the Council of Constance, had been a court musician of Carlo Malatesta da Rimini, and served as a musician in the *familia* of Luis Aleman. Indeed, as I have noted elsewhere, he was probably recruited for Aleman by Robert Auclou in an effort to emulate the sophisticated chapel maintained by Alfonso Carrillo, one of Aleman's recent predecessors as legate of Bologna,[31] and Du Fay's documented compositions during his two years in Bologna, which include the *Missa Sancti Jacobi*, *Rite maiorem*, *Apostolo glorioso*, and most likely *Vergene bella*, form an impressive group. The decade that Du Fay spent in papal service was also an impressively productive era for him, and were we to have no works written after 1437 we would still have more music by him than we have from many of his contemporaries. These works include a number of 'papal' motets: *O beate Sebastiane*, most likely composed at the time of

[29] On this see Tomasello, *Music and Ritual at Papal Avignon*, 123–50.

[30] See Keith Mixter, 'Johannes Brassart: A Biographical and Bibliographical Study', *MD* 18 (1964), 37–62, and 19 (1965), 99–108.

[31] Planchart, 'Guillaume Du Fay's Benefices', 126–7.

the plague in Rome in 1429, *Ecclesiae militantis*, perhaps for the coronation of Eugene IV on 11 March 1431, *Balsamus et munda cera*, for the papal distribution of the Agnus Dei on 7 April 1431, *Supremum est mortalibus bonum*, for the entry of King Sigismund into Rome on 21 May 1433, and *Nuper rosarum flores*, for the dedication of Santa Maria del Fiore by Eugene IV on 25 March 1436. Two other works, *Salve flos Tuscae gentis* and *Mirandas parit haec urbs florentina puellas*, although not for papal ceremonies, must date from 1436 and therefore have been written while Du Fay was in the papal chapel. This is an astonishing group of works to be performed by the members of the papal chapel, unmatched by those of any other composer before Josquin, but they are not music for the papal chapel *per se* as an institution, and thus fall outside the scope of this study.[32] They are ample evidence, however, of Du Fay's activity as a composer during his years in the chapel. They are also proof that the singers of the papal chapel could sing complex polyphony, but from what music is left that may in some way reflect the chapel's polyphonic repertory, it appears that in the early fifteenth century the singing of polyphony was exceptional in that institution. In this, however, the papal chapel does not appear to be much different from most of the other princely chapels of its time.[33]

Three categories of music offer themselves as logical possibilities for the papal repertory among Du Fay's works: settings of the proper of the mass, settings of the ordinary, and settings of liturgical music for the office. Apart from the propers of the *Missa Sancti Jacobi*, works that apparently had very little circulation, the period when Du Fay composed most of his music for the *proprium missae* is the decade between 1440 and 1450, when there was apparently little communication between him and Rome.[34] But there is a group of prose settings that do appear to date from the 1430s, that is from his period in papal service. These are given in Table 3.3. I have included not only the works with an ascription to Du Fay but four other proses as well, one that was mistakenly reported as having an ascription to him in Guillaume de Van's inventory of Bologna Q 15,[35] and was discussed as an authentic work by Charles Hamm,[36]

[32] An extended discussion of the genesis and context of these pieces appears in Laurenz Lütteken, *Guillaume Dufay und die isorhythmische Motette: Gattungstradition und Werkcharakter an der Schwelle zur Neuzeit* (Schriften zur Musikwissenschaft aus Münster, 4; Hamburg, 1993). On *Nuper rosarum flores* see also Craig Wright, 'Du Fay's *Nuper rosarum flores* and King Solomon's Temple', *JAMS* 47 (1994), 395–441.

[33] To this day we have no clear view of the actual incidence of polyphonic singing in the chapels of the princes or in the cathedrals of northern Europe in the early 15th c. Much remains to be done in this respect.

[34] See Planchart, 'Guillaume Du Fay's Benefices', 141–52, for an account of what is known of Du Fay's propers.

[35] Guillaume de Van, 'An Inventory of the Manuscript Bologna, Liceo Musicale, Q 15 (*olim* 37)', *MD* 2 (1948), 231–57.

[36] Charles Hamm, 'Dating a Group of Dufay Works', *JAMS* 15 (1962), 65–71, and Hamm, *A Chronology of the Works of Guillaume Dufay Based on a Study of Mensural Practice* (Princeton Studies in Music, 1; Princeton, 1964), 76–8.

TABLE 3.3. Proses ascribed to Guillaume Du Fay

No.	Incipit and sources	Feast
1	*Laetabundus exsultet fidelis chorus* Bologna Q 15, no. 316 (du fay) Trent 92, fo. 66ᵛ	Christmas *de nativitate domini* prosa
2	*Epiphaniam domini canamus* Trent 87, fo. 63ᵛ (G dufay)	Epiphany *In epiphania domini*
3	*Victimae paschali laudes* Munich 14274, fo. 59ᵛ Trent 92, fo. 23ᵛ (dufay)	Easter
4	*Rex omnipotens die hodierna* Trent 87, fo. 65ᵛ (G dufay)	Ascension *In ascensione domini*
5	*Veni sancte spiritus* Trent 92, fo. 100ᵛ (du fay)	Pentecost
6	*Lauda Sion salvatorem* Munich 14274, fo. 67ᵛ Trent 90, fo. 98ᵛ (G dufay) Trent 93, fo. 290ᵛ	Corpus Christi
7	*Isti sunt duae olivae* Trent 87, fo. 61ᵛ (G. dufay)	SS Peter and Paul

Anonymous prose (possible complement to no. 5)

No.	Incipit and sources	Feast
8	*Veni sancte spiritus* Bologna Q 15, no. 325b Aosta, fo. 185ᵛ Munich 14274, fo. 67ᵛ	Pentecost

Proses ascribed to Du Fay by Charles Hamm[a]

No.	Incipit and sources	Feast
9	*Laetabundus exsultet fidelis chorus* Trent 92, fo. 68ᵛ	Christmas
10	*Mittit ad virginem* Bologna Q 15, no. 336 Trent 92, fo. 67ᵛ	Visitation
11	*Sancti spiritus adsit nobis* Trent 92, fo. 36ᵛ	Pentecost

[a] Hamm, *Chronology*, 76–8.

and a group of three proses for which Hamm made a careful case as works by Du Fay. I have not included, however, the first of the pieces published as a prose in the complete works, *Ave virgo quae de caelis*,[37] since, as I noted in an earlier study, the piece is not a prose but a cantilena motet.[38] I also wish to

[37] Dufay, *Opera omnia*, ed. Heinrich Besseler, 6 vols. (CMM 1; Rome, 1950–96), v. 1–4.
[38] Alejandro Enrique Planchart, 'What's in a Name? Reflections on Some Works of Guillaume Du Fay', *EM* 16 (1988), 165–75.

reject Hamm's attribution of the setting of *Laetabundus exsultet* found in Trent 92 (no. 9 in Table 3.3) despite its position within a group of Du Fay works. There is a wide stylistic gulf between this work and the others in the table. Du Fay did not use C mensuration in the way this piece uses it in any of his works from this period, and neither did he write any treble-dominated plainsong setting for three low voices. Further, even in his modally more adventurous settings of the 1440s he never transposed a chant by a whole step, as happens in this work. The remaining proses, however, are indeed likely to be his work, as Hamm has suggested. In the case of the anonymous *Veni sancte spiritus* in Bologna Q 15 both Hamm and Fallows have noted that it is stylistically very close to the setting ascribed to Du Fay in Trent 92, and sets the verses not set in that version,[39] so that it may well be a complement to the ascribed work and intended to be sung in lieu of the chanted sections of that piece.

We can tell very little about the origin of Du Fay's surviving proses, however. The manuscript transmission suggests that all of them originated during the 1430s, and some may have been composed in Rome or later in Florence, Bologna, and Savoy and thus could have been used by the papal chapel. All but one of them are settings of the most widespread prose texts, used all over Europe and thus also in Rome, but there are two exceptions to this in terms of Roman use. The first is the attributed work *Sancti spiritus adsit nobis gratiae*, for Pentecost. To be sure, Notker's poem with its magnificent west Frankish tune was known and sung in Italy and in Rome itself from very early on. It appears not only in every Italian Gradual and sequentiary, north and south, including the Beneventan and the Ravennatic sources, but it even made it into the eleventh-century Graduals with Old Roman chant from the Lateran Basilica and Santa Cecilia in Trastevere,[40] so that it did form part of the papal liturgy in the eleventh century. But from the thirteenth century on it was replaced in a number of centres, and particularly in Rome itself, by *Veni sancte spiritus*, which medieval tradition ascribed to Pope Innocent III (1198–1216),[41] so that in the fifteenth century there was no place in the papal liturgy for Notker's piece. If Du Fay wrote this work, it was not for the papal choir. The other prose that must be excluded from any putative papal canon of Du Fay's works is, ironically, *Isti sunt duae olivae*, for SS Peter and Paul, the archetypal Roman saints. Heinrich Besseler, in his study 'Dufay in Rom', placed this piece during

[39] Hamm, *Chronology*, 76; David Fallows, *Dufay* (London, 1982), 230.

[40] Cologny-Geneva, Bodmer Library, MS 74, fo. 104ᵛ, facsimile in Max Lütolf (ed.), *Das Graduale von Santa Cecilia in Trastevere (cod. Bodmer 74)*, 2 vols. (Cologny-Geneva, 1987), and BAV, Vat. lat. 5319, fo. 158ʳ, in Stäblein and Landwehr-Melnicki (eds.), *Die Gesänge des altrömischen Graduale Vat. lat. 5319*.

[41] On the different ascriptions, and an evaluation of their worth, see Clemens Blume and Henry Marriott Bannister (eds.), *Liturgische Prosen des Übergangsstiles und der zweiten Epoche* (Analecta Hymnica, 54; Leipzig, 1915, repr. New York, 1961), 237–9, where the editors indicate that indeed Innocent III is the probable author.

Du Fay's Roman years on stylistic and notational grounds,[42] a dating questioned by Hamm on similar grounds,[43] but there is, in fact, a further detail that not only excludes Rome or the papal chapel as the locus for this prose, but also gives us an indication of when and where Du Fay composed the piece: it is the chant itself on which it is based. Both the chant and its text had a very small circulation and were all but unknown except in the dioceses of Lausanne and Geneva.[44] Du Fay was a canon at Lausanne from 1431 to 1439, and during these years made a number of fruitless efforts to obtain a canonicate in Geneva.[45] *Isti sunt duae olivae*, then, was surely written for Lausanne or for the ducal singers of Savoy to sing during the court's stay in the Swiss cantons.[46] It differs markedly from his other proses in that it uses a number of different mensurations and changes of textures. It represents a special effort by Du Fay, something that is consonant with what we know about his relations with Lausanne and Geneva.

The other proses, for whatever institution they may have been written, were probably used by the papal singers at least during Du Fay's last years in the chapel, after his return from Savoy. This, perhaps, explains the existence of the anonymous complement to his *Veni sancte spiritus* found in Bologna Q 15. The evidence of the settings of the Magnificat in the late fifteenth and early sixteenth centuries suggests that there was no strong tradition of alternatim singing in the papal chapel, with the exception of hymn settings, and thus this prose, a papal work *par excellence*, may have been brought into line with the prevailing performance tradition of the papal chapel by the added verses, but this in itself would show that the work was not originally written for the chapel.

Du Fay's settings of the ordinary of the mass outside the complete cycles do not present a pattern of transmission that shows any coherence, but it would appear nonetheless that many of his isolated Kyries were part of an apparently systematic attempt to provide a polyphonic Kyriale for the entire liturgical year. A few years ago Lia Laor tried to establish the liturgical function of Du

---

[42] Heinrich Besseler, 'Dufay in Rom', *AfMw* 15 (1958), 1–19; repr. with additions in *Miscelánea en homenaje a monseñor Higinio Anglés,* 2 vols. (Barcelona, 1958–61), i. 111–34.

[43] Hamm, *Chronology,* 64–5.

[44] See e.g. the concordance of text sources in Henry Marriott Bannister (ed.), *Sequentiae Ineditae: Liturgische Prosen des Mittelalters aus Handschriften und Frühdrucken* (Analecta Hymnica, 40; Leipzig, 1902, repr. New York, 1962), 275. Note that the prose text, but not the melody, begins like a very common office antiphon that was used in Rome and is cited at the end of the motet *Supremum est mortalibus.* The antiphon and the prose, however, have very different transmissions.

[45] Planchart, 'Guillaume Du Fay's Benefices', 132–3.

[46] The Savoy court, travelling as it did from Chambéry to Geneva, and to Turin, went across several boundaries in terms of liturgical usage. Probably the court, since it was based mostly at Chambéry, followed for the most part the use of Besançon. The Sainte-Chapelle at Chambéry certainly did so. See Alexis de Jussieu, *La Sainte-Chapelle du Château du Chambéry* (Chambéry, 1868), 29–48.

Fay's early ordinary settings,[47] but her attempt was hindered by a fundamental misunderstanding of the liturgical categories for the ordinary of the mass, as opposed to the propers. She sought, for the most part, to associate a given work with a specific feast. Instead, in the fourteenth century, as the plainsong propers began to be grouped into cycles in the manuscripts, an effort was made to assign them to a given category of feasts.[48] Assignments varied from place to place, following local liturgical traditions, but by and large they are reasonably consistent for a number of the older and more widely used Kyrie melodies, though even within a single source duplicate assignments are common. In any event, a summary of common late fourteenth- and early fifteenth-century assignments drawn from some two hundred sources is given in Table 3.4.

Some of the surviving Kyries by Du Fay give evidence of being part of a cycle of polyphonic Kyries for the whole year. Du Fay's Kyries, with their sources

TABLE 3.4. Common liturgical Kyrie assignments in the fourteenth and fifteenth centuries

Feast	Kyrie
Pascha Domini	*Lux et origo lucis*
Maior duplex[a]	*Fons bonitatis*
Minor duplex	*Cunctipotens genitor deus*
Maior semiduplex	*Pater cuncta, Rex genitor ingenite*
Minor semiduplex	*Jesu redemptor omnium*
Dominica	*Orbis factor*
Simplex	Various melodies without names (Melnicki 144, 172, etc.)
Minor simplex	Various melodies without names (Melnicki 144, 172, etc.)
Beatae Mariae Virginis	*Cum iubilo, Cunctipotens genitor*[b]
Apostolorum	*Cunctipotens genitor, Jesu redemptor*
Martyrum	*Orbis factor, Pater cuncta*
Confessorum	*Rex deus aeterne*
Virginum	*Cunctipotens genitor,*[c] *Orbis factor*

   [a] In most chant sources feasts of the duplex rank are referred to as *sollemne* or a similar term.

   [b] Sometimes with trope *Rex virginum amator*, which survived in use until the late 15th c. even outside England.

   [c] As an extension of its assignment for feasts of the BVM.

[47] Lia Laor, 'Concerning the Liturgical Usage of Dufay's Fragmentary Masses', *Current Musicology*, 37–8 (1984), 49–58.

[48] Dominique Catta, 'Aux origines du Kyriale', *Revue Grégorienne*, 34 (1955), 175–82, and Leo Schrade, 'The Cycle of the Ordinarium Missae', in Higinio Anglés *et al.* (eds.), *In Memoriam Jacques Handschin* (Strasburg, 1962), 87–96.

and rubrics, are given in Table 3.5, followed by an assignment to the categories in Table 3.4 based both upon the plainsong melody used and the rubrics given in the source. I have excluded the Kyries of the *Missa Resveilliez vous* and the *Missa Sancti Jacobi*, even though both were transmitted—the second in partial form—as independent settings, but have included the Kyries of the two *Missae breves* by Du Fay that survive, all the more so because Kyrie no. 13 in Table 3.5 is one piece that I am certain was written to be performed by the conciliar chapel in Constance in 1416 or 1417. It is interesting to note that the three Kyries that give no hint of a liturgical classification consist of the two pieces found that form part of *Missae breves* and one that may be unauthentic. In any case they do not seem part, as the others do, of a systematic attempt at composing a cycle of Kyries for use throughout the year.

Among the remaining Kyries there seems to be a division between the pieces for the *temporale*, which use no alternation, and those for the *sanctorale*, which do. The exceptional treatment of the Easter Kyrie, which survives in three forms—one without alternation, one with the full alternation, and one with a chant intonation—is consonant with the special position that this Kyrie had in the liturgical tradition by the fifteenth century. It is worth noting that the plainsongs set by Du Fay are among those with the most stable assignments across every liturgical tradition in the Continent, so that the liturgical assignments found in the rubrics are entirely consonant with the classification most often found for the melodies. In any event, the stylistic division between *temporale* and *sanctorale* may explain the two settings of the Kyrie *Orbis factor*, which is one of the Kyrie melodies most often given double assignments in the plainsong manuscripts. If this is correct, the conflicting rubric for this Kyrie in Trent 92 may be regarded as unauthentic but understandable.

I would also propose that the liturgical impulse leading to the production of such a cycle is most likely a product of Du Fay's work in the papal chapel rather than his work for a secular prince, even one as devout as Amadeus of Savoy, and thus I would propose that, in their liturgical organization, Du Fay's Kyries do represent music that was composed for the papal chapel itself. It is also worth noting that we are probably missing at least three pieces from this group, namely a Kyrie *in semiduplicibus minoribus*, as well as Kyries for confessors and for virgins. It is possible that they have survived anonymously, as did some of Du Fay's mass propers from the 1440s, but at this point we have no way of identifying them short of finding a concordance or a citation by a theorist.

Another group of early works by Du Fay that exhibits the same kind of large-scale liturgical organization found in the Kyries and to an even more obvious degree is the hymns. The genesis of Du Fay's *liber hymnorum* is very

TABLE 3.5. Guillaume Du Fay's Kyrie settings

No.	Kyrie and sources	Edition	Remarks
1	Kyrie (*Cum iubilo*)	CW 5:14	alternatim
	Bologna Q 15, no. 124bis (du fay)		
	Munich 14274, fo. 57ʳ		
	Trent 90, fo. 85ʳ		
	Trent 92, fo. 64ᵛ		
	Trent 93, fo. 117		
2	Kyrie (*Cunctipotens genitor*)	CW 5:10	non-alternatim
	Aosta, fo. 22ʳ		
	Bologna 2216, p. 83		
	Bologna Q 15, no. 157b (du fay)		
	Munich 14274, fo. 31ᵛ		
	Trent 92, fo. 27ʳ (dufay)		
	Trent 93, fo. 98ᵛ		*sollempne*
3	Kyrie (*Fons bonitatis*)	CW 5:16	non-alternatim
	Bologna Q 15, no. 127 (du fay)		*kyrie fons bonitatis*
	Munich 14274, fo. 127ᵛ		*sollenne*
	Trent 90, fo. 64ᵛ		*fons bonitatis*
	Trent 93, fo. 93ᵛ		*fons bonitatis*
4	Kyrie (*Fons bonitatis*)[a]	CW 5:17	non-alternatim
	Trent 87, fo. 94ᵛ (G dufay)		*kyrie in summis festivitatibus*
5	Kyrie (*Jesu redemptor*)	CW 5:13	alternatim
	Munich 14274, fo. 102ᵛ		
	Trent 87, fo. 101ᵛ (G dufay)		*de apostolis*
	Trent 87, fo. 93ᵛ (G dufay)		*de apostolis*
6	Kyrie (*Lux et origo*)	CW 4:15	chant opening[b]
	Aosta, fo. 23ᵛ (G du fay)		
	Munich 14274, fo. 34ᵛ		*paschale*
	Trent 90, fo. 75ʳ		*aliud paschale*
	Trent 92, fo. 24ʳ		
	Trent 93, fo. 106ʳ		*paschale*
7	Kyrie (*Orbis factor*)	CW 4:11	alternatim
	Aosta, fo. 27ᵛ		
	Munich 14274, fo. 33ᵛ		*de martyribus*
	Trent 87, fo. 94ʳ (G dufay)		*de martyribus*
	Trent 90, fo. 81ᵛ (duffay)		*de martyribus*
	Trent 92, fo. 38ᵛ		*in diebus dominicis*
	Trent 93, fo. 112ᵛ (Duffay)		*de martyribus*
8	Kyrie (*Orbis factor*)	CW 4:12	non-alternatim
	Bologna Q 15, no. 126 (du fay)		*in dominicis diebus*
9	Kyrie (*Pater cuncta*)	CW 4:9	non-alternatim
	Aosta, fo. 21ᵛ (G du fay)		
	Aosta, fo. 56ᵛ		
	Trent 92, fo. 132		
	Trent 93, fo. 120ʳ		
	Trent 93, fo. 125ᵛ		
10	Kyrie (*Rex genitor*)	CW 4:18	non-alternatim
	Bologna Q 15, no. 128 (du fay)		*in semiduplicibus maioris*

No. Kyrie and sources	Edition	Remarks
11 Kyrie (no plainsong)[c] Cambrai 6, fo. 4^v Cambrai 11, fo. 2^v Trent 90, fo. 90^v Trent 92, fo. 144^r (dufay) Trent 93, fo. 122^v	CW 4:19	non-alternatim
12 Kyrie (no plainsong) Aosta, fo. 49^r (du Fay) Aosta, fo. 25^r (G dufay) Bologna Q 15,[d] no. 187 (du Fay) Cambrai 6, fo. 1^v Cambrai 11, fo. 2^r Munich 14274, fo. 31^r (dufay) Venice 145, fo. 2$^{v\,e}$	CW 4:1	non-alternatim
13 Kyrie (no plainsong?)[f] Aosta, fo. 24^r (G dufay) Bologna Q 15[g], no. 17 (du fay)	CW 4:2	non-alternatim

Assignments of the Du Fay Kyries

Pascha Domini	6
Maior duplex	3, 4
Minor duplex	2
Maior semiduplex	9, 10
Minor semiduplex	—
Dominica	8
Simplex	—
Minor simplex	—
Beatae Mariae Virginis	1
Apostolorum	5
Martyrum	7
Confessorum	—
Virginum	—

Kyries with no clear liturgical assignment: nos. 11 and 12.[h]

---

[a] The scribe labels it *Magne deus*, a melody that begins like that of *Fons bonitatis* but has an entirely different ending and modal classification.

[b] Trent 92 has chant for the first invocation; Munich 14274 has a full set of alternatim chants, Aosta, Trent 90, and Trent 93 have no chant.

[c] Perhaps unauthentic; see Craig Monson, 'Stylistic Inconsistencies in a Kyrie Attributed to Dufay', *JAMS* 28 (1975), 245–67.

[d] Associated in this source with a Gloria and a Credo found also in Aosta but as independent movements; all three movements, however, are in *cursiva* style and probably do belong together.

[e] Fragmentary, 2vv, textless.

[f] The Sanctus and Agnus associated with this Kyrie in Bologna Q 15 have as cantus firmus the *cantus fractus* 'vineux', but the one source for this cantus firmus from Cambrai (LADN, MS 134), is now only a bifolium.

[g] Associated in this source with a Sanctus and Agnus by Du Fay based on the tenor *vineux* found only in Bologna Q 15; most likely all three movements belong together and date from 1416.

[h] Their position in Cambrai 6 and Cambrai 11 suggests that they were considered at Cambrai to be for solemn feasts.

complex, and it has not been helped by the kinds of *obiter dicta* favoured by Besseler in discussing these works, in particular his dismissal of some of the occasional hymns as unauthentic, all the more so since we do have documentary evidence that Du Fay continued to write isolated hymns to the end of his life.[49] The Du Fay hymns and their sources copied during the composer's lifetime appear in the Appendix.

Unlike the Kyries, the hymns, as they have come down to us, consist of a complete cycle for the entire year. If anything may be missing at all it is the hymn for Sundays throughout the year outside Lent, *Lucis creator optime*.[50] There are, in Du Fay's canon, also a few occasional hymns, most of which seem to be arrangements by someone else of Du Fay's melodies, but three of which are surely authentic: nos. 10a, 13b, and 25a. The hymn cycle apparently was composed in two stages and probably revised a number of times. The two main stages of its composition are reflected in their transmission in Bologna Q 15 and Modena α.X.1.11 and are given in Table 3.6. The cycle as found in Bologna Q 15 has a gap going from the Purification, for which *Ave maris stella* would have been used, to Ascension and St John Baptist. The gap is not large in terms of the number of pieces, but includes the most important feast in the entire liturgical year, for it goes from the first Sunday in Lent to Easter inclusive. In liturgical terms, then, the gap is astonishing in what is clearly a systematic collection, and indeed, with the exception of a hymn for apostles and a hymn for Lauds at Christmas, all the new hymns in Modena α.X.1.11 simply fill this gap.

As I have suggested in the case of the Kyries, the fact that the hymns are a cycle for the entire year suggests to me that they were intended for the papal chapel rather than for a princely court, where not all vespers were celebrated with the same consistency. The difficulty, noted by Tom Ward years ago, is that the melodies used by Du Fay seem to be a slightly heterogeneous collection: they do not fit what Ward has called 'the monophonic tradition of the papal court',[51] which is largely a Franciscan one,[52] but neither do they fit the uses of Savoy, Cambrai, or any of the churches where Du Fay worked during his life. They represent an exceptional tradition dominated largely by main north

[49] See the entry in the fabric accounts for 1463–4 in Houdoy, *Histoire artistique*, 195. Rudolf Bockholdt, 'Die Hymnen der Handschrift Cambrai 6: Zwei unbekannte Vertonungen von Dufay?', *TVNM* 29 (1979), 75–91, proposes that the setting of *O quam glorifica* in Cambrai 6 is the hymn by Du Fay mentioned in the fabric accounts. This is imposible; the hymn of 1463–4 is described as 'newly composed', and Cambrai 6 dates from some two decades earlier.

[50] That Du Fay apparently never set this hymn is suggested by the presence of an interpolated setting by Benoit in the hymn section of Modena α.X.1.11, but perhaps a setting by Du Fay is hiding behind the elaboration of a *fauxbourdon* setting in Vatican CS 15, fos. 12ᵛ–13ʳ.

[51] Tom R. Ward, 'Hymn. III. Polyphonic Latin', *New Grove*, viii. 841.

[52] The fundamental work on this is Stephen J. P. van Dijk, *The Sources of the Modern Roman Liturgy*, 2 vols. (Leiden, 1963).

TABLE 3.6. Layers of composition in Du Fay's hymns

No.	Hymn	Type	Feast
Layer 1			
1a	*Conditor alme siderum*	FB	Advent
2a	*Christe redemptor omnium*	FB	Christmas
4a	*Hostis Herodes impie*	3v	Epiphany
9a	*Jesu nostra redemptio*	3v	Ascension
11a	*Veni creator spiritus*	3v	Pentecost
12a	*O lux beata trinitas*	3v	Trinity
13a	*Pange lingua gloriosi*	3v	Corpus Christi
14a	*Urbs beata Jerusalem*	3v	Dedication
15a	*Ave maris stella*	FB	BVM
15b	*Ave maris stella*	3v	BVM
16a	*Christe redemptor omnium*	FB	All Saints
16b	*Christe redemptor omnium*	3v	All Saints
17a	*Tibi Christe splendor*	FB	Angels (St Michael)
18a	*Ut queant laxis resonare*	3v	St John Baptist
19a	*Aurea luce et decore*	3v	SS Peter and Paul
20a	*Exsultet caelum laudibus*	FB	Apostles
21a	*Deus tuorum militum*	FB	One martyr
22a	*Sanctorum meritis inclita*	3v	Several martyrs
23a	*Iste confessor domini*	FB	Confessors
24a	*Jesu corona virginum*	FB	Virgins
Layer 2			
2b	*Christe redemptor omnium*	3v	Christmas
3a	*A solis ortus cardine*	3v	Christmas
5a	*Audi benigne conditor*	3v	Quadragesima 1
6a	*Aures ad nostras deitatis*	3v	Quadragesima 2–4
7a	*Vexilla regis prodeunt*	3v	Passion Sunday
8a	*Ad caenam agni providi*	3v	Easter
8b	*Ad caenam agni providi*	FB	Easter
20b	*Exsultet caelum laudibus*	FB	Apostles
Occasional Hymns			
6b	*Aures ad nostras deitatis*[a]	3v	Quadragesima 2–4
8c	*Ad caenam agni providi*[b]	FB	Easter
10a	*Festum nunc celebre*[c]	3v	Ascension
13b	*Pange lingua gloriosi*[c]	3v	Corpus Christi
15c	*Ave maris stella*[d]	3v	BVM
21b	*Deus tuorum militum*[e]	3v	One martyr
25a	*Proles de caelo dedit*[f]	3v	St Francis

[a] Probably an incorrect attribution in Montecassino 871.

[b] Two versions derived from no. 8b, probably the work of an anonymous arranger.

[c] An authentic early hymn, not part of the cycle.

[d] Two voices composed for the superius of no. 15a. The rubric suggests they are the work of another composer.

[e] Two voices composed for the superius of no. 21a, perhaps by Du Fay, perhaps by an anonymous arranger.

[f] An authentic hymn probably dating from the 1440s.

Italian melodies, with three exceptions that fall in the Common of Saints: *Sanctorum meritis* (Stäblein 70),[53] a Cistercian melody that did find its way to Italian sources outside the Order; *Iste confessor domini* (Stäblein 146), a melody spread by the Dominicans in France and Germany, though rarely in Italy (Stäblein knew no early sources); and *Jesu corona virginum* (Stäblein 115), found in northern Italy with this text. The origins of this tradition seem to be in the chapel of Martin V, where the only liturgical book produced in the chapel itself for which we have records is precisely a book of hymns: on 7 September 1428 Jehan Pigouche, *custos iocalium* of the chapel, was paid 12 florins and 35 solidi for the 'factura unius libri ymnorum ad usum dicte capelle'.[54]

The gap in Du Fay's hymn cycle points to two possible times when he might have composed the first layer. Chronologically the first of these is the six months from August 1433 to February 1434, immediately after he left the papal chapel but before he became *maestro di cappella* in Savoy on 1 February 1434.[55] We have no idea where he was during that time, but he may have written the hymns piecemeal and sent them on to Rome since he had retained his official post as a papal singer. One of the most intriguing aspects of this hypothesis is that, in terms of the liturgical calendar, these six months cover exactly the period for which we have Du Fay hymns in Bologna Q 15, that is from Advent until shortly before Purification. The beginning of his duties in Savoy, including the wedding of Louis and Anne of Lusignan, may have precluded his completion of the cycle in time for the rest of the hymns to be available to the scribe of Bologna Q 15.

In this respect it is worth noting that Du Fay clearly wanted to keep his connection with the papal chapel and his prerogatives there alive during his absence, which he regarded as a temporary leave. This can be gathered from a declaration the pope made in 1435, stating that an unnamed number of his singers then absent were to be treated as if they were present, as long as they had been in the chapel in July of 1434, when Du Fay was absent, and then appending a clause that mentions Du Fay and a few others to be included as well.[56] This language indicates that Du Fay, like the other singers, had taken some action before leaving to ensure the continuity of his connection with the chapel.

---

[53] Melody numbers in Bruno Stäblein (ed.), *Hymnen I. Die mittelalterlichen Hymnenmelodien des Abendlandes* (MMMA 1; Kassel, 1956).

[54] ASV, IE 387, fo. 75ᵛ. Pigouche is referred there as *clericus capelle*, but time and again he also refers to himself as the custodian of the jewels.

[55] The last order of payment for Du Fay's salary in Rome is 8 July 1432, and is for the month of July, so presumably he was in the chapel until the end of that month (ASR, Fondo Camerale I, 827, fo. 101ᵛ). His first payment in Savoy, dated 21 Mar. 1434, mentions that he had been *maestro di cappella* there since 1 Feb. (AST, Sezione II, Inventario 16, Pacco 35, Registro 79, fo. 464ᵛ).

[56] ASV, RS 303, fos. 90ʳ–91ʳ.

More plausible as a date for the first section of the hymn cycle, however, is the period going from the summer of 1435 to Easter of 1436. Du Fay returned from his leave in Savoy in early June of 1435. He may have written some of the hymns in Savoy, particularly the three pieces that do not follow the main Italian melodic tradition. But the writing of the cycle *per se* would have begun in this case with Ascension and St John Baptist, continuing throughout that year and the early winter of 1436. But as Easter of 1436 approached a number of circumstances arose that may well have deflected him from finishing the cycle, circumstances connected with Eugene's decision to break with tradition and officiate at the dedication of Santa Maria del Fiore, as well as the decision to transfer the curia to Bologna at about the same time. The outward sign of the first of those decisions was the presentation of the golden rose to the cathedral itself, which took place on Sunday, 18 March, but preparations for such a momentous event probably involved the curia and left little time for other preparations.[57] Unless we assume that Du Fay could write a work as complicated as *Nuper rosarum flores*, which refers to that event, in less than a week, he probably knew the plans before 18 March. Further, as Craig Wright has shown in his recent study of *Nuper rosarum flores*, Du Fay also wrote the plainsong *prosa* for that ceremony.[58] In 1436 the first Sunday in Lent fell on 26 February, Palm Sunday on 1 April (it was a leap year), Easter on 8 April. Less than a fortnight after Easter, on 18 April, the papal court left Florence for Bologna. Even though the hymns are very modest works that could be quickly written, it is also easy to see why, under the circumstances, Du Fay may have decided to put aside the cycle for a short time. If he finished it in 1437, then the additional hymns, unlike one or two pieces that may be slightly later but do appear in Bologna Q 15, did not reach the compiler of that source.

In any event, that the papal chapel regarded Du Fay's hymns as theirs is also suggested by the presence of virtually the entire cycle, along with a number of derived works, in the earliest collection of music for the office we have from the papal chapel, namely Vatican CS 15, which opens with Du Fay's cycle, including his settings of *Sanctorum meritis*, *Iste confessor domini*, and *Jesu corona virginum*, the three hymns where he used as a cantus firmus a melody from outside the main Italian tradition (see Table 3.7).[59] Otherwise he uses the

[57] In this respect it is worth noting that Du Fay's use of the plural, 'rosarum flores', is correct in that the actual object, several examples of which survive, had more than one bud. See Charles Burns, *Golden Rose and Blessed Sword: Papal Gifts to Scottish Monarchs* (Glasgow, 1970), pls. ii and vi. The recipient of the rose was supposed to be a secret, but the news might have leaked out.

[58] Wright, 'Du Fay's *Nuper rosarum flores*'.

[59] See Tom R. Ward, *The Polyphonic Office Hymn, 1400–1520: A Descriptive Catalogue* (Renaissance Manuscript Studies 3; Neuhausen, 1980), 15–17.

TABLE 3.7. Hymns of Du Fay and derived pieces in Vatican CS 15

Fo.	Incipit	Layer	No. in Appendix
4ᵛ	*Conditor alme siderum*	1	= 1a
5ᵛ	*Christe redemptor omnium / ex patre*	1	= 2a
7ᵛ	*Christe redemptor omnium / conserva*	1	= 16b -4
15ᵛ	*Audi benigne conditor*	2	= 5a
18ᵛ	*Aures ad nostras deitatis*	2	= 6a
20ᵛ	*Vexilla regis prodeunt*	2	cf. 7a (S: Du Fay, T: new, FB?)
22ᵛ	*Vexilla regis prodeunt*	2	= 7a
23ᵛ	*Ad caenam agni providi*	2	= 8a
29ᵛ	*Veni creator spiritus*	1	= 11a
29ᵛ	*Veni creator spiritus*	1	cf. 11a (S: Du Fay, T: new, FB)
32ᵛ	*O lux beata trinitas*	1	= 12a
34ᵛ	*Pange lingua gloriosi*	1	= 13a
37ᵛ	*Ut queant laxis resonare*	1	= 18a
39ᵛ	*Aurea luce et decore roseo*	1	= 19a
41ᵛ	*Aurea luce et decore roseo*	1	= 19a
50ᵛ	*Christe redemptor omnium / conserva*	1	= 16b
53ᵛ	*Exsultet caelum laudibus*	1	= 20a
55ᵛ	*Exsultet caelum laudibus*	1	= 20b
56ᵛ	*Deus tuorum militum*	1	= 21a
56ᵛ	*Deus tuorum militum*	1	cf. 21a (S: Du Fay, T, A, B: new)
58ᵛ	*Sanctorum meritis inclita*	1	= 22a
62ᵛ	*Iste confessor*	1	cf. 23a (S: Du Fay, T, CT: new)
62ᵛ	*Iste confessor domini*	1	= 23a
63ᵛ	*Iste confessor*	1	cf. 23a (S: Du Fay, T, CT: new)[a]
66ᵛ	*Jesu corona virginum*	1	cf. 24a (S: Du Fay, T, CT: new)
67b	*Jesu corona virginum*	1	cf. 24a (S, T: Fay, A, B: new)
67ᵛ	*Jesu corona virginum*	1	= 24a
68ᵛ	*Urbs beata Jerusalem*	1	cf. 14a (S: Du Fay, T: new, FB)
69ᵛ	*Urbs beata Jerusalem*	1	= 14a
69ᵛ new)	*Urbs beata Jerusalem*	1	cf. 14a (S: Du Fay, T: new,[b] A, B:

ᵃ Duplicate of the version on fo. 62ᵛ.

ᵇ Tenor is the new tenor added on fo. 62ᵛ.

Italian melodic tradition. In this respect we must remember that the years 1433–8 represent an extremely unstable period for the papal curia, and it is unwise to expect what Tom Ward has called 'the monophonic tradition of the papal court'[60] to be reflected in Du Fay's settings at a time when the papal court was using by and large Florentine chant books. The hymns, I believe, do

[60] Ward, 'Hymn. III. Polyphonic Latin'.

represent Du Fay's largest contribution to the repertory of the papal chapel while he was a member, and this was in fact the perception of the papal singers at the end of the fifteenth century.

A special problem is presented by the one piece by Du Fay that has a rubric associating it with the papal chapel, namely the Sanctus 'Ave verum corpus', found in Bologna Q 15 and Trent 90, 92, and 93,[61] which carries the rubric 'papale' in Trent 92. In a perceptive study of the piece David Fallows suggested that it was intended for an alternation of two ensembles, one consisting of choristers and their master and the other an adult choir. The coexistence of such ensembles, though not their performance together in a piece as elaborate as Du Fay's Sanctus, is documented for numerous northern churches in the early fifteenth century, but choristers were not employed by the papal chapel except for two periods. The first goes from June 1425 to November 1427, when, as mentioned, a number of choristers under the tutelage of Nicholas Grenon were part of the chapel. At this time, however, Du Fay was in Laon and Bologna, and he did not arrive in Rome until nearly a year after Grenon's departure. The second period when choristers were used was in Bologna, where the cameral mandates record for the first time in October 1437 a payment to four choristers, three from Liège—Guillaume Scoblant, Pierre de Bomel, and Jan Jonckin—and one from Narni, Lodovico Bernardi. Unlike the previous experiment with choristers, which ended abruptly if amicably with the departure of Grenon and all his charges except Poignare, the second group petered out gradually. Scoblant left in March 1438 and was not replaced, Lodovico's voice changed and he became an adult member of the chapel in January 1439, Jonckin's did the same in April 1441, and the lone chorister, Pierre de Bomel, left the chapel in November of that year.[62] This period does not overlap with Du Fay's stay in the chapel, which ceased at the end of May 1437. But our primary source for information about the membership of the chapel, the series of *Mandata cameralia* and the corresponding series of *Introitus et exitus* in the Vatican Archives and the Archivio di Stato in Rome, do not always tell the whole story. We know that Du Fay was in the papal chapel in some capacity before his first payment is recorded, and where we know the dates of induction of singers from the *Liber officialis*,[63] we can see that in some cases there is a lapse of several months before the first salary is recorded. Further, I have found something like half a dozen members of the curia who in supplications do refer to themselves as papal singers, but whose

---

[61] Bologna Q 15, nos. 135–7, Trent 90, fos. 277ᵛ–279ʳ, Trent 92, fos. 213ᵛ–215ʳ, Trent 93, fos. 350ʳ–352ᵛ.

[62] ASR, Fondo Camerale I, Registro 828, fos. 136ʳ–234ᵛ, *passim*, Registro 829, fos. 2ʳ–110ᵛ, *passim*. More likely Pierre de Bomel rejoined the papal chapel as adult singer in October 1442 (ASR 829, fo. 182ʳ), when one Petrus Langhe begins his service.

[63] Ibid., Registro 1711, fos. 90ʳ–92ʳ, *passim*.

names are never given in the monthly salary lists. These may have been the extraordinary singers whose services were requested only on certain occasions. In any case, one entry unrelated to the chapel in the *Introitus et exitus* for December 1436 indicates that the choristers were already in Bologna. In a single entry it records the payment on 28 December 1436 of twelve florins to Du Fay for his robes, and ten florins to Master Filippo da Rimini, 'pro docendo grammaticam pueris cappellae'.[64] In other words, there were choristers in the papal chapel in early 1437, and Du Fay may have used them for his Sanctus. This piece is probably his valedictory to the chapel itself. May 1437 was his last month as a papal singer, and thus the last major papal ceremony in which he ever sang was the Feast of Corpus Christi, which in 1437 fell on 30 May and for which this Sanctus with its trope is uniquely appropriate.

This date, however, may be too late for the Sanctus, which is copied in Bologna Q 15. Another possibility is that in fact the Sanctus was written in Bologna to be performed by the papal singers with the choirboys. On 20 February 1426, shortly after Du Fay's arrival in Bologna (I assume he came to Bologna together with Robert Auclou), Auclou signed an order of payment for Toussaint de la Ruelle, a papal singer who had stayed in the city on his way to Rome, bringing with him two new choirboys for the papal chapel, Guibert Nettelet and Pierre Chareton.[65] Given that Du Fay was working for the papal legate, that the master of the children in the papal chapel was Grenon, and that all the choristers, including the two new recruits, were from Cambrai, he may have composed the Sanctus either for Corpus Christi 1426 or 1427. Sending the piece to Rome would have been the simplest thing at the time since there was throughout the period a constant stream of couriers going back and forth between Aleman's court and the curia. The possibility of the Sanctus being composed in 1427 is interesting also in that, despite stylistic differences between this piece and the *Missa Sancti Jacobi*, they are the only two works in Du Fay's canon where certain textural experiments were carried out by the composer.[66]

Du Fay, however, is an exception to the pattern of papal singers in the early fifteenth century. For the most part they were not composers and I do not believe that the chapel itself was then an institution where a composer would have found artistic as opposed to purely ecclesiastic patronage. In this respect the dukes of Savoy presented him with a more encouraging environment, and his loyalty to them, which was to last across the long decade of the Schism and

[64] Mandate of payment ibid., Registro 828, fo. 108ᵛ, payment recorded in ASV, IE 400, fo. 80ᵛ.
[65] Planchart, 'Du Fay's Benefices', 127 n. 40.
[66] See Alejandro Enrique Planchart, 'Parts with Words and without Words: The Evidence for Multiple Texts in Fifteenth-Century Masses', in Stanley Boorman (ed.), *Studies in the Performance of Late Medieval Music* (Cambridge, 1983), 237–42.

beyond, shows to what extent this was important to him. Nevertheless, he did contribute some of the earliest monuments of polyphonic music we have that were specifically written for the papal chapel, just as in later decades he apparently continued to send his works to Rome—much to our benefit, since it is only from Roman sources that we have such a work as his *Ave regina* of 1464. The Roman curia may not always have understood the works of their musicians, but they saved them from destruction even long after they were obsolete, and for this, among other things, we must always be grateful to the countless archivists and librarians that kept this extraordinary heritage for us.

Appendix: The Hymns of Guillaume Du Fay

No.	Hymn and sources[a]	Type	Feast
1a	*Conditor alme siderum* (23)[b] Bologna Q 15, no. 311b (du fay) Modena α.X.1.11, fo. 1ʳ (Dufay) Munich 14274, fo. 81ᵛ Trent 92, fo. 61ʳ (dufay)	FB	Advent *in adventu domini* *Sabbato in adventu domini ad vesperas*
2a	*Christe redemptor omnium/ex patre* (71) Bologna Q 15, no. 313 (du fay) Montecassino 871, p. 295 Trent 92, fo. 134ʳ (dufay)	FB	Christmas *in natale domini*
2b	*Christe redemptor omnium/ex patre* (71) Modena α.X.1.11, fo. 1ᵛ (Dufay)	3v	Christmas *In nativitate domini ad vesperas*
3a	*A solis ortus cardine* (53)[c] Aosta, fo. 219ʳ Modena α.X.1.11, fo. 2ᵛ (Dufay) Trent 92, fo. 238ᵛ ᵈ (G dufay)	3v	Christmas *Ad laudes*
4a	*Hostis Herodes impie* (53) Bologna Q 15, no. 313bis (du fay) Modena α.X.1.11, fo. 3ᵛ (Dufay) Trent 92, fo. 238ᵛ (G dufay)	3v	Epiphany *in epiphania* *In epiphania domini ad vesperas*
5a	*Audi benigne conditor* (55) Cambrai 29, fo. 157ᵛ Modena α.X.1.11, fo. 5ᵛ (Dufay) Montecassino 871, p. 298	3v	Quadragesima *In quadragesima*
6a	*Aures ad nostras deitatis preces* (714) Modena α.X.1.11, fo. 6ʳ (Dufay) Vatican SP B 80, fo. 228ᵛ	3v	Quadragesima *In diebus dominicis in xlma*

No.	Hymn and sources[a]	Type	Feast
6b	*Aures ad nostras deitatis preces* (714)[c] Montecassino 871, p. 297 (G. Dufay)	3v	Quadragesima
7a	*Vexilla regis prodeunt* (32₉) Cambrai 29, fo. 259ᵛ (-4th) Great St Bernard, fo. 1r (-4th) Modena α.X.1.11, fo. 6ᵛᶠ (Dufay) Montecassino 871, p. 299 Trent 92, fo. 72ʳ (-4th)	3v	Passion Sunday
8a	*Ad caenam agni providi* (3₆) Modena α.X.1.11, fo. 7ᵛ (Dufay) Trent 89, fo. 377ᵛ	3v	Easter
8b	*Ad caenam agni providi* (3₆) Modena α.X.1.11, fo. 8ʳ	FB	Easter
8c	*Ad caenam agni providi* (3₆)[g] Cividale 101, fo. 82ᵛ Merseburg, fo. 3ʳ Trent 89, fo. 377ᵛ	FB	Easter
9a	*Jesu nostra redemptio* (513) Bologna Q 15, no. 314bis (du fay) Modena α.X.1.11, fo. 8ᵛ (Dufay)	3v	Ascension *in ascensione domini* *In ascensione domini*
10a	*Festum nunc celebre* (512) Munich 14274, fo. 151ᵛ (Duffay) Trent 87, fo. 166ᵛ	3v	Ascension
11a	*Veni creator spiritus* (17) Bologna Q 15, no. 315 (du fay) Florence 112bis, fo. 5ᵛ (Dufay) Modena α.X.1.11, fo. 9ᵛ (Dufay) Montecassino 871, p. 305 Munich 14274, fo. 55ʳ (-5th) Trent 92, fo. 30ʳ (Dufay) Trent 93, fo. 357ᵛ (no ct) Vatican SP B 80, fo. 184ʳ	3v	Pentecost *in pentecosten* *In festo pentecostes* *de sancto spiritu*
12a	*O lux beata trinitas* (22₃) Bologna Q 15, no. 315bis (du fay) Modena α.X.1.11, fo. 11ᵛ (Dufay) Montecassino 871, p. 309 (G dufay) Trent 92, fo. 14ʳ (Dufay) Vatican SP B 80, fo. 184ᵛ	3v	Trinity *in festo sanctissimae trinitatis* *In festo trinitatis*
13a	*Pange lingua gloriose* (56) Bologna Q 15, no. 316bis Modena α.X.1.11, fo. 10ᵛ (Dufay) Trent 92, fo. 236ʳ (Dufay)	3v	Corpus Christi *In festo corporis christi*

No.	Hymn and sources[a]	Type	Feast
13b	*Pange lingua gloriose* (56) Trent 92, fo. 238[v] (Dufay)	3v	Corpus Christi
14a	*Urbs beata Jerusalem* (140) Bologna Q 15, no. 317bis (du fay) Modena α.X.1.11, fo. 14[v] (Dufay)	3v	Dedication *in dedicatione ecclesiae* *In dedicatione ecclesiae*
15a	*Ave maris stella* (67) Bologna Q 15, no. 318 Bologna 2216, p. 25 Munich 14274, fo. 81[v]	FB	BVM
15b	*Ave maris stella* (67) Bologna Q 15, no. 318b Modena α.X.1.11, fo. 4[v] (Dufay)	3v[h]	BVM *in festivitatibus gloriosae virginis mariae*
15c	*Ave maris stella* (67) Trent 92, fo. 236[vi] (dufay)	3v	BVM
16a	*Christe redemptor omnium/conserva* (71) Bologna Q 15, no. 318bis (du fay) Vatican SP B 80, fo. 182[r]	FB	All Saints *in honore omnium sanctorum* *In festo omnium sanctorum*
16b	*Christe redemptor omnium/conserva* (71) Bologna Q 15, no. 319 (du fay) Modena α.X.1.11, fo. 15[v] (Dufay) Montecassino 871, p. 328 Trent 90, fo. 1[r] Trent 92, fo. 96[r] (Dufay) Trent 92, fo. 237[r] Verona 759, fo. 96[v]	3v[j]	All Saints *in honore omnium sanctorum* *In festo omnium sanctorum*
17a	*Tibi Christe splendor patris* (112) Bologna Q 15, no. 319bis (du fay)	FB	Angels (St. Michael) *in honore angelorum*
18a	*Ut queant laxis resonare* (151) Bologna Q 15, no. 320 (du fay) Modena α.X.1.11, fo. 12[v] (Dufay) Trent 92, fo. 239[v]	3v	St. John Baptist *in honore sancti iohannis baptistae* *In nativitate sancti iohannis baptistae*
19a	*Aurea luce et decore roseo* (152) Bologna Q 15, no. 320bis (du fay) Modena α.X.1.11, fo. 13[v] (Dufay) Vatican SP B 80, fo. 186[r]	3v	SS Peter and Paul *in honore apostolorum petri et pauli* *In festo apostolorum petri et pauli*
20a	*Exsultet caelum laudibus* (114) Bologna Q 15, no. 321 (du fay) Modena α.X.1.11, fo. 17[v] (Dufay) Munich 14274, fo. 71[r] Vatican SP B 80, fo. 189[v]	3v	Apostles *in honore apostolorum* *In festo unius apostoli vel plurimorum apostolorum* *de apostolis*

No.	Hymn and sources[a]	Type	Feast
20b	*Exsultet caelum laudibus* (114)	FB	Apostles
	Bologna Q 15, no. 321 (du fay)		*in honore apostolorum*
	Florence 112bis, fo. 11[r]		
	Modena α.X.1.11, fo. 17[v k] (Dufay)		*In festo unius apostoli vel plurimorum*
	Munich 14274, fo. 73[r]		*apostolorum*
21a	*Deus tuorum militum* (115)	FB	Martyr
	Bologna Q 15, no. 321bis (du fay)		*in natale unius martyris*
	Modena α.X.1.11, fo. 19[v] (du fay)		
	Trent 88, fo. 387[r]		
21b	*Deus tuorum militum* (115)	3v[l]	Martyr
	Vatican SP B 80, fo. 187[v m]		
22a	*Sanctorum meritis inclita* (70)	3v	Martyrs
	Bologna Q 15, no. 322 (du fay)		*in natale plurimorum martyrum*
	Modena α.X.1.11, fo. 18[v] (Dufay)		*In festo plurimorum martyrum*
	Trent 92, fo. 237[v] (G dufay)		*plurimorum martyrum*
23a	*Iste confessor domini* (146)	FB	Confessor
	Bologna Q 15, no. 322bis (du fay)		*in natale confessorum*
	Modena α.X.1.11, fo. 20[r] (Dufay)		*In festo unius confessoris*
	Trent 92, fo. 238[r] (G dufay)		*unius confessoris*
24a	*Jesu corona virginum* (115)[n]	FB	Virgins
	Bologna Q 15, no. 323bis (du fay)		*in natale virginis*
	Modena α.X.1.11, fo. 20[v] (Dufay)		*In festo unius virginis*
25a	*Proles de caelo dedit* (751)	3v	St Francis
	Modena α.X.1.11, fo. 21[v] (Dufay)		*De beato francisco*

[a] The versions in Vatican CS 15 are omitted in this table.

[b] Number in parentheses is the melody number in Stäblein, *Hymnen I*.

[c] Same music as no. 4a, *Hostis Herodes impie*.

[d] Indicated by a rubric at the end of *Hostis Herodes impie*.

[e] Probably an incorrect attribution in Montecassino 871.

[f] Has a polyphonic amen in addition to the chanted one.

[g] These are slightly different versions that seem derived from no. 8b; they are most likely the work of other composers.

[h] A contratenor to be added in place of fauxbourdon to the superius and tenor of no. 15a.

[i] Lower voices only: *Tenor, Contratenor super ave maris stella dufay sine faulxbourdon*. Space for the cantus left on fo. 237[r], but it was never entered. The rubric suggests they are the work of another composer.

[j] Texture consisting of two superius and tenor. Du Fay uses this texture in some of the sequence settings but in no other hymn.

[k] An alternate tenor 'a faulx bourdon' for the melody of no. 20a, copied on fo. 18[r].

[l] The melody of no. 21a provided with a new tenor and a contratenor, perhaps by Du Fay, perhaps by an anonymous arranger.

[m] Du Fay's superius with two new lower voices.

[n] Melody of *Deus tuorum militum*.

4

Liturgical (and Paraliturgical) Music in the Papal Chapel towards the End of the Fifteenth Century: A Repertory in Embryo

ADALBERT ROTH

> Those who delight the hearts of the audience with a certain sweet chant and for the rest of us as we celebrate the divine service, they render our acts of worship more pleasing and joyful.

WITH these words in the *arenga* of the first bull of privileges in favour of the college of the papal chapel, published in June 1473, Sixtus IV became the first pope in the fifteenth century to express his contentment with the musical services of the most consistent corporate group in his court chapel.[1] Never before in an official document of the Holy See had a pope referred explicitly to the musical duties of his singers.[2] This is not merely the rhetoric of some versatile papal secretary, but the pope himself who speaks to us, as the history of the papal chapel during the second half of the fifteenth century clearly testifies. Sixtus IV was not the real founder of the college of the

I gratefully acknowledge the kind assistance of Father Leonard E. Boyle, OP, who shared with me some of his vast learning.

[1] Sixtus IV, *Et si cunctis ecclesiasticis personis*, bull published 20 June 1473 (ASV, RV 662, fos. 312ʳ–313ᵛ): 'illi quadam suavi melodia audientium corda letificant ac ceteris gratiora et iocundiora obsequia celebrando divina officia nobis impendunt.' The college of the papal chapel as it emerged together with other colleges in the Roman curia during the decades after the return of Eugenius IV to Rome in 1442 was by no means merely a musical institution but primarily a liturgical one and was formed not only of singing chaplains (*cantores capellani*) but also of a group of officials whose duties exclusively concerned liturgical aspects of the service and/or administration: the chapel-master (*magister capellae*), the sacristan (*sacrista capellae*), the chaplains (*capellani missarum*), the masters of ceremonies (*clerici cerimoniarum*), and the clerics (*clerici campanarum*). This group was considerably reinforced during the first decades of the 16th c., when new permanent offices were established in the college. References hereafter to the papal chapel always comprise the entire personnel; this is essential for everything that follows.

[2] There is additional evidence for the interest the first Della Rovere pope took in his chapel, as opposed to his predecessors. See Adalbert Roth, *Studien zum frühen Repertoire der päpstlichen Kapelle unter dem Pontifikat Sixtus' IV. (1471–1484): Die Chorbücher 14 und 51 des Fondo Cappella Sistina der Biblioteca Apostolica Vaticana* (Capellae Apostolicae Sixtinaeque Collectanea Acta Monumenta, 1; Vatican City, 1991), 374–5.

papal chapel, or its reformer, as I have explained elsewhere, but of all popes of that century he was beyond doubt its most determined promoter.[3] His pontificate is of key importance for the history of perhaps the most venerable and influential institution in European musical history. At the request of his *cantores et capellani capellae* Sixtus IV published no fewer than four bulls, in which he principally confirmed the privileges of the college; in the history of the papal chapel no other pope had issued as many.[4] This alone is a clear demonstration of the extraordinary disposition of this pope to satisfy the particular requirements and wishes of his singers and of the other members of the college. Three of these bulls were published during the period between 1477 and 1483,[5] crucial years, as we shall see, for the history of the college.

During the last five years of Sixtus's pontificate, fundamental changes occurred in the composition of the college: between May 1479 and December 1483 sixteen new singers entered the service of the pope and their total number was increased from fourteen to twenty-four. Only eight of the *cantores capellani capellae* listed in May 1479 were still present in December 1483, which means that two-thirds of the musical establishment in the college consisted of fresh forces, at least half of whom had formerly been in the service of Ercole d'Este and Galeazzo Maria Sforza, in Ferrara and Milan, respectively.[6] Neither before nor during the remainder of the fifteenth century, with the possible exception of the Holy Year 1450, did the composition of the choir of the papal chapel change so radically within such a short period of time, namely three and a half years.[7] There is no question that the conspicuous increase of

---

[3] Adalbert Roth, 'Zur "Reform" der päpstlichen Kapelle unter dem Pontifikat Sixtus' IV. (1471–1484)', in Jörg O. Fichte, Karl-Heinz Göller, and Bernhard Schimmelpfennig (eds.), *Zusammenhänge, Einflüsse, Wirkungen: Kongreßakten zum ersten Symposion der Mediävisten in Tübingen, 1984* (Berlin and New York, 1986), 168–95 at 173–4; id., '"Primus in Petri aede Sixtus perpetuae harmoniae cantores introduxit": alcune osservazioni sul patronato musicale di Sisto IV', in Massimo Miglio *et al.* (eds.), *Un pontificato ed una città: Sisto IV (1471–1484). Atti del convegno Roma 3–7 dicembre 1984* (Istituto storico italiano per il Medio Evo, Studi storici, fasc. 154–62; Rome, 1986), 217–41; id., 'La storia della Cappella Pontificia nel Quattrocento rispecchiata nel Fondo Camerale I dell'Archivio di Stato di Roma', in Bianca Maria Antolini, Arnaldo Morelli, and Vera Vita Spagnuolo (eds.), *La musica a Roma attraverso le fonti d'archivio. Atti del Convegno internationale Roma 4–7 giugno 1992* (Lucca, 1994), 446–51.

[4] See Roth, 'Zur "Reform" der päpstlichen Kapelle', 178 ff. The confirmation of privileges, especially those of the curial colleges, belonged to a long series of administrative duties a newly elected pontiff had to undertake. The publication of the first bull in favour of the chapel was therefore a common administrative act and cannot be interpreted as a particular favour granted by the pope to the members of the papal chapel. In such a context it becomes evident that the institutional history of the college of the papal chapel cannot be studied without taking into account the curia as a whole. Only in this context will many, if not most, papal measures concerning the chapel find an adequate historical explanation.

[5] Ibid. 184–8.   [6] Ibid. 190–1.

[7] During the Holy Year of 1450 the fluctuation in the chapel, which at this point counted an average of fifteen *cantores capellani*, was more intense than usual: seven singers, who died or left the chapel, were replaced and only nine singers remained. Cf. ASR, Cam. I, 831, fos. 131ᵛ–178ʳ and the following footnote. The fluctuation before and after 1450 moved within normal limits: fewer than half the singers were replaced every three or four years. Nevertheless, the circumstances in 1450 were not comparable to those during the last years of the

the budget of the college by almost 50 per cent necessitated the consent of the competent curial authorities; it was probably ordered by the pope himself.[8]

Another event of great importance, contemporaneous with the remarkable changes in the college of the papal chapel, was the construction of a large new chapel in the Vatican palace, which, since the pontificate of Nicholas V, had been the papal residence in Rome. Although Nicholas's ambitious building project already included, as part of a completely rebuilt palace on the *Mons saccorum*, 'a sort of large chapel with a great vestibule',[9] it was only Sixtus IV who realized the project of a splendid new palace chapel.[10] Needless to say, the former general of the Franciscan order was not inspired by the lofty humanistic but unrealistic concepts of architecture described by Leon Battista Alberti in his famous treatise *De re aedificatoria*. Rather, he tackled the building project in a pragmatic manner. The new chapel was constructed on the foundations of the medieval chapel wing.[11] The demolition of the medieval *capella magna* probably began during the second half of 1475, since the construction of the new chapel must already have been under way early in 1476.[12] While the outer building was finished in 1481 at the latest, the interior furnishing and the decoration of the chapel continued until the summer of 1483. At the beginning of August the *novum maius sacrarium* finally became accessible and the pontiff did not hesitate to take advantage of the first opportunity to hear 'extra ordinem', that is, contrary to the ceremonial regulations, Vespers on the vigil of Saint Lawrence the Martyr (9 August) in his new chapel, whose construction he had eagerly followed at every stage.[13]

pontificate of Sixtus IV. These remarks are based on an examination of all extant payrolls of the papal chapel from the 15th c., preserved in two different series of registers kept by the officials of the Apostolic Chamber. A critical edition of these payrolls will be included in my forthcoming documentation for the history of the papal chapel 1417–1503. Some chapel rosters have already been made available by Pamela F. Starr for the years 1447–64 and by Richard Sherr for the period between 1484 and 1509. See Pamela F. Starr, 'Music and Music Patronage at the Papal Court, 1447–1464' (Ph.D. diss., Yale University, 1987), 269–86; Sherr, 'The Papal Chapel ca. 1492–1513 and its Polyphonic Sources' (Ph.D. diss., Princeton University, 1975), 25–42.

[8] The sum rose from fl. 161 in May 1479 (ASR, Cam. I, 847, fo. 3ᵛ) to fl. 241 in Dec. 1483 (849, fo. 245ʳ). See Roth, 'La storia della Cappella Pontificia', 446–7.

[9] Carroll W. Westfall, *In this Most Perfect Paradise: Alberti, Nicholas V and the Invention of Conscious Urban Planning in Rome 1447–55* (London, 1974), 149.

[10] Anna Maria Voci and Adalbert Roth, 'Anmerkungen zur Baugeschichte der alten und der neuen *capella magna* des apostolischen Palastes bei Sankt Peter', in *Collectanea II*, 13–102.

[11] Cf. Franz Ehrle and Hermann Egger, *Der vatikanische Palast in seiner Entwicklung bis zur Mitte des XV. Jahrhunderts* (Studi e testi per la storia del Palazzo Apostolico Vaticano, 2; Vatican City, 1935), 71–2; John Shearman, 'La costruzione della cappella e la prima decorazione al tempo di Sisto IV', in *La Cappella Sistina: I primi restauri, la scoperta del colore* (Novara, 1986), 26; Voci and Roth, 'Anmerkungen zur Baugeschichte', 58–61.

[12] On the medieval *capella magna* see A. M. Voci, *Nord o sud? Note per la storia del medioevale Palatium Apostolicum apud sanctum Petrum e delle sue capelle* (Capellae Apostolicae Sixtinaeque Collectanea Acta Monumenta, 2; Vatican City, 1992), *passim*; and Voci and Roth, 'Anmerkungen zur Baugeschichte', 52–5.

[13] *Il Diario romano di Jacopo Gherardi da Volterra dal vii settembre MCCCCLXXIX al xii agosto MCCCCLXXXIV*, ed. Evaristo Carusi (Rerum Italicarum Scriptores, 23/3; Città di Castello, 1904–6), 121, and Voci and Roth, 'Anmerkungen zur Baugeschichte', 64–71.

In March 1488 the two masters of ceremonies Agostino Patrizi and Johannes Burckard presented to Innocent VIII, successor of Sixtus IV on the *cathedra Petri*, the first normative text of the *Caeremoniale Romanae Curiae*, with which the highly complex and somewhat chaotic late medieval tradition of ceremonial texts, traceable back to the twelfth century, was brought to completion.[14] Their 'three books on ceremonies of the Roman curia' remained *de facto* effective until the Second Vatican Council. In the dedicatory letter to Innocent VIII, Patrizi explains the prime motives for the compilation of the new Ceremonial, which he describes as an extremely complicated and laborious task:[15]

1. The performance of the papal ceremonies had been characterized by uncertainty and confusion mainly caused by a chaotic and ambiguous late medieval tradition, which was open to contradictory interpretations.[16]

2. Papal ceremonies had been subject to continuous and drastic changes, which necessitated the emendation and compilation of new guidelines in a new Ceremonial.[17]

Patrizi explicitly alludes to the experience he had acquired in two decades of daily service in the papal chapel to underline his exceptional competence to undertake the task, which implies that the profound changes he refers to happened at least in part during the pontificate of Sixtus IV.[18] His remark is of great significance because it clearly shows that, along with the turnover in the singing personnel, the liturgy and ceremonial at the court of the first Della Rovere pope underwent so many important modifications as to make the redaction of a new papal ceremonial necessary.[19] That these three events—the building of the new palace chapel, the most radical renewal of the musical

---

[14] For a modern edition, which unfortunately has proved to be unreliable owing to problematic, if not incorrect, readings, see Marc Dykmans, *L'Œuvre d'Agostino Patrizi Piccolomini ou le cérémonial papal de la première renaissance*, 2 vols. (Studi e testi, 293–4; Vatican City, 1980–2). See also Bernhard Schimmelpfennig, *Die Zeremonienbücher der römischen Kurie im Mittelalter* (Bibliothek des deutschen historischen Instituts in Rom, 10; Tübingen, 1973), 136–40 and *passim*; Niels Krogh Rasmussen, '*Maiestas Pontificia*: A Liturgical Reading of Étienne Dupérac's Engraving of the *Capella Sixtina* from 1578', *Analecta Romana Instituti Danici*, 12 (1983), 109–48 at 114.

[15] Dykmans, *L'Œuvre d'Agostino Patrizi Piccolomini*, i. 58.   [16] Ibid. 5.   [17] Ibid. 6–7.

[18] Ibid. 6. The darkest period in the history of the papal chapel in the 15th c. was the pontificate of Paul II (1464–71), the predecessor of Sixtus IV. The archival sources indicate, for the first and only time in the century, a remarkable reduction of the singing personnel of the college during almost the entire pontificate. Even more significant, the office of the *magister capellae* remained vacant from Apr. 1465 to the end of his pontificate; and Jean Puyllois, a minor composer of the Ockeghem generation and member of the chapel since 1447, left papal service in 1468. See Roth, 'Zur "Reform" der päpstlichen Kapelle', 184 and 190; id., 'La storia della Cappella Pontificia', 452.

[19] An analytical study of the development of the ceremonial and the liturgy at the papal court during the 15th c. is still needed. Dykmans does not provide such a study in his edition. Instead, he presents summaries in French of the Latin texts of the ceremonial. There can be no doubt that a significant transformation of the papal ceremonial occurred during the second half of the 15th c., especially under the pontificate of Sixtus IV, and that this transformation was accompanied by changes in the musical practice in the chapel, a process that did not begin before the seventh if not the eighth decade of the Quattrocento.

personnel of the chapel in the fifteenth century, accompanied by magnanimous administrative measures, and the compilation of the first normative Ceremonial for the papal court—were not only contemporaneous but were interconnected, indeed part of a more comprehensive plan, is, in my opinion, much more than a mere supposition. This hypothesis is supported by a fourth event, which I consider an integral part of this evolution, embedded of course in a specific historical context. Around 1487 at the latest, more or less at the same time that the masters of ceremonies were about to complete their epochal opus, the singers began to create almost systematically and, as far as I can see, for the first time in the history of this institution, a repertory of polyphonic liturgical and paraliturgical music.

That all these singular events (and others not mentioned) were synchronized was not coincidental. Taken as a whole, they are the expression of a new papacy with representational requirements that had changed fundamentally.[20] After the Great Schism and the turbulent conciliar period, after decades of serious dissention, weakened both in spiritual authority and temporal power, during the pontificate of Nicholas V the papacy entered into a phase of restoration. By then confined to the territory of the Papal States by the councils, the papacy emerged as a temporal power in central Italy. From that time onwards the pontiffs concentrated almost all their political and economic ambitions on the Papal States, which became the most important and readily expandable source of revenue for the Renaissance papacy.[21] The popes, in short, became temporal rulers, who did not differ in the least from all the other competing sovereigns on the peninsula in terms of temporal government and consequently in terms of self-aggrandizement or self-representation.[22] It is therefore little wonder that the sovereign of the Patrimony of St Peter considered it unacceptable to be second, for example, to the dukes of Milan and Ferrara, who at the beginning of the 1470s began to build up their own court chapels with frenetic zeal.[23] By then it had become fashionable on the Italian peninsula to maintain costly musical institutions.

[20] The following outline of church history is based mainly on Hubert Jedin (ed.), *Handbuch der Kirchengeschichte*, iii/2 (Freiburg i. Br., 1968), 625 ff.; Erich Meuthen, *Das 15. Jahrhundert* (Oldenbourg Grundriß der Geschichte, 9; Munich, 1984), 75 ff.

[21] Bernhard Schimmelpfennig, 'Der Papst als Territorialherr im 15. Jahrhundert', in Ferdinand Seibt and Winfried Eberhardt (eds.), *Europa 1500. Integrationsprozesse im Widerstreit. Staaten, Regionen, Personen-Verbände, Christenheit* (Stuttgart, 1986), 84–95; and Peter Partner, 'The "Budget" of the Roman Church in the Renaissance Period', in Ernest F. Jacob (ed.), *Italian Renaissance Studies: A Tribute to the Late Cecilia M. Ady* (London, 1960), 256–77.

[22] This is my rendering of the German term 'Selbstdarstellung'.

[23] On the chapel of Galeazzo Maria Sforza see Guglielmo Barblan, 'Vita musicale alla corte sforzesca', in *Storia di Milano*, ix: *L'epoca di Carlo V (1536–1559)* (Milan, 1961), 787–852; William F. Prizer, 'Music at the Court of the Sforza: The Birth and Death of a Musical Center', *MD* 43 (1989), 141–94. On Ferrara, see Lewis Lockwood, *Music in Renaissance Ferrara 1400–1505: The Creation of a Musical Centre in the Fifteenth Century* (Oxford, 1984).

The first attempt to raise the papal chapel to the musical standard of the other court chapels in Italy, on the occasion of the Holy Year of 1475, was brought to naught by the plague, which raged in the Eternal City throughout 1476 and 1477.[24] More successful, on the other hand, was the second attempt during the last five years of Sixtus's pontificate, when the pope spent the considerable sum of approximately 9,400 gold florins exclusively on his singers; in comparison, Eugene IV spent roughly the same amount on the singers of the chapel during the almost sixteen years of his pontificate.[25] It is symptomatic of the spiritually and politically weak Renaissance papacy that enormous sums were invested in huge building programmes and in urban projects, in the promotion of science and culture, in representational purposes, etc., to create, or to correct and to project, a new—what we would call today—image of the papacy, despite the dramatic financial difficulties of the Roman curia.[26] Lavish patronage was not always synonymous with true wealth and abundance.[27]

Sixtus IV was the first pope of the fifteenth century who clearly took a personal interest in his court chapel, and during his pontificate, apparently for the first time, polyphonic liturgical music was considered an essential element of the papal profile, the display of the *maiestas pontificalis* or *maiestas pontificia*.[28] This exhibition of splendour and pomp took place principally during the *capellae papales* or *pontificales*, those solemn liturgical functions (Masses, Vespers, etc.) that the pope celebrated with his court in the course of the Church year on nearly fifty different feast-days.[29] During the late fifteenth and almost the entire sixteenth century, the normal setting for the *capellae papales* was the Cappella Sistina and only on special occasions the basilica of St Peter.[30] Needless to say, the polyphonic liturgical repertoire was created mainly for the *capellae papales*, which had been redefined in their liturgical and ceremonial

---

[24] Roth, *Studien zum frühen Repertoire*, 363.   [25] Roth, 'La storia della Cappella Pontificia', 450.

[26] For the *cantores capellani capellae*, papal impecuniosity proved to have rather unpleasant consequences under the pontificate of Innocent VIII, when the members of the college had to wait not just the usual one, two, or three weeks, but almost three years to be paid by the Apostolic Chamber (ASR, Cam. I, 851, fos. 142ᵛ and 160ᵛ; ASV, IE 518, fo. 138ʳ). During the period between July 1487 and Aug. 1491 they did not receive any money at all from the hands of the papal bankers (Cam. I, 852–4, *passim*; IE, 516–23, *passim*). This situation changed only with the accession of Rodrigo Borgia to the *cathedra Petri*. In the course of the eleven years of his pontificate, the college was again paid promptly and regularly by the Apostolic Chamber (Cam. I, 855, *passim*; IE, 524–35, *passim*).

[27] As far as the arts are concerned see Arnold Esch, 'Über den Zusammenhang von Kunst und Wirtschaft in der italienischen Renaissance: Ein Forschungsbericht', *Zeitschrift für historische Forschung*, 8 (1981), 179–222.

[28] *Maiestas pontificalis* is the term Agostino Patrizi used in the preface of his *Caeremoniale* addressed to Innocent VIII. See Dykmans, *L'Œuvre d'Agostino Patrizi Piccolomini*, i. 5. Almost a century later the concept had not changed, the expression only slightly: 'Maiestatis pontificiae dum in capella Xisti sacra peraguntur accurata delineatio' is the title of Étienne Dupérac's famous engraving from 1578. Cf. Rasmussen, '*Maiestas Pontificia*', *passim*.

[29] Cf. Bernhard Schimmelpfennig, 'Die Funktion der Cappella Sistina im Zeremoniell der Renaissancepäpste', in *Collectanea II*, 123–74.

[30] Ibid. 127–8 and 150–74.

aspects in the new *Caeremoniale Romanae Curiae* presented to Innocent VIII in 1488.[31]

The first choirbook that was compiled by the singers of the papal chapel is Vatican CS 35. Its compilation can be dated with precision: the oldest quire in the codex, which from the outset had been intended to open the choirbook, must have been copied in the middle of September 1487.[32] This is the oldest datable quire produced by a member of the chapel in the former archive of the Cappella Pontificia. The main corpus of CS 35 (fos. 23–187) was copied by a single scribe and was completed probably around 1490 or 1491, whereas the quires preceding or following the main corpus, copied in part by other hands, can be roughly dated in the first half of the 1490s. Thus, the compilation of the main corpus of the choirbook covered a time-span of about three or four years, while the addition of the remaining quires and the binding of the codex cannot have occurred before August 1492, but probably shortly thereafter.[33]

A glance at the codicological composition of the choirbook will help us understand how the singers of the papal chapel proceeded practically with the creation of a repertory. The main corpus of the codex consists of eleven independent single-quire booklets (or isolated codicological units), which were put together and linked to each other in part by attaching or inserting five other quires (which I call coherently attached or inserted codicological units) during the process of compilation.[34] The result is three fascicles (comprised of two or more quires) that together form the main corpus of CS 35.[35]

When CS 35 was put together, not all the single-quire manuscripts extant in the papal chapel were taken into account.[36] This means that the papal singers

[31] We shall see below that polyphony was not restricted to the *capellae papales*, but was also sung during Vespers of other important feasts that were celebrated by the college of the papal chapel.

[32] See A. Roth, 'Zur Datierung der frühen Chorbücher der päpstlichen Kapelle', in Ludwig Finscher (ed.), *Quellenstudien zur Musik der Renaissance*, 2: *Datierung und Filiation von Musikhandschriften der Josquin-Zeit* (Wolfenbütteler Forschungen, 26; Wolfenbüttel, 1983), 239–68 at 250.

[33] Adalbert Roth, 'Die Entstehung des ältesten Chorbuches mit polyphoner Musik der päpstlichen Kapelle: Città del Vaticano, Biblioteca Apostolica Vaticana, Fondo Cappella Sistina, Ms. 35', paper read at the conference *Die Entstehung einer musikalischen Quelle im 15. und im 16. Jahrhundert*, Herzog August Bibliothek, Wolfenbüttel, 13–17 Sept. 1992, in press.

[34] By 'quire' (in German: *Lage*) I understand (in accordance with *The Oxford English Dictionary*) any collection or gathering of leaves. A 'fascicle' on the other hand always consists, as we shall see, of more than one quire. A booklet is a manuscript consisting of one quire, e.g. quintern, sextern, septern, etc. A codicological unit is a gathering of leaves having its own identity irrespective of whether there is a text or not. With regard to choirbooks I should like to propose a more content-oriented definition: a codicological unit represents one or more complete pieces of music copied by one or more scribes in a continuous process on one distinct quire.

[35] A fascicle is always composed of two or more quires not necessarily written consecutively, that is of more than one codicological unit copied—immediately or subsequently—one after the other.

[36] This was, for example, the case with the single-quire manuscript CS 51, fos. 196–215. It contains the *Missa Salve diva parens* of Jacob Obrecht and was copied by the compiler of CS 35 approximately at the same time he began to put together the material for the first choirbook compiled in the papal chapel. Cf. Roth, *Studien zum frühen Repertoire*, 33–4.

performed not only out of choirbooks, but also out of single-quire manu-scripts.[37] One such single-quire manuscript (CS 197 with Josquin's *Missa L'homme armé super voces musicales*) has survived in the former archive of the papal chapel; others later were bound into other choirbooks of the *fondo Cappella Sistina*.[38] In at least one case this occurred more than eight decades after the particular single-quire manuscript had been copied.[39] This situation began to change only in 1497 when the post of a chapel scribe was estab-lished; thereafter the preparation of the performing material (choirbooks, single-quire manuscripts, etc.) followed a more organized and homogeneous course.[40]

It seems that the papal choir, in an effort to compile a repertoire of poly-phonic liturgical music, concentrated first on compositions of the ordinary of the Mass, which makes sense, since the majority of the *capellae papales* were Masses.[41] CS 35 and a considerable number of originally single-quire manu-scripts produced by a number of scribes during the years 1487 until around 1495 exemplify this effort. These were the first manuscripts of polyphony cer-tainly compiled in the papal chapel.

Regardless of differing opinions about the provenance and date of CS 14 and the main corpus of CS 51, these two choirbooks, whose importance was long underestimated, if not ignored, were not compiled in the papal chapel.[42] In any case, merely a decade after important changes in the papal chapel had

[37] Whereas plainchant was sung in the papal chapel as everywhere else out of choirbooks, polyphonic music for the most part was not. This practice is not only illustrated by the physical makeup of most of the older choir-books containing the polyphonic repertoires, but also by the tendency in later periods to prepare rather thin booklets or fascicles for special occasions. At least in the papal chapel, voluminous choirbooks were put together only during the late 15th and 16th cc., apparently as repositories for polyphonic repertoires that in greater part had become obsolete. I shall treat this question more extensively in a forthcoming publication.

[38] The choirbooks in question are CS 15, 41, 49, 51, 63, and 64. A detailed analysis of the genesis of the old-est repertory of polyphonic music preserved from the pontificates of Innocent VIII and Alexander VI is the sub-ject of a forthcoming study. Meanwhile, see José M. Llorens, *Capellae Sixtinae Codices musicis notis instructi sive manu scripti sive praelo excussi* (Studi e testi, 202; Vatican City, 1960), 21–9, 81–3, 100–2, 119–21; Sherr, 'The Papal Chapel', 214–17, 225–33, 253–6; id., *Papal Music Manuscripts in the Late Fifteenth and Early Sixteenth Centuries* (Renaissance Manuscript Studies, 5; Neuhausen-Stuttgart, 1996), 76–131, 145–56, and 192–200; Roth, *Studien zum frühen Repertoire*, 388 ff. and *passim*.

[39] This happened to the single-quire manuscript CS 64, fos. 3–13, containing the *Missa L'homme armé* of Marbrianus de Orto. It was incorporated in a choirbook that had been compiled during the 1570s by Johannes Parvus, scribe of the papal chapel *c.*1538–80. See Mitchell P. Brauner, 'The Parvus Manuscripts: A Study of Vatican Polyphony, ca. 1535 to 1580' (Ph.D. diss., Brandeis University, 1982), 23, 226, and 243–55.

[40] Rich illustrative material is provided by the choirbooks compiled by the chapel's scribes Jean Orceau and Johannes Parvus. See Sherr, 'The Papal Chapel', *passim*, and *Papal Music Manuscripts*; Jeffrey Dean, 'The Scribes of the Sistine Chapel 1501–1527' (Ph.D. diss., University of Chicago, 1984); and Brauner, 'The Parvus Manuscripts', *passim*.

[41] Schimmelpfennig, 'Die Funktion der Cappella Sistina', 150–70, lists fifty *capellae papales*, of which forty-three were *missae papales*.

[42] Roth, *Studien zum frühen Repertoire, passim*; Adalbert Roth, 'Napoli o Firenze? Dove sono stati compilati i manoscritti CS 14 e CS 51?', in Piero Gargiulo (ed.), *La musica a Firenze al tempo di Lorenzo il Magnifico: Congresso Internazionale di Studi, Firenze 15–17 giugno 1992* (Florence, 1993), 69–100.

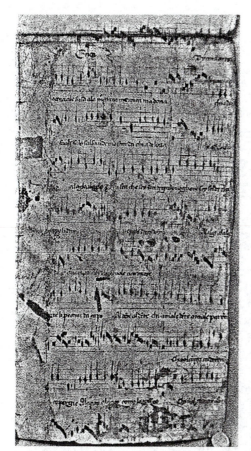

Plate 1. Egidi, fo. 1ʳ, Zacara: *Caciando per guastar/Ay cinci ay toppi*

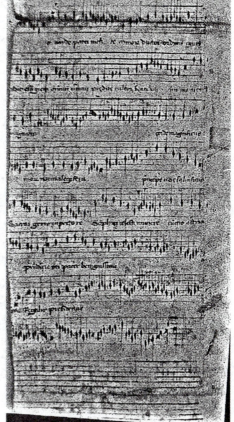

Plate 2. Egidi, fo. 1ᵛ, *Leonarde pater inclite*

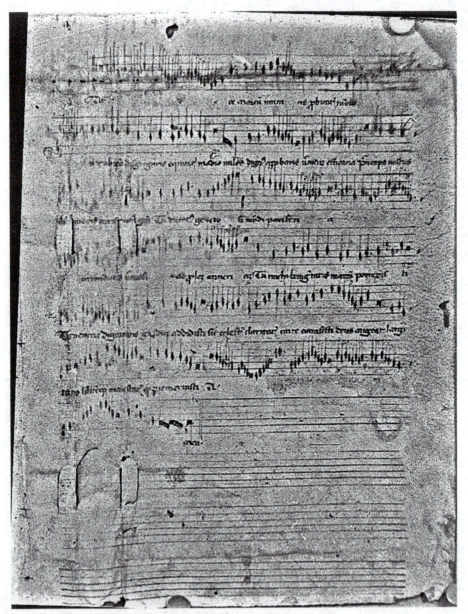

Plate 3. Egidi, fo. 2ʳ, *Marce Marcum imitaris*

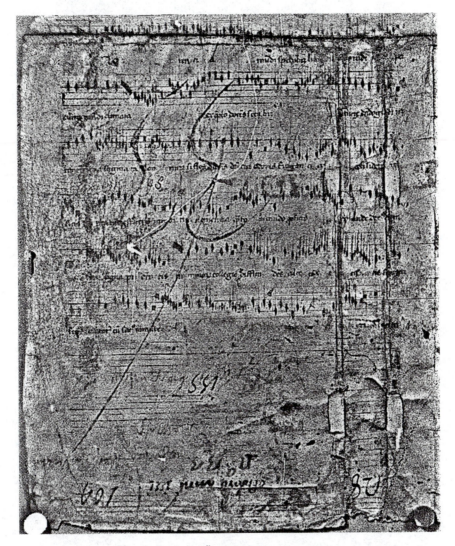

Plate 4. Egidi, fo. 2^v, *Florencia mundi speculum*

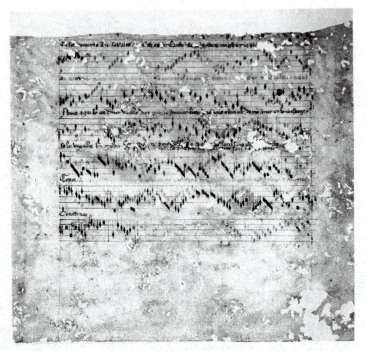

Plate 5. Cortona 2, fo. 1^r

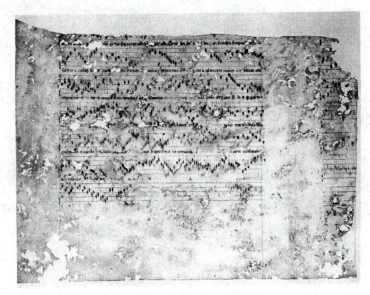

Plate 6. Cortona 2, fo. 1^v

Plate 7. Cortona 2, fo. 2ʳ

Plate 8. Cortona 2, fo. 2ᵛ

Pate 9. Cortona 1, offsetting of the recto side of the leaf onto the leather cover

Plate 10. The *maestro di cappella*, Ludovico Magnasco, receiving the Constitution of the papal chapel from Paul III. Photo, Biblioteca Vaticana, Vatican CS 611, fo. 1ᵛ

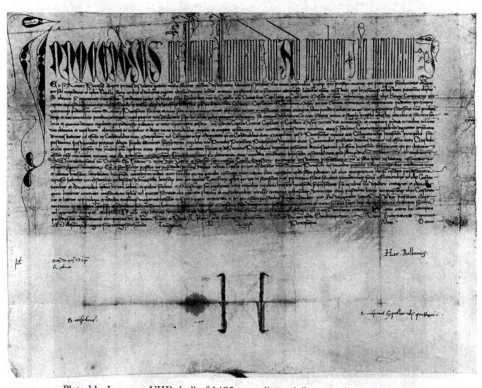

Plate 11. Innocent VIII's bull of 1492 according privileges to the papal chapel.
Photo, Biblioteca Vaticana, Vatican CS 703, no. 8

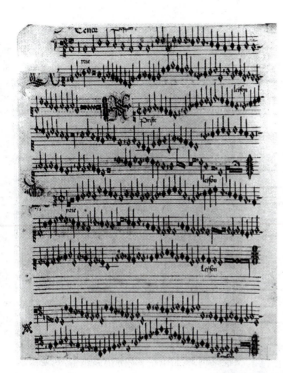

Plate 12(*a*). Josquin, *Missa L'homme armé super voces musicales*, Kyrie. Photo, Biblioteca Vaticana, Vatican CS 197, fo. 1[v]

(*b*). Josquin, *Missa L'homme armé super voces musicales*, Kyrie. Photo, Biblioteca Vaticana, Vatican CS 197, fo. 2[r]

Plate 13 (*top left*). Initial in Tenor of Agnus Dei III of Josquin, *Missa L'homme armé super voces musicales*. Photo, Biblioteca Vaticana, Vatican CS 197, fo. 10 verso

Plate 14 (*top right*). Initial in Cantus of Agnus Dei III of Josquin, *Missa L'homme armé super voces musicales*. Photo, Biblioteca Vaticana, Vatican CS 154, fo. 25 verso

Plate 15 (*left*). Initial in Bassus of Kyrie of Josquin, *Missa L'homme armé super voces musicales*. Photo, Biblioteca Vaticana, Vatican CS 154, fo. 3^v

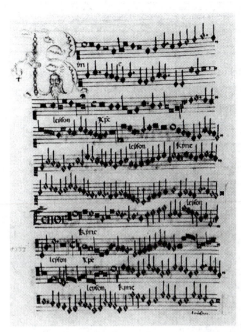

Plate 16(*a*). Josquin, *Missa La sol fa re mi*, Kyrie. Vatican CS 41, fo. 38ᵛ

(*b*). Josquin, *Missa La sol fa re mi*, Kyrie. Vatican CS 41, fo. 39ʳ

In gradus vnde nos descendant multiplicantes
Consimiliqz modo crescant antipodes vno.

Plate 17. Josquin, *Missa Fortuna desperata*, Agnus Dei I (T, B). *Misse Josquin* (Venice, 1502), fo. 13ᵛ

Plate 18. Josquin, *Missa Fortuna desperata*, Agnus Dei I (A, B). Photo, Biblioteca Vaticana, Vatican CS 41, fo. 60ʳ

Plate 19. Josquin, *Missa L'homme armé sexti toni*, Agnus Dei III (T, B). *Misse Josquin* (Venice, 1502), T, fo. 13ʳ; B, fo. 16

Plate 20. Josquin, *Missa L'homme armé sexti toni*, Agnus Dei III. Photo, Biblioteca Vaticana, Vatican CS 41, fo. 36ᵛ

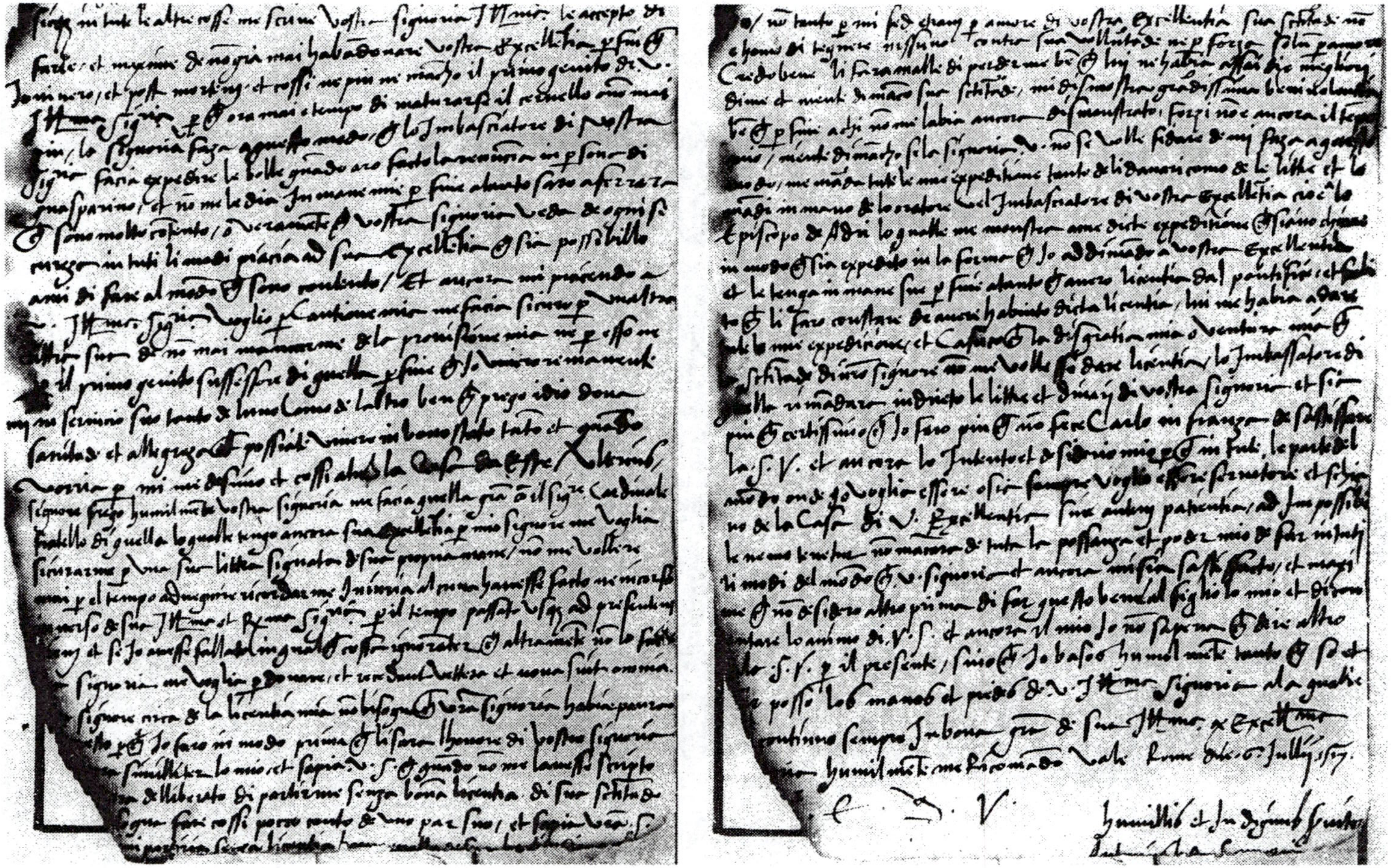

Plate 21. Letter of 6 July 1517 from Antonio Bidon to Duke Alfonso I d'Este. Modena, Archivio di Stato, Particolari, 'Bidone'

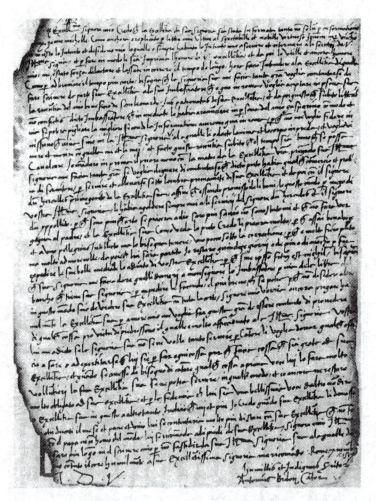

Plate 22. Letter of 7 November 1517 from Antonio Bidon to Duke Alfonso
I d'Este. Modena, Archivio di Stato, Particolari, 'Bidone'

occurred, a noteworthy international repertoire of more than sixty polyphonic cycles of the ordinary of the Mass was in use in the papal chapel.

A considerable number of the *capellae papales* were Vespers celebrated on the evening before particular feasts.[43] Indeed, during the first half of the 1490s the busy singers began to add polyphonic music for those occasions to their collection. This time their efforts resulted in CS 15, divided into three distinct sections. The first section (fos. 2–70) contains the most complete and by far the largest cycle of polyphonic hymns extant from the fifteenth century.[44] Based on Du Fay's famous hymn cycle, which was not completely incorporated by the compilers and does not cover all the Vespers celebrated normally at the papal court during the period in question, the cycle offers a separate musical setting for every strophe to be executed polyphonically.[45] Because of these gaps, Marbrianus de Orto and Josquin des Prez were called to the scene to compose some alternative or new hymn-settings.[46] Interestingly enough, these were copied by a different hand working in collaboration with the main scribe of the hymn section, and the task must have been accomplished within a short time, as the palaeographical and codicological analysis clearly shows. Richard Sherr originally dated the copying of the hymn section *c.*1492–5, but later proposed 1495–7.[47]

But the size of the hymn section suggests that the creation of the cycle in CS 15 covered a much greater span of time than the whole process of compilation. Even if we take into consideration that, apart from Du Fay's pieces, other hymns were of non-Roman origin or predate the events contemporary with the construction of the large new palace chapel (and this is the subject of this contribution), it is logical that the greater part of the anonymous settings were composed by members of the papal chapel.[48] The question inevitably arises

---

[43] The table offered by Schimmelpfennig, 'Die Funktion der Cappella Sistina', 150–70, is not complete as far as the late 15th c. is concerned. For example, only five of the twelve *vesperae papales* regularly celebrated are recorded.

[44] Rudolf Gerber, 'Römische Hymnenzyklen des späten 15. Jahrhunderts', *AfMw* 12 (1955), 50–73.

[45] It is the first collection in which the traditional alternatim practice in the performance of hymns, i.e. the alternation of chant and polyphonic settings, was systematically realized. Moreover, it is by far the largest cycle extant from the 15th c. (76 settings, 24 by Du Fay), which illustrates once again the ambitious endeavour of the papal singers to create an up-to-date repertoire of polyphonic liturgical music adequate to the papacy, whose representational needs had so radically changed. There seem to be good reasons to believe, however, that Du Fay did not compose his hymn cycle in Rome; it does not fit the liturgy of the papal court and uses a non-Italian melodic tradition. See Tom R. Ward, 'The Polyphonic Office Hymn and the Liturgy of Fifteenth-Century Italy', *MD* 26 (1972), 161–88 at 185. [For a different view, see Alejandro Planchart's contribution to this volume, Ch. 3.—Ed.]

[46] See Martin Picker, 'The Career of Marbrianus de Orto (ca. 1450–1529)', in *Collectanea II*, 529–57. More than half the settings form the earliest layer of the collection. According to Gerber most of these pieces were written at the end of the century ('Römische Hymnenzyklen', 50–73).

[47] Sherr, 'The Papal Chapel', 204–8; *Papal Music Manuscripts*, 65.

[48] It is noteworthy in this context that almost all the anonymous hymn settings that cannot be attributed to Du Fay (24) are ascribed to Josquin des Prez (2) or Marbrianus de Orto (3) in the source, and appear uniquely

whether the pieces ascribed to De Orto and to Josquin des Prez were the only ones composed on the occasion of the compilation of the hymn section in CS 15. Since this possibility also has to be taken into serious consideration on the grounds of the stylistic heterogeneity that characterizes the collection, one might further ask if other singers of the college of the papal chapel were not involved in the project. The first name that might be mentioned in this context is that of Gaspar van Weerbecke, who became a papal singer in February 1481 and played a leading role in the reorganization of the singers of the college during the first half of the 1480s.[49] But I am thinking also of minor figures like Bertrand Vacqueras, who entered the college as a singer in November 1483,[50] and—why not—even of Johannes Stockem *alias* de Prato, to whom is attributed a two-voice setting of *Ave maris stella* and who only figures in the payment rolls for thirteen months, that is, from September 1486 until September 1487.[51]

There is sufficient reason to assume that the project of creating the hymn cycle probably reached back into the pontificate of Innocent VIII (1484–92). As we have seen, all the known composers of the chapel became members of the college between 1481 and 1486, with the exception of Josquin des Prez, who entered the papal service only in June 1489. But the year 1489 is not only the *terminus post quem* for the settings ascribed to Josquin.[52] It has already been pointed out that they were copied together with the settings attributed to Marbrianus de Orto by a second scribe, when the main copyist of the hymn section was already at work.[53] This seems to suggest

in CS 15. See Tom R. Ward, *The Polyphonic Office Hymn, 1400–1520: A Descriptive Catalogue* (Renaissance Manuscript Studies 3; Neuhausen, 1980), *passim*.

[49] Cf. Gerhard Croll, 'Weerbeke, Gaspar van', *New Grove*, xx. 290–2.

[50] Cf. Richard Sherr, 'Vaqueras, Bertrandus', *New Grove*, xix. 528–9.

[51] Cf. Albert Seay, 'Stokem, Johannes de', *New Grove*, xviii. 165–6, and id., 'An "Ave maris stella" by Johannes Stochem', *Revue belge de musicologie*, 11 (1957), 93–108. The setting does not appear in CS 15, nor is it listed in Ward, *The Polyphonic Office Hymn 1400–1520*. Fr. X. Haberl, *Die römische 'schola cantorum' und die päpstlichen Kapellsänger bis zur Mitte des 16. Jahrhunderts* (Bausteine für Musikgeschichte, 3; Leipzig, 1888), was convinced that the 'Jo. de Prat.' who appears in the payment records for this period was Josquin des Prez and he has been followed in this by all other scholars. The knowledge that 'Jo. de Prat.' is really Johannes Stockem means that Josquin did not enter the chapel until June 1489, where he appears on payrolls as 'Judo. de Prez', and is listed under some variant of this name in all lists until Mar. 1494. A critical edition of all the extant payment rolls until 1503 will be included in my forthcoming documentation for the history of the college of the papal chapel during the 15th c., which will clarify statements concerning the personnel in Haberl, *Die römische 'schola cantorum'*. [On this subject, see also Pamela F. Starr, 'Josquin, Rome, and a Case of Mistaken Identity', *Journal of Musicology* 15 (1997), 43–65.—Ed.]

[52] The numbers in square brackets refer to the numeration in Ward, *The Polyphonic Office Hymn 1400–1520*: (1) *Ave maris stella* (Feasts of the Virgin): [104] *Monstra te esse matrem*, 4 voc. (strophe 4), fos. 43ᵛ–44ʳ. (2) *Nardi Maria pistici* (St Mary Magdalen): [409] *Honor decus imperium*, 4 voc. (strophe 2), fos. 46ᵛ–47ʳ.

[53] The numbers in square brackets refer again to the numeration in Ward, *The Polyphonic Office Hymn*: (1) *Lucis creator optime* (Sundays *per annum*): [392] *Quia mane iunctum*, 4 voc. (strophe 2), fos. 10ᵛ–11ʳ; [393] *Celorum pulset intimum*, 4 voc. (strophe 4), fos. 11ᵛ–12ʳ. (2) *Ut queant laxis* (St John Baptist): [603] *Ventris obstruso*, 4 voc. (strophe 4), fos. 38ᵛ–39ʳ.

that the two composers wrote the pieces explicitly attributed to them in CS 15 at a late stage, when the compilation of the hymn section was well under way.[54]

I cannot conclude my remarks on the hymn section without at least mentioning one important aspect: the hymn cycle in CS 15 is not restricted exclusively to *vesperae papales*,[55] but provides in addition polyphonic hymn settings for feasts—and this is the great majority—for which the papal Ceremonial did not prescribe any such liturgical function.[56] Does this mean that the effort of the compilers of the hymn section was at least in part in vain? Certainly not. On the contrary, since the hymn cycle in CS 15 covers the whole Church year it provides us with a clue to understanding the essential function of the college of the papal chapel: to provide the daily liturgical service in the papal palace.[57] The *capellae papales*, of which the *vesperae papales* were only one element, constituted only a part of this service, although an essential one. The important point is that the hymns were not only performed polyphonically in the course of the *vesperae papales*, but also during those Vespers which were celebrated by the members of the college on all other occasions, usually in the small palace chapel.[58] Consequently we have to ask ourselves if the performance of

[54] Interestingly enough, some of the settings concern hymns that are specific to Roman use. See above, n. 45.

[55] According to the testimony of Johannes Burckard, master of ceremonies of the papal chapel (1483–1506), during the last two decades of the 15th c. *vesperae papales* were celebrated on the following occasions: Vigil of Christmas [152, 162, 170], Circumcision [60 and 65 or 385 and 386 or 392 and 393], Epiphany [298, 300], Easter [Vespers in chant], Ascension [370–1], Pentecost [622, 642–4], Trinity Sunday [418–19], Corpus Christi [451, 452a, 471], St John Baptist [592, 603], SS Peter and Paul [66–7], All Saints [152, 154–5], All Souls [Vespers in chant]. In addition the Ceremonial of the papal court provided *vesperae papales* for Annunciation [83, 104–6], Assumption [83, 104–6], Nativity of the Virgin [83, 104–6], and Dedication of the Basilicas of St Peter, St John Lateran, and St Paul [567–9]. Cf. Johannes Burckard, *Liber Notarum ab anno MCCCCLXXXIII usque ad annum MDVI*, ed. Enrich Celani, 2 vols. (Rerum italicarum scriptores, 32/12; Città di Castello, 1906), i. 91–2 and *passim*; Dykmans, *L'Œuvre d'Agostino Patrizi Piccolomini*, ii. 318–19 and *passim*. The numbers in square brackets refer to the numeration in Ward, *The Polyphonic Office Hymn*.

[56] These are all the hymn settings for the Sundays of Advent [184, 192–4], Sundays *per annum* [385–6, 392–3], weekdays of Lent [60, 65], Sundays of Lent [72, 80–1], Passion Sunday [682, 687–8], Octave of Easter [1a, 810], Saturdays *per annum* [418–19], St Mary Magdalen [409], *Cathedra Petri* [495], St Michael [562–3], Common of Apostles [231a, 231b, 237], Common of One Martyr [208–9, 215], Common of Many Martyrs [545–6, 548], Common of One Confessor [335–6, 344–5], and Common of One Virgin [208, 349–50]. The numbers in square brackets refer to the numeration in Ward, *The Polyphonic Office Hymn*.

[57] The constitutions, confirmed by Paul III with a brief dated 17 Nov. 1545, are still preserved in the former archives of the papal chapel in the MS CS 611, and have been published most recently by Haberl, *Die römische 'schola cantorum'*, 96–108. Chapters XLIII–LLX (ibid. 106–8) meticulously describe the daily liturgical service the college had to render.

[58] In 1493 Johannes Burckard refers explicitly to daily liturgical duties of the college (cited from *Liber Notarum*, 454): 'Dominica IIII adventus, que fuit XXII dicti mensis decembris, SS. D. N. Rome existente, non fuit missa publica more solito in capella maiore celebrata propter periculum pestis, sed in capella parva per cantores, prout in privatis diebus fieri solet. . . . In festis sanctorum Stefani et Ioannis evangeliste non fuit habita capella propter periculum pestis; sed in parva capella palatii cantores cum capellano dixerunt missam ordinariam prout in privatis diebus fieri consuevit.' Eight years earlier Burckard refers to the omission of the *vesperae papales* or, as he used to call them on other occasions, of the *officium vespertinum* on All Souls' Day 1485 (ibid. 121–2): 'Die

polyphonic liturgical music was actually restricted to the *capellae papales*. But this argument and other subjects associated with it merit a more thorough examination in a separate study.

The year 1495 was politically one of the most turbulent in the pontificate of Alexander VI, yet it was also one of the most memorable for the singers of the papal chapel, since in that year, shortly before the advent of the new century, they were provided with the opportunity to meet with their colleagues in the French royal chapel.[59] Clearly related to this event, as Richard Sherr has shown, is the compilation of the second section of CS 15 (fos. 71–160), which contains fourteen settings of the Magnificat, mostly copied by a French hand, perhaps of a member of the French royal chapel who may have remained in Rome when Charles VIII set out for Naples. Thus a part of the Magnificat settings may be considered as French repertoire.[60] About the third section of CS 15 (fos. 161–269), I would only wish to observe that roughly 40 per cent of the pieces are polyphonic settings of Marian antiphons, which perfectly fit the purpose explained above.[61]

What I have delineated is only the beginning of a development from the first signs to the first concrete steps, so to speak, in the course of which polyphonic liturgical music became a regular practice in the papal chapel to enrich the solemn *capellae papales* with a more sophisticated, more splendid, acoustical dimension.[62] Around the middle of the 1490s the conditions for such a

sequenti, 1 novembris, festo omnium sanctorum . . . hora vesperorum, papa, paratus . . . venit ad capellam predictam . . ., ubi omissis vesperis festi a cantoribus dicte sunt vespere pro defunctis . . .'.

These remarks of the master of ceremonies—many others could be cited—not only show that the everyday duties of the college described in the constitutions of 1545 had long been a reality, they also call to mind the principal function of every ecclesiastical institution, which is to organize and guarantee the liturgical service, the *cultus divinus* mentioned in so many papal documents relevant in this regard.

[59] For the most detailed description of these events see Ludwig von Pastor, *Geschichte der Päpste seit dem Ausgang des Mittelalters*, iii: *Geschichte der Päpste im Zeitalter der Renaissance von der Wahl Innozenz VIII. bis zum Tode Julius II. Erste Abteilung: Innozenz VIII. und Alexander VI.* (Freiburg i. Br., 1924), 407–16; Kenneth M. Setton, *The Papacy and the Levant (1204–1571)*, ii: *The Fifteenth Century* (Memoirs of the American Philosophical Society, 127; Philadelphia, 1978), 448–82. At least a part of the personnel of the French royal chapel accompanied Charles VIII on his expedition into Italy during the years 1494 and 1495. See Lewis Lockwood, 'Music at Ferrara in the Period of Ercole I d'Este', *Studi musicali*, 1 (1972), 101–31 at 129–30.

[60] Sherr, 'The Papal Chapel', 158–9 and 214–15; *Papal Music Manuscripts*, 9–20, 60–5; Roth, *Studien zum frühen Repertoire*, 389–91.

[61] It is beyond the scope of this contribution to discuss such an intricate question as the use of what we call today 'motet' in papal liturgy and at the curia in general. Obviously, no problem exists for those pieces based on liturgical chant. These settings of antiphons, tracts, etc. should not be considered under this category. At this point, I should like to limit myself to proposing that especially those pieces that escape any unequivocal liturgical classification might have been performed more or less exclusively in a non-liturgical context, allowing us to enter into a more private sphere of the papal household, constituting something like what later was called *musica riservata*.

[62] The goal here is not to question whether the papal singers performed any polyphony before the last two decades of the century. There is no doubt that polyphony was occasionally performed in the papal chapel as far back as the 14th c. or even earlier. The aim of this contribution is to show that a series of essential interconnected parameters changed radically at the curia mainly during the pontificate of Sixtus IV, and that these new

practice had been created. The papal chapel disposed of a remarkable repertoire of polyphonic liturgical music for Mass and Vespers and even for other occasions or events, liturgical and non-liturgical, not mentioned here. But we should never forget that polyphony was always an exception, reserved for special occasions. Plainchant was, so to speak, the daily musical bread that even Josquin had to eat. And it was, I fear, plainchant to which Sixtus IV was referring in the *arenga* of the first bull of privileges published in favour of the college of the papal chapel.

conditions had a direct impact on the college of the papal chapel, leading to concrete consequences creating the prerequisites for what I have called in an earlier publication 'a regular practice of polyphony'. By this I mean that polyphony was regularly performed during the *capellae papales* and (this is a new suggestion or working hypothesis) even occasionally during the ordinary liturgical services the college had to guarantee every day. Pamela F. Starr's criticism of my view is based on a misunderstanding of the concept 'regelmäßigen Praxis polyphoner Vokalmusik', which she translates simply as 'practice of polyphony'. See Roth, 'Zur "Reform" der päpstlichen Kapelle', 189–94; Pamela F. Starr, 'Towards the Cappella Sistina: A Profile of the *Cappella Pontificia* during the Pontificates of Nicolas V, Calixtus III, Pius II, and Paul II (1447–1471)', in *Collectanea II*, 451–75 at 459–60 n. 27.

5

The Evolution of a Canon at the Papal Chapel: The Importance of Old Music in the Fifteenth and Sixteenth Centuries

JEFFREY DEAN

THE whole body of music performed by the singers of the papal chapel in the fifteenth and sixteenth centuries can be separated into three categories, distinguished by the varying degrees of permanence of individual compositions within the repertory. At one extreme we can place the very fluid body of 'new' music (new in the sense of its availability to the singers, not necessarily newly composed). Only a fraction of this music is apparent to us now. It was expensive to copy pieces into the big booklets and choirbooks that survive in the *fondo* Cappella Sistina: a typical mass of fourteen openings would have cost over 4 scudi around 1540, at a time when the monthly salary of singers in the papal chapel (among the best paid in Italy) was about 9 scudi and a printed book containing five masses could be bought for 1.20 scudi.[1] In

I wish to record my gratitude to the *musicorum collegium* at Oxford for their cogent and stimulating criticisms of this essay in draft form, and also to Richard Sherr for the generous and collegial spirit he has extended to me since the inception of my work on the papal chapel in 1979.

[1] Before 1530 the chief unit of the Roman currency was the gold ducato di camera; in 1504 Pope Julius II instituted a new silver coin, valued at one-tenth of a ducat, the julio or giulio (sometimes called carlino after an earlier Neapolitan coin). The julio was in turn equivalent to 10 silver baiocchi (b.). In 1530 the ducat was replaced by the scudo d'oro in oro (V). Around 1540 there was a revision in the relation between gold and silver, which ended in the scudo d'oro in oro being equal to 11 julii; the confusingly named scudo di moneta (literally 'in coin') of 10 julii continued as a money of account (since payments were actually made in silver). It is this scudo of 10 julii or 100 baiocchi that is used in the documents cited here.

The payment records for the copying of the two MSS Vatican CG XII.5 and XII.6 in 1539–41 (see Mitchell Brauner, 'The Parvus Manuscripts: A Study of Vatican Polyphony, ca. 1535 to 1580' (Ph.D. diss., Brandeis University, 1982), 67–71, 135–8) show that paper cost b.45 per quire of five sheets, plus ruling at b.20 per quire. The scribe Johannes Parvus was paid b.20 per verse for copying sixteen Magnificats of nine verses each, rounded up to V29; the Magnificats occupy 187 openings, making the rate per opening approximately b.15½. Fourteen openings require fifteen sheets, making the cost of ruled paper alone V1 b.95, and the copying would come to V2 b.17, for a total of V4 b.12.

The salary of the Sistine singers was raised from V8 to V9 in Dec. 1540 (see Richard Sherr, 'The Singers of the Papal Chapel and Liturgical Ceremonies in the Early Sixteenth Century: Some Documentary Evidence', in

consequence, what we now have are the compositions that passed from the first category into the second, the repertory proper: those pieces that, having been tried out, were deemed worthy of being sung again. It seems probable that most of this music continued to be used for some years but was fairly soon retired from the active repertory, and that most of the repertory was in a continual process of replacement. The subject of this paper is the third category, at the other extreme: those pieces that continued to be performed for such a long time that their style of composition came to seem noticeably old-fashioned.

When a body of such privileged works, which have 'stood the test of time' and remain employed on a regular basis as a living part of their culture, comes to dominate the repertory to which it belongs, it constitutes a canon. The word 'canon' has only recently come to have this kind of significance, by extension from official lists: it was used for the first time by Eusebius of Caesarea about AD 325 for the canon of books in the Bible, later for the Catholic canon of saints. In 1768 David Ruhnken applied the word to the selective lists of the foremost Greek writers prepared in the Hellenistic era, though the word was not used in this way in antiquity.[2] The broader present-day usage seems to have originated not long afterwards.[3]

Cultural canons differ from those just mentioned in that they are arrived at tacitly and consensually, rather than by a formal process of codification. The canons of Western music in performance at the present time are determined by a process of supply and demand, not by the fiat of any person or body, and the same is true of other canons, say of painting or English literature. The canons are, however, embodied in formal lists, such as the year's operas planned for Covent Garden, or the syllabus for the course in Western Civilization at Stanford University. These are not the canons themselves, but abstractions from (or expressions of) them.

Canons of vernacular literature seem to have come into being during the fourteenth and fifteenth centuries, when Dante, Petrarch, and Boccaccio became the cynosures of Italian literature, Chaucer, Gower, and Lydgate of English. A sixteenth-century canon of painting is embodied in Vasari's *Lives of the Painters*. But practical music had no such general canon (or canons) before the eighteenth century.[4] In the words of Jacques Chailley, 'Until the middle of

---

Paul A. Ramsey (ed.), *Rome in the Renaissance: The City and the Myth* (Medieval and Renaissance Texts and Studies 18; Binghamton, NY, 1982), 249–64 at 250). The Cappella Giulia paid Vl b.20 for the *Liber primus missarum* of Carpentras (Avignon, 1532; RISM G 1571) in 1539 (see José M. Llorens, *Le opere musicali della Cappella Giulia* (Studi e testi, 265; Vatican City, 1971), p. xx).

[2] Rudolf Pfeiffer, *History of Classical Scholarship from the Beginnings to the End of the Hellenistic Age* (Oxford, 1968), 206–7.

[3] See the *Oxford English Dictionary*, s.v. 'Canonical' 4.

[4] See William Weber, *The Rise of Musical Classics in Eighteenth-Century England: A Study in Canon, Ritual, and Ideology* (Oxford, 1992).

the eighteenth century . . . there was only one kind of "live" music that aroused any interest, and that was modern music. . . . Fifty years was the maximum period during which a work remained in circulation. After that, it was forgotten and replaced by something else.'[5] But there is one major exception to this generalization: by the middle of the seventeenth century, the performing repertory of the papal chapel had come to be thoroughly dominated by the music of Palestrina. His masses, motets, hymns, and other ritual polyphony were employed far more often than the works of more recent composers; but when newer music like (to take only the most notorious example) Gregorio Allegri's *Miserere* became accepted, it too became quasi-permanent.[6] Though circumscribed to a single institution, this is arguably the oldest instance of a canon in Western music.

Much of the debate in the last few years over the canons of Western civilization seems to imply that a canon is something very rigid and immutable. This is exaggerated; canons are continuously evolving, and enormous changes occur over the span of a single generation.[7] Room is made for new works, and older ones are continually re-evaluated. Take the performing canon of opera, for example: from the late nineteenth century to the middle of the twentieth the operas of Gluck were central to the canon, and those of Donizetti were merely historical curiosities seldom performed. Since then that situation has been reversed, while the operas of Britten, for instance, have found a secure place in the canon.

Because one of the essential characteristics of a canon is *domination*, it is entirely appropriate that criticism of present-day canons should focus on mechanisms of domination, and particularly on the ways canons *exclude* certain categories of works.[8] But faulty canons are rectified by the *inclusion* of previously excluded works, and whether or not the process is deliberate, canons always evolve by inclusion rather than exclusion *per se*. This distinction is especially important in the present context, for I wish to examine the pre-history of the papal chapel canon: the process by which individual works came to achieve canonical status even though there was not yet a canon, the repertory being dominated by recently composed music.

---

[5] Jacques Chailley, *40,000 Years of Music: Man in Search of Music*, trans. R. Myers (New York, 1964), 3.

[6] A concrete expression of the canon of motets (unfortunately other categories of polyphony are not specified) around 1700 is provided in Andrea Adami, *Osservazioni per ben regolare il coro de i cantori della Cappella Pontificia* (Rome, 1711; facs. edn., Musurgiana, 1; Lucca, 1988), *passim*.

[7] See George P. Landow, *Hypertext: The Convergence of Contemporary Critical Theory and Technology* (Parallax: Re-Visions of Culture and Society; Baltimore and London, 1992), 'Reconceiving Canon and Curriculum', 149–60, esp. 155–6. The section as a whole has been very stimulating to me.

[8] An especially fine critique, focusing on the inadequate treatment of late-medieval women's writing in 20th-c. criticism, is presented in Paula Higgins, 'Parisian Nobles, a Scottish Princess, and the Woman's Voice in Late Medieval Song', *EMH* 10 (1991), 145–200.

We have every reason not to expect to find evidence of a canon of practical music in the fifteenth and sixteenth centuries. Tinctoris notoriously declared in 1477 that 'there does not exist a single piece of music, not composed within the last forty years, that is regarded by the learned as worth hearing';[9] in 1547 Glareanus assigned music older than seventy years to the first of his three ages of music: 'Nor indeed (so far as we can be certain) is this art much more ancient.'[10] In a survey of fourteen writers on music from the late fifteenth century to the early seventeenth, Jessie Ann Owens concluded that: 'Even given the very real limits to our understanding of the musical "canon" at various times and places, it is clear that musicians in the fifteenth and sixteenth centuries—at least judging from this particular group of writers—had a restricted view of the past. Music had an immediate past, but no distant past beyond the span of human memory.'[11]

But at the papal chapel, beginning early in the fifteenth century and in increasing quantity throughout our period, some pieces were accepted as well-nigh permanent, continuing in performance for a far longer period than we tend to regard as normal. During the fifteenth and sixteenth centuries the process was already operating by which the Palestrinian canon of the seventeenth and later centuries came into being. In investigating the possible canonical status of a given work, we must not require it to have entered the performing repertory once and for all, never to be discarded. It is also important not to assume that in order for a work to have been accorded canonical status in the past it must have qualities that would lead us to grant it that status ourselves. At the papal chapel the earliest compositions to be canonized were not works in the high style such as masses or motets but modest pieces of substitution polyphony: hymns and the like.

The evidence we have for the long-continued performance of certain pieces at the papal chapel during the fifteenth and sixteenth centuries is both sparse and various, and most of it is inferential rather than definite. What would be most helpful is documentary testimony that such-and-such a piece was performed on such-and-such an occasion. The *Diarii Sistini*, the day-to-day records of the singers' attendance at services in the papal chapel, which survive

---

[9] 'Neque quod satis admirari nequeo quippiam compositum nisi citra annos quadraginta extat quod auditu dignum ab eruditis existimetur.' Johannes Tinctoris, *Liber de arte contrapuncti*, in his *Opera theoretica*, ed. Albert Seay, 2 vols. (CSM 22; American Insitute of Musicology, 1975–8), ii. 11–157 at 12; translation from Oliver Strunk, *Source Readings in Music History*, 5 vols. (New York, 1965), ii. 9.

[10] 'Neque enim (quantum nobis constat) haec ars est multo vetustior.' Henricus Loris Glareanus, *Dodekachordon* (Basle, 1547; facs. edn., Monuments of Music and Music Literature in Facsimile, 2/65; New York, 1967), bk. 3, ch. 13, p. 240.

[11] Jessie Ann Owens, 'Music Historiography and the Definition of "Renaissance"', *Notes*, 47 (1990), 205–30 at 324. The writers surveyed are Tinctoris, Aaron, Lanfranco, Heyden, Glareanus, Coclico, Finck, Dressler, Bartoli, L. Guicciardini, Gaetano, Zacconi, G. C. Monteverdi, and Nucius.

nearly continuously beginning in 1535, are a mine of such information in the seventeenth century—but unfortunately not before.[12] Another set of diaries, those of the papal masters of ceremonies, which extend from 1483 without a break until 1688, frequently refer to the performance of polyphony, but usually their references are vague ('a Credo *in cantu figurato*', 'a motet', and so on), and when they are more precise the compositions they describe cannot be identified in the surviving choirbooks.[13] The one really informative document comes from the second half of the sixteenth century, and it will be discussed presently.

In the absence of documents we must turn to the musical sources themselves. Although the corrosive action of their ink has rendered the manuscripts of the Vatican choirs very fragile after the lapse of centuries, they were copied on strong and heavy paper, and it is evident that many of them continued in practical use for decades, as is shown by alterations to the notes or (more often) the words made many years after the music was originally copied. But because of the expense of copying mentioned at the beginning of this chapter, it is the recopying of pieces long after they were first composed that affords the best evidence of their persistence in the active repertory. And this is the sort of evidence we must rely on for knowledge of the earliest stages of the evolution of the Sistine canon.

Although the institutional history of the papal chapel is continuous from early in the fifteenth century,[14] the earliest of its polyphonic sources to survive

[12] Raffaele Casimiri (ed.), *I Diarii Sistini: I primi 25 anni (1535–1559)*, (Rome, 1939; originally published in *Note d'archivio per la storia musicale*, 1924–39); Herman-Walther Frey (ed.), *Die Diarien der Sixtinischen Kapelle in Rom der Jahre 1560 und 1561* (Düsseldorf, 1959); id. (ed.), 'Das Diarium der Sixtinischen Sängerkapelle in Rom für das Jahr 1594 (Nr. 19)', *Analecta musicologica*, 14 (1974), 445–505; id. (ed.), 'Das Diarium der Sixtinischen Sängerkapelle in Rom für das Jahr 1596 (Nr. 21)', *Analecta musicologica*, 23 (1985), 129–204; id., 'Die Gesänge der Sixtinischen Kapelle an den Sonntagen und hohen Kirchenfesten des Jahres 1616', in *Mélanges Eugène Tisserant*, 7 vols. (Studi e testi, 231–7; Vatican City, 1964), vi. 395–437.

[13] The diaries of the first master of ceremonies in the sequence, Johannes Burckard, have been published in *Liber Notarum ab anno MCCCLXXXIII usque ad annum MDVI*, ed. Enrico Celani, 2 vols. (Rerum italicarum scriptores, 32; Città di Castello, 1906–13). So have portions of the diaries of Burckard's successor, Paride de' Grassi, in Luigi Frati (ed.), *Le due spedizioni militari di Giulio II* (Bologna, 1886); I have used a late 16th-c. MS copy of Grassi's complete diaries, covering 1504–21, Rome Cas. 2141–4, and also a MS copy of the diaries of Grassi's successor Biagio da Cesena, covering 1518–34, BAV, Vat. lat. 12422. Biagio has next to nothing to say about musical performance, and his successors are progressively more laconic in their entries. Burckard's diaries were first brought to the attention of musicologists by Arnold Schering, 'Musikalisches aus Joh. Burkhards Liber Notarum', in *Festschrift Johannes Wolf* (Berlin, 1929), 171–5; both Burckard and Grassi have been thoroughly and profitably exploited by Richard Sherr, 'The Papal Chapel ca. 1492–1513 and its Polyphonic Sources' (Ph.D. diss., Princeton University, 1975), 85–104; and Sherr, 'The Singers of the Papal Chapel' (see p. 261 n. 18 for reference to some further partial editions of Grassi, less extensive and less useful than Frati's). A notable instance of how frustrating these diaries can be, cited by both Schering and Sherr, is Burckard's mention of a motet by Johannes Tinctoris offered in honour of Pope Alexander VI in 1492; Burckard even provides the complete text, but the music does not survive (*Liber notarum*, i. 376).

[14] See Manfred Schuler, 'Die Musik in Konstanz während des Konzils, 1414–1418', *Acta musicologica*, 38 (1966), 150–68; id., 'Zur Geschichte der Kapelle Papst Martins V', *AfMw* 25 (1968), 30–45; id., 'Zur Geschichte der Kapelle Papst Eugens IV', *Acta musicologica*, 40 (1968), 220–7; Pamela Starr, 'Music and Music Patronage at the Papal Court, 1447–1464' (Ph.D. diss., Yale University, 1987).

are two large manuscripts of music for the ordinary of the Mass, which apparently entered the chapel sometime in the 1470s or early 1480s.[15] There are thus no early fifteenth-century manuscripts stemming from the papal chapel, and it is late recopying that bears witness to the earliest music to achieve canonical status there: some modest pieces of substitution polyphony (settings of plainchant items that took the place of those chants in the ritual) for Vespers and the Mass.

Du Fay's extraordinary cycle of hymn settings *per circulum anni* has for its latest source the manuscript CS 15, copied in the 1490s, by which time the cycle had been considerably augmented by other composers.[16] Heinrich Besseler proposed that the original cycle was composed during the period when Du Fay was a member of the papal chapel in Rome, 1428–33. But Charles Hamm dated the hymns slightly later, 1433–5, on the grounds of their use of mensurations, and Tom Ward showed that the melodies used for two of the hymns are not to be found in Italian chant books, so that Hamm's date, embracing the period when Du Fay was employed at the court of Savoy, has been accepted by most later scholars.[17] The composer returned to the papal chapel, now in Florence, in mid-1435, and undoubtedly brought his hymn cycle with him.[18] It continued to be performed at least until the 1490s, and probably was ousted from the repertory during the 1530s by the hymn cycle of Costanzo Festa.[19]

[15] See Adalbert Roth, *Studien zum frühen Repertoire der päpstlichen Kapelle unter dem Pontifikat Sixtus' IV. (1471–1484): Die Chorbücher 14 und 51 des Fondo Cappella Sistina der Biblioteca Apostolica Vaticana* (Capellae Apostolicae Sixtinaeque Collectanea Acta Monumenta, 1; Vatican City, 1991). Roth's conclusions have been contested by Flynn Warmington, who offers persuasive evidence that the MSS were executed in Venice or the Veneto *c.*1480 (Flynn Warmington, '*Abeo semper Fortuna regressum*: Evidence for the Venetian Origin of the Manuscripts Cappella Sistina 14 and 51', unpublished paper presented at the 22nd Conference on Medieval and Renaissance Music, Glasgow, 10 July 1994, and elsewhere).

[16] The date is from Sherr, 'Papal Chapel', 204–8; he dates the subsequent fascicles of Magnificats and motets to *c.*1495 and (in the main) *c.*1495–1501 respectively (pp. 209–13). And see now Sherr, *Papal Music Manuscripts in the Late Fifteenth and Early Sixteenth Centuries* (Renaissance Manuscript Studies, 5; Neuhausen-Stuttgart, 1996), 58–67.

[17] Heinrich Besseler, 'Dufay in Rom', *AfMw* 15 (1958), 1–19; Charles Hamm, *A Chronology of the Works of Guillaume Dufay Based on a Study of Mensural Practice* (Princeton Studies in Music, 1; Princeton, 1964), 80–1; Tom R. Ward, 'The Polyphonic Office Hymn and the Liturgy of Fifteenth Century Italy', *MD* 26 (1972), 161–88 at 181–6.

[18] A word of caution: Margaret Bent's proposed very early date and place of origin of the earliest MS of the cycle, Bologna Q 15 (see below), taken together with the inherent imprecision of Hamm's method and the certainty that the cycle was long used by the papal chapel despite the two alien hymn melodies, may necessitate a revision of the current scholarly consensus concerning the cycle's composition—Besseler may have been right after all. This essay is not, however, an appropriate place to develop this suspicion, and I shall proceed on the presumption that the theory of the cycle's composition in Savoy between 1433 and 1435 is correct.

[19] The earliest source of Festa's cycle of thirty hymns is CS 18, which dates from 1538 (Brauner, 'Parvus Manuscripts', 123–8); it was probably newly composed (along with the companion cycle of Magnificats in the same MS), since a prominent commission to copy the same cycles for the Cappella Giulia was made in the following year (ibid. 135–43). An earlier cycle of forty-six hymns had been composed by Carpentras (Elzéar

The hypothesis that the papal chapel acquired Du Fay's hymn cycle from the composer himself accounts elegantly for the present state of preservation of the cycle as such (individual hymns are preserved in isolation elsewhere): its earliest source is a layer of Bologna Q 15 copied in Vicenza not long after 1433; the next is Modena α.X.1.11, copied for the Ferrarese court chapel in the late 1440s, which includes three new hymns attributed to Du Fay; the third source is Vatican SP B 80, copied for the chapter of St Peter's in the Vatican about 1475 and reproducing a manuscript prepared in 1458, which is much augmented by anonymous settings; the last is CS 15 from the 1490s, in which the cycle is independently expanded to a much greater extent.[20] Pope Eugene IV spent the greater part of his papacy away from Rome, chiefly in Florence and Bologna; both were important commercial centres of manuscript production, which might have provided the exemplar from which Bologna Q 15 was transcribed. A document shows Du Fay to have been in touch with the Ferrarese court some time before May 1437 (at the end of which month he quitted the papal court), and he may have given his hymns directly to the Ferrarese chapel; certainly he would have had the opportunity to compose the three added settings, 'stylistically quite different from the earlier ones', by this time.[21] But the papal court spent the year of 1438 in Ferrara on account of the opening of the Council of Ferrara, and this seems a more likely occasion for the transmission of Du Fay's hymn cycle there.[22] Eugene and his court finally returned to Rome

---

Genet), the favoured musician of Leo X, who led the papal chapel from 1514 to 1521 (he had earlier been a member of the chapel in 1508–11, and may have returned briefly in 1525–6). No copy of his hymn cycle survives in the Cappella Sistina collection; it was printed under the composer's supervision as *Liber Hymnorum usus Romae ecclesiae* (Avignon, [1535]; RISM G 1573). Only thirteen of Carpentras's hymns were copied (following all of Festa's) into CG XII.6 in 1540 by the papal chapel scribe Johannes Parvus (see Brauner, 'Parvus Manuscripts', 109–43), evidently not from the print; see Albert Seay's Introduction to Genet (Carpentras), *Opera omnia*, iii (CMM 58; American Institute of Musicology, 1972), p. xix. Carpentras states in the dedicatory epistle to his masses of 1532, the first of four volumes printed under his own direction, that the music of all four had been composed during the preceding five years as therapy for a debilitating attack of tinnitus ('morbus (ni fallor) hactenus inauditus . . . caput (partem corporis nobilissimam) ita mihi repente invasit: ut assiduis illud sibilis vexare, cerebrum quasi ventis inter se pugnantibus agitare non desinat'); see ibid. xii. Probably the thirteen hymns in CG XII.6 had already been composed in 1514–21 (I presume they would have been interpolated into the Du Fay cycle), and the rest of Carpentras's cycle was added in 1527–32.

[20] For the date of Bologna Q 15 see Margaret Bent, 'A Contemporary Perception of Early Fifteenth-Century Style: Bologna Q15 as a Document of Scribal Editorial Initiative', *MD* 41 (1987), 183–201 at 185–7; I am grateful to Dr Bent for sharing her as yet unpublished conclusions about the place of origin (its earliest layer was copied in Padua, and it was later taken by the same scribe to Vicenza; the Du Fay hymn cycle is in the later part of the second of the MS's three layers). On Modena α.X.1.11 see Charles Hamm and Ann Besser Scott, 'A Study and Inventory of the Manuscript Modena, Biblioteca Estense Alpha X.1.11', *MD* 26 (1972), 101–43; Lewis Lockwood, *Music in Renaissance Ferrara, 1400–1505: The Creation of a Musical Centre in the Fifteenth Century* (Oxford, 1984), 51–63. On Rome SP B 80 see Christopher Reynolds, 'The Origins of San Pietro B 80 and the Development of a Roman Sacred Repertory', *EMH* 1 (1981), 257–304, and id., *Papal Patronage and the Music of St. Peter's, 1380–1513* (Berkeley, 1995).

[21] David Fallows, *Dufay*, rev. edn. (London, 1987), 47–8, 145.

[22] See Lockwood, *Music in Ferrara*, 56–7.

in 1443, which would be when the hymns came into the possession of the chapter of St Peter's.

Du Fay's sequences, which (like the hymns) are very homogeneous in contrapuntal style and so almost certainly composed as a cycle, have been connected by Besseler and David Fallows with the periods of his employment at the papal chapel in 1428–33 or 1435–7 respectively.[23] Fallows separates the composition of the sequence cycle from that of the hymn cycle on the cogent grounds that in the hymns the compass of the contratenor and tenor is separated from that of the discantus by an octave, whereas in the sequences they are separated by a fifth, suggesting composition 'for the needs of different institutions with different vocal resources'; and the Savoyard chapel employed boy choristers while the papal chapel did not.[24] But despite their wide scoring the papal chapel seems to have adopted the hymns at an early date; and it is unlikely that the sequences were composed for the papal chapel, for sequences were used very sparingly in the papal ritual.

Of Du Fay's settings, *Victime paschali laudes*, *Veni sancte spiritus*, and *Lauda Sion* are sequences used at the papal chapel, and *Rex omnipotens* had in the thirteenth century replaced the hymn at Second Vespers of the Ascension.[25] On the other hand, *Letabundus*, *Epiphaniam Domino*, and *Isti sunt due olive*, as well as *Sancti spiritus assit nobis* and *Mittit ad virginem* (attributed to Du Fay by Hamm), have no attestation in any ritual source connected with the papacy at any time. The non-papal sequences might have been used at the papal chapel, perhaps substituting for hymns in the manner of *Rex omnipotens*, but it seems most probable that the sequence cycle was composed for an institution that could employ them all as sequences. Unlike the hymns, there is no evidence in musical sources that any of Du Fay's sequences was known at the papal chapel or any other Roman musical institution.[26]

A composition very similar to Du Fay's hymns and sequences seems to have entered the Sistine repertory about the same time as the hymn cycle, and to have continued in use as long. Since this piece has hardly been studied by musicologists, I propose to take the opportunity to examine it rather closely. An

---

[23] Besseler, 'Dufay in Rom', 1–19; Fallows, *Dufay*, 43, 146–7.   [24] Ibid. 146.

[25] 'In secundis vesperis. si est Rome vel etiam alibi. consueverunt cantores de scola loco ymni prosam cantare. *Rex omnipotens*. cum melodiis', 'Ordinal of Gregory X, c. 1274', in Stephen J. P. van Dijk and Joan Hazelden Walker (eds.), *The Ordinal of the Papal Court from Innocent III to Boniface VIII and Related Documents* (Spicilegium Friburgense, 22; Fribourg, 1975), 533–91 at 566. Whether the practice was still observed in the 1430s is not apparent; the ceremonial of the papal chapel, [Agostino Patrizi], *Rituum ecclesiasticorum sive sacrarum cerimoniarum .S.S. romanae ecclesiae libri tres*, ed. Cristoforo Marcello (Venice, 1516; issued in MS in 1488), facs. edn. (Ridgewood, NJ, 1965), fo. 112^{r–v}, is silent on this matter, as is CS 9 (a partial antiphoner copied for the Sistine Chapel in 1545), fos. 59^{v}–63^{r}.

[26] It was announced at the Library of Congress conference that one of Du Fay's sequences is preserved in Lucca A 8, copied by the papal chapel scribe Johannes Parvus in 1576 (cf. Brauner, 'Parvus Manuscripts', 257–63, 295, 409). The identification of the setting as Du Fay's is unfortunately mistaken.

anonymous setting in three and four voices of the antiphon-with-canticle *Lumen ad revelationem gentium/Nunc dimittis* was copied around 1510 and is now incorporated in the manuscript CS 46; a score appears as the Appendix to this chapter.[27] This composition is based on the chant that accompanies the distribution of candles before the procession and Mass on the feast of the Purification (2 February), one of the services classified as of 'papal' rank, meaning that the pope was expected to be present in state.[28] The chant is one of the rare survivors of the ancient practice of repeating an antiphon in its entirety between every pair of verses of its canticle as well as before and after; so the antiphon is stated six times, surrounding the five verses of the Nunc dimittis and doxology.[29] The polyphonic composition in CS 46 mirrors this structure: each of the six statements of the antiphon is given its own polyphonic setting, as is the second half of each verse of the canticle (the first half of which is chanted).

CS 46 is not the unique source for the setting: the sections for three voices (though not those for four) are preserved in the third layer of the Aosta manuscript, in a gathering whose paper has been dated 1435.[30] Laurence Feininger conjectured that the three-voice sections (though not those for four) were the work of Du Fay—and although Feininger was ready to attribute an enormous quantity of anonymous music to Du Fay, he was sometimes right.[31] But close inspection shows that the three-voice *Lumen ad revelationem* is unlikely to be Du Fay's work: he would not have committed exposed parallel fifths like those between the two upper voices (discantus and contratenor), marked with asterisks in the Appendix. Still, comparison with available scores shows the counterpoint of *Lumen ad revelationem* in its Aosta state to resemble

---

[27] The original source is reproduced in facsimile in Jeffrey Dean (ed.), *Vatican City, Biblioteca Apostolica Vaticana, Cappella Sistina MS 46* (Renaissance Music in Facsimile, 21; New York and London, 1986), fos. 59ᵛ–64ʳ. It was copied by the Sistine scribe Johannes Orceau *c.*1509–12; see Jeffrey Dean, 'The Scribes of the Sistine Chapel, 1501–1527' (Ph.D. diss., University of Chicago, 1984), 244.

[28] The distribution was held at a chapel or church 'in loco conveniente' and was followed by a procession to a different church or chapel where Mass was to be sung; see Patrizi, *Ritus ecclesiastici*, fos. 88ᵛ–89ᵛ; also the Roman gradual CS 5 (copied for Cardinal Pietro Barbo, later Pope Paul II, *c.*1458), fo. 6ʳ⁻ᵛ. The location of the distribution ceremony seems normally to have been the Sistine Chapel itself: see *I Diarii Sistini*, ed. Casimiri, *passim*; Frey (ed.), 'Das Diarium für 1596', 131. For the 'papal' ranking of feasts see Sherr, 'Singers of the Papal Chapel', 252–4.

[29] *Liber Usualis* (Tournai and New York, 1961), 1357–8.

[30] Fos. 190ᵛ–191ʳ; for the date see Tsutomu Sasaki, 'The Dating of the Aosta Manuscript from Watermarks', *Acta musicologica*, 64 (1992), 1–16.

[31] Most notably in the case of the cycles of mass propers in Trent 88; see Fallows, *Dufay*, 188–90; Alejandro Enrique Planchart, 'Guillaume Du Fay's Benefices and his Relationship to the Court of Burgundy', *EMH* 8 (1988), 117–71 at 142–5, 151–8. Feininger's conjectured attribution of the *Lumen ad revelationem* appears in a thirteen-volume collection of unpublished transcriptions now in Rome, Pontificio Istituto di Musica Sacra (two further volumes are in Trent, Museo Provinciale d'Arte, Castello del Buon Consiglio), which was drawn on extensively though without acknowledgement by José M. Llorens in his preparation of the catalogue of the Sistine MSS: *Capellae Sixtinae codices musicis notis instructi, sive manu scripti sive praelo excussi* (Studi e testi, 202; Vatican City, 1960), 19, where the whole composition is attributed to Du Fay.

that of Du Fay's sequence settings more than any other similar music bearing a paraphrased chant melody in the discantus.

The anonymous *Lumen ad revelationem* was certainly part of the repertory of the papal chapel some seventy-five years after its composition, as the augmented copy now in CS 46 attests, and it undoubtedly continued to be sung on Candlemas until the 1530s, when settings by Jean Conseil and Costanzo Festa were composed.[32] The open question is when the piece began to be sung by the papal singers. The second and third layers of its earlier source, the Aosta manuscript, which share their scribes but are distinct in contents and date, contain a great deal of English music and have also been seen as drawing on the repertory of the papal chapels of Martin V and Eugene IV.[33] England and the papal chapel also seem to have been the two places where the polyphonic *Lumen ad revelationem* was cultivated: I know of five other substitution settings of this chant, two of them in English manuscripts (one copied in the 1460s and the other in the 1490s),[34] the other three from the sixteenth-century papal chapel (those mentioned by Conseil and Festa, and another by either Palestrina or Felice Anerio).[35]

Given that the piece in question was part of the papal chapel repertory later on, that it most closely resembles similar compositions of Du Fay's, and that

[32] Conseil's earliest datable composition is *O desolatorum consolator*, copied in CS 55 *c.*1523–5 (Dean, 'Scribes of the Sistine Chapel', 250); his unpublished four/five-voice *Lumen ad revelationem*, in the mid-18th-c. part-books CS 484–9, no. 43, must have been composed before his death at the beginning of 1535. I believe Festa's four-voice setting to have been composed shortly before it was copied in CS 20, fos. 128ᵛ–134ʳ, *c.*1539 (Brauner, 'Parvus Manuscripts', 128–34); it is published in Costanzo Festa, *Opera Omnia*, ed. Alexander Main and Albert Seay, 8 vols. (CMM 25; American Institute of Musicology, 1962–79), iv. 117–26. Festa's setting was still in use in 1616; see Frey, 'Gesänge des Jahres 1616', 405.

[33] Marian Cobin, 'The Aosta Manuscript: A Central Source of Early Fifteenth-Century Sacred Music' (Ph.D. diss., New York University, 1978). Cobin's dating has been refined by Sasaki, 'Dating of the Aosta Manuscript'.

[34] Cambridge, Magdalene College, Pepys Library, MS 1236 (Kent, *c.*1460–5), fos. 55ᵛ–56ʳ, three voices; published in Sydney R. Charles (ed.), *The Music of the Pepys Ms. 1236* (CMM 40; American Institute of Musicology, 1967), 83–4. London, British Library, Add. MS 5665 (the 'Ritson MS', Devon, in a layer copied 'about the end of the [15th] century'), fos. 62ᵛ–64ʳ, by Thomas Packe, five voices; unpublished. See Frank Ll. Harrison, *Music in Medieval Britain*, 2nd edn. (London, 1963), 278 n. 4 (for the date of Ritson), 353 (Pepys setting 'One of the earliest examples' of the polyphonic ritual antiphon, with excerpt). Both English pieces, unlike the one in question or the later ones from the papal chapel, provide only a single setting of the antiphon.

[35] The late 16th-c. four/five-voice setting is in CS 71 (1631), fos. 1ᵛ–34ʳ, anon.; BAV Ottob. lat. 3388 (17th c.), attributed to Anerio; and CS 484–9 (*c.*1750), no. 62, attributed to Palestrina. It is published in Giovanni Pierluigi da Palestrina, *Werke*, ed. Fr. X. Haberl *et al.* (Leipzig, 1862–1903), xxxii. 143–54; Haberl believed it to be a work of Anerio's (ibid., p. vi n.). There is also in CS 484–9, no. 33, a four-voice *Lumen ad revelationem* by François Roussel (Rossello), who worked in Rome in 1548–50 and 1562–75, though not at the papal chapel (*New Grove*, xvi. 276–7). Llorens classifies this as a motet and not as an antiphon; similarly he calls Conseil's setting an antiphon but does not state that it includes the canticle *Nunc dimittis* as he does in the case of the Palestrina/Anerio setting. See *Capellae Sixtinae codices*, 436–7. I also know of a four-voice motet by Maistre Jan in RISM 1543⁴ and four German motets: by Matthias Eckel in Budapest, Országos Széchényi Könyvtár, MS Bártfa 22 (Wittenberg, *c.*1550; probably composed before 1540), for four voices; Leipzig, Universitätsbibliothek, MS Thomaskirche 49 (Leipzig, *c.*1558), fos. 205ʳ, 212ᵛ, both for four voices; Regensburg, Bischöfliche Zentralbibliothek, MS A.R 1018 (south or central Germany, *c.*1563), no. 21, for five voices.

the earliest certain English example dates from a quarter of a century later, it seems most probable that it was composed for the papal chapel shortly after Du Fay's return in 1435 and under his influence. The mensurations used in the original three-voice setting are O, $\mathirm{\Cenglish}$, and $\mathirm{\Cenglish}3$ (given as $\Phi 3$ in CS 46); Du Fay seems to have used $\mathirm{\Cenglish}3$ for the first time in *Supremum est mortalibus* in 1433, and Hamm believes 'pieces using $\mathirm{\Cenglish}$ probably were not written' before 1435.[36] This would make 1435 the *terminus post quem* for the composition of *Lumen ad revelationem*, but 1435 is precisely the date of the paper on which it appears in the Aosta manuscript. This must therefore be a very early copy indeed.[37]

In its earliest state, as preserved in Aosta, the antiphon was given only three settings, each of which was to be repeated in a manner familiar from early fifteenth-century Magnificats to give a pattern AABBCC (see Table 5.1). But in CS 46 the even-numbered iterations of the antiphon have been provided with entirely new settings for four voices, so no music is repeated.[38] What is

TABLE 5.1. Concordance of polyphonic sections in *Lumen ad revelationem* between Aosta and CS 46

Text	Aosta	CS 46[a]
Lumen ad revelationem gentium: et gloriam plebis tue Israel.	A	A
Nunc dimittis servum tuum, Domine	–	–
secundum verbum tuum in pace.	a^1	a^1
Lumen ad revelationem gentium: et gloriam plebis tue Israel.	A	I
Quia viderunt oculi mei	–	–
salutare tuum.	a^2	1
Lumen ad revelationem gentium: et gloriam plebis tue Israel.	B	B
Quod parasti	–	–
ante faciem omnium populorum	a^3	a^3
Lumen ad revelationem gentium: et gloriam plebis tue Israel.	B	II
Gloria Patri, et Filio,	–	–
et Spiritui Sancto.	a^4	(a^2)
Lumen ad revelationem gentium: et gloriam plebis tue Israel.	C	C
Sicut erat in principio, et nunc, et semper,	–	–
et in secula seculorum. Amen.	a^5	2
Lumen ad revelationem gentium: et gloriam plebis tue Israel.	C	III

[a] Dashes indicate plainchant. Use of the same letters denotes identical music. The use of roman or arabic numerals in the CS column denotes the substitution of new music.

[36] Hamm, *Chronology of the Works of Dufay*, 57, 82.

[37] If, however, Du Fay's hymn cycle had been composed earlier than 1433 (see above, n. 18), then *Lumen ad revelationem* might have been composed a few years before 1435 (though surely not many). Hamm's stricture against the use of $\mathirm{\Cenglish}$ before 1435 must not be taken too rigidly.

[38] Furthermore, in Aosta the half-verses of the canticle are all variants of the same counterpoint, adjusted to fit the varying mensuration and number of syllables; some of these as well have been recomposed in CS 46 (see Table 5.1).

more, there appear to be at least two separate layers within the four-voice music: the setting for the second statement of the antiphon is rhythmically and contrapuntally more animated than those for the fourth and sixth statements, and it is in Φ whereas they are both in $\mathbb{C}$. Each of the new settings treats the chant melody differently: in the second statement it is at original pitch in the tenor, in the fourth it is transposed up an octave in the discantus (as in the three-voice statements), and in the sixth it is up a fifth in the contratenor. Contrapuntal style leads me to conjecture that the second antiphon was composed in the 1470s, the fourth around 1490, the sixth perhaps a little later.

A further striking aspect of this setting of *Lumen ad revelationem* as it is given in CS 46 is the prescription for the first half of each verse of the Nunc dimittis to be chanted in octaves (the chanted half-verses are not given in Aosta). This is unique among the Sistine manuscripts, and so far as I am aware among all sources of fifteenth- and sixteenth-century music. I believe this may provide an explanation for the perplexing designation 'great plainchant' (*cantus planus maior*) called for in the invitatory of Christmas Matins in the Constitutions of the College of Singers at the papal chapel: 'the invitatory [antiphon] of these matins, *Christus natus est nobis*, must be sung by two soprano singers. And the chorus must repeat it the first time in great plainchant, and the last time the chorus will similarly continue *Venite adoremus* in great plainchant, as is the custom.'[39]

We can now discern two groups of pieces that entered the repertory of the papal chapel about 1435 and continued to be sung regularly well into the sixteenth century: the anonymous *Lumen ad revelationem* and Du Fay's cycle of hymns. But if the hymns and *Lumen ad revelationem* had achieved canonical status, they had not been canonized in the way we should expect nowadays, to become inviolable 'classics'. Evidently at more than one point during their working life it was thought appropriate to augment them, in some sense to bring them up to date. For the same attitude we have seen in *Lumen ad revelationem* was applied to the whole cycle of Du Fay's hymns in CS 15: there are not only replacements of Du Fay's fauxbourdon settings with independent settings of Du Fay's chant-paraphrase discantus, but again and again one verse of a hymn uses Du Fay's setting while the next has been set by someone more

---

[39] 'cantandum est Invitatorium dicti Matutini Videlicet, Christus natus est nobis, &c. per duos Supranos Cantores. Et Chorus debet replicare idem in cantu plano maiori prima vice, et ultima vice Chorus similiter continuabit, Venite adoremus, &c. in cantu plano maiori (ut est consuetum)'; 'Constitutiones Capellae Pontificiae', CS 611 (1545), 'De Matutino noctis Nativitatis Domini', p. 28; published with orthographical alterations in F. X. Haberl, *Die römische 'schola cantorum' und die päpstlichen Kapellsänger bis zur Mitte des 16. Jahrhunderts* (Bausteine für Musikgeschichte, 3; Leipzig, 1888; repr. Hildesheim, 1971), 96–108 at 107. Also present with orthographical differences in CS 687, fos. 160ʳ–166ᵛ (c.1507–25) at 164ᵛ. The manner of alternating the invitatory *Venite exsultemus* and its antiphon *Christus natus est* with second part *Venite adoremus* (which is similar to the alternation of *Nunc dimittis* and *Lumen ad revelationem*) is shown in the *Liber Usualis*, 368–71.

recent—De Orto and Josquin are the only composers who are named in this portion of the manuscript.[40]

It is notable that all the music in this earliest identifiable phase of the papal chapel repertory is substitution polyphony. As Adalbert Roth points out in his contribution to this volume (Ch. 4), there is scant evidence for the cultivation of the more substantial genres of sacred polyphony, the cyclic mass and the motet (apart from a few occasional motets), at the papal chapel before the reforms of Sixtus IV in the 1470s. The late fifteenth- and early sixteenth-century manuscripts of the chapel show a vigorous policy of acquiring masses and motets.[41] Some of this music was supplied by composers who were singers in the chapel, such as Josquin des Prez, Gaspar van Weerbecke, Marbriano de Orto, and Bertrand Vacqueras; but more was imported from without, and the chief source seems to have been the royal chapel of France.

Two French royal composers of masses and motets whose work entered the papal chapel repertory at the earliest level and remained there for an unusually long time are Johannes Ockeghem and Philippe Basiron. Both the earliest pair of mass manuscripts acquired by the chapel, CS 14 and 51 of *c*.1480, and the earliest manuscript prepared within the chapel, CS 35 of the 1480s and early 1490s, contain several works by each composer. Ockeghem's *Missa My my* was still being sung shortly before 1520, as the copy in CS 41 shows: the one opening in the mass that had been inadequately supplied with words by its original scribe has had the omission made good, and a misplaced page-turn in the music of the bass has been rectified.[42] About the same time, the superb calligrapher whose chief monument is the Medici Codex prepared a booklet, now part of CS 46, that begins with Ockeghem's *Alma redemptoris mater* and Basiron's *Salve regina*.[43]

Ockeghem and Basiron both died during the 1490s. The masses and motets of two French composers in royal service who lived until about 1520, Loyset Compère and Jean Mouton, had an even longer currency in the repertory of the papal chapel. A mass of Compère's (*L'homme armé*) was copied into CS 35 during the 1480s or early 1490s, and half a dozen works of his are preserved

---

[40] See Rudolf Gerber, 'Römische Hymnenzyklen des späten 15. Jahrhunderts', *AfMw* 12 (1955), 40–73.

[41] CS 14 and 51, brought into the papal chapel in the 1470s or early 1480s, are studied in Roth, *Studien zum frühen Repertoire*. CS 35, the first MS prepared within the chapel during the 1480s and early 1490s, has not been the subject of a published study (though Roth has studied it and has communicated some of his findings informally); it is inventoried in Llorens, *Capellae Sixtinae codices*, 69–72. CS 15 and the scattered 15th-c. booklets embedded within MSS chiefly copied in the 16th c. are studied in Sherr, 'Papal Chapel' and *Papal Music Manuscripts*. The early 16th-c. MSS are studied in Dean, 'Scribes of the Sistine Chapel' (with some overlap with Sherr).

[42] Fos. 121ᵛ–122ʳ, 123ʳ; Dean, 'Scribes of the Sistine Chapel', 187–93.

[43] Fos. 116ᵛ–119ʳ, 119ᵛ–121ʳ. The 'Medici Codex' is Florence, Biblioteca Medicea Laurenziana, Acq. e doni 666; for the scribe see ibid. 110–19.

in CS 15, in layers that appear to reflect the presence of the French royal chapel (Compère himself among them) in Rome in January 1495.[44] The latest date of copying among the Sistine manuscripts for any piece of Compère's is *c*.1508–9 for *O genitrix gloriosa* in CS 46.[45] Mouton's music appears in Sistine manuscripts for the first time *c*.1503–4 with *Sancte Sebastiane* in CS 63, and (to judge from the frequency with which his masses and motets were copied) he seems to have been the composer whose music was most cultivated in the papal chapel during the papacy of Leo X.[46] One motet of Mouton's, *Queramus cum pastoribus*, had its refrain 'Noe, noe' revised to 'Alleluia' sometime after 1570, and was recopied as late as *c*.1620.[47]

But for these two composers in particular we do not depend on the evidence of copying alone. For once there is a documentary witness: a two-page memorandum compiled by the Sistine singer Giovanni Antonio Merlo in 1568. Along with various items of plainsong and extemporized counterpoint, some eighteen polyphonic compositions are mentioned (see Table 5.2).[48] Merlo writes in several cases that such-and-such 'is sung' or 'it is customary to sing', and I am quite sure he is describing a living part of the repertory. Only two of the eighteen pieces listed (both motets of Mouton's) were copied more recently than 1545, some twenty years before Merlo drew up the memorandum; at the other extreme, the two identifiable works by Compère both come from fifteenth-century manuscripts.

Of course, the eighteen pieces in the list can only represent the tip of the iceberg: not only are they unrepresentative of *all* the music being sung at the papal chapel in 1568 (for the singers must have been singing a good deal of recently composed music), they must also be insufficiently representative of the other old music then being performed. But Merlo's memorandum is unique, and we have no choice but to depend on it. It is striking that Compère and Mouton are not only two of the oldest composers on the list, but far and away the best represented: Mouton has four or five pieces (depending on

---

[44] See Sherr, 'Papal Chapel', 164–5.   [45] See Dean, 'Scribes of the Sistine Chapel', 245.

[46] Ibid. 251; 95, 138–9.

[47] The text of *Queramus* in CS 46, fos. 34ᵛ–36ʳ, was altered by the same hand that replaced the text of the Marian Gloria trope 'Spiritus et alme orphanorum paraclite', abolished by the reformed Missal of 1570, in Costanzo Festa's *Missa de domina nostra* (CS 26, fos. 5ᵛ–7ʳ); see Dean, 'Scribes of the Sistine Chapel', 205, 230, 243. The copy of *c*.1620 is CS 77, fos. 4ᵛ–12ʳ. This extremely lovely and popular motet, which survives in twenty-four vocal sources and eleven instrumental intabulations, had an astonishing distribution in space as well as time: no fewer than three of its sources were copied at missions in the mountains of western Guatemala (Bloomington, Indiana University, Lilly Library, Latin American Manuscripts, Guatemala, Music MSS 4, 8, 9). See Robert Stevenson, 'European Music in 16th-Century Guatemala', *Musical Quarterly*, 50 (1964), 345–6; Stevenson, *Renaissance and Baroque Musical Sources in the Americas* (Washington, DC, 1970), 50–62.

[48] See Richard Sherr, 'From the Diary of a 16th-Century Papal Singer', *Current Musicology*, 25 (1978), 83–98 at 91–4; Sherr (ed.), 'The Diary of the Papal Singer Giovanni Antonio Merlo', *Analecta musicologica*, 23 (1985), 75–128 at 122–3; Dean, 'Scribes of the Sistine Chapel', 207–14, from which (with corrections) Table 5.2 is digested.

TABLE 5.2. Compositions mentioned in the Merlo memorandum (in order of copying date)

Title		Composer	Source/no.	Date[a]
1.	*Missa L'homme armé*	Loyset Compère	CS 35/9	1482/92 S
2.	*Ave Maria*	Loyset Compère	CS 15/54	1495/1501 S
3.	*Missa L'homme armé*	Matthaeus Pipelare	CS 41/2	1503/4 D
4.	*Missus est Gabriel angelus*	Josquin des Prez	CS 63/7	1504/7 D
	or *Missus est Gabriel angelus*	Jean Mouton	CS 42/6	1509/12 D
	or *Missus est angelus Gabriel*	Jean Mouton	CS 19/14	1536/7 B
5.	*Missa Le villain jalloux*	Robert de Févin	CS 23/7	1507/8 D
	or *Missa Ave Maria*	Robert de Févin	CS 26/2	1517/19 D
6.	*Missa La chastagnia*	?	'messa vecchia'[b]	
7.	*Factum est cum baptizaretur*	Johannes Prioris	CS 42/12	1509/12 D
8.	'Infra ottava epifania cie			
	un motetto de compere'	Loyset Compère	(probably before 1510)[c]	
9.	*Missa Alma redemptoris mater*	Jean Mouton	CS 45/5	1511/12 D
10.	*Illuminare, illuminare Jerusalem*	Jean Mouton	CS 46/14	1514/15 D
11.	*Veni, Sancte Spiritus*	Jean Brunet	CS 46/19	1514/15 D
	or *Veni, Sancte Spiritus*	Loyset Piéton	CS 64/5	1538/9 B
			or CS 24/18	1545 B
	or *Veni, Sancte Spiritus*	Hesdin	CS 24/6	1545 B
12.	*Quem dicunt homines*	Jean Richafort	CS 46/23	1518 D
13.	*Veni Domine*	Cristóbal de Morales	CS 19/15	1536 B
14.	*Corona aurea*	Jacques Arcadelt	CS 24/9	1538/9 B
15.	*Alma redemptoris mater*	Costanzo Festa	CS 20/7 *or* 26	1539 B
16.	*O beata infantia*	Loyset Piéton	CS 24/10	1545 B
17.	*Benedicam Dominum*	Jean Mouton	CS 38/12	1560 B
18.	*Confitemini Domino*	Jean Mouton	CS 38/11	1562/3 B

[a] Dates followed by B are taken from Brauner, 'Parvus Manuscripts', those by D from Dean, 'Scribes of the Sistine Chapel', those by S from Sherr, 'Papal Chapel'. All dates are approximate, and refer to copying, not composition.

[b] The entries for nos. 5–6 are actually 'Una messa vecchia de rubreto fevino nel libro vecchio; Un'altra chiamata la Chastagnia'.

[c] None of Compère's motets surviving in Sistine MSS seems to be related to the Epiphany.

which setting of *Missus est* Merlo had in mind), and Compère three; only one other composer may have as many as two (Piéton, if Merlo was thinking of his *Veni, sancte spiritus*). Between them they account for nearly half the compositions on the list.

It seems certain that the music of Compère and Mouton was accorded canonical status at the papal chapel during the greater part of the sixteenth century. Their great contemporary Josquin, who had spent an appreciable time as a singer in the chapel, occupied a similar position, but apparently as a French rather than a papal composer. Few of his pieces can be assigned to his tenure at the papal chapel with any assurance: the hymn verses 'Monstra te esse matrem' from *Ave maris stella* and 'Honor, decus, imperium' from *Nardi Maria pistici* in CS 15, the tract *Domine, non secundum peccata nostra*, the motet *Illibata Dei Virgo nutrix*, the mass *L'homme armé super voces musicales*.[49] Only the last of these shows signs of having become a canonical composition: it was recopied in the early 1550s.

There are half a dozen of Josquin's motets, all of them likely to postdate his service in the papal chapel, in CS 38, copied between the early 1550s and 1563.[50] None of the motets in this manuscript has an earlier concordant source in the Sistine library, but the volume is dominated by composers copied there chiefly in the early sixteenth century—Josquin, Mouton, Festa, De Silva, Richafort, Moulu, La Fage—and so probably represents a rather large-scale programme of replacement of worn-out copies of music still being regularly performed. Merlo may refer to Josquin's *Missus est Gabriel* (if he does not intend one of Mouton's two motets with the same incipit). And in the 1570s someone erased the no longer tolerated text of the trope 'Spiritus et alme' from the Gloria of Josquin's *Missa de domina nostra* in CS 45, and Johannes Parvus altered the text underlay of his *Mittit ad Virginem* in CS 46; these two pieces were still being sung half a century after Josquin's death.[51] Finally, the *Diarii Sistini* for 1616 tell us that the motet at the Offertory on the second Sunday of Lent was Josquin's *Qui habitat*.[52]

But in the 1560s the stage was being set for a revolution. As Richard Sherr has pointed out, Merlo's list of 1568 coincides with the well-known augmentation of Palestrina's pension in 1565 'on account of various musical compositions that he has already composed and shall compose for the use of the chapel'—but Palestrina's compositions are noticeably absent from the memorandum, along with those of other contemporary Roman composers.[53] Merlo

---

[49] The hymn verses are unique to CS 15 and are obviously integrated into the hymn cycle there. For *Domine, non secundum* and *Illibata* see Richard Sherr, '*Illibata Dei Virgo Nutrix* and Josquin's Roman Style', *JAMS* 41 (1988), 434–64. For the *Missa L'homme armé* (whose designation 'super voces musicales' seems to stem from Petrucci, who had to distinguish two 'L'homme armé' masses by the same composer in the same print), see the contributions to this volume by Mitchell Brauner (Ch. 6) and James Haar (Ch. 9).

[50] The motets are *In principio erat Verbum*, fos. 4ᵛ–11ʳ; *In exitu Israel de Egypto*, fos. 11ᵛ–21ʳ; *Qui habitat in adiutorio altissimi*, fos. 21ᵛ–28ʳ; *In illo tempore: Assumpsit Jesus duodecim discipuli*, fos. 32ᵛ–34ʳ; *Miserere mei Deus*, fos. 44ᵛ–53ʳ; *Planxit autem David*, fos. 66ᵛ–76ʳ; *De profundis* a 5, fos. 109ᵛ–113ʳ. On the copying of CS 38, see Brauner, 'Parvus Manuscripts', 186–203. At the Library of Congress conference Louise Litterick suggested that *Planxit autem David* may be a work of Ninot le Petit, to whom it is attributed in Florence II.I.232, an earlier source than any that attribute it to Josquin.

[51] CS 45, fos. 6ᵛ–8ʳ; CS 46, fos. 131ᵛ, 132ᵛ. See Dean, 'Scribes of the Sistine Chapel', 204–6, 241, 246.

[52] Frey, 'Gesänge des Jahres 1616', 407.

[53] Sherr, 'From the Diary', 93. The quotation is cited in Giuseppe Baini, *Memorie storico-critiche della vita e delle opere di Giovanni Pierluigi da Palestrina*, 2 vols. (Rome, 1828; repr. Hildesheim, 1966), i. 242: 'ex causa diversarum compositionum musicalium, quas hactenus edidit, et est editurus ad commodum capellae'.

gives us a glimpse of part of the proto-canon of music being performed at the papal chapel during Palestrina's prime: an entrenched body of notably older music within which individual works by Palestrina and his contemporaries could be accommodated. But within a few years this situation was to be overturned by the Tridentine reform of the ritual, promulgated in the Breviary of 1568 and the Missal of 1570; this appears to have stimulated an enormous outpouring of new music from Palestrina, self-consciously and comprehensively organized by genre, that in the course of the seventeenth century came to form the nucleus of the papal chapel canon *en masse*.[54]

Like all canons, this evolved over time: works by composers more recent than Palestrina, most famously Allegri's *Miserere*, made their way into the canon, and one older composer, Cristóbal de Morales, was represented by a number of motets until well into the eighteenth century, though he seems then to have gone out of fashion.[55] But in the canon of the papal chapel the music of Palestrina has never yielded pride of place even into our own time.

[54] For the position of Palestrina's music in relation to the core repertories of the Cappella Sistina and the Cappella Giulia around 1570, see Jeffrey Dean, 'The Repertory of the Cappella Giulia in the 1560s', *JAMS* 41 (1988), 465–90 at 485–8.

[55] CS 484–9, copied *c.*1750, contains Morales's *Lamentabatur Jacob*, no. 37; *O sacrum convivium*, no. 44; *Inter vestibulum et altare*, no. 45; and *Veni, Domine*, no. 52. *Lamentabatur Jacob* is dated 1794 in CS 313, fo. 20^r; this seems to have been the only piece by Morales still sung from the late 18th c.

The Anonymous *Lumen ad revelationem* in CS 46

Sources: Aosta, fos. 190ᵛ–191ʳ (copied in the upper Rhine region, *c.*1435–9)
BAV, CS 46, fos. 59ᵛ–64ʳ (copied for the papal chapel by Johannes Orceau, *c.*1509–12)

The score here presented is transcribed from CS 46. Spelling, punctuation, and capitalization of words have been normalized. *Minor color* is not recorded. The words of the cantus firmus have been underlaid to mirror the plainchant, and those of the other voices have been brought into near coincidence with this, often requiring ligatures to be ignored. Asterisks mark parallel fifths between discantus and contratenor (see above, p. 146).Other peculiarities of the transcription should be self-explanatory.

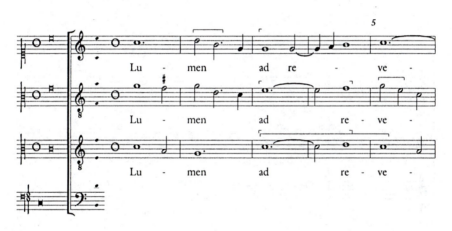

Jeffrey Dean

Nunc di- mit- tis ser- vum tu- um, Do- mi- ne, se- cun- dum ver- bum tu-

Nunc di- mit- tis ser- vum tu- um, Do- mi- ne, se- cun- dum ver- bum tu-

Nunc di- mit- tis ser- vum tu- um, Do- mi- ne, se- cun- dum ver- bum tu-

Nunc di- mit- tis ser- vum tu- um, Do- mi- ne,

- um in pa - - - - ce.

- um in pa - - - - ce.

- um in pa - - - - ce.

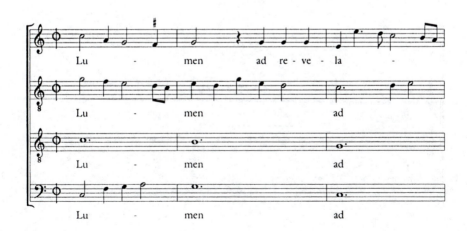

Lu - men ad re- ve- la -

Lu - men ad

Lu - men ad

Lu - men ad

am · · · · · · · · · · · · ple - - - bis
am · · · · · · · · · ple - bis
am · · · · · · · · · ple - bis
am · · · · · · · · · ple - bis

tu - e Is - ra - - - el.
tu - e Is - ra - el.
tu - e Is - ra - el.
tu - e Is - ra - el.

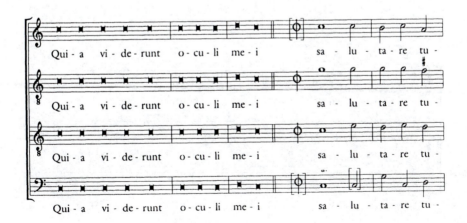

Qui - a vi - de - runt o - cu - li me - i sa - lu - ta - re tu -
Qui - a vi - de - runt o - cu - li me - i sa - lu - ta - re tu -
Qui - a vi - de - runt o - cu - li me - i sa - lu - ta - re tu -
Qui - a vi - de - runt o - cu - li me - i sa - lu - ta - re tu -

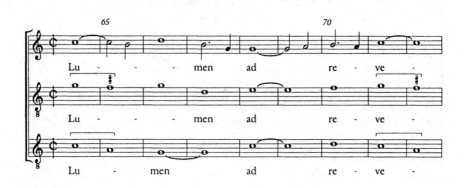

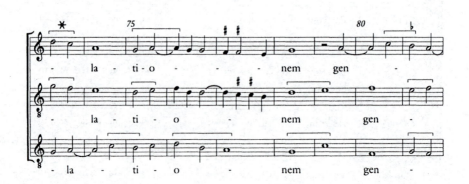

Jeffrey Dean

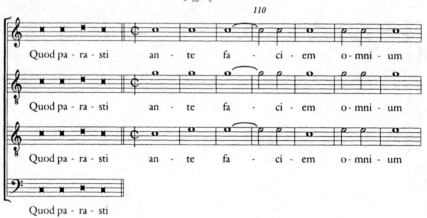

Quod pa - ra - sti an - te fa - ci - em o - mni - um

Quod pa - ra - sti an - te fa - ci - em o - mni - um

Quod pa - ra - sti an - te fa - ci - em o - mni - um

Quod pa - ra - sti

po - pu - lo - - - - - - rum.

po - pu - lo - - - - - rum.

po - pu - lo - - - - - - rum.

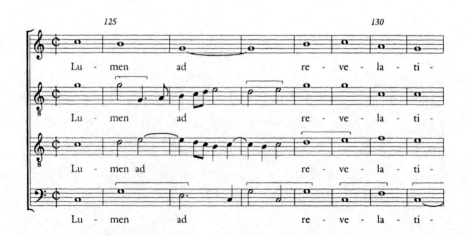

Lu - men ad re - ve - la - ti -

Lu - men ad re - ve - la - ti -

Lu - men ad re - ve - la - ti -

Lu - men ad re - ve - la - ti -

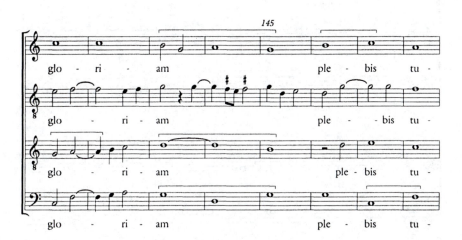

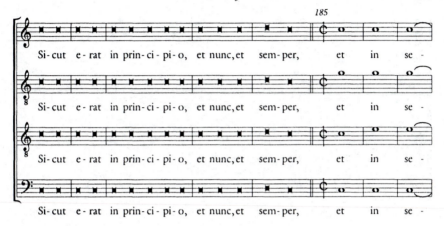

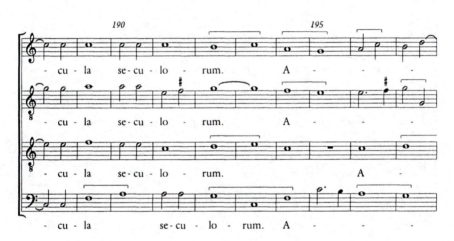

Jeffrey Dean

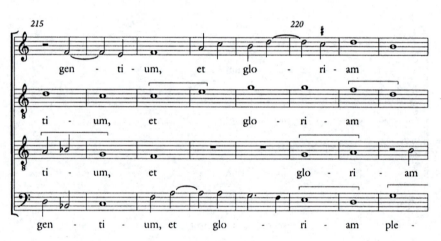

6

Traditions in the Repertory of the Papal Choir in the Fifteenth and Sixteenth Centuries

❦

MITCHELL P. BRAUNER

To define the traditions in the papal choir's repertory between the pap-
acies of Sixtus IV and Sixtus V, one cannot simply discuss those works
that were established in that repertory over a period of time. That
would be a discussion of a canon of works. Rather, one should put a slightly
different slant on the notion of canon and discuss not only particular pieces in
the repertory but also the types of pieces to which were attached ceremony,
lore, and symbolism—in other words, tradition.

Moreover, it is not so much the particular works or the work of particular
composers that should be called traditional but categories of works. Within
the categories one finds representative pieces and composers that bear the tradition. There were short-term traditions, those that were born and died within
a generation or two—in some cases made obsolete by liturgical change—and
surprisingly long-lived traditions, maintained even after new music was introduced into the repertory. We can get a sense of what older works were thought
to be worthy of singing and passing along from various sources: the Merlo
memorandum,[1] the information on works performed published by Frey[2] and
Lionnet[3] for the seventeenth century, and of course Baini.[4] Also, much of what
I believe to be part of the performance traditions of the choir entailed music
that was not copied into the Sistine choirbooks.

---

[1] See Richard Sherr, 'From the Diary of a 16th-Century Papal Singer', *Current Musicology*, 25 (1978), 83–98
at 91–3.

[2] Herman-Walther Frey, 'Die Gesänge der Sixtinischen Kapelle an den Sonntagen und hohen Kirchenfesten
des Jahres 1616', in *Mélanges Eugène Tisserant*, 7 vols. (Studi e testi 231–7; Vatican City, 1964), vi. 395–437.

[3] Jean Lionnet, 'Performing Practice in the Papal Chapel during the 17th Century', *EM* 15 (1987), 3–15, and
id., 'Palestrina e la Cappella Pontificia', in Lino Bianchi and Giancarlo Rostirola (eds.), *Atti del Convegno internazionale di studi palestriniani: Palestrina e la sua presenza nella musica e nella cultura europea da suo tempo ad oggi,
Anno Europeo della Musica 3–5 maggio 1986* (Palestrina, 1991), 127–35.

[4] Giuseppe Baini, *Memorie storico-critiche della vita e delle opere di Giovanni Pierluigi da Palestrina*, 2 vols.
(Rome, 1828; repr. Hildesheim, 1966).

As our point of departure, let us designate the traditional genres of music. In doing so it will become clear that some specific works were considered traditional, some composers' works were considered traditional, and most interestingly, that these traditional works themselves and the traditions that they carried were connected directly to the traditions and ceremonies of the papacy.

First, most musical institutions sang the Magnificat alternating verses of chant and polyphony. The pontifical choir sang the Vespers canticle with each verse set polyphonically, with only a chant incipit intoning the title word. The beginnings of this practice, before the appearance of the extant manuscript repertory in the late fifteenth century, are shadowy. The earliest sources, Vatican CS 15 and CS 44,[5] reflect the practice, which entailed adapting what were originally alternatim cycles by repeating verses. Further, these sets are miscellanies, compilations of the settings by many composers, some associated with the chapel, some not.[6]

There are three complete Magnificat cycles attributed to papal choir composers in our period of consideration: Carpentras (Elzéar Genet), Costanzo Festa, and Cristóbal de Morales. Carpentras's cycle, though copied by the chapel scribe Johannes Parvus for the Cappella Giulia at St Peter's in 1539–40 (in CG XII.5),[7] is not extant in a Cappella Sistina source and is untraceable in the earliest chapel catalogues. Festa's is to be found in CS 18, prepared at the composer's behest in 1539–40.[8] The earliest Sistine source for Morales's Magnificats is CS 21, prepared in 1576.[9] Without doubt, both the Carpentras and Morales cycles must have been available to the singers from the time of each composer's residence in the chapel, even though large, formal choirbook copies were not prepared during those periods.

As Jeffrey Dean describes in this volume (see Ch. 5), the practice of singing the canticle *Nunc dimittis* and its antiphon *Lumen ad revelationem* on the Feast of the Purification of the Virgin (2 February) in alternating chant and polyphony can be dated back to the fifteenth century. There are also a number

---

[5] On the dating of these MSS see Richard Sherr, 'The Papal Chapel ca. 1492–1513 and its Polyphonic Sources' (Ph.D. diss., Princeton University, 1975), 204–15 and 247–51, and now *Papal Music Manuscripts in the Late Fifteenth and Early Sixteenth Centuries* (Renaissance Manuscript Studies, 5; Neuhausen-Stuttgart, 1996), 25. Jeffrey Dean has offered a refined relative chronology of the same manuscripts, though in some cases with less convincing dates, in his 'Scribes of the Sistine Chapel, 1501–1527' (Ph.D. diss., University of Chicago, 1984). On these particular manuscripts see pp. 44–5, 48–59, and esp. 239–40.

[6] These and all Cappella Sistina manuscripts are inventoried by José M. Llorens in *Le opere musicali della Cappella Giulia, i: Manoscritti e edizioni fino al '700* (Studi e testi, 265; Vatican City, 1971) and id., *Capellae Sixtinae Codices musicis notis instructi sive manu scripti sive praelo excussi* (Studi e testi, 202; Vatican City, 1960).

[7] See Mitchell Brauner, 'Music from the Cappella Sistina at the Cappella Giulia', *Journal of Musicology*, 3 (1984), 287–311 at 289–90.

[8] Mitchell P. Brauner, 'The Parvus Manuscripts: A Study of Vatican Polyphony, ca. 1535 to 1580' (Ph.D. diss., Brandeis University, 1982), 123–8.

[9] Ibid. 222–3.

of sixteenth-century settings of the antiphon and canticle by Festa, Jean du Conseil, and, finally, Palestrina. Festa's setting was copied into the choirbook CS 20 and is recorded as having been performed in 1616.[10] Conseil's and Palestrina's survive in a set of partbooks from the eighteenth century (CS 484–9); Palestrina's was also copied in the seventeenth century (CS 71). The singing of these antiphon and canticle sets is thus documented from the fifteenth century right to the time of Baini.

The practice of singing of the Vespers hymns alternating polyphony and chant on the major feasts over the whole year dates from at least the fifteenth century. CS 15 contains a composite cycle and forms the earliest known repertory in this genre. Festa's cycle in CS 18 probably replaced it but was certainly not the only one available to the singers. Carpentras's hymns, published *c*.1535, and copied in 1541 for the Cappella Giulia (into CG XII.6) but not for the Cappella Sistina, could have been part of the repertory as well.[11]

The Lamentations with alternating chant and polyphony during Tenebrae services in Holy Week are among the best known and most highly documented parts of the polyphonic liturgy sung by the papal choir.[12] We cannot be sure whose Lamentation settings were used before the pontificate of Leo X. From that time we have documentation that the choir sang the settings by Carpentras, who states that he wrote them for Leo X, but that they were eventually copied without his consent in corrupted form.[13] This means that Carpentras's settings had become a staple in the repertory for quite some time before the corrected dedicatory copy he had prepared arrived in Rome (i.e. CS 163).

Although it is unclear if the singers actually performed from CS 163, this illuminated parchment manuscript is definitely the source of the three lessons by Carpentras in Rome Cas. 1671, a folio manuscript from the early 1540s that was prepared as a kind of performance collection.[14] It contains six lessons by Festa, in addition to the three by Carpentras, and two Passions, to be discussed shortly. The nine lessons thus formed the core of the Lamentation repertory sung by the papal choir until the late 1570s. At that time, probably within a year after Pope Gregory XIII commissioned Palestrina and Annibale

---

[10] Frey 'Die Gesänge der Sixtinischen Kapelle', 406. CS 20 is to be dated 1540–1. This is a slight revision from that in my dissertation ('The Parvus Manuscripts', 128–33).

[11] Brauner, 'Music from the Cappella Sistina', 289–90.

[12] The documentation can be found in the *Diarii Sistini* from 1535 onward, transcribed by Raffaele Casimiri in all volumes of *Note d'archivio* (1925–43); Frey's and Lionnet's studies of these documents for the 17th c.; references throughout Baini's *Memorie storico-critiche* for the 16th to 19th cc.; and most recently in Richard Boursy, 'The Mystique of the Sistine Chapel Choir in the Romantic Era', *Journal of Musicology*, 11 (1993), 277–329.

[13] The first indication comes from Carpentras's own dedication in CS 163, transcribed in Llorens, *Capellae Sixtinae Codices*, 191.

[14] See Brauner, 'The Parvus Manuscripts', 420–30. A more complete and accurate description is forthcoming in a revised edition of my dissertation.

Zoilo on 25 October 1577 to bring the antiphoners, graduals, and psalters, and other chants into line with the post-Tridentine liturgy,[15] the Casanatense Lamentations were replaced, in part, with edited versions by Festa and Morales—and indeed, the texts of these edited Lamentations coincide with the *Editio Medicaea*.[16] The editing of Morales's settings, in turn, implies they were sung before then as well, though there are no sources from the Cappella Sistina before these copies. In sum, then, for most of the sixteenth century, the choir sang Lamentations during Holy Week by Carpentras, Festa, and Morales.

Richard Sherr has recently noted the tradition of singing of the Passions in a manner described as Spanish by the papal masters of ceremonies, setting the words of Jesus on the Cross in three-part polyphony.[17] This may date from the papacy of the Borgia Pope Alexander VI (1492–1503) or even that of his uncle Calixtus III (1455–8).[18] Sherr suggests that the two Passions in Cas. 1671 might have been composed by the Spanish singer Juan Escribano. Given that the source dates from the early 1540s, it is just as likely that the composers were of a younger generation, perhaps Bartolomé Escobedo or Cristóbal de Morales. The chapel sang the parts of the Passion *a 3* at least into the seventeenth century: the *Diarii Sistini* record such performances in Holy Week of 1616.[19]

It is clear that the pontifical choir sang all or part of the Mass ordinary in polyphony. There is a significant amount of Mass music by papal composers from the late fourteenth through the sixteenth centuries and beyond. Performance of ferial Masses and festal cycles are amply documented.[20] At times the Credo was not sung polyphonically and sometimes a Credo from another cycle was substituted. There are numerous instances recorded of these practices; I shall simply cite some from the seventeenth century involving sixteenth-century works. In 1624, as Lionnet has written, displeasure arose over the choice of a Morales mass with a secular cantus firmus. The singer who made the choice was told at the end of the Gloria to pick a different Sanctus and Agnus, implying that the Credo was either not to be sung polyphonically, or had already been chosen from another cycle.[21] For 1616, Frey records no

---

[15] The papal brief commissioning Palestrina and Zoilo is best known in English from Oliver Strunk's translation in *Source Readings in Music History* (New York, 1950), 358–9.

[16] See Brauner, 'The Parvus Manuscripts', 349–53.

[17] Richard Sherr, 'The "Spanish Nation" in the Papal Chapel, 1492–1521', *EM* 20 (1992), 601–9 at 602.

[18] On Calixtus and music, see Pamela Starr, 'Music and Music Patronage at the Papal Court, 1447–1464' (Ph.D. diss., Yale University, 1987), 7–10.

[19] See Frey, 'Die Gesänge der Sixtinischen Kapelle', 411 and 413.

[20] See John Nádas, 'Further Notes on Magister Antonius dictus Zacharias de Teramo', *Studi musicali*, 15 (1986), 167–82, on the composers who were papal singers in Italy during the Great Schism. On polyphony for the Avignon papacy see Andrew Tomasello, *Music and Ritual at Papal Avignon, 1309–1403* (Ann Arbor, 1983). Other references are to be gleaned from the *Diarii* (including the studies by Frey and Lionnet).

[21] Lionnet, 'Performance Practice in the Papal Chapel', 11.

fewer than nine instances in which the Credo of one mass was substituted for that of the mass being sung that day. Even the Credo of the *Missa Papae Marcelli* was not exempt from replacement.[22]

Certain specific genres and sub-genres of polyphonic masses were also traditional. Two of particular interest are a form of polyphonic mass for the Blessed Virgin and the *Missa L'homme armé*. During the papacy of Leo X, Vatican composers started to use a specific formula in the composition of the *Missa de Beata Virgine*,[23] paraphrasing the Gregorian Kyrie and Gloria IX and Sanctus and Agnus XVII and setting the Credo in five voices with a fully texted Marian cantus firmus in the tenor. In keeping with late medieval practice, the *Spiritus et alme* trope is set in the Gloria.[24] Indeed, nearly all the Lady Masses in the earlier Cappella Sistina manuscripts have the trope. In many of these the trope texts have been erased or covered over, which implies post-Tridentine use. The polytextual Credos may have continued to be sung as well, perhaps without the added text, although, given the common practice, the singers may have simply substituted different Credos.

The composition of this type of Lady Mass stops in the 1540s. Arcadelt's mass, copied then, has a five-voice Credo (without a separate Marian chant as cantus firmus) in an otherwise four-voice cycle.[25] Later *Missae de Beata Virgine* do not follow the formula. Even though the compositional formula seems to have had a relatively short life, the performance of these works obviously lasted beyond the period of reform. The institution, thus, hung on to its traditions, even as Church polyphony moved either to the radically new and complex, or to the very simple and utilitarian in the seventeenth century.

Irrespective of the origins of the *L'homme armé* masses—indeed, irrespective of the origins of the earliest sources of these masses in the choir's library—it is the Cappella Sistina that perpetuated the *L'homme armé* mass tradition to the end of the fifteenth century and into the next. Of the Vatican composers who wrote *L'homme armé* masses while in the papal choir two are of particular note

[22] Frey, 'Die Gesänge der Sixtinischen Kapelle', *passim*. The Credo of the *Missa Papae Marcelli* was replaced by that from Palestrina's *Missa Brevis* on the Tuesday after Easter, 5 April. I have come across a notice in which the Credo of the *Missa Papae Marcelli* was replaced by that from Noel Bauldeweyn's *Missa En douleur et tristesse*, both in CS 22. My notes, however, are incomplete, and I have been unable to verify the reference. I simply report it, then, as an uncorroborated observation.

[23] The masses in question are those by Misonne and d'Argentil in CS 13; Beausseron and Morales in CS 19; Festa in CS 26 (though his does not completely conform to the model), Michot in CS 55, and the conflation by Josquin d'Or and Beausseron also in CS 55.

[24] This type of mass is discussed in Nors Josephson, 'The *Missa de Beata Virgine* of the Sixteenth Century' (Ph.D. diss., University of California at Berkeley, 1970), 191–203.

[25] Arcadelt's mass is found in CS 155 and dates from *c*.1542–3. This dating is also revised from my dissertation.

for our purposes here.[26] The mass by Marbriano de Orto perhaps dates from
the time of Innocent VIII. It was copied into a libretto (that is a booklet or
fascicle manuscript) and left unbound until at least the 1570s if not much later.
At the time it was bound, a new first leaf replaced the original, prepared either
from the original, or as a reconstruction. There would be no reason to prepare
this new first leaf had that piece not still been in use.[27]

The other cycle, Josquin's *Missa L'homme armé super voces musicales*, was
copied into a libretto in the early 1490s that has remained separate and intact
ever since (CS 197).[28] It has miniatures on the first opening and the depiction
of an armed man (St Michael?) slaying a dragon at the beginning of Agnus III
(see below, Pl. 13). There is another Sistine copy of the work, in CS 154—the
only reading of the mass that has an *Et in spiritum* section in the Credo, and an
added fifth part to the third Agnus (attributed to Johannes Abbate, a chapel
member). In all other respects, including the unusual placement of a miniature
at the beginning of the third Agnus (see below, Pl. 14), the readings in CS 197
and 154 are almost identical.[29] Clearly the latter was copied from the former.
The completion of the Credo brought the work into conformity with common practice, and the additional voice in the last section updated it to mid-
sixteenth-century style. CS 154 was copied almost entirely before 1555 but
was not actually completed until about 1560.[30] Thus, the updating of this
apparently beloved work fell during the period of reform, at least sixty years
after its composition.[31]

As to motets and motet-like compositions, it became traditional—and
remained so into the seventeenth century—to sing motets after the offertory.
The practice is detailed by Anthony Cummings in his 1981 study on the motet
in the early sixteenth century and is corroborated by Frey and Lionnet for the
seventeenth century.[32] In addition, as I suggested in my article on the so-called

[26] The masses by Du Fay, Busnois, Regis, Caron, and Faugues are in CS 14, which probably dates from the
1480s (my thanks to Flynn Warmington for sharing this and other soon to be published information on this
MS). Those by Compère, Tinctoris, Basiron, and Ockeghem were copied into CS 35, the earliest extant choirbook actually copied in the Vatican for the chapel's use. CS 14 came into the chapel's library with CS 51 before
or at about the same time that CS 35 was copied in the late 1480s. Four others were copied in slightly later MSS:
those by Brumel (CS 49), Vacqueras (CS 49), and Pipelare (CS 41), and Josquin's *Missa L'homme armé sexti toni*
(CS 41). Josquin's mass *super voces musicales* and de Orto's will be discussed presently.

[27] The libretto is found at the beginning of CS 64. See Brauner, 'The Parvus Manuscripts', 226 and 243–55,
for the dating of this MS. Adalbert Roth has identified the scribe of the libretto as the main contributor to CS
35 (personal communication).

[28] Sherr ('The Papal Chapel, ca. 1492–1513', 191–2, 204–7, and 214–15) identifies the scribe as one who
contributes to the hymn cycle in CS 15 and dates these contributions at *c.*1492–5.

[29] See James Haar's discussion, below, Ch. 9.

[30] See Brauner, 'The Parvus Manuscripts', 163–8 and 172–5.   [31] Roughly 1489 to 1495.

[32] Anthony M. Cummings, 'Toward an Interpretation of the Sixteenth-Century Motet', *JAMS* 34 (1981),
43–59; Frey 'Die Gesänge der Sixtinischen Kapelle', and Lionnet, 'Performance Practice in the Papal Chapel'.
Also see Hartmuth Möller, 'Motetten nach dem Offertorium im 17. und 18. Jahrhundert', in *Collectanea II*,
289–331.

Panuzzi Catalogue of 1687, sequences and Marian antiphons were used as votive hymns.[33] The settings of *Corona aurea*, especially those by Arcadelt and Palestrina, were performed at the investiture of bishops, the coronation of popes, and the anniversaries of the popes' coronations.[34] Festa's *Te Deum* also must be considered among the traditional works in the repertory. Baini reports that it was performed regularly into the nineteenth century.[35]

Particular motet-like compositions with chant incipits sometimes replaced the corresponding chant. Examples are the Magnificat antiphons for certain feasts, like SS Peter and Paul, but most pointedly the tract for Ash Wednesday, *Domine non secundum peccata*, whose polyphonic performance and composition can be dated from the time of Innocent VIII to the post-Tridentine era. As Richard Sherr has outlined, the ceremony of the papal Mass for Ash Wednesday required the pope to move from his throne to the faldstool in the centre of the chapel and back again during the performance of the tract, these movements to be co-ordinated with the singing of certain parts of the text. The need to relate music and ceremonial action caused the various settings of *Domine non secundum* that originated in the Vatican to have a certain distinctive structure, adhered to more or less throughout the period that the papal composers wrote these pieces. The ones in CS 35, including Josquin's, are the earliest. The last to appear was by Bartolomé Escobedo in CS 24, copied in the late 1540s, perhaps even close to 1550.[36] A survey of the repertory as a whole, even into the eighteenth century, revealed that there were no *Domine non secundum* settings copied after the Council of Trent. The practice and tradition of singing it in polyphony must have declined under the influence of Church reform. Sherr cites a document showing that singing even only part of the tract polyphonically in 1578 was considered inappropriate.[37]

It is clear from the foregoing discussion that the music of certain composers comprised the greatest percentage of the papal choir's repertorial traditions. The names of the composers regarded as traditional are well known and not unexpected: Josquin, Carpentras, Festa, Morales, Arcadelt, and ultimately Palestrina. Other composers' works also fit into the traditional role as well. In the case of Josquin, however, while his music was copied from the time of his

[33] Mitchell Brauner, 'The Catalogue of Raffaele Panuzzi and the Repertory of the Papal Chapel in the 15th and 16th Centuries', *Journal of Musicology*, 8 (1990), 427–43 at 434–5.

[34] See José M. Llorens, 'The Musical Codexes of the Sistine Chapel Written through the Generosity of the Pauline Popes', in James W. Pruett (ed.), *Studies in Musicology: Essays in the History, Style, and Bibliography of Music in Memory of Glen Haydon* (Chapel Hill, NC, 1969), 18–50 at 33, and Sherr, 'From the Diary of a Papal Singer', 91–3. Also see Brauner, 'The Catalogue of Raffaele Panuzzi', 441.

[35] Baini, *Memorie storico-critiche*, i. 215. It was also sung on 9 Jan. 1616 (Frey, 'Die Gesänge der Sixtinischen Kapelle', 402).

[36] On the date of this MS see Brauner, 'The Parvus Manuscripts', 152–72.

[37] See Richard Sherr, '*Illibata Dei Virgo nutrix* and Josquin's Roman Style', *JAMS* 41 (1988), 434–64 at 455–62.

membership in the choir, beginning in 1489,[38] to the last sessions of the Council of Trent, in 1563, very few works—and perhaps only one, the *Missa L'homme armé super voces musicales*—really have the hallmark of tradition.

Finally, I wish to discuss the performance of works not copied into the archival collections. This implies a hidden repertory, and a tradition of using repertory not to be copied into the volumes of the chapel's library. For the fifteenth century one can argue that the papal singers did not have choirbooks and did not regularly employ scribes. The music of composers like Puyllois would thus not have been copied into any contemporary archival collection.[39] Even in the later period, when the chapel had scribes regularly on the payroll, music by chapel composers did not always get copied down. A composer like Conseil, who spent his whole compositional career in the employ of the papacy, only had three of his twenty or so sacred works copied into chapel books, and only one in his lifetime.[40] Morales's Magnificats were not copied into an extant book until thirty years after his departure from its ranks (in CS 21, dated 1576). The so-called corrupt versions of Carpentras's Lamentations appear not in a Cappella Sistina book but only in CG XII.3 (dated 1543). Clearly, they must have used some sort of performance materials, but certainly not an archival choirbook. And what of other works we have not even mentioned, like Festa's alternatim setting of the burial responsory, the *Libera me*? No Cappella Sistina copies have come down to us from this period.[41] Performance of the *Libera me* was required of the singers at funerals of their own members and members of the curia, though not necessarily in polyphony. One might expect to have, or have some record of, at least some form of archival copy, even if not in a large choirbook. The 'underground' repertory constitutes the most intriguing tradition of the papal choir. It implies that we do not know even half of what we think we know to be traditional.

[38] This revised date of Josquin's entry into the papal chapel was reported by Pamela Starr in 'Josquin in Rome, and a Case of Mistaken Identity', read at the annual meeting of the American Musicological Society, Baltimore, 1996.

[39] On Puyllois see Starr, 'Music and Music Patronage', 167–75 and 287–8. Only one of Puyllois's sacred works, *Flos de spina*, is represented in a chapel MS, CS 15, fos. 166ᵛ–168ʳ, where it is without attribution.

[40] On this composer see Mitchell Brauner, 'Jean du Conseil (Johannes Consilium): His Life and Motets' (M.F.A. thesis, Brandeis University, 1978).

[41] It is to be found in Rome, S. Maria Maggiore, MS G.IV.26, and Lucca, Seminario Arcivescovile, MS A.8.

PART II

The Papal Choir as Institution

7

Strange Obituaries: The Historical Uses of the *per obitum* Supplication

❦

PAMELA F. STARR

WHEN the Renaissance musician breathed his last, we must hope that he died at peace, surrounded by mourning colleagues and family; perhaps, as Du Fay had planned, to the cadences of his own specially chosen polyphony. But it is also likely that the onlookers included someone less concerned with final farewells than with passing along information of the decease to a person with a fast horse to Rome. Even as the obsequies were in progress, it is likely that a petition was being rushed to the papal court with a request for an ecclesiastical benefice that had been held by the deceased musician. If the petition reached the curia and was processed before any other petition for the same benefice, its success was probable. The key was priority of dating: the earliest petition had priority in canon law.[1] The instrument containing this petition was called a *per obitum* supplication, a request for a benefice relinquished by the decease of the holder. It is by far the most common type of supplication: tens of thousands are found in the Registers of Supplications (Registra Supplicationum) in the Vatican Archives.[2] These

This essay is a slightly expanded version of the one originally presented. It has benefited from subsequent discoveries made in the Archivio Segreto Vaticano in the summer of 1993, with research grants generously provided by the American Philosophical Society and the Research Council of the University of Nebraska. This version was read at the Fifty-Ninth Annual Meeting of the American Musicological Society, Montreal, 4–7 November 1993. All 15th-c. dates are given in modern style.

[1] On the importance of priority of dating, see Léon Célier, *Les Dataires du XVe siècle et les origines de la Daterie apostolique* (Bibliothèque des Écoles Françaises d'Athènes et de Rome, 103; Paris, 1910), 71 ff; and Thomas Frenz, *Die Kanzlei der Päpste der Hochrenaissance (1471–1527)* (Bibliothek des Deutschen Historischen Instituts in Rom, 63; Tübingen, 1986), 97–100. Roberto Bizzochi describes the practice of planting 'spies' at the bedside of a dying cleric, 'exploratores industrios circum aegrotantis cubiculum', who would speed the news to an expectant beneficiary in Rome. See his *Chiesa e potere nella Toscana del Quattrocento* (Annali dell'Istituto Storico Italo-Germanico, 6; Bologna, 1987), 107.

[2] I have treated the subject of papal provisions through supplications at length in my article 'Rome as the Centre of the Universe: Papal Grace and Music Patronage', *EMH* 11 (1992), 223–62, esp. 225–34 and the bibliographical citations contained therein. Before the papacy of Innocent VIII, the use of the specific designation 'per obitum' for this type of supplication was sporadic. The more usual designation was 'nova provisio'.

supplications testify to far more than the cupidity for preferment of Renaissance clerics. In them, we find definitive information concerning the many otherwise enigmatic careers of papal singers and other Renaissance musicians, both illustrious and obscure.

Perhaps the simplest and most obvious kind of information to be gleaned from the *per obitum* supplication is a musician's date of death. For most musicians, this has been, up till now, an open question. The new information from the Vatican presents the precise year of death and even allows us to conjecture an approximate month of the year for some individuals. The period from the mid-1440s to the early 1470s saw, as we might expect, the decease of many composers and musicians of the 'generation of *c.*1400', that is, the composers and performers active in the first two or three decades of the fifteenth century. The Vatican registers record the deaths of no fewer than eleven former papal singers of the reign of Martin V and the early years of his successor, Eugene IV. For most of these musicians, the death date has never been established.[3] I shall single out four here, for whom the supplications also yielded additional useful data: Johannes Dornart (d. 1447), Johannes Vincenet (d. 1447), Johannes Brassart (d. 1455), and Nicolaus Zacharie (d. 1466).

The confirmation of Vincenet's date of death will probably invite the most attention. With it, we can finally put to rest one of the most persistent Doppelmeister issues of the fifteenth century: the identification of the one-time singer in the chapel of Martin V, Johannes Vincenet, with the composer Vincenet, a musician associated with the chapel of Ferrante, King of Naples. Although it has been viewed with increasing scepticism in recent years, this problematic identification continues to haunt the secondary literature concerning Vincenet.[4] From the Vatican Archives we have no fewer than three supplications of the *per obitum* type dated April 1447, in which benefices held by the recently deceased former papal musician, Johannes Vincenetius, are

---

[3] For comprehensive biographical information on musicians of the papal court during the 15th c., see Pamela Starr, 'Music and Music Patronage at the Papal Court, 1447–1464' (Ph.D. diss., Yale University, 1987), 114–98 and my forthcoming study: *Storia della Cappella Pontificia, dal Concilio di Costanza al pontificato di Giulio II* (monograph to be published by the Fondazione Palestrina as part of the series Storia della Cappella musicale Pontificia (1300–1990), ed. Giancarlo Rostirolla (Palestrina, 1994–)). Musicians serving during the first two decades of the 15th c. will be discussed in the forthcoming monograph by John Nádas and Giuliano di Bacco, to be published in the same series. For information about musicians serving at the end of the century, see also Richard Sherr, 'The Papal Chapel ca. 1492–1513 and its Polyphonic Sources' (Ph.D. diss., Princeton University, 1975).

[4] See, for example, Manfred Schuler, 'Zur Geschichte der Kapelle Papst Martins V', *AfMw* 25 (1968), 30–45; Vincenet, *The Collected Works*, ed. Bertran Davis (RRMMA 9–10; Madison, 1978), vii–x; Tom Ward, 'Vincenet, Johannes', *New Grove*, xix. 781–2; Allan Atlas, *Music at the Aragonese Court of Naples* (Cambridge, 1985), 69–71 (the first author to present a strong case against the two musicians being the same individual); Adalbert Roth, *Studien zum frühen Repertoire der päpstlichen Kapelle unter dem Pontifikat Sixtus' IV. (1471–1484)* (Capellae Apostolicae Sixtinaeque Collectanea Acta Monumenta, 1; Vatican City, 1991), 28; and Reinhard Strohm, *The Rise of European Music, 1380–1500* (Cambridge, 1993), 601.

requested by other clerics.[5] As the composer Vincenet's works clearly date from the 1460s and 1470s, he and the papal singer cannot be one and the same.[6]

Moreover, the Vatican has yielded two additional documents that finally provide a surname and a partial biography for the composer Vincenet. His full name was Vincentius du Bruecquet, organist and singer in the ducal chapel of Savoy between 1450 and 1464.[7] The composer probably went directly from Savoy to Ferrante's court at Naples, where he made the acquaintance of Jachetto da Marvilla before 1469, and where, in 1470, he resigned his benefices, perhaps in order to contract marriage. Within nine years, Vincentius du Bruecquet had died, leaving a widow, Vannella.[8]

Nicolaus Zacharie's death date in 1466 testifies to an extraordinarily long life-span for these times.[9] Like most of his colleagues in the chapel of Martin V,

---

[5] See ASV, RS 416, fo. 93ᵛ (dated 17 Apr. 1447, a supplication for Vincenet's canonry at the cathedral of Metz); fo. 119ʳ (dated 16 Apr. 1447, for his canonry in the collegiate church Dei Custodia in Toul); and fos. 223ʳ–224ʳ (dated 16 Apr. 1447, for his canonry at the cathedral of Toul).

[6] I present here an aside about Vincenet's *obit* that both reflects the lighter side of archival research and urges caution with even the presumably authoritative documents of the Vatican Archives. During the proceedings of the conference reported in the present volume, Alejandro Planchart contradicted this information on Vincenet in a paper of his own, presenting the composer's death date as 1438. Which was the correct death date? During the summer of 1993, at the Vatican Archives, Professor Planchart and I together were able to resolve this conundrum. In 1438, Vincenet was indeed presumed dead by a cleric requesting one of his benefices (ASV, RS 350, fo. 201ʳ⁻ᵛ, dated 6 Sept. 1438, for a parish church in the diocese of Toul, held by Vincenet). The petitioner, Guillermus Johannis, a cleric of that diocese, evidently had been misinformed about the gravity of Vincenet's illness. In 1443, Vincenet himself demonstrated that rumours of his death had been greatly exaggerated by sending to the pope a petition of his own (ASV, RS 385, fo. 199ʳ, dated 27 Oct. 1443). Finally, in 1447 Vincenet once again was placed—definitively, this time—in his grave.

[7] ASV, RS 657, fos. 163ᵛ–164ʳ (dated 23 May 1470) and RS 664, fo. 46ʳ (dated 19 Jan. 1471). Both supplications concern the resignation of Du Bruecquet's benefices in the dioceses of Geneva and Tarantaise to Johannes de Dortenco, a familiar of Cardinal Caraffa, Ordinary of the diocese of Naples. Du Bruecquet described himself as a cleric of the diocese of Cambrai, which fits well with a contemporary description of the composer Vincenet as being from the province of Hainaut.

On Du Bruecquet's career in Savoy, see Marie-Thérèse Bouquet, 'La cappella musicale dei duchi di Savoia dal 1450 al 1500', *Rivista italiana di musicologia*, 3 (1968), 233–85. My thanks to David Fallows for sharing with me his long-standing hypothesis that the composer Vincenet and the musician Vincenet du Bruecquet were the same individual. He discusses this in the preface to Geneviève Thibault (ed.), *Chansonnier de Jean de Montchenu* (Paris, 1991), p. cviii. I am pleased to be able to confirm Dr Fallows's hypothesis.

[8] On the career of the composer Vincenet, see Atlas, *Music at the Aragonese Court of Naples*, and Frank A. D'Accone, 'The Singers of San Giovanni in Florence during the 15th Century', *JAMS* 14 (1961), 307–58, esp. 324–5. It is an interesting coincidence that both the composer Vincenet and his one-time double Johannes Vincenet shared the experience of having worked alongside Guillaume Du Fay, the former when Du Fay served as *maître de chapelle* for Louis of Savoy in the early 1450s, and the latter as a colleague of Du Fay's in the chapel of Martin V in the late 1420s. It is certainly possible that Du Fay, who had at least one connection in Naples in the 1450s, helped to procure the position at the Aragonese court for Du Bruecquet. And it is also possible that Du Bruecquet served as a conduit for Du Fay's works into the repertory of the chapel and manuscripts of Neapolitan provenance from the 1460s and 1470s. I thank Alejandro Planchart for drawing my attention to these possibilities, as well as for having recently reconfirmed the spelling of Du Bruecquet's name in the Vatican documents.

[9] ASV, RS 602, fo. 133ᵛ (dated 26 Sept. 1466); RS 604, fos. 166ᵛ–167ʳ and 181ʳ (dated 8 Dec. 1466); and RS 629, fos. 265ᵛ–266ʳ (dated 3 Sept. 1468). All supplications concern one benefice. See below for discussion of these supplications.

Nicolaus was probably born in the 1390s, and thus he had easily accomplished the biblical span of three score and ten at his demise.[10]

Sometimes, as with the papal musician Henricus Rosa de Zelle, we can pin-point the date of death almost to the day. The earliest supplication for one of Rosa's benefices, submitted by another member of the pope's household, is dated 17 July 1468.[11] Rosa died *intra romanam curiam*, and was paid his monthly chapel stipend on 1 July. So he must have died while still serving as a member of the *capella pontificia*, sometime close to 17 July, when the first *per obitum* supplication was lodged in the papal curia.

The *per obitum* supplication also presents information about the musician when alive. For example, we can learn of positions, both musical and non-musical, held by former and currently serving members of the papal chapel and other music institutions of the fifteenth century. In the supplication for Johannes Brassart's canonry at St-Paul in Liège, he is described as having held the title of *rector principalis*, or head of the Imperial chapel of Frederick III.[12] Johannes Dornart apparently held the position of *ceremoniarius* while serving as *cantor-capellanus* in the papal chapel.[13] This was a highly accountable position, involving special responsibility for liturgy and ceremony: it was normally held by a highly educated and high-ranking cleric.[14] Ricardus Herbare, a musician serving three popes successively, from 1432 to 1456, died *intra romanam curiam* while simultaneously holding down two demanding positions: those of *cantor-capellanus* and *procurator litterae contradictarum audientiae* in the papal chancery.[15] The latter office was venal; its sale in 1503 brought 750 ducats to the papal coffers. (Herbare apparently found the office so time-consuming that he was frequently fined for delinquency in his chapel duties.)[16]

We can also determine from the *per obitum* supplications the place of origin of a musician. Several documents help to clarify the diocesan origin of the papal

[10] When Nicolaus died, a person was considered to be 'old' at anywhere from thirty-five to fifty years. Death commonly came before the age of sixty. See G. Creighton, 'When Did a Man in the Renaissance Grow Old?', *Studies in the Renaissance*, 14 (1967), 7–32.

[11] ASV, RS 627, fo. 180ʳ (for a parish church in Laeken, diocese of Cambrai).

[12] ASV, RS 485, fo. 253ʳ (dated 22 Oct. 1455). For further discussion of this new information on Brassart, see my Communication to *Plainsong and Medieval Music* 2 (1993), 215–16.

[13] ASV, RS 417, fo. 78ʳ (dated 13 May 1447, a supplication for Dornart's canonry in the collegiate church of Werny in the diocese of Tournai); RS 424, fo. 189ʳ (dated 21 Mar. 1447, for his canonry at St-Pierre in Lille, in the diocese of Tournai).

[14] Information and bibliography on the office of *clericus ceremoniarum* can be found in Andrew Tomasello, *Music and Ritual at Papal Avignon, 1309–1403* (Ann Arbor, 1983), 122; and Starr, 'Music and Music Patronage', 226–30.

[15] ASV, RS 479, fos. 52ᵛ–53ʳ (dated 31 Mar. 1456, a supplication for Herbare's office of *procurator litterae audientiae* by Ludovicus Thora, a papal secretary).

[16] For the venality of the office, see Frenz, *Die Kanzlei der Päpste*, 215–16; for pluralistic office-holding and absenteeism, see Peter Partner, *The Pope's Men* (Oxford, 1990), esp. 56–61 and 106–9. That Herbare actually served in both offices is demonstrated in RS 469, fo. 175ᵛ (see Starr, 'Music and Music Patronage', 189–90 for a discussion of the implications of this document).

singer Johannes Dornart, incorrectly assigned to Rouen by Haberl, and, follow-ing Haberl, by Manfred Schuler and others.[17] The documents point, instead, to an origin in Tournai, in the heart of Burgundian territory. Indeed, one of his benefices in that diocese was requested by a councillor of Philip of Burgundy.[18]

Similarly, one supplication, lodged at the time of his death, reveals the prob-able home town of another papal musician, Sigerius Nerin (d. 1463). His name in this petition is uniquely given as Sigerius de Nederhem, very likely a curial abbreviation of Neder-Heembeek, a village in the ancient duchy of Brabant (and now a suburb of Brussels).[19]

Living musicians have also left us information about themselves through the medium of *per obitum* supplications for benefices relinquished by deceased clerics. Turning to a composer active at the end of the fifteenth century, we dis-cover the probable diocese of origin of Antoine Brumel. The diocese of Chartres had been suggested most recently as the birthplace of this com-poser.[20] However, in a *per obitum* supplication he submitted in 1488, while serving as the Master of the Innocents at a collegiate church in Geneva, Brumel describes himself as a 'clericus laudunensis', a cleric from the diocese of Laon.[21] Still later, following a time-honoured practice of professional musicians in the Renaissance, Brumel returned to the scene of his earliest training, accepting installation as a canon of the cathedral of Laon.[22]

Another composer of note may have unknowingly informed historians of his place of origin. In a *per obitum* petition drawn up when he was a member of the chapel of the duke of Ferrara, Johannes Martini designated himself 'Johannes Martinus Luce' (or 'Lute'; chancery scribes often confused the two letters), 'clericus cameracensis'.[23] I would suggest that the additional surname or sobriquet might refer to the town of Martini's birth: Leuze, located in the province of Brabant, in the diocese of Cambrai.[24]

[17] Fr. X. Haberl, *Die römische 'schola cantorum' und die päpstlichen Kapellsänger bis zur Mitte des 16. Jahrhunderts* (Bausteine für Musikgeschichte, 3; Leipzig, 1888; repr. Hildesheim, 1971), 31. See also Martin Schuler, 'Die Musik in Konstanz wärend des Konzils, 1414–1418', *Acta musicologica* 38 (1966), 150–68 at 156; and John Nádas, following Schuler, private communication. The error apparently arose through a confusion of the papal singers Johannes Dornart and Johannes Dore. The latter was certainly from Rouen.

[18] ASV, RS 424, fo. 189r (dated 21 Mar. 1447, a supplication by Symon de Moekerke).

[19] ASV, RS 566, fo. 78r (dated 19 Aug. 1463, a supplication for a parish church in Haesedonck, a village near Neder-Heembeek, by another cleric from the diocese of Cambrai).

[20] Barton Hudson, 'Antoine Brumel', *New Grove*, iii. 377.

[21] ASV, RS 894, fo. 257r (dated 20 Nov. 1488, a request for a chaplaincy in the collegiate church of St-Blaise, diocese of Geneva, vacant *per obitum Johannis de Bichis*).

[22] Hudson, ('Brumel', 377), indicates that the composer was a canon of the chapter of the cathedral of Laon in 1497.

[23] ASV, RS 894, fo. 65r (dated 5 Nov. 1488, a petition for a canonry at the cathedral of Reggio Emilia, vacated by the death of Geroldus de Bonzanis).

[24] This hypothesis is supported by information presented in Lewis Lockwood, *Music in Renaissance Ferrara, 1400–1505: The Creation of a Musical Centre in the Fifteenth Century* (Oxford, 1984), 167, that Martini 'was regularly called in Ferrarese records "Johannes Martini de Brabantia" or "Barbante"'.

The social condition of Renaissance musicians is another enigma for modern historians. We generally assume that the professional musician was originally a member of the artisan or peasant classes, elevating his social status through cathedral training and lucrative employment in the secular chapels, cathedrals, and collegiate churches of Europe. To my knowledge, there was only one member of the pope's music chapel in the fifteenth century who could boast membership in the aristocracy: Thomas Leporis, who described himself in a *per obitum* petition for the benefice of a deceased colleague as 'de nobile genere procreatus'.[25]

Ecclesiastical benefices were the prizes that preoccupied clergy, musicians and non-musicians alike. It is, of course, this preoccupation with preferment that produced the many *per obitum* supplications; and these, in turn, are more informative than any other source about a musician's success in the pursuit of benefices. Consider again Henricus Rosa, as a good example of a musician whose decease revealed that he had succeeded to nearly all the benefices requested of his employer, the pope. He died possessed of four benefices in his native diocese of Cambrai, including a desirable canonry at St-Géry.[26] The total annual income from these benefices was 110 small pounds of Tours—a very impressive income for those times.[27] Only two benefices eluded this musician: a canonry at St-Gertrude in Nivelles, requested shortly before his death, and one of the most keenly sought-after of all benefices, a canonry at the cathedral of Cambrai.[28]

The *per obitum* supplications can also be used to supplement records in archives of cathedrals and collegiate churches. For example, at the death in 1457 of Hugolinus Madoche, another retired member of the papal chapel, four different clerics petitioned for his chaplaincy at the altar of the Blessed Virgin at St Niklaas in Brussels, a benefice that yielded at that time 15 small pounds of Tours.[29] The records at St Niklaas omit mention of Madoche's

[25] ASV, RS 627, fo. 237ʳ (dated 23 July 1468, a petition for a canonry at St-Géry in Cambrai). For more on the career of Leporis, both as papal singer, and as singer-recruiter for the duke of Milan, see Starr, 'Music and Music Patronage', 191–6.

[26] ASV, RS 627, fo. 180ʳ (dated 17 July, a petition for the parish church of Laeken) and fo. 237ʳ (dated 23 July, for Rosa's canonry at St-Géry); RS 628, fo. 180ʳ (dated 18 Aug., for a chaplaincy in the parish church of Kappelkerk, in Brussels); and RS 629, fos. 152ᵛ–153ʳ (dated 9 Sept., another petition for the parish church in Brussels). All supplications bear the date 1468, and all are for benefices in the diocese of Cambrai.

[27] It should be noted, however, that the value of the income of a benefice is usually given as the highest estimated amount ('whose income by common estimation does not exceed . . .' is the usual formula). The real income might be less than that estimated, but probably not by a great deal.

[28] ASV, RS 602, fos. 292ʳ–293ʳ and RS 626, fo. 62ʳ (dated 28 Oct. 1466 and 25 May 1468, respectively, both involving litigation for the canonry at St Gertrude in Nivelles). Supplications in RS 533, fo. 140ʳ (dated 22 Aug. 1461); RS 553, fos. 225ʳ–226ᵛ (dated 31 Aug. 1462); RS 572, fo. 60ʳ (dated 1 Mar. 1464); RS 585, fo. 280ᵛ (dated 2 Jan. 1465) and fo. 295ʳ (dated 17 Jan. 1465) testify to Rosa's prolonged and ultimately unsuccessful attempt to secure a canonry at the cathedral of Cambrai.

[29] ASV, RS 492, fo. 160ᵛ and fo. 255ʳ (both dated 19 Aug. 1457); RS 493, fo. 31ʳ and fos. 81ᵛ–82ʳ (dated 21 Aug. and 15 Aug. 1457, respectively).

incumbency and the value of the benefice.[30] His successor was the petitioner with the earliest dated supplication, Jacobus Boni, another papal musician. Boni held the chaplaincy, which would see a precipitous decline in value, well into the 1470s.[31]

When so many benefices relinquished in death by papal musicians were then requested by and eventually provided to their colleagues (at least forty in the period under discussion), one immediately suspects that the dying musicians had found a way to 'beat the system', as it were—to arrange for the transmission of benefices to friends or colleagues even after death. This practice was, of course, forbidden in canon law.[32] Historians cite numerous papal edicts from the fifteenth and sixteenth century aimed at squelching this abuse. In 1530 Clement VII, for example, issued a bull prohibiting sons 'born from the fornication of prelates and priests from obtaining the benefices of their fathers'.[33] One method employed frequently by clergy in their last illness was to resign all benefices in favour of a family member. Chancery rules were promulgated to combat this practice. They decreed that if a cleric should die within twenty days of the date of a request for the resignation of a benefice, it would revert to the pope or to a local collator for provision.[34] The need for such edicts, however, always testifies to the persistence of abuse.

The case of the *quondam* papal singer Nicolaus Zacharie is but one example of such abuse. When he died in 1466, three clerics asked for the one and only benefice he had managed to obtain while serving in the papal chapel: a chaplaincy at the altar of B. Maria de Candeloro in the parish church B. Maria in Ceglie, in the diocese of Brindisi.[35] Of these, a priest from Brindisi with the suggestive name Barnoliano Zacharie was the successful petitioner. He triumphed even over a papal familiar whose supplication had the earliest date. Another cleric from Brindisi with an expectative for that benefice peppered the curia for years with petitions for the recall of Zacharie, who, he claimed, had succeeded to the benefice through fraudulent means. Whether fraud was involved or not, it seems clear that someone at the papal curia pulled strings to

---

[30] See Barbara Haggh, 'Music, Liturgy, and Ceremony in Brussels, 1350–1500' (Ph.D. diss., University of Illinois, 1988), 743.

[31] Haggh, and ASV, RS 493, fos. 81ᵛ–82ʳ (dated 15 Aug., the earliest supplication for that benefice).

[32] See F. Gillmann, 'Die Resignation der Benefizien', *Archiv für Katholischen Kirchenrecht*, 80 (1900), 361–3, for a discussion of early canonical sanctions against the practice.

[33] Barbara McClung Hallman, *Italian Cardinals, Reform, and the Church as Property* (Berkeley, 1985), 124. Other authors who deal with the forbidden practice of spoliation and attempts at reform include Pier Giovanni Caron, *La Rinuncia all'ufficio ecclesiastico* (Milan, 1946), 274 ff.; Bizzochi, *Chiesa et potere*, 107 ff.; Willibald Plöchel, *Geschichte der Kirchenrecht* (Vienna, 1953–4), ii. 381–3; Étienne Delaruelle et al., *L'Église au temps du Grand Schisme et de crise conciliare (1378–1449)* (Paris, 1962), 308–9; and Gillmann, 'Resignation'.

[34] Gillmann, 'Resignation', 368–9.

[35] See the documents cited in n. 9.

ensure that a relative of the deceased papal musician Nicolaus Zacharie received his benefice.

Many benefices relinquished by deceased papal singers were conferred upon their colleagues. Frequently these were younger musicians from the same diocese as the deceased. In the earlier version of this study, I could only speculate about an informal system operating within the chapel that perhaps made it possible to manipulate the beneficial process to the advantage of chapel members. Additional research in the Vatican Archives has confirmed this hypothesis. In the series of documents pertaining to the Cappella Sistina located in the Biblioteca Apostolica Vaticana, there is a papal bull, *Etsi Romanus Pontifex*, dated 20 July 1492.[36] In this document, Innocent VIII promises to grant the *per obitum* petitions of the musicians of his chapel for benefices of deceased chapel members, provided they had been duly authorized and presented by the *magister capellae*.

I also uncovered indisputable evidence that the bull merely legalized a practice that had been occurring informally for some years. Within days of the death of the papal singer Pascasius Le Kent, on or about 20 November 1485, his colleagues lined up to dissect his beneficial *Nachlass*: his canonry at Comines was given to Marbrianus de Orto, his chaplaincy at the Beguinhof in Antwerp to Antonius Baneston, a parish church in Arras to Remigius Mastaing, and so on.[37] One presumes that this equitable dispersal of their colleague's benefices took place under the careful·supervision of the *magister capellae*, Bartholomeus Maraschis. Other papal familiars were crowded out, and non-curialists apparently did not even bother to apply for the benefices released by the papal singer. The system could come unglued, however, when a *magister capellae*, through inattention or favouritism, passed over the claims of a chapel member. In 1490 Eustachius Havresse complained in a supplication to Innocent VIII that the *magister capellae* had prevented him from receiving his fair share of the beneficial leavings of a deceased colleague.[38] It may even have been this complaint that prompted the promulgation of *Etsi Romanus Pontifex* in 1492. The right of succession to benefices held by deceased members of the papal chapel was yet another perquisite granted by

---

[36] BAV, CS 703, no. 8. I am grateful to Richard Sherr for having drawn my attention to this document, which is transcribed in the appendix to his contribution to this volume (Ch. 8). For additional discussion of the significance of *Etsi Romanus pontifex*, see also Sherr's recent article 'A Biographical Miscellany: Josquin, Tinctoris, Obrecht, Brumel', in Siegfried Gmeinwieser *et al.* (eds.), *Musicologia Humana: Studies in Honor of Warren and Ursula Kirkendale* (Florence, 1994), 65–72.

[37] ASV, RS 852, fos. 207ʳ, 219ʳ, 229ʳ, 242ʳ 246ʳ.

[38] ASV, RS 914, fo. 62 (dated 2 Jan. 1490). The *magister capellae* was now Christophorus, bishop of Cortona, the successor to Maraschis, who died in 1487. See Haberl, *Die römische 'schola cantorum'*, 56 and Conrad Eubel, *Hierarchia catholica medii aevi*, ii (Regensburg, 1914), 130 and 138.

their employer and jealously guarded by the college of papal singers in the late fifteenth century.[39]

One immutable requirement in the *per obitum* supplication for a benefice ought to have been the actual, certifiable decease of the former incumbent. However, even this requirement was sometimes sidestepped. I shall present one more example, which concerns one of the most illustrious of Renaissance composers, Guillaume Du Fay. We have long been aware of his death date, 27 November 1474. Nevertheless, one of the supplications submitted soon after the composer's death contains a surprise. The earliest such petition came from Egidius de le Coquerie, a canon at St-Géry who was deeply interested in the canonry at the cathedral of Cambrai that had been vacated at the death of 'magister Guillermus Du Fay'. This supplication was processed at the papal court under the date 5 December 1474, just eight days after the death of Du Fay.[40] In the absence of such modern conveniences as the fax machine or telephone, Egidius surely must have sent off his supplication prior to the actual demise of Du Fay, perhaps in early October, when the composer took to his bed; or even as early as July 1474, when Du Fay drew up his will.[41] Coquerie must have deemed the canonry at Cambrai worth a lie, and in the end, events did justify his premature action. With a little effort, one can visualize Du Fay's final moments as he had intended them, the strains of the hymn *Magno salutis gaudio* sounding,[42] and all but one person intent on the dying figure. That one was probably rushing out to inform a relieved Coquerie that the composer had breathed his last, and that the canonry at Cambrai was finally vacant 'per obitum quondam Magistri Guillermi Du Fay', as Coquerie had claimed in his supplication to the pope.

The picture of acquisitive clerics circling—as one fellow vaticanist has put it—like buzzards around the figure of a dying colleague is not particularly

---

[39] Richard Sherr reminds me that it was the singers' custom in the 16th c. to decide among themselves the candidates for such benefices, presenting the names to the *magister capellae*, who would then communicate them to the pope. The practice, which they claimed 'had been active since time immemorial', was codified in an early 16th-c. constitution. (Personal communication; see also below, Ch. 8).

[40] ASV, RS 712, fos. 149ᵛ–150ʳ.

[41] David Fallows, *Dufay* (2nd edn., New York, 1988), 79, 224. It is difficult to estimate how long it would have taken for Coquerie's request for the benefice to reach the point in the process when the supplication was signed and dated. There are many cases of supplications by members of the papal chapel and other officers of the curia that required less than a month to be signed and dated (as in the example of Henricus de Rosa discussed above). But if the petition from Coquerie was coming from Cambrai, one would have to count travel time to Rome, the time required for the drafting of the supplication by a procurator at the papal court, and, of course, the time spent in the queue of similar supplications awaiting the attention of the officials in the Apostolic Signature (see Starr, 'Music and Music Patronage', 40–50). Eight days would not have sufficed.

[42] Fallows, *Dufay*, 79. Because of the death of another canon earlier in the day, Du Fay's carefully planned death-bed arrangements were not in fact followed. See Craig Wright, 'Dufay at Cambrai: Discoveries and Revisions', *JAMS* 28 (1975), 175–229 at 219.

attractive. Nevertheless, the results, in the form of the thousands of *per obitum* supplications lodged in Rome, are extraordinarily attractive for music historians of the Renaissance. They provide for us a range of biographical detail previously unknown for our period. They also furnish a kind of obituary for the Renaissance musician, the only one he was likely to receive.

8

A Curious Incident in the Institutional History of the Papal Choir

RICHARD SHERR

THE papal singers occupied a somewhat unique position among choirs of the sixteenth century in that they were organized as a college; that is, even though they were technically the pope's private singers and merely one group within the *capella papalis*[1] under the jurisdiction of the papally appointed *maestro di cappella* (until 1586 a high cleric, usually a bishop, who was not a musician),[2] they had a particular corporate structure, headed by a dean, internal rules and procedures codified in documents but also sanctioned by custom, and a collection of papal privileges granted to them as a group. As a college, they were directly subject to the pope, and acted corporately, constantly defending their privileges against attacks by other similar corporate entities (the apostolic scriptors, abbreviators, etc.). In these matters the *maestro di cappella* had basically no authority over the singers, a situation, if we are to believe the testimony of the singers given in the middle of the sixteenth century, that had existed since time immemorial (meaning at least the early sixteenth century). But something radical and disturbing to the status quo happened in the 1540s and this is the subject of the following discussion, of interest because it set the singers against their own *maestro di cappella*, and of even more interest because they were successful in achieving their goal, which was nothing less than the removal of the maestro. This is something like a faculty forcing the removal of a college president. The dispute also sheds

---

[1] The papal chapel technically consisted of everybody who was necessary for the celebration of the liturgy (sacristan, subdeacons, chaplains, bell-ringers). It should also be mentioned that the papal bulls granting privileges to the chapel do not refer to a 'College of Singers' and instead grant the privileges to all members of the chapel. While this conglomeration of people may have been considered a 'college' in the 15th c. (see Adalbert Roth's contribution to this volume, Ch. 4), it is clear from 16th-c. documents that the 'College of Singers' existed and was recognized as a legal entity. I shall therefore use the term 'college' to refer exclusively to the singers.

[2] The one exception being Elzéar Genet, known as Carpentras, who was appointed *maestro di cappella* in the reign of the music-loving Leo X (1513–21).

some light on the organization and workings of the College of Singers in a period for which we have no extant documentation. The crisis erupted into the open in 1550 as a final, almost desperate, reaction to the successful attempt of the then *maestro di cappella* to change to his own advantage the rules and procedures under which the singers lived. A main bone of contention, it turns out, was the most famous document connected with the papal choir, the Constitution granted them by Pope Paul III in 1545.

The *Diarii Sistini* report that on 6 April 1545 the singers had appointed a delegation (as always, containing representatives of the three 'nations' of the chapel: French, Italian, and Spanish) to meet with the *maestro di cappella*, Ludovico Magnasco, Bishop of Assisi, for the purpose of discussing the preparation of a new constitution.[3] The document was produced in seven months; by 17 November 1545 it was complete, as a papal breve attests.[4]

This is the Constitution that has come down to us in the sumptuous manuscript Vatican CS 611 and has long been available in transcription.[5] It is claimed in the papal breve of 17 November 1545, and also in the Preamble to the Constitution itself, that because all earlier constitutions had been destroyed in the Sack of Rome of 1527, a new one was needed, and that the present Constitution had been constructed 'from memory' with certain new additions.[6] The opening miniature of CS 611, showing a kneeling Magnasco at the head of the papal singers receiving the Constitution from the hands of Pope Paul III, is visual testimony to their happy acceptance of this much needed document (see Pl. 10).[7]

---

[3] The singers deputized to meet with the *maestro di cappella* about the new Constitution were Giovanni Francesco Felici and Giovanni Antonio de Magnanis (Italian); Charles d'Argentil and Antoine Loyal (French); and Antonio Calasans and Juan Sanchez de Tineo (Spanish). See BAV, Diarii Sistini 2, fo. 1ʳ, published in Raffaele Casimiri, 'I Diarii Sistini: I primi 25 Anni (1535–1559)', *Note d'archivio*, 9 (1932), 55.

[4] BAV, CS 684, fo. 74ʳ⁻ᵛ; see below, App., no. 1.

[5] The Constitution is published in Fr. X. Haberl, *Die römische 'schola cantorum' und die päpstlichen Kapellsänger bis zur Mitte des 16. Jahrhunderts* (Bausteine für Musikgeschichte, 3; Leipzig, 1888), 96–108. See also José M. Llorens, 'Reglamentación del Colegio de Cantores Pontificios: las *Constitutiones Apostolicae* y el *Liber Punctorum Capellae*', *Anuario Musical*, 30 (1975), 97–107.

[6] The Preamble to the Constitution of 1545 reads as follows: 'Pauli III. Pontificis maximi anno XI MDXLV cantorum pontificii systematis in maiore sacrario Constitutiones. Roma capta, et in direptionem impiis data, tempore Clementis VII. Praedecessoris nostri, etiam scripta, quae nulli usui in rapinam fuere, igne absumpta sunt. Inter haec et Musicorum maioris sacrarii leges periere. Quae igitur vel memoria retentae sunt, vel etiam innovandae sunt visae, Pauli III. Pontificis maximi jussu curaque R. D. Ludovici Assisiensis Episcopi, dictae capellae cantorum Magistri instauratae, innovatae, stabilitatae in perpetuam memoriam editae hujusmodi sunt, videlicet . . .'.

[7] It is possible that the miniature shows Magnasco giving the Constitution to the pope, but the other scenario seems more likely. Clearly visible behind Magnasco are three singers who are probably the three highest dignitaries of the college in 1545: the Dean, Bernardo Pisano (probably the middle figure with [red] trim on his sleeves), the abbot, Pedro Ordóñez, and the punctator, Giovanni Francesco Felici (probably the figure holding a roll of paper—the punctator assigned and recorded fines to be paid by other singers). Llorens identifies the figure with the roll of paper as the composer Cristóbal de Morales, and indeed the face has a certain resemblance to Morales's, as seen in Andrea Adami, *Osservazioni per ben regolare il coro dei cantori della Cappella Pontificia*

Actually, the singers do not look all that happy in the miniature, and this may be because the miniaturist was reflecting reality. For the excuse for the new constitution was based on a lie and the document had been forced down the singers' throats by the *maestro di cappella*, who had managed to convince the pope to grant him unheard-of authority over the College of Singers. Only through other documents can it be discovered that the new Constitution was the direct expression of a blatant power grab, violently resented by the singers, on the part of Ludovico Magnasco, who wished to and did gain total control over the most important aspects of the singers' lives. He achieved this in typical curial fashion by using papal authority to override established rules and customs, in this case through the instrument of a papal breve promulgated by Pope Paul III on 27 July 1545 (before the completion of the Constitution) that defined Magnasco's position as head of the papal chapel and of the College of Singers.[8]

The breve begins innocuously enough by confirming that Magnasco had been appointed maestro of the papal chapel on the death of Bartholomeus Croto[9] and stating that this appointment had been made *ad vitam*. But the heart of the document may be found in the following phrase:

et insuper tibi ut quoscumque et quotcumque de quibus tibi videbitur in cantores et capellanos ac clericos et alios ministros dicte capelle recipere et admittere, ac tam admittendos quam etiam admissos, quando tibi placuerit ex suo loco amovere et repellere ac alios substituere et subdeputare necnon quascumque lites tam beneficiales quam profanas inter eos tunc et pro semper ubicumque residentes audire terminos et decidere possis plenam et liberam licentiam et facultatem auctoritate nostra et tenor premissis concedimus, mandamus in odiernis et pro semper existentibus cantoribus capellanis clericis et aliis ministris capelle huiusmodi ut tibi monitis et mandatis pareant et obediant.[10]

By these words, the pope specifically assigns to Magnasco the power to admit or remove any member of the chapel, including singers, entirely on his own volition, further making him the final authority in all disputes, sacred (over benefices) and secular. The breve ends with clauses abrogating whatever rights and privileges the College of Singers might have that would stand contrary to

(Rome, 1711, repr. Lucca, 1988), 164; but Morales was not the punctator in 1545. See José M. Llorens, 'Cristóbal de Morales, cantor en la Capilla Pontificia de Paulo III (1535–1545)', *Anuario Musical*, 8 (1953), 39–69 at 42.

   [8] ASV, Arm. 41, vol. 33, fo. 337ᵛ. The breve is partially transcribed in Llorens, 'Cristóbal Morales', 43, and in id., 'Los Maestros de la Capilla Apostólica hasta el Pontificado de Sixto V (1585–1590)', *Anuario Musical*, 43 (1988), 35–66. Most of the documents discussed in this study were known to Llorens, but he has not, to my knowledge, published an extensive account of this incident.

   [9] On Magnasco, see Llorens, 'Los Maestros'. According to Llorens, Croto died in Jan. or Feb. 1541, but Magnasco is listed as maestro as early as Nov. 1540; See ASR, Camerale I (mandati camerali) 870, fo. 408ʳ.

   [10] See Llorens, 'Los Maestros', 29, Doc. XXVIII.

the papal will. The effect of the breve was to give the *maestro di cappella* complete executive authority over the two crucial aspects of the singers' professional lives (hiring and firing) and control of the most important source of their extra income (benefices). The maestro had by this truly become, as the singers later bitterly complained, the 'ruler' of the papal chapel. Magnasco acted quickly to exert his new powers; in fact, we learn that it was on the authority of this breve and without the consent of the singers that he had ordered the preparation of a new constitution of the papal chapel.[11]

The stated excuse for ordering the new constitution, that no earlier written constitutions had survived the Sack of Rome, was pure fiction. Earlier written constitutions did exist in 1545. Two are extant in CS 687 on fos. 146r–153r (a complete constitution, hereafter A) and 160r–166v (an extended fragment, hereafter B).[12] From internal evidence, it can be shown that A dates from before 1540: ch. 7 of this constitution states that the salary of the papal singers was 8 ducats a month; in December 1540 the official salary was raised to 9 ducats a month and so it remained until 1586.[13] B is even earlier. Its nineteenth chapter refers to Juan Scribano as someone who is 'now' the secretary of the College.[14] Scribano had joined the choir in the reign of Julius II, is demonstrably a member for the entire reign of Leo X, yet is absent from the first extant list after the Sack of Rome (1529); he had probably left Rome shortly before or after the Sack in 1527. When he returns in 1531, he is the Dean of the College of Singers. This makes it almost certain that B predates the Sack of Rome, while the mention of Matteo Alzate and Gaspar van Weerbecke in its eleventh chapter suggests that it may date from as early as the reign of Leo X.[15]

---

[11] Apparently he acted on the authority of the breve even before it was officially promulgated, since the negotiations for the new constitution had begun in Apr. 1545.

[12] I hope to publish these documents in due course. A has the following title: *Constitutiones sive Ordinationes Capelle sacri palatii apostolici per Collegium Reverendorum Dominorum Cantorum observande* (CS 687, fo. 146r).

[13] 'De salario consignando novo cantori. In capella sanctissimi domini nostri pape pro salario sive provisione ordinaria consignantur unicuique cantori quolibet mense ducati octo auri in auro de camera' (CS 687, fo. 147v). The rise to 9 ducats is first recorded in the pay list for Dec. 1540; see ASR, Camerale I (mandati camerali) 870, fo. 422r–v.

[14] 'Dominus Johannes Scribanus canonicus Salamantinus de presenti et qui pro tempore fuerit secretarius collegii cantorum unicuique cantori noviter recepto et admisso legere tenetur omnes constitutiones collegii et capelle predictorum tam temporales quam spirituales in pleno capitulo congregando post admissionem dicti cantoris per duos seu tres dies' (CS 687, fo. 162r).

[15] 'Qualiter inter cantores dividenda sunt regalia. Cum cantor noviter admissus solverit regalia sua ut supradictum est videlicet ducatos x in una et ducatos duos in alia manibus constituentes in totum ducatos xii auri de camera ipsa regalia dividantur inter cantores participantes et interessantes admissioni cantoris predicti et interpresentes hoc est Rome commorantes etiam si in infirmitate constituti essent dummodo ipsa infirmitas non esset tam grandis seu periculosa ad vitam quod non possent cantores infirmi servire nec accedere ad quottidianum offitium ut fuit in Domino Gaspare Vebret et in Domino Matheo de Alzate' (CS 687, fos. 160v–161r). Weerbecke had joined the chapel in 1481 and served with interruptions into the reign of Leo X (he was a member in 1517). Alzate was a member of the chapel by 1504 and served until at least 1521.

When put together, A and B contain almost all the chapters now found in the Constitution of 1545. Indeed, the numerous marginal changes and additions in the documents, many in the hand of Antonio Calasans (bass singer from Lérida, Spain who had joined the chapel in 1529 and had a forty-three-year career in the choir, and who seems to have been consistently entrusted with the prosecution of their legal disputes), indicate that it was from these 'working documents' rather than from 'memory' that the new constitution was prepared.[16] The various constitutions agree on many basic points, although they differ in details of wording; yet a careful reading of the Constitution of 1545 against the earlier constitutions reveals a fundamental change in the authority of the *maestro di cappella* regarding punishments. As an example, take the chapter of A concerning singers who create 'scandal' (a frequent occurrence):

De cantore scandalum faciente
Quia optimum est obviare scandalis ut inter cantores pax observetur maxime in dicta capella ubi quottidie predictos cantores divina officia celebrantur ideo prout ab antiquis predecessoribus ordinatum et observatum extitit quicunque cantorum existens intus dictam capellam tam durante officio divino quam in congregationem prefatorum cantorum pro negociis capelle peragendis aut alio quocunque tempore quovismodo aut quovis quesito colore verba iniuriosa adversus seu contra alium cantorem dixerit punctabitur in jul. decem et si de huiusmodi verbis sequeretur notabile scandalum punctabitur in scutos quatuor. Et si aliquis cantor intus dictam capellam ut prefertur existens inductus persuasionibus seu verbis alicuius cantoris pugno calce[17] vel armis alium cantorem percusserit vel alias quovismodo in eum manus violentas iniecerit [*debet privari de loco suo et non censetur esse amplius de collegio cantorum sed de mandato S.mo D.no nostro et ad libitum prefatorum cantorum de novo intrabit et in ultimo loco sedebit ac sua regalia solvet tanquam novus cantor et cantor qui dederit occasionem vel[18] induxerit dictum cantorem ad huiusmodi scandalum faciendum pro prima vice perditus de scutos sexdecim et pro secundam intrabit de novo et erit tanquam novus cantor*—crossed out] [*deprivabit in salario sex mensium et cantor provocans alium cantorem ad huiusmodi scandalum faciendum condempnabitur in salario trium mensium si vero extra dictam capellam inter cantores fiet scandalum eum condempnabitur arbitrio collegii cantorum*—added in the margin] (CS 687, fo. 151ʳ)

The corresponding chapter in the Constitution of 1545 reads as follows:

XVII. De cantore scandalum faciente
Quia optimum est obviare scandalis ut inter cantores pax observetur maxime in dicta capella ubi quotidie per dictos cantores divina officia celebrantur ideo prout ab antiquis

---

[16] That the extant *Diarii Sistini* with their records of fines actually begin in 1535, ten years before the promulgation of the 1545 constitution, is another indication that the singers had a perfectly good set of working procedures in place.

[17] *baculo*—written above.   [18] Something crossed out—*induxerit*—written above.

praedecessoribus ordinatum et observatum extitit quicunque cantor existens in dicta capella tam durante officio divino quam in congregationibus praefatorum cantorum pro negotiis capellae peragendis aut alio quocunque tempore quovis modis aut quovis quaesito colore verba injuriosa adversus seu contra alium cantorem dixerit etiam quod scandalum ait punctabitur arbitrio societatis cantorum et si hujusmodi notabile scandalum oriatur in praesentia papae aut r. cardinalium sive magistri capellae punctabitur *arbitrio ejusdem magistri capellae cum collegio cantorum*. et si aliquis cantor intra vel extra dictam capellam persuasionibus seu provocatus verbis alicujus cantoris pugno calce baculo vel armis alium cantorem percusserit vel alias quovismodo in eum manus violentas injecerit condemnabitur *arbitrio magistri* tantum et cantor provocans alium cantorem ad hujusmodi scandalum faciendum similiter condemnabitur *arbitrio magistri cum collegio*. si vero extra dictam capellam inter cantores fiet scandalum condemnabuntur arbitrio collegii cantorum *semper interveniente magistro capellae*.[emphasis mine]

These examples show clearly how A was used as the working copy to produce the Constitution of 1545 and how Magnasco made his influence felt. For instance, the original wording of A is quite strict in its punishment for a singer who actually gets into a physical fight with another, effectively expelling him from the College, then readmitting him as if he were a newly appointed singer (depriving him of his seniority and forcing him to pay again the 13-ducat entrance fee that was required of all new singers). This is, however, changed in A itself by crossing out the relevant lines and inserting language that substitutes a fine of six months' salary (48 ducats—this might have been worse punishment) if the fight was in the chapel and an undetermined fine, to be assigned 'at the will of the College of Singers', if the fight was outside the chapel. This is basically the version that was adopted in the chapter in the Constitution of 1545, except that here the specific value of the fine is omitted. But more strikingly, in the Constitution of 1545, the *maestro di cappella* is prominently inserted at key points of the punishment process (indicated by italic). In other chapters concerning punishments in the 1545 document, it can be seen that the *maestro di cappella* has been added to decision-making that had been reserved solely to the College of Singers; he is either said to be acting in concert with them or having his own special authority. Effectively then, the maestro had arrogated to himself the power to impose extraordinary fines and punishments that had heretofore resided solely in the purview of the College of Singers.

A more important source of conflict between the *maestro di cappella* and the singers is to be found, however, in things that do not appear in the Constitution of 1545. For instance, Chapters 1–4 of the Constitution of 1545 state that new singers were appointed with lifetime tenure only after an audition and a two-thirds plus one vote of the other singers, the *maestro di cappella*'s function being to investigate the character of the applicant and to preside over the meeting.[19] Yet in reality, the papal breve of July 1545 had given the *maestro di cappella* the power to admit singers entirely of his own volition, ignoring the procedures of the constitution. It is not clear to what extent Magnasco actually availed himself of this authority, but the singers did claim that he had forced the acceptance of Ottaviano Gemelli, a man of bad moral character who was later suspended from the choir for thievery.[20] Furthermore, they claimed that he had held back the salaries of singers and threatened singers with suspension and outright dismissal, powers not specified in the Constitution of 1545 but granted by the papal breve.

In effective control of crucial aspects of the singers' careers, Magnasco also moved to exert his authority over their most cherished form of extra income, ecclesiastical benefices. The pursuit of benefices always formed an important part of the career of any singer. In the fifteenth century this appears to have been largely as the result of individual initiative, but in 1492 Pope Innocent VIII changed the situation radically. In his bull *Etsi Romanus Pontifex* of 20 July 1492, Innocent declared that the *maestro di cappella* would have the right to present members of the chapel (basically the singers) for benefices vacated by the death of any (past or present) member (see Pl. 11).[21]

This was arguably the most important privilege regarding benefices that the College had ever received: it effectively established a perpetual fund of benefices available to the members of the choir, gave them a strong legal claim to those benefices, helping also to cement their close relations with places like Cambrai, which had long provided singers to the pope. For the early sixteenth century, the major evidence of the force of the Indult can be found in individual supplications submitted by singers asking for a 'new provision' to a benefice and explaining that it had originally been granted by virtue of the Indult. But A has two chapters specifying the manner in which the Indult of Innocent VIII was actually to be applied. Both are crossed out in A and neither appears in the Constitution of 1545.[22] It is clear from these that even though the papal bull had reserved only to the *maestro di cappella* the right to

---

[19] Haberl, 96.

[20] See App., no. 3. Gemelli was admitted in Nov. 1542 and disappears from the lists in June 1547.

[21] CS 703, no. 8; see App., no. 2.

[22] 'Modus eligendi et presentandi ad beneficia per obitum cantorum vacantia. Si per obitum alicuius cantoris vel alterius persone dicte capelle aliqua beneficia vacare contigerit decanus cantorum pro tempore existens in loco per eum deputando omnes cantores collegialiter congregare debet quibus sic ut prefertur collegialiter congregatis debet proponere vacacionem dictorum beneficiorum et habita noticia de vacatione et qualitate dictorum beneficiorum unum cantorem ex illa patria seu natione unde beneficia reperiuntur vacare ut ab antiquis observatum exstitit eligere debent et R.p.d. magister capelle ad quem presentatio huiusmodi beneficiorum pleno jure pertinet cantorem sic ut prefertur electum iuxta privilegia dicte capelle Sanctissimo domino nostro presentabit et cantor ut prefertur electus et presentatus a Sanctissimo domino nostro institutionis seu novam provisionem impetrabit et beneficia huiusmodi ad libitum et ordinationem dicti collegii distribuentur videlicet antiquioribus et benemeritis [*dummodo* — in margin] tituli dictorum beneficiorum inter cantores illius patrie seu nationis

present chapel members for the benefices of deceased colleagues, the practice (one that may stretch back to the very year of the bull, 1492) was for the singers to meet, with or without the maestro, and to elect one or more singers who had served the chapel for three years or more and were 'of the same nation' as the incumbent to receive the benefices, while the *maestro di cappella* then merely transmitted the name or names to the pope for action. The absence of these chapters from the new constitution coupled with the specific authority concerning intervention in the question of benefices that had been granted by the papal breve was extremely significant. It took away from the College control over an important source of outside income and vested it entirely in the hands of the executive administrator.

In short, the written and unwritten rules put into effect at the time of the Constitution of 1545 were a bold attack on the most cherished privileges of the College of Singers and were viewed by them as an unmitigated disaster. But as long as his patron Pope Paul III was alive, there were no actions that the singers could effectively take against Magnasco. In late 1549, however, Paul III had the bad grace to die. The singers saw their window of opportunity and jumped right through it.

The evidence can begin with a document filed in the private archives of the papal singers, its author, Antonio Calasans, and its intended recipient, an unnamed cardinal. It is an outpouring of pent-up bile, of passionate complaint, of appeal to (somewhat shaky) historical authority, ending with an earnest plea for relief in the most drastic sense.[23] A résumé follows:

Most Reverend Lord:
Since the time of Urban VI until the time of Paul III [1378–1549] singers were always admitted for life and were immediately subject to the pontiff, and as a College that did not include the *maestro di cappella* they were governed by certain statutes, and singers deviating from the statutes could be fined only by the other singers and the *maestro di cappella* never interfered. When Sixtus IV created the post of *maestro di cappella* these arrangements were not altered.[24] The maestro's job concerned the Divine Service; he

---

ubi beneficia reperiuntur vacare distribuantur et de huiusmodi beneficiis non debent esse participes nisi cantores qui ad vacationem dictorum beneficiorum per triennium dicte capelle inse[rv]ierint' (CS 687, fos. 149ᵛ–150ʳ).

'Qualiter sunt dividenda beneficia vacantia in capella. De beneficiis ad electionem collegii cantorum et presentationem magistri dicte capelle spectantibus dummodo fructus dictorum beneficiorum summam xl ducatorum non ascendant [*recte* excedant] etiam si in dicta capella non reperirentur nisi unus vel duo cantores aliis [illius] patrie seu nationis unde beneficia reperiuntur vacare ac etiam per triennium dicte capelle non inservierint nullus cantor alienigena de dictis beneficiis aliquam partem habebit. Si vero summam quadraginta ducatorum excedant vel infra triennium bis contigerit beneficia vacare in una et eadem patria etiam si non excedant dictam summam distribuentur in regula [? r.a] vacatione duntaxat ad libitum collegii cantorum videlicet antiquioribus et benemerentibus ut supradictum est in precedente capitulo' (fo. 150ʳ).

23 CS 680, fos. 96ʳ–97ʳ; see App., no. 3.

24 Actually, it was Calixtus III who instituted (or rather, revived) the post of *maestro di cappella* in 1455. See Pamela Starr, 'Music and Music Patronage at the Papal Court, 1447–1464' (Ph.D. diss., Yale University, 1987), 81.

also protected the rights and privileges of the chapel and interceded with the pope on behalf of the singers. He was therefore to act for the utility of the chapel and not to destroy it, and even less to teach the singers about music 'since all of them are more than capable of teaching the *maestro di cappella* about the art of singing'.

But this relationship was shattered when Ludovico Magnasco, Bishop of Assisi, was appointed *maestro di cappella* by Paul III in 1540. In 1545 he received a breve from Paul III that gave him the power to hire and fire members of the chapel of his own volition, and he introduced a number of abuses, 'which are not difficult to specify'.

There now follow two facing pages; on one the ancient privileges are stated, each connected by a line to the other page, entitled 'Abuses introduced by the *maestro di cappella*' (*Abusus introducti per magistrum capelle*), where the relevant abuse is spelled out.

1. Singers were always admitted *ad vitam* by papal order after having their characters examined by the maestro and their abilities examined by the singers. ABUSE: Without consulting the pope, with the singers in opposition, and advised of his notoriety, he admitted into the papal chapel Ottaviano [Gemelli], infamous singer, who was [later] publicly suspended from duty.[25]

2. When any member of the chapel died, the College of Singers selected from among the more senior and deserving singers, those to be presented by the *maestro di cappella* for the newly vacant benefices. ABUSE: He presented Federigo Lazizio, a recently hired singer, for the benefices in Pesaro [vacant] by the death of Girolamo Arduini,[26] preferring Lazizio to the more senior singers, saying to the singers who asked him about this: 'I want the new singer to be considered first and the senior singer last because I am the Boss'.[27] He presented the chaplain of the Mass Antonio de Olmedo for the benefices of the late Pedro de los Ottones and refused to present Juan Sanchez [de Tineo] who had been elected by the singers.[28] He distributed the benefices of Matteo Fioran,[29] Girolamo Arduini, and Pedro de los Ottones without consulting the College of Singers, contrary to the statutes of the chapel, saying in all cases: 'I am the Boss'.

---

[25] See above, n. 20.

[26] Listed as a member of the choir from July to Sept. 1529, who must have died after leaving Rome.

[27] 'Volo ego quod primi sint novissimi et novissimi primi quia ego dominus' (literally, 'I will that the first shall be the last and the last shall be the first for I am the Lord'). As Leofranc Holford-Strevens pointed out in a private communication, this is a mixture of biblical quotations (cf. Matt. 19: 30 ('Multi erunt primi novissimi, et novissimi primi') and also Matt. 20: 16; Mark 10: 31, Luke 13: 30, and Exodus 10:2 and other places for 'quia ego dominus'), which is clever but is also blasphemous. It is possible, however, that the exchange was really in Italian and Magnasco used a word like 'padrone' (master) and Calasans in a fit of spite turned him into a blasphemer. In any case, I have decided to render 'dominus' as 'the Boss' in an attempt to capture what was probably the sense in which the singers understood Magnasco's statement.

[28] Ottones cannot be found in any chapel list, but Olmedo became a *capellanus missarum* in June 1549. Sanchez began his chequered career in the chapel in 1525.

[29] Died 21 Feb. 1547.

3. If any singer were to be fined it was to be done wholly at the will of the College of Singers and the *maestro di cappella* never interfered. ABUSE: Without consulting the College of Singers and without legitimate reason, he held back the salaries of Giovanni Francesco Felici, Bernardo Pauli [Pisano], Yves Barry, and Pablo Bursano, singers in the chapel. He ordered certain singers not to enter the chapel on pain of punishment of his choosing, and this for the flimsiest of reasons; he threatened others that he wanted to expel them from the papal chapel at his discretion, saying in all cases: 'I am the Boss'.

4. Extended leaves of absence were to be granted only after receiving permission from the pope, the College of Singers, and the maestro, but a singer who wanted permission for only a few days' absence received this from the College of Singers alone. ABUSE: He gave permission to several singers to leave Rome without consulting the College of Singers, and he revoked the leave of absence of Yves Barry, who had obtained it from Paul III of blessed memory and the College of Singers, on pain of punishment of his choosing, and made Barry return from Bologna to Rome.

5. Since time immemorial the chapel had been governed by constitutions. ABUSE: By the authority granted to him by a Breve of Pope Paul III of blessed memory, he had a new constitution written in which on the authority of that Breve he boasted that he was the ruler of the papal chapel and had the power of punishing and fining singers according to his discretion; horrible words which up to now had never been heard.

The document ends with a plea to intercede with the pope to provide the singers with another maestro because, as the Latin has it, 'ulterius pati non possunt', which I presume could be translated as: 'they can't stand it any longer'. This document, however, is clearly a draft, and one could argue that it was not sent and had no effect. But it was followed by something very official.

The date is 10 March 1550, Paul III has been dead for four months, and the new pope Julius III has ruled for one; the place, the office of Johannes Baptista Cicada, Bishop of Albenga and auditor of the Apostolic Chamber. Before him, giving sworn testimony about the ancient privileges of the College of Singers, especially regarding their relationship to the *maestro di cappella*, are present and former members of the papal chapel, chief among them Antonio Calasans. He is followed by a number of witnesses, including Giovanni Francesco Felici, the Dean of the College of Singers. All claimed to have intimate knowledge of the state of things in the chapel in the early sixteenth century; in fact, Felici had actually entered the chapel during the reign of Leo X (he joined the chapel in 1519). The purpose of the testimony was to prove that the *maestro di cappella* had never held any authority over the singers, that he had never been able to hire and fire, that he had never been able to assign fines, that he had never been able to decide who was to get benefices; in short that the *maestro di cappella* had never had any of the powers now being exercised by Ludovico Magnasco.[30] A summary follows:

THE TESTIMONY
10 March 1550: Witness I

Antonio Calasans, papal singer acting for the College of Singers, explains how things had always been and makes seven specific points (basically the same points made in the draft petition).

1. For ten, twenty, thirty, and forty years, indeed for as long as anybody could remember, the singers had constituted a College with a Dean and the *maestro di cappella*.[31]

2. The College of Singers had always been directly subject to the pope. The *maestro di cappella* never interfered in the meetings of the College except in matters concerning the Divine Service, and the singers had the right to and did congregate without the presence of the maestro.

3. The *maestro di cappella* did not have the right to admit singers to the choir or expel singers from the choir without the approbation of the College as expressed in a vote, and any singer who is removed should be given recompense.

4. The *maestro di cappella* did not have the right to hold back the salary of any singer, much less did he have the right to punish singers, for the right to assign such punishment rested entirely with the College.

5. The College of Singers had the right to fine any member of the chapel who committed offences, without consulting the *maestro di cappella*.

6. When a benefice became vacant through the death of a singer or any other member of the chapel, the singers met in congregation and nominated a person to be given the vacant benefice, and the *maestro di cappella* presented that person to the pope, and in no way could the *maestro di cappella* present another person or distribute the fruits of the benefice.

7. If a singer wished to absent himself from Rome for a few days, he had to request permission from the College, not from the *maestro di cappella*. And if a singer was absent without permission of the College, the College, and not the maestro, had the right to fine him.

13 March 1550: Witness II

Jacobus Fanturius, cleric of Ravenna, about 50 years old, gives corroborative testimony on the points raised by Calasans.

---

[30] A copy of the notarial act is preserved in CS 703, no. 14.
[31] That is, from the beginning of the 16th c.

1. In his time as clerk of the chapel, which began in 1528 (a year after the Sack of Rome), he observed that the singers formed a College with a Dean and Abbot and a *maestro di cappella*, and this College held private meetings.

2. In the ten or eleven years that he was a member of the chapel, he observed that the *maestro di cappella* had no jurisdiction over the singers and did not attend their meetings unless asked to; in particular when benefices were to be distributed, the singers met without the maestro to decide whom the maestro would present to the pope. The maestro only interfered in matters of the Divine Service, such as telling the singers when they should sing faster or slower, and if the singers did something the pope did not like, the maestro would tell them about it. And he confirms this not only from his own experience but also from having talked to Tommaso Fazanis, Bernardo Pisano, and Blas Núñez.[32]

3. He confirms that the maestro could not admit singers to the choir without receiving the permission first of the pope and then of the College of Singers, and if singers were expelled it could only be for important reasons and the singer was to be given recompense.

4. He had observed occasions when a singer owed money and the College had retained his salary in order to pay the debt, and it was true that such punishment, that is monetary punishment, was in the entire purview of the College and the maestro did not interfere.

5. On the question of leaves of absence, he remembered an occasion when Costanzo Festa requested permission to attend the marriage of a member of the Orsini family.

13 March 1550: Witness III

Ludovicus de Perlinis, cleric of Oviedo, about 60 years old, gives corroborating testimony.

1. As a servant of Juan Scribano during the reigns of Leo X, Adrian VI, and Clement VII, he observed that the singers constituted a College of ten, twenty, or twenty-five members at the wish of the pontiff, with a Dean and a *maestro di cappella*.

2. Scribano had told him that the maestro only dealt with matters concerning service to the pope and the Divine Service, and had no jurisdiction over the singers, and if singers made errors then the College would fine them and the maestro would not interfere. He had himself observed many times when the singers would meet after Mass or Vespers without the presence of the *maestro di cappella*.

---

[32] Fazanis was a member of the choir from 1502 to 1530; Pisano was a member from 1514 to 1548; Núñez was a member from 1520 to 1563. I give the names in the vernacular where known.

3. He remembered that during the reign of Clement VII, Garsias Salinas and several other Spanish singers had been removed from the choir because of farsightedness or because they did not have good voices, and that they were given recompense in the form of benefices in Spain. And he remembered that Juan Hillanis had been removed because of farsightedness in the reign of Leo X and given recompense. And no one could expel a singer unless it be the pope and the singer was given recompense.[33]

4. Punishment and fines for bad behaviour, except for the crime of lèse-majesté, which concerned only the pope, were in the purview of the College and the maestro did not interfere.

5. When he was in Scribano's service, he had heard from Scribano that there were many times when benefices became vacant by the death of singers or chaplains, and the singers would meet without the maestro and distribute the benefices to Italian, French, or Spanish singers, and the maestro did not interfere, and the maestro would then present those nominated by the singers for the benefices.

6. He had many times heard singers ask his master (Scribano) to petition the College to give them leave to absent themselves from Rome, and this permission was never requested from the *maestro di cappella*.

20 March 1550: Witness IV

Giovanni Battista de Comitibus, deacon of the chapel, about 46 years old, gives corroborating testimony.

1. He had joined the chapel in 1529 and agreed with what was said earlier about the makeup of the choir.

2. He had many times seen the singers meet without the *maestro di cappella* and sometimes he had seen the maestro take part; he does not know if the maestro should have jurisdiction over the singers.

3. He had never seen or heard of an occasion when the maestro on his own authority had admitted a singer to the choir or expelled a singer, and it was true that if a singer were removed he was given recompense.

4. He had observed the singers meet without the maestro and decide to retain part of the salary of a delinquent singer, but he does not know if the maestro has the power to do this or not.

5. During his time in the chapel he had often seen the singers and the maestro meet to consider the distribution of benefices, but he does not know what happened at the meetings.

6. He agreed with what others have said about leaves of absence.

---

[33] See Richard Sherr, 'The "Spanish Nation" in the Papal Chapel, 1492–1521', *EM* 20 (1992), 601–9.

26 March 1550: Witness V

Giovanni Francesco Felici, dean of the Chapel, more than 69 years old, gives corroborative testimony.

1. Concerning the makeup of the chapel, he confirms what the others have said from his thirty-one years of experience and from having talked with his older colleagues.

2. Ever since Ludovico, Bishop of Assisi, had become the *maestro di cappella*, he had not observed the ancient constitutions and customs, and had admitted singers to the choir without papal permission and without audition, and especially he had admitted one Ottavio Gemelli who was later suspended because he was a thief. And this *maestro di cappella* had held back the salaries of several singers and had prohibited others from entering the Sistine Chapel, all this contrary to all customs and constitutions that had been in effect before he became *maestro di cappella*.

3. Concerning fines, he remembered when Antonio Ribera had left Rome without the College's permission, and when he returned, was fined by the College without the interference of the *maestro di cappella*.

The entire document was duly registered on 27 March 1550.

Things must have reached a very serious juncture for the singers to take such open action against their *maestro di cappella*; more to the point, they would not have dared to make such sworn public accusations if they had not known that the new pope had no great desire to support a creature of his predecessor. Without political support and faced with an open revolt, Magnasco was forced to compromise. Negotiations were opened with the College of Singers. Documents were exchanged. The singers demanded changes in key chapters of the Constitution concerning punishment and leaves of absence.[34] Magnasco refused to change the wording of the Constitution, but offered a series of concessions and suggestions, ending his document on a bitter note of frustration that indicates that he knew he had lost the battle: 'Et si questi capitoli non vi satisfanno ni contentano che si observino totalmente le constitutioni vechie et si busino [= bruccino] le nuove et non la intendo altramente et risolvetevi como vi piace' (And if these clauses do not satisfy or content you then observe totally the old constitutions and burn the new ones and I don't intend anything different, and make up your own minds as you wish).[35]

A final document was drawn up between Magnasco and representatives of the College of Singers (Yves Barry and Jacques Arcadelt for the French, Antonio Calasans and Juan Sanchez de Tineo for the Spanish, Giovanni

---

[34] See CS 680, fos. 79ʳ–79ᵛ.   [35] Ibid., fo. 82ʳ⁻ᵛ.

Abbate and Giovanni Antonio de Magnanis for the Italians).[36] The parties agreed that:

1. The *maestro di cappella* would not use the authority to admit and expel singers that had been granted by the breve of Paul III, nor would he interfere in disputes between members of the chapel in beneficial or other matters.

2. The College of Singers alone had the right to punish delinquent singers, and only if they did not act within ten days of receiving notice of the problem could the *maestro di cappella* (along with the College) impose punishment.

3. Only in the case where the crime resulted in bloodshed and in no other could the *maestro di cappella* (along with the College), within ten days of the incident, impose punishment.

4. No singer could appeal a punishment unless it was more than 4 gold ducats.

5. No words could be deleted from or added to the Constitution of 1545 without consulting the *maestro di cappella* or the pope on pain of expulsion from the chapel.

6. The *maestro di cappella* could not intervene in meetings of the College except in the above cases and in matters that concerned the Divine Service.

7. The constitutions and other chapel documents should be kept in an archive under the custody of three senior singers, one from each of the nations of the chapel, and they could not remove and retain documents for more than a month on pain of a fine.

8. These three singers could not remove documents from the archive without receiving permission, expressed by a vote of the College, and could not give the documents to anybody without receiving permission from the *maestro di cappella* and the College. The person wishing to remove a document had to leave a monetary deposit.

9. No singer could be absent from Rome for three or more days without the permission of the College.

10. If a benefice should become vacant through the death of a member of the chapel the singers were to nominate one of their number for the benefice and the *maestro di cappella* would present that man and no other to the pope for the benefice, nor could the maestro distribute the fruits of benefices.

11. The oath that new singers swear should have its ancient wording.[37]

Magnasco had lost the battle. Soon, he was to lose the war. In December 1550 his name disappears from the chapel lists, replaced by Girolamo Maccabei, Bishop of Castro. The breve that appointed Maccabei, dated 5

---

[36] CS 679, fos. 31ʳ–32ᵛ; see App., no. 4.

[37] The wording does not seem to differ significantly from the wording of the oath in the Constitution of 1545. See App., no. 4.

November 1550, leaves little doubt that Magnasco had in fact been summar-
ily dismissed, his appointment *ad vitam* cancelled by the order of Pope Julius
III.[38]

The singers had clearly won this particular dispute. They had forced the
removal of an ambitious and hated administrator, achieved the reinstatement
of their ancient privileges, and took control again over their most important
concerns. At the same time, none of this was codified in the Constitution, not
a word of which was changed (as later copies attest). This is not surprising
since the greatest abuses that Magnasco had introduced involved things that
were not in the Constitution, but it also clearly was not considered necessary
officially to amend the 1545 document in order to return to the old procedures; in fact, the singers agreed with Magnasco that nothing should be
changed in the Constitution without the permission of the maestro or the
pope. This can only mean that the College was governed by a number of documents of which the Constitution was the most important but only one; in fact,
the singers constantly refer to their constitution*s*.[39]

That the old method of distributing the benefices of dead members of the
chapel was reinstated can be seen from documents recording the decisions of
the College of Singers in the years following 1550. For instance, a notarial
document relates that on 11 December 1569 the singers met to discuss the
benefices that had become vacant on the death of the deacon and *capellanus
missarum* Johannes Angelus de Johanninis. As the benefices were in Rome, the
Roman singers were excluded from the meeting. The singers then voted that
the benefices would be distributed to the Roman singers in order of their
seniority. The *maestro di cappella* attended this meeting but merely confirmed
what the singers had decided.[40] In 1563 the College got involved in a detailed
dispute with the papal domestic chaplains concerning the benefices made
vacant on the death of Antonio de Olmedo; again it was clearly the College of
Singers who made all the relevant decisions in the case, even though the
maestro di cappella officially signed various of the documents.[41]

The singers' victory seemed to be secure in the matter of benefices. But they
were much less successful in controlling the membership of the choir; for what
they had taken away from the *maestro di cappella* was soon appropriated by cardinals and popes. As I have outlined elsewhere, no less a person than Julius III
himself was responsible for a major erosion of the singers' right to choose their

---

[38] ASV, Arm. 41, vol. 58, fo. 186ʳ; see App., no. 5.

[39] The extreme concern for the preservation of these documents is expressed in clauses 7–8 of the articles of
agreement between Magnasco and the singers.

[40] CS 679, fos. 24ʳ–25ʳ.

[41] The details of this case are too complicated to go into here.

own membership, with disastrous consequences.[42] Next came an attack on their special relationship with the pope. In 1560 Paul's nephew Cardinal Carlo Caraffa suddenly announced to the singers that he had a motu proprio making him the Cardinal Protector of the Chapel with the right to admit and expel singers (the very powers the singers had so laboriously taken from Magnasco). He immediately exercised this power by presenting Francesco Nardo for admission, permitting the singers at least to hear his voice and to vote.[43] Nardo was approved by a unanimous vote on 25 February 1560.

This was an ominous development. Ten years after the singers had succeeded in stripping the *maestro di cappella* of almost all his rights to interfere with their privileges, they now were faced with a much more powerful prelate, a cardinal, with precisely these same rights. Needless to say, the singers were very concerned. They asked to be given a copy of the motu proprio to study (actually to see how they could overturn it and also have Caraffa removed as protector).[44] They did not have to worry long about Cardinal Caraffa; he was soon arrested, imprisoned, and executed by Pope Pius IV.[45] Pius, however, did not give up the idea of a cardinal protector of the Chapel as a person to whom the College and the *maestro di cappella* could bring their various concerns, rather than bothering the pope. Accordingly, he promoted Cardinal Bartolomé de la Cueva to the post; this protector, however, was admonished to uphold the constitutions and customs of the College and no mention is made of the authority to admit and expel singers.[46] During the next decades, occasional mention is made of a cardinal protector, but the powers of the

---

[42] Richard Sherr, 'Competence and Incompetence in the Papal Chapel in the Age of Palestrina', *EM* 22 (1994), 606–30.

[43] 'Finita missa comparuit Rev.mus cardinalis Carafa una cum magistro capelle et congregatis cantoribus omnibus exceptis infirmis predictis dictus Rev.mus presentavit unum motum proprium manu Sanctissimi signatum cuius vigore fuit deputatus protector capelle cum potestate admittendi et expellendi quoscumque cantores etc., committens cantoribus predictis et quibusvis aliis, ad quos spectat, ut obediant sub pena excommunicationis et aliis in eodem contentis; quo motu proprio lecto et intellecto omnes cantores una cum magistro dederunt obedientiam deosculantes manum Rev.mi protectoris.

Item fecit cantare bassum Bononiensem Franciscum Nardum, ut audiretur vox eiusdem, que fuit laudata et commendata ab omnibus.' *Diarii Sistini* 5, fo. 159ᵛ, entry dated 10 Feb. 1560; transcribed in Herman-Walther Frey, *Die Diarien der Sixtinischen Kapelle in Rom der Jahre 1560 und 1561 (Diarium 5 fo. 156–192, Diarium 6)* (Düsseldorf, 1959), 14.

[44] 'Finita missa congregatis cantoribus comparuit R.p.d. magister capelle et retulit se locutum fuisse cum Rev.mo Caraffa super eo, quod impetraverat protectoriatum capelle cum derogationibus privilegiorum et constitutionum eiusdem in grave preiuditium collegii et qualiter petierat copiam dicti motu proprii et quod responderat, si totum collegium id peteret, daret copiam, sed eoquod tantum duo vel tres illam volebat [*sic*] nolebat dare. Quare fuit conclusum per vota publica data per unumquemque singulum cantorem, quod omnes unanimes dictam copiam desiderabant, causa illam reformandi et annichilandi, si possibile foret, et fuit conclusum ab omnibus tunc presentibus, quod omnes simul vel separatim informarent cardinales Borromeum et Fulginatensem ceterosque alios ipsis benevisos ac etiam pontificem super hac causa etc., attento quod numquam visum fuit, collegium predictum habere alium protectorem quam collegium Rev.morum cardinalium.' Ibid., fo. 160ʳ, entry dated 12 Feb. 1560 (transcribed in Frey, *Die Diarien*, 14).

[45] He was executed in the Castel Sant'Angelo on 6 Mar. 1561.   [46] See CS 679, fo. 9ʳ⁻ᵛ.

protector are not made clear. All this changed with the accession of Pope Sixtus V (r. 1585–90). In the bull *In suprema militantis ecclesiae* of 1 September 1586—the same bull that, for the first time, formally established the College of Singers as a legal entity, completely reorganized their finances, and declared that officially henceforth the *maestro di cappella* was to be a singer elected by his peers—the position of cardinal protector with complete authority over all matters secular and beneficial concerning the College of Singers was officially instituted in perpetuity.[47] With this, thirty-six years after their successful prosecution of Magnasco, the singers were finally rid of their outside administrator, the *maestro di cappella*; however, their immediate relationship to the Supreme Pontiff (the legal basis for all their complaining to the pope about Magnasco in the first place) was now for ever to be replaced by direct subordination to the cardinal protector. A chapter in their centuries-old institutional history had closed.

Appendix: Documents Concerning the College of Singers

1. BAV, CS 684, fo. 74[r–v]. Copy of a papal breve dated 17 November 1545. Pope Paul III confirms the new Constitution to the Chapel.

Paulus Papa III
Ad futuram rei memoriam. Romanus pontifex Christi vicarius, et Beati Petri successor cupiens domino devotius famulari, iis quae et ex pia fidelium devotione in favorem divini cultus, et ad pia opera exercenda provide ordinata, seu aliquo tempore deperdita eorum opera instaurata comperit, ut illibata persistant, libenter cum ab eo petitur apostolici muniminis praesidium impartitur. Sane pro parte venerabilis fratris Ludovici Episcopi Assissinatensis magistri capellae nostrae, necnon dilectorum filiorum universorum cantorum cappellanorum et clericorum in eadem capella nostra nobis nuper fuit expositum, quod cum in direptione almae urbis statuta et ordinationes dictae capellae inter alia receptionem cantorum capellanorum et clericorum in eadem capella et ea, ad que in illam cantores capellani et clerici pro tempore recepti tenerentur ad divinum cultum et alias pias causas concernentia deperdita fuissent, statuta et ordinationes huiusmodi ab aliquibus memoria retenta jussu et cura dicti Ludovici episcopi pro salubri directione cantorum capellanorum, nec non clericorum praedictorum eiusdem capellae ac illorum status conservatione restaurata et per eundem Ludovicum episcopum de novo edita et ordinata fuerunt. Quare pro parte eorumdem Ludovici episcopi ac universorum cantorum capellanorum et clericorum predictorum nobis fuit humiliter supplicatum, ut statutis et ordinationibus huiusmodi pro eorum subsistentia firmiori, et ut efficacius observentur, robur nostrae approbationis adiicere et alias in premissis oppor-

---

[47] The original bull is preserved in CS 703, no. 21.

tune providere de benignitate apostolica dignaremur. Nos igitur dictae nostrae capellae, ac illius personarum tranquillum statum, et profectum ac felicem successum paterno zelantes affectu, ac dictorum statutorum et ordinationum veriores tenores presentibus pro sufficienter expressis haberi volentes, huiusmodi supplicationibus inclinati statuta et ordinationes huiusmodi, ac omnia et singula in eis contenta, licita tamen et honesta, ac sacris canonibus non contraria auctoritate apostolica tenore presentium approbamus et confirmamus, ac illa perpetuo firmiter observari debere decernimus, supplentes omnes et singulos iuris et facti defectus si qui forsan in illorum editione intervenerint. Et nichilominus eidem Ludovico episcopo et pro tempore existenti in dicta capella magistro per presentes committimus et mandamus, quatenus statuta et ordinationes huiusmodi iuxta illorum ac approbationis, et confirmationis huiusmodi tenorem firmiter observari faciant, contradictores per censuram ecclesiaticam et alia opportuna juris remedia, et prout ex tenore dictorum statutorum et ordinationum possunt auctoritate nostra appellatione posposita compescendo invocato etiam ad hoc si opus fuerit auxilio brachiis secularis. Non obstantibus constitutionibus et ordinationibus contrariis quibuscunque aut si aliquibus communiter vel divisim ab apostolica sit sede indultum quod interdici, suspendi, vel excommunicari non possint per literas apostolicas non facientes plenam et expressam ac de verbo ad verbum de indulto huiusmodi mentionem. Datum Rome apud Sanctum Petrum sub annulo piscatoris die 17 Novembris 1545 Pontificatus Nostri Anno Duodecimo.

2. CS 703, no. 8. Bull dated 20 July 1492 (see Pl. 11). Innocent VIII reserves to the Master of the Papal Chapel the right to present members of that chapel to benefices made vacant by the death of former members.

INNOCENTIUS EPISCOPUS SERVUS SERVORUM DEI AD PERPETUAM REI MEMORIAM. Etsi Romanus Pontifex ad quem pertinet distributio gratiarum cunctis fidelibus in illarum distributione liberalem se exhibeat, illos tamen amplioribus gratiis ipsum prosequi convenit qui preter grata familiaritatis obsequiis que sibi impendunt in apostolica capella sonoris vocibus et dulcibus organis altissimo divinas laudes continue persolvunt ut eo ferventius attentiusque laudibus eisdem insistant quo beneficiorumque ecclesiasticorum provisione ab apostolica sede uberius se cognoverint circunfultive.

Intendentes igitur ut dilectis filiis familiaribus nostris in capella nostra cantoribus capellanis, ac capellanis missarum, et clericis cerimoniarum, necnon aliis clericis campanariis nuncupatis et presertim benemeritis eiusdem capelle etiam < non > nullis aliis, de beneficiis ecclesiasticis que per obitum aliorum cantorum capellanorum, et capellanorum missarum, necnon clericorum cerimoniarum et campanariorum predictorum qui tempore quorumcunque predecessorum nostrorum Romanorum Pontificum fuerunt et nunc sunt ac pro tempore erunt, ad presens vacant et in futurum vacare contigerit libere provideri valeat, et ne nos aut pro tempore sucessores nostros per aliquem decipi et non merentibus provideri contingat,

motu proprio, non ad alicuius super hec oblate nobis petitionis instantiam sed ex mera deliberatione et certa scientia, omnia et singula beneficia ecclesiastica cum cura et sine cura secularia et quorumvis ordinum regularia que predecessorum predictorum ac

nunc et pro tempore existere < > nostri in dicta capella cantores capellani, et capellani missarum, necnon dicti < clerici > ceremoniarum et campanarii predicti, in titulum
vel commendam obtinent et imposterum obtinebunt, ac in quibus et ad que ius eis
quomodolibet competit et competet in futurum, nunc vacantia et imposterum
vacatura, etiam si secularia, canonicatus et prebende dignitates personatus administrationes, vel officia in cathedralibus etiam metropolitanis vel collegiatis ecclesiis, et dignitates ipse in cathedralibus etiam metropolitanis post pontificales maiores aut
collegiatis ecclesiis huiusmodi principales, seu prestimonia prestimoniales portiones
obligea fercula addi < ta > menta supplementa, regularia vero prioratus prepositure
prepositatus dignitates etiam conventuales personatus administrationes, vel officia
etiam claustralia, et alia quecunque beneficia tam secularia quam regularia etiam quocunque nomine nuncupata fuerint, et ad prioratus preposituras dignitates personatus
administrationes vel officia huiusmodi consueverint qui per electionem assumi eisque
cura immineat animarum cum illa per decessum in Romana curia vel extra eam illa obti-
nentium, etiam commendis commendatorum huiusmodi cessantibus etiam apud
sedem predictam vacabunt,

Venerabilis fratis nostri Cristofori episcopi Cortonensis nunc dicte capelle et successo-
rum suorum eiusdem capelle magistrorum pro tempore existentium presentationi ac
nostre et sedis apostolice institutioni reservamus, eisdemque episcopo et successoribus
prefatis ius presentandi personas ydoneas ex dicta capella per nos et successores nostros
Romanos pontifices instituendis perpetuis futuris temporibus concedimus, veros et
ultimos beneficiorum commendatorum huiusmodi vacantium modos, etiam si ex illis
quevis generalis reservatio etiam ratione illorum vacationis apud sedem predictam vel
alias in corpore iuris clausa resultet pro sufficienter expressis habentes, non obstantibus
quibuscunque de huiusmodi beneficiis tam per regulas cancellarie apostolice per nos et
successores nostros pro tempore factas, seu alias quomodocunque factis reservation-
ibus, ac aliis constitutionibus et ordinationibus apostolicis necnon ecclesiarum in
quibus secularia et monasteriorum seu regularium locorum in quibus regularia beneficia huiusmodi forsan fuerint, seu a quibus illa dependere contigerit et ordinationibus
quorum extiterint iuramento confirmatione apostolica vel quavis firmitate alia robo-
ratis statutis et consuetudinibus ceterisque contrariis quibuscunque, decernentes etiam
presentibus litteris per quascunque alias constitutiones et litteras ac privilegia et indulta
quascunque derogatorias clausulas in se pro tempore continentia et per que eisdem presentibus derogari videretur aut illis derogaretur expresse nisi de data presentium illaque
toto tenore in eis mentio specifica et individua fiat et trina litterarum expeditione diver-
sis mensibus facta derogari non possit necnon irritum et inane si secus super hiis a quo-
quam quavis auctoritate scienter vel ignoranter contigerit attemptari.

Nulli ergo omnino hominum liceat hanc paginam nostre concessionis et constitutionis
infringere vel ei ausu temerario contraire. Si quis autem hoc attemptare presumpserit
indignationem omnipotentis dei ac beatorum Petri et Pauli apostolorum eius se noverit
incursurum. Datum Rome apud Sanctum Petrum anno incarnationis dominice millesimo quadringentesimo nonagesimo secundo terciodecimo kalendas augusti pontificatus nostri anno octavo.

3. CS 680, fos. 96ʳ–97ʳ. Memorandum without date (1550). The singers complain about the abuses perpetrated by Ludovico Magnasco.

Reverendissime Domine
A tempore felicis recordationis Urbani Pape Sexti reperitur memoria cantorum cappel-lanorum capelle apostolice a quo tempore citra usque ad pontificatum fe. re. Pauli Pape 3 dicti cantores cappellani semper fuerunt admissi ad vitam et fuerunt immediate subiecti summo pontifici, et tanquam collegium sine magistro capelle fuerunt inter se plura statuta et ordinationes quibus gubernabantur, que inter dictos cantores fuerunt inconcusse observata et cantor qui contra dicta statuta et ordinationes delinquebat mulctabatur et puniebatur arbitrio dictorum cantorum cappellanorum et punitio sive mulcta huiusmodi facta per cantores mandabatur essecutioni absque eo quod in aliquo intervenisset magister capelle.

Et videlicet fe. re. Sixtus Papa 4us creaverit officium magistratus capelle nichilominus prefati cantores cappellani semper in eadem consuetudine permansserunt, absque eo quod predecessores R.p.d. episcopi Assissinatensis moderni magistri capelle super huiusmodi consuetudine aliquam molestiam cantoribus dedissent.

Est admittendum pro intelligentia consuetudinis capelle offitium magistratus capelle fuit erectum ad effectum quod magister capelle haberet curam ne cantores pro suis aut capelle negotiis pretermitterent officium divinum in capella et defenderet prerogativas et privilegia capelle et intercederet apud pontificem pro cantoribus. Itaque offitium magistratus capelle fuit erectum pro utilitate capelle non autem ad illam dissipandum neque ad docendum cantores cum omnes sunt suficientissimi ad docendum magistrum capelle in arte canendi.

Anno 1540 prefatus R.p.d. episcopus Assissinatensis successit in magistratu capelle et videlicet in dicta capella invenerit dictam consuetudinem in viridi observantia nichilominus haspirans in eversionem capelle de anno 1545 impetravit a fe. re. Paulo 3.o quoddam breve in quo atribuntur sibi facultas expellendi cantores et alias personas a dicta capella et loco eorum alios de novo admittere ad beneplacitum suum, cuius vig-ore contra privilegia, statuta et consuetudines capelle intentavit introducere innum-merabiles et varios abusus in dicta capella de quibus aliqui specificantur, quia non esset dificile specificare omnes abusus per magistrum introductus.

Primo. Fuit et est statutum in capella apostolica ab immemorabili tempore citra incon-cusse observatum quod cantores admittuntur ad vittam in dicta capella de mandato pontificis et facto examine tam de moribus et vita per magistrum capelle quam de voce et suficientia per cantores dicte capelle, contra huiusmodi statutum magister capelle inconsulto pontifice, invitis cantoribus, et avisatus de infamia, admisit in capella apos-tolica Ottavianum [Gemelli] cantorem infamem qui publice fuit suspensus.

2.o. Per summos pontifices fuit concessum privilegium cappelle apostolice, in qua magister capelle videlicet ius presentandi personas idoneas ex dicta capella ad elec-tionem cantorum ad benefitia vacantia per obitum cantorum etc., et benefitia huius-modi ac fructus et emolumenta eorundem distribuuntur arbitrio collegii cantorum videlicet antiquioribus et benemerentibus etc., contra dictum privilegium magister capelle presentavit ad benefitia Pisauriensis per obitum Hieronimi Arduini Federicum Lazizum modernum cantorem preferendo eum antiquioribus cantoribus ac dicendo cantoribus conquerentibus de huiusmodi presentatione volo ego quod primi sint novissimi et novissimi primi quia ego dominus. Presentavit ad benefitia quondam Petri de los Ottones Antonium de Olmedo cappellanum missarum et recusavit presentare Johannes Sanchez electum per cantores. Distribuit benefitia Mathei Florani, concordavit et distribuit benefitia Hieronimi Arduini et Petri de los Ottones inconsulto collegio cantorum contra statuta capelle dicens in omnibus ego dominus.

3.o. Est consuetudo in dicta capella quod quando aliquis cantor venit puniendus sive mulctandus, in quocunque casu talis cantor punitur sive mulctatur per collegium cantorum sine magistro capelle, et prefatus magister non potest imponere penam pecuniariam occurere mulcte seu pene neque retinere salarium cantoribus inconsulto collegio cantorum, contra huiusmodi consuetudinem magister capelle inconsulto collegio cantorum sine legitima causa mandavit retineri salarium Johanni Francisci Felicis, Bernardi Pauli, Yvonis Barry et Pauli de Bursanis cantores capelle. Fecit monitorium contra nonnullos cantores quatenus non intrent in capellam sub pena arbitrii sui et hoc per levissimus causis; alios minavit se velle expellere a capella apostolica ad libitum suum et in omnibus dicens, ego dominus.

4.o. Est statutum in capella apostolica quod nullus cantor potest recedere ab urbe sine licentia pontificis et collegii cantorum ac magistri capelle si vult ire ad partes si vero causa recreationis per tres quatuor aut pluries dies, obtenta licentiam a collegio, contra dictum statutum magister capelle pluries dedit licentiam cantoribus recedendi ab urbe inconsulto collegio cantorum, et Yvoni Bary qui obtinerat licentiam a fe. re. Paulo 3.o et a collegio cantorum eundi ad partes dictam licentiam revocavit sub pena arbitrio sui et a civitate Bononiensi fecit eum regredi Romam.

5.o. In capella apostolica sunt constitutiones que fuerunt et sunt inviridi observantia quibus ab immemorabile tempore citra cantores dicte capelle fuerunt gubernati, contra dictas constitutiones magister capelle vigore cuiusdam brevis per fe. re. Paulum Papam Tertium sibi concessi fecit scribi novas constitutiones, quarum ex dicti brevis vigore iactatur se esse dominus capelle apostolice, et habere potestatem puniendi et mulctandi cantores ad libitum suum quod horridum verbum hactenus non fuit auditum.

Ideo supplicatur domine vestre Reverendissime pro parte cantorum capelle dignetur facere verbum cum Sanctissimo quatenus Sanctitas Sua provideat cantoribus de opportuno remedio aliud magistrum eis concedendo nam gubernium magistri capelle quem in presentiarum habent cantores ulterius pati non possunt, cum non sperent in futurum dictum magistrum nec mores neque modum administratio posse mutare, cum ipse magister pluries dixerit cantoribus se velle esse sibi proprium quam capelle et cantoribus et a decem annis citra nec semel tantum accessit ad capellam pro utilitate cantorum sed semper dicti cantores fuerunt sibi invisi causu quare ignoravimus.

4. CS 679, fos. 31^r–32^v. Memorandum without date (1550). The relevant clauses of the final agreement between the singers and Ludovico Magnasco.

Capitula inita inter magistrum et cantores capelle pape

Primo quod de facultate prefato R.p.d. magistro capelle per fe. re. Paulum iii vigore brevis eidem d. magistro capelle concessi seu vigore quarumcunque aliarum litterarum et indultorum quomodolibet attributis idem magister capelle non utatur quo ad admittendis et expellendis cantores nisi iuxta antiquam consuetudinem videlicet consultis cantoribus et de eorum voto sive consensu neque se intromittat in cognoscendis causis beneficialibus neque profanis inter cantores neque alias persona dicte capelle.

Item quod in quorumcunque casu collegium cantorum habeat facultatem puniendi et mulctandi cantorem deliquentem iuxta antiquam consuetudinem ab innummerabili tempore citra inconcusse observatam infra decem dies a die notitie et casu quo infra dictos decem dies collegium cantorum non punierit cantorem delinquentem magister capelle unanimiter collegio cantorum possit eum punire.

Item quod in eventum in quem delictum commissum per cantorem fuerit cum effusione sanguinis in tali casu sive eventu et non alias prefatus magister capelle unanimiter collegio cantorum infra decem dies etiam in ipso instanti et fragranti delicto possit punire sive mulctare cantorem delinquentem.

Item quod nullus cantor mulctatus sive punitus per collegium cantorum possit appellare nisi punitio sive mulcta huiusmodi excesserit summam quatuor scutorum auri.

Item quod in novis constitutionibus capelle per fe. re. Paulum papam iii confirmatis non possit cassari neque addi aliquod verbum nisi consulto prefato magistro capelle aut summo pontifice pro tempore existente sub pena privationis capelle.

Item quod magister capelle non possit intervenire in congregationibus et capitulis cantorum nisi in casibus supradictis aut concernentibus servitium capelle et summi pontificis videlicet iuxta officium divinum.

Item quod observentur consuetudo antiqua super capsa sive archivio et custodiatura per tres cantores antiquiores unum videlicet ex qualibet trium nationum qui fa[ciant— hole in page] fideliter custodiri in dicto archivio omnia privilegia constitutiones et scripturas commodum et utilitatem capelle concernentes que non possint retinere extra dictum archivium ultra mensem et si secus factum fuit mulctabuntur arbitrio collegii cantorum dicti antiquiores cantores si negligentes erunt in monendo et requirendo habentes privilegia huiusmodi quatenus illa restituant vel recusans restituere mulctabitur arbitrio collegii cantorum.

Item quod prefati tres antiquiores cantores non possint neque debeant extrahere dicta privilegia sive scripturas a dicto archivio nisi consultis cantoribus collegialiter congregatis et de eorum voto sive consensu neque debeant neque possint ea consignare nisi prefato magistro aut cantori dicte capelle habita prius apocha manu recipientis privilegia huiusmodi et dato pignere auri vel argenti quod pignus ponatur in archivio donec privilegia seu scriptura restituantur in locus suum.

Item quod in dandis licentiam eundi extra urbem servetur consuetudo antiqua videlicet quod nullus cantor possit recedere ab urbe per tres aut pluries dies inconsulto collegio sine licentiam collegii alias punctetur prout hactenus consuetum est.

Item quod occurrente vacatione alicuius beneficii per obitum cantoris seu capellani seu alterius persone de dicta capella semper fuit consuetum quod cantores insimul congregati unum nominent et ab eis nominatus et nullus alius solet presentari per magistrum capelle ad beneficium huiusmodi sibi per papam conferendum et nullo modo possit magister capelle alium presentare quam nominatum a collegio minusque possit distribuere magister capelle fructus beneficii huiusmodi sed illorum distributio atque pars cuique ex cantoribus assignanda ad ipsum collegium cantorum libere spectet et ita voluerunt quod inconcusse deinceps observetur quocumque alio abusu remoto.

Et quia a paucis annis citra forma iuramenti quam in suo ingressu cantores observare solent ab eo quod antiquitus observabatur alterata fuit ideo voluerunt quod in futurum cantores in primo suo ingressu prestent iuramentum secundum formam et consuetudinem antiquam hoc videlicet modo

Ego N clericus N ab hac hora in antea fidelis ero S.mo d.n. n.o pape et obediens d.n. magistro capelle, d. decanum, ceteres cantores et illorum collegium venerabor, constitutiones et consuetudines dicte capelle observabo, et secreta que in capitulis et congregationibus collegii cantorum tractari contigerit non revelabo, sic me Deus adiuvet et hec Sancta Dei Evangelia.

5. ASV, Arm. 41, vol. 58, fo. 186ʳ. Minute of the breve dated 5 November 1550. Julius III makes Girolamo Maccabei, Bishop of Castro, the *maestro di cappella*.

Venerabili fratri Hieronimo Episcopo Castrensis Prelato nostro domestico
Venerabilis fratri salutem. De tua probitate, virtute, ac diligentia, et in rebus sacris experientia de quibus etiam per antiquam familiaritatem tuam plenam notitiam habemus, confisi, ac sperantes quod ea que tibi commiserimus ad Dei omnipotentis honorem et nostram satisfactionem laudabilem exequeris, te capellam nostram magistrum cum omnibus et singulis honoribus oneribus iuribus, obventionibus emolumentis ac commodis solitis et consuetis ad beneplacitum nostrum ex nunc inchoanda facimus et deputamus per presentes. Mandantes dilectis filiis cantoribus et capellanis ac aliis eiusdem capellae ministris ut te in ipsius capellae magistrum recipiant tibique tanquam dictae capellae magistro reverentiam et obedientiam solitis exhibeant, et ad quod spectat ut de solitis ac consuetis emolumentis et aliis debitis suo tempore respondeant. Non obstantibus constitutionibus et ordinationibus apostolicis ac deputatione de venerabili fratre Ludovico episcopo Assisiensi per fe. re. Paulum Papam III predecessorem nostrem in dicta capella magistrum ad eius vitam facta, et per nos forsan confirmata quam rationabilibus moti causis ex nunc revocamus, ceterisque contrariis quibuscumque. Datum Romae etc. V Novembris 1550 Anno Primo.

PART III

Studies of Individuals

9

Josquin in Rome: Some Evidence from the Masses

❦

JAMES HAAR

IT would be gratifying to be able to announce that I have new documentation concerning Josquin des Prez's service in the papal chapel, a period thought to extend from June 1489 until some time in 1495 or perhaps longer, with some internal gaps.[1] Unfortunately I do not. My purpose here is more indirect and more modest; I wish to suggest that some of Josquin's masses were known in Rome before their printing by Ottaviano de' Petrucci, and that regardless of their date of copying in Roman manuscripts they were known in versions differing from Petrucci's sources, in a few instances versions that may lay claim to being specifically Roman and thus possibly close to the composer himself.

My investigation has been limited to the five masses contained in Petrucci's *Misse Josquin* of 1502: *Missa L'homme armé super voces musicales*, *Missa La sol fa re mi*, *Missa Gaudeamus*, *Missa Fortuna desperata*, and *Missa L'homme armé sexti toni*. All these works are to be found in Roman manuscripts dating from *c*.1490–1520. I shall take them up in Petrucci's ordering, an arrangement made with some care.

The *Missa L'homme armé super voces musicales* was, to judge from its wide dissemination in manuscript and print, one of the most if not the most celebrated of Josquin's masses among his contemporaries and immediate successors.[2]

I am grateful to Richard Sherr and Mitchell Brauner for the loan of microfilmed materials, which aided me in preparing this chapter.

[1] See Helmuth Osthoff, *Josquin Desprez*, 2 vols. (Tutzing, 1962–5), i, ch. 2: 'Die römische Zeit'; Jeremy Noble, 'New Light on Josquin's Benefices', in Lowinsky and Blackburn (eds.), *Josquin des Prez: Proceedings*, 76–102; and above, Ch. 4 n. 51.

[2] To the manuscript sources for the complete mass listed in Josquin des Prez, *Werken*, ed. Albert Smijers, Missen, Deel I/1 (Amsterdam, 1926) (in addition to the three Roman sources, on which see below, Smijers cites Basle, F.IX.25 a–d; Jena 32; Modena α.M.1.2; Vienna 11778) should be added the following: Frankfurt am Main, Stadt- und Universitätsbibliothek, Mus. fol. 2; Regensburg, Bischöfliche Zentralbibliothek, MSS A.R. 878–882 and C 100; and Toledo, Biblioteca Capitolar, MS B 9. Individual sections were printed as examples in various treatises beginning with the *Dodekachordon* of Henricus Glareanus (Basle, 1547); see Smijers, op. cit., p. vii.

This may be due to its virtuosic character, to a renewed vogue for *L'homme armé* pieces at the end of the fifteenth century, or to both. Scribes and compilers as well as printers placed it at the opening of volumes, so it seems appropriate to begin with it. Given the evident popularity of the theme in late fifteenth-century Rome, and the fact that several of Josquin's contemporaries wrote masses on it, one might speculate that Josquin wrote this work in a climate of emulation similar to the 'motet competition' so suggestively hypothesized by Richard Sherr as background for the motet *Illibata Dei Virgo nutrix*.[3]

The *Missa L'homme armé super voces musicales* is found in three Roman manuscripts, two from the Cappella Sistina (Vatican CS 197 and 154) and one from the Cappella Giulia (Vatican CG XII.2). No precise date of composition is known for this or any of the other masses under consideration; but the earliest surviving source would appear to be CS 197, a single fascicle containing only this work and probably copied during the 1490s.[4] This manuscript, presumably never bound into a choirbook volume, is the careful and rather handsome work of a scribe whose hand has been identified in a few other Cappella Sistina sources, all of early date.[5] The appearance of the music in this source is very different from Petrucci's printing, enough to mask the fact that there are not many substantial variants. As in all the masses under consideration here, the manuscripts differ from Petrucci in text underlay, in agglomeration vs. fragmentation of note-values, and in use of ligatures (there are many more in the manuscripts, an indication on the one hand of scribal ease and perhaps pleasure in writing them as opposed to the obvious difficulties of reproducing them in type, on the other hand an attitude towards notation as immediately ready reading material—the prints—as opposed to notation viewed as the preserve of professional singers, the manuscripts). The one substantive variant occurs in the Cantus part at the opening of the Confiteor of the Credo, a difference from Petrucci's text shared by all the other important manuscript sources of the work.[6]

More interesting than any of this is the presentation of the work in CS 197. In the Kyrie the Tenor is combined with the opening of the Cantus (Kyrie I),

[3] Richard Sherr, '*Illibata Dei virgo nutrix* and Josquin's Roman Style', *JAMS* 41 (1988), 434–64.

[4] Richard Sherr, 'The Papal Chapel ca. 1492–1513 and its Polyphonic Sources' (Ph.D. diss., Princeton University, 1975), 191–2; id., *Papal Music Manuscripts in the Late Fifteenth and Early Sixteenth Centuries* (Renaissance Manuscript Studies, 5; Neuhausen-Stuttgart, 1996), 211; Jeffrey Dean, 'The Scribes of the Sistine Chapel, 1501–1527' (Ph.D. diss., University of Chicago, 1984), 3. See also Mitchell P. Brauner, 'The Catalogue of Raffaele Panuzzi and the Repertory of the Papal Chapel in the 15th and 16th Centuries', *Journal of Musicology*, 8 (1990), 427–43, esp. 431. The scribe who copied CS 197 used some notational archaisms, prominent among them a double-tailed figure (♦) representing a fusa.

[5] Sherr, 'The Papal Chapel', 192.

[6] For this variant, found as well in CS 154, Basle F.IX.25, Jena 32, Modena α.M.1.2, and Vienna 11778, see Josquin, *Werken*, Missen I/1, p. xxii.

with that of the Altus (Christe), and with the Bass (Kyrie II), each having two clefs and two mensural signatures (Pl. 12). This visual device, showing the whole of the *L'homme armé* melody in two voices at once, is an economical notation of canonic procedure; it also establishes the theme both as cantus firmus and as motto for the whole work and demonstrates graphically the theorem on which the mass is based, a contest of mode and hexachord, the armed man locked in internal combat. Its vivid appearance suggests something further, namely the peculiar aptness of the *L'homme armé* melody, particularly its opening phrase, for the words of the Kyrie. Whether or not it was sung this way (no source shows syllabic underlay), composers—including the first one, whoever he was—using the melody as basis for a mass must have noticed this correspondence. Pl. 12 also shows citation of a part of the *L'homme armé* chanson text in the Christe, a citation that reappears in the Tenor in the Patrem and Osanna of the mass.[7]

The varied permutations of the Tenor have idiosyncratic rubrics in CS 197; for example, cancrizans motion is indicated in the Qui tollis of the Gloria by 'Verte cito', a phrase ordinarily meaning 'turn [the page] quickly', and by placement of the words 'Qui tollis' at the end rather than the beginning.[8] At the end of the mass Agnus III has the Cantus rubric 'Clama ne cesses', referring to the fact that rests above the value of a minim are to be omitted, found in a number of sources; it also has an illuminated Tenor capital (Pl. 13) showing an armed nobleman (note the plumes in the helmet) grasping a serpent with one hand and with the other impaling it on a sword. This *homme armé* could also be seen as St George, suggesting the Order of the Garter, or even the Archangel Michael, although there are no angelic attributes.[9] Given the revival of crusader enthusiasm in the Rome of Alexander VI, particularly at the time of Charles VIII's visit to the city early in 1495, one might conclude that this

---

[7] The text phrase 'On a fait par tout crier' is also found in the Christe and Osanna of Vienna 11778. On the use of these mottos and of various canonic inscriptions dealing with the 'armed man' motif in the Naples *L'homme armé* masses see Judith Cohen, *The Six L'homme armé Masses in Naples, Biblioteca Nazionale, MS VI E 40* (American Institute of Musicology, 1968), 23, 28–30.

[8] This rubric, used in the Et incarnatus est of the Credo as well, is also found in Basle F.IX.25 and Jena 32. Petrucci here has 'Cancrizet et supra dicta notet', found in several other sources, including Vatican CG XII.2. The Tenor in the Confiteor of the Credo has the rubric 'reverte citius', indicating a diminished reversal of the preceding cancrizans Tenor, followed by a resolution 'ad longum'; Petrucci has only the word 'equaliter', accompanied by a *resolutio*. See Richard Sherr, 'The Performance of Josquin's *L'homme armé* Masses', *EM* 19 (1991), 261–8.

[9] Louis XI founded an Order of St Michael, emulating the Burgundian Order of the Golden Fleece, in 1469; see P. M. Kendall, *Louis XI* (New York, 1971), 226; cf. Adalbert Roth, 'L'homme armé, le doubté turcq, L'ordre de la toison d'or: Zur "Begleitmusik" der letzten grossen Kreuzzugsbewegung nach dem Fall von Konstantinopel', in Detlev von Altenberg, Jörg Jarmut, and Hans-Hugo Steinhoff (eds.), *Festen und Feiern im Mittelalter* (Sigmaringen, 1991), 469–79, esp. 478 n. Roth also notes (478–9) the foundation in 1465 of a Neapolitan chivalric order dedicated to St Michael. The *L'homme armé* mass of Regis uses as text for its cantus firmus Tenor the Magnificat antiphon for the feast of the Archangel Michael. See Johannes Regis, *Opera Omnia*, ed. Cornelius Lindenburg (CMM 9; American Institute of Musicology, 1956), i, p. iv.

illustration had particular as well as general relevance to the 'armed man' subject of the mass; it would also be appropriate for the larger context of *L'homme armé*, recently proposed by Flynn Warmington.[10]

The *Missa L'homme armé super voces musicales* appears in a second Cappella Sistina manuscript, CS 154, copied by Johannes Parvus. The coat of arms of Pope Julius III (r. 1550–5) on the first opening of the mass suggests that it was copied during his pontificate.[11] Here it may be noted that Palestrina, later to publish two *L'homme armé* masses of his own, was a singer in the Cappella Sistina in 1555.[12]

CS 154 is clearly copied from CS 197. Its musical text is identical except for a very occasional ligature change and for some additions (see below). Its scribe improved upon the model in layout; he modernized the notation by eliminating nearly all the *minor color*; and he clarified the mensuration canon of Agnus Dei II by changing the clef from the c1 clef used in CS 197 to f3 and by placing the three mensuration signs on the correct stave-lines for their realization.[13] Agnus Dei III in the newer source is once again illustrated by an armed man and serpent (Pl. 14), now placed correctly with the cantus firmus in the top voice, and updated by replacement of fifteenth-century armour with Roman military garb, including a breastplate *alla romana*, armour already seen without its wearer in an illumination at the opening of the mass (Pl. 15).[14] The scribe of CS 154 surely saw the Cappella Giulia copy (see below) and perhaps printed copies of the mass as well, replacing some of the Tenor rubrics in CS 197 with those found in Petrucci. Finally, in CS 154 the text underlay of CS

[10] See Flynn Warmington, 'The Mass of the Ceremony of the Armed Man: The Sword and the Altar', in Paula Higgins (ed.), *Antoine Busnoys: Method, Meaning, and Context in Late Medieval Music* (Oxford; forthcoming); I am grateful to the author for letting me see the paper in advance of its publication. Warmington's paper contains much fascinating information on traditions of an armed man, often a ruler, attending Mass with sword drawn at the Gospel. Of special interest is a ceremony at the Duomo in Cividale del Friuli, documented as early as 1433, in which the deacon is armed and wears a helmet (plumed, at least in modern observances). The presence of the dragon in CS 197 would seem to tie its illustration to St Michael (or St George); but the Armed Man could refer as well to the ceremonies described by Warmington.

[11] Mitchell P. Brauner, 'The Parvus Manuscripts: A Study of Vatican Polyphony ca. 1535 to 1580' (Ph.D. diss., Brandeis University, 1982), 163, 172–3, 310.

[12] Lewis Lockwood, 'Palestrina', *New Grove*, xiv. 119–20. Of course the two *L'homme armé* masses of Morales, published in 1544, may have been Palestrina's immediate inspiration; but Morales was no longer in Rome in the 1550s. On relationships between the masses of Morales and those of Francisco Guerrero see Owen Rees, 'Guerrero's *L'homme armé* Masses and their Models', *EMH* 12 (1993), 19–54. The MS CG XII.2 (see below) may also have been known to Palestrina. The Morales *L'homme armé* masses as printed by Valerio Dorico in Rome contain woodcut illustrations in the Cantus parts of their opening Kyries, one depicting the Emperor Charles V as a warrior, the other a helmeted soldier. See Robert Stevenson, *Spanish Cathedral Music in the Golden Age* (Berkeley, 1961), 57–8. For further discussion of Palestrina's masses, see James Haar, 'Palestrina as Historicist: The Two *L'homme armé* Masses', *Journal of the Royal Musical Association* 121 (1996), 191–205.

[13] None of the other sources, even Glareanus, gives the Agnus II in this form.

[14] The opening of Busnoys's *Missa L'homme armé* in the Chigi Codex (Vatican C VIII 234), fo. 213ᵛ, shows two male heads wearing helmets (at the bottom of the page). The Kyrie of the same mass in SMM 26, fo. 154ᵛ, is decorated with a figure armed with bow and arrow.

197 is altered and improved, not necessarily in accord with those sources; it draws upon additions and alterations made in a cursive hand in CS 197.[15]

The closeness of CS 154 to CS 197 indicates respect for the earlier source, amounting to a desire to reproduce it without substantial alteration. Why the need then for a new chapel copy? Archaisms in the older source could not alone explain it; the answer I think is in the presence of added music. CS 154 contains a setting of the Et in Spiritum section of the Credo, omitted in CS 197 and in all other sources. The crusader-influenced desire to avoid offence to the Eastern Church, which this portion of the Credo might give, was clearly no longer relevant to the Tridentine Roman Church of the 1550s.[16] The added section is surely not by Josquin; its composer might well be the 'Jo. Abbat', a papal singer of the time, whose name appears next to a *si placet* fifth voice in CS 154's version of Agnus Dei III of the mass.[17]

A third Roman source for this mass is CG XII.2. In this version, copied *c*.1519–20, the basic musical text is that of CS 197, but there are signs that Petrucci's print was also used as source.[18] And there is some evidence, chiefly an idiosyncratic passage in the Qui tollis of the Gloria, that yet another exemplar, now lost, may have been used.[19] There are no pictures and no *L'homme armé* mottos here; the Rome of Leo X was not that of the 1490s, nor was the makeup of the Cappella Giulia anything like that of the Sistine Chapel.

The *Missa La sol fa re mi* also survives in three manuscripts of Roman provenance: CS 41, probably the earliest extant source for the work; Santa Maria Maggiore 26 (Vatican, SMM 26), originating in the chapel of that church but now in the Vatican Library; and Berlin 40091, a manuscript originally copied for the church of San Luigi dei Francesi in Rome.[20] Some years ago I wrote an article on this mass, trying among other things to deal with Glareanus's anecdote about the origin of the work.[21] In that study I mentioned CS 41 and

[15] It is tempting to speculate that the scribe of CS 154 made these additions and corrections in CS 197 himself prior to starting his recopying, even though they are not invariably followed in his copy of the mass.

[16] See Ruth Hannas, 'Concerning Deletions in the Polyphonic Mass Credo', *JAMS* 5 (1952), 155–86, esp. 158–69.

[17] Giovanni Abbate was admitted to the papal choir on 6 July 1535, after having served for a year in the Cappella Giulia. He remained a member of the papal choir until his death in Rome on 28 Oct. 1568.

[18] Dean, 'The Scribes of the Sistine Chapel', 253. In the opinion of Dean (285) the version of the mass in CG XII.2 derives from a tradition independent of CS 197, but I do not agree. CS 154, it might be noted, uses some of the same canonic rubrics seen in CG XII.2.

[19] See Josquin, *Werken*, Missen, Deel I/1, p. xxiii.

[20] On CS 41 see Sherr, 'The Papal Chapel', 223–6; id., *Papal Music Manuscripts*, 145–56; Dean, 'The Scribes of the Sistine Chapel', 233. For SMM 26 see Barton Hudson, 'A Neglected Source of Renaissance Polyphony: Rome, Santa Maria Maggiore JJ.III.4', *Acta musicologica*, 48 (1976), 166–80. On Berlin 40091 see Martin Staehelin, 'Zum Schicksal des alten Musikalien-Fonds von San Luigi dei Francesi in Rom', *Fontes Artis Musicae*, 17 (1970), 120–7, esp. 125–6; cf. Leeman Perkins, 'Notes bibliographiques au sujet de l'ancien fond musical de L'Église de Saint Louis des Français à Rome', *Fontes Artis Musicae*, 16 (1969), 57–71.

[21] James Haar, 'Some Remarks on the "Missa La sol fa re mi" ', in Lowinsky and Blackburn, *Josquin des Prez: Proceedings*, 564–88.

drew attention to the illuminations on its opening pages, one a capital containing the head of a bearded man and a scroll with the illuminator's (?) name on it (Pl. 16(*a*)), and the other an independent portrait of a seated figure dressed *alla turchesca* and holding a scroll with the Franco-Italian motto 'Lesse faire a mi' written on it (Pl. 16(*b*)). At the time I could identify neither figure. The bearded man still eludes me, and indeed may be nobody in particular; but my own subsequent work, conversations with Joshua Rifkin and Adalbert Roth, and especially the published research of Dawson Kiang have convinced me that the turbaned figure represents Prince Jem, son of the conqueror of Constantinople Mohammed II and half-brother of Bayazid II, sultan from 1481 to 1512.[22] Jem spent thirteen years in the West as guest/prisoner, in France from 1482 to 1489, in Rome—after Innocent VIII had more or less purchased him—from 1489 to the end of January 1495, and in the possession of Charles VIII of France in Naples until his death there in February 1495. He was well fed and well-heeled (note the coins, apparently French, at his waist), and an important pawn in international politics, who promised among other things to give up Constantinople to the crusading West if he were placed on the Turkish throne.[23] The motto in his hand could be an attempt to reproduce the way he pronounced either French or Italian, or a stab at the latter language by a French artist.

Kiang speculates interestingly on when and where René II of Anjou, a sometime patron of Josquin who was keenly interested in Jem's fortunes, might have commissioned the mass.[24] But I think it unlikely that such a commission would have come, however indirectly, from a Turkish prince, however disaffected; and I think it better to separate the composition of the mass from its copying for the Cappella Sistina repertory. Whoever may have commissioned the mass, the barzelletta 'Lassa fare a mi', current *c*.1490, is likely to be its proximate source, even though no musical setting of the poem itself survives.[25] The significance of the portrait miniature in CS 41 is perhaps to be found in the same crusader-mania, prevalent in 1490s Rome, that occasioned the 'armed man' portrait in CS 197. Papal dreams for a crusade were shattered by the French invasion of Italy in 1494; and if the work was copied then, or even during January of 1495 when Charles VIII was in Rome, taking possession of Jem *inter alia*, the illustration could even have had a satiric intention

---

[22] Dawson Kiang, 'Josquin Desprez and a Possible Portrait of the Ottoman Prince Jem in Cappella Sistina Ms 41', *Bibliothèque d'humanisme et Renaissance*, 54 (1990), 411–26.

[23] Kenneth M. Setton, *The Papacy and the Levant (1204–1571)*, ii: *The Fifteenth Century* (Philadelphia, 1978), 383, 412. When Charles VIII was in Italy he seemed intent on a crusade, and rumours circulated that he would seize the former Byzantine crown. After Jem's death Charles's plans for a crusade were dropped. Setton's book is full of fascinating details on Jem's relationships with the papacy and the French crown.

[24] Osthoff, *Josquin Desprez*, 421–3.   [25] See Haar, 'Some Remarks', 568–72.

behind it,[26] one coinciding in spirit at least with Glareanus's tale about the mass.

The work as transmitted in CS 41 differs from Petrucci's version in the usual details of ligatures, prevalence of *minor color*, text underlay, and ornamental figures. There are several more substantive differences; two of these, a phrase in the Cantus near the end of the Qui tollis in the Gloria and one in the Altus of the Sanctus, set the Cappella Sistina redaction distinctly apart from Petrucci's version.[27]

If, as it would appear, the fascicle of CS 41 containing the *Missa La sol fa re mi* was copied *c.*1494–5, we have a Roman version of the mass close to the composer and clearly independent of the source used by Petrucci. The other Roman sources for the work are later. Vatican SMM 26 (*olim* JJ.III.4) is a large and complex manuscript of nearly 300 folios, with at least four scribal hands responsible for its contents, chiefly masses with a few motets interspersed.[28] It is full of mottos, devices, and occasional illuminations, including an armed man at the beginning of Busnoys's *Missa L'homme armé* (fo. 154ᵛ), and the French royal arms (fo. 180ᵛ). Particularly interesting is a depiction of the Della Rovere arms surmounted by a cardinal's hat (fo. 135ᵛ), occurring in the middle of a Brumel mass. This is probably the device of Leonardo Grosso della Rovere da Savona, nephew of Pope Julius II, created cardinal in December 1505, and made *arciprete* of Santa Maria Maggiore in 1511; he died in Rome in 1520.[29] The manuscript was probably compiled during the latter part of his incumbency at S. Maria Maggiore, in any event before 1520. The *Missa La sol fa re mi* as entered in this source is not a direct or at any rate not a slavish copy of CS 41; there are many small variants. The two substantive differences from Petrucci found in CS 41 are, however, here as well, and this source would then appear to be part of the Roman tradition for the mass.

The version contained in Berlin 40091, according to Martin Staehelin a manuscript copied at San Luigi dei Francesi *c.*1516 by a scribe with connections to the Cappella Sistina, is a different matter.[30] Apart from the usual small variants the *Missa La sol fa re mi* shows, at the crucial passages identified above, dependence on the Petrucci tradition rather than that of CS 41. This does not necessarily mean that it was copied from a print; but it does indicate the presence of more than one Roman tradition for the mass.

---

[26] Jem's 'acquisition' by Charles VIII of France ended his usefulness to Alexander VI as the focus of a crusade; see above, and n. 23.

[27] For these passages, bb. 105–6 of the Gloria and bb. 17–18 of the Sanctus in Smijers's edition, see *Werken*, Missen, Deel I/2, pp. xi–xv.

[28] For a good preliminary study of this manuscript see Hudson, 'A Neglected Source'.

[29] See Lorenzo Cardella, *Memorie storiche de' Cardinali della santa romana chiesa*, 9 vols. (Rome, 1792–7), iii. 313–14; Antoine Aubery, *Histoire générale des cardinaux*, 5 vols. (Paris, 1642–9), iii., 99–100.

[30] Staehelin, 'Zum Schicksal', 125–6.

About the *Missa Gaudeamus* there is much less to say. Of the relatively small number of extant sources for this work, there is only one Roman one, a fascicle of CS 23 copied by the papal scribe Johannes Orceau during the period 1503/4–7, thus after the appearance of Petrucci's first Josquin volume.[31] The mass as found in this manuscript shows signs, particularly in the earlier movements, of consultation of Petrucci or at any rate of a source close to that of the printer; even the ligatures are similar. There are nonetheless differences—in *ficta*, in division or assimilation of note-values, in text underlay; if Orceau was using Petrucci as exemplar he was doing so freely. The elevenfold repetition of a Tenor pattern in the Et in terra of the Gloria, indicated by a canon in Petrucci, is written out in the manuscript—not what one would expect. There are one or two differences of slightly more substance, possibly indicating correction of the exemplar.[32] Nevertheless I see no evidence here for a separate Roman tradition for this mass, of which in any event no source earlier than the first decade of the sixteenth century appears to survive.

For the *Missa Fortuna desperata* the situation is different. The date of composition of this mass has been assigned to the early 1480s (Lowinsky), to 'before 1486' (Osthoff), and, most interestingly, to a date prior to Obrecht's mass of the same name, which can be dated 1487–8 (Hudson).[33] Its earliest surviving copy would appear to be its one Roman source, CS 41, in a fascicle dated by Sherr as *c*.1492–5.[34] Once again the mass as transmitted here has few substantive differences from Petrucci's version, but those few are of real interest.

To begin with, the CS 41 copy has no flat in the signature, a feature shared only with the MS Modena α.M.1.2, a source that may be close to the composer.[35] In the Et in terra the Tenor, as in Petrucci, has a repeat sign at its end; it appears at first inspection to lack the double signature ₵, ₵2 indicating diminution in the repeat, but what may be a '2' is to be seen below the ₵. In CS 41 the rubrics for canons in this mass are consistently different from those

[31] Sherr, 'The Papal Chapel', 216; id., *Papal Music Manuscripts*, 133–4; Dean, 'The Scribes of the Sistine Chapel', 228.

[32] Examples are to be found in the Osanna (Tenor, bb. 58–9) and Agnus I (Cantus, b. 26). See *Werken, Missen*, Deel I/3, p. xiv.

[33] See Edward E. Lowinsky, 'Ascanio Sforza's Life: A Key to Josquin's Biography and an Aid to the Chronology of his Works', in Lowinsky and Blackburn, *Josquin des Prez: Proceedings*, 31–75 at 60–3, 65–7; Osthoff, *Josquin Desprez*, i. 151; Barton Hudson, 'Two Ferrarese Masses by Jacob Obrecht', *Journal of Musicology*, 4 (1985–6), 276–302, esp. 298–9. Cf. Myroslaw Antonowytsch, 'Renaissance-Tendenzen in den Fortuna-desperata-Messen von Josquin und Obrecht', *Die Musikforschung*, 9 (1956), 1–26.

[34] Sherr, 'The Papal Chapel', 223, 225. Sherr has now modified the date to the late 15th c. and points out that the mass is copied by two scribes; fos. 50–4 are in the hand of the scribe of CS 197 (Sherr's Scribe B) and fos. 55–61 are in the hand of a scribe who may have produced some folios in CS 35 (Sherr's Scribe F). See Sherr, *Papal Music Manuscripts*, 148.

[35] Hudson, 'Two Ferrarese Masses', 298, describes Modena α.M.1.2 as originating in Ferrara *c*.1505, a time close to that of Josquin's residence in Ferrara.

of Petrucci. Even the mensural signs are not the same; for example, in the Et in Spiritum–Confiteor of the Credo, where Petrucci has ₵3—₵[2 (Cantus only)], CS 41 has 3—Ɔ). At this point in the mass something of the very practical nature of the source shows itself. Petrucci brings the preceding Et incarnatus est section to a close with fermata-crowned longas followed by 'verte' signs to turn the page. The CS 41 scribe ends the page on the penultimate notes (in A, T, and B) of the Et incarnatus est, gives the rubric 'verte cito folium' (turn the page quickly), then conflates the last notes of the section with the identical first notes of the Et in Spiritum, thus indicating an attacca performance.

Most interesting is the first Agnus Dei of this mass. The Bass presents the cantus firmus in the superius register, in breves and semibreves. Petrucci gives it thus, followed by a pretentious and incomprehensible canonic rubric, adding a very necessary *resolutio*, which leaves the opening note on the same space but transposes the melody down by an eleventh, quadruples its note-values, and inverts all its intervals (Pl. 17).[36] In CS 41 the canonic rubric is the biblical 'Crescite et multiplicamini'[37] accompanied by a cabbalistic-looking inscription which I interpreted in various fanciful ways before my colleague John Nádas pointed out that it might be—as it surely is—'dei Agnus' upside-down and written in part in a crabbed book-hand. Better, but not enough so; for once in these sources a *resolutio ad longum* is supplied (Pl. 18). The Modena manuscript version of this canon reads 'Crescite et multiplicamini et inebriamini eam', striking if not completely biblical, and perhaps the composer's original choice.[38] The singers of the Cappella Sistina may have been spared the verbal injunction about drunkenness, but the laboured book-hand Agnus dei inverted in word order and turned on its head was surely its graphic equivalent.

A final note about this Agnus Dei, something that may well have been observed by others but that struck me newly and forcibly: the canon used by Josquin is very similar in effect if not in wording of the rubric to that used for Agnus Dei I and III of Busnoys's *Missa L'homme armé*, where a canon in contrary motion results in the tenor descending more than two octaves below its written pitch.[39] All roads in this paper lead, it would seem, to the Roman 'armed man'.

---

[36] RISM 1539¹, *Liber Quindecim Missarum* (Nuremberg: Petreius), has the inscription 'Celsa canens imis commuta quadruplicando'; Glareanus, *Dodekachordon*, 389, has Petrucci's rubric, preceded by a Greek motto ὺʙ⁻ ῦὲὲΆΑe⁻ ·ΥΌὲΆ᷄· (the Riddle of the Sphinx).

[37] Gen. 1: 22: 'Crescite et multiplicamini, et replete aquas maris; avesque multiplicentur super terram.'

[38] Cf. Gen. 1: 28: 'Crescite et multiplicamini, et replete terram, et subjicite eam'; Gen. 9: 21: '[Noe] bibensque inebriatus est'.

[39] See Antoine Busnoys, *Collected Works*, Part 2: *The Latin-Texted Works*, ed. Richard Taruskin (New York, 1990), 41; Part 3, *Commentary*, 34.

This brings us to the last mass of Petrucci's first volume, the *Missa L'homme armé sexti toni*. There are almost as many sources for this work as there are for the *super voces musicales* mass; but only one of them is of Roman provenance, and it is again CS 41, in a fascicle copied by Orceau and dated *c*.1505–7 by Sherr, 1503–4 by Dean.[40] By this time the mass was already published; but earlier manuscript sources for the work exist,[41] and in this instance there is little reason to think that Orceau turned to Petrucci. Apart from the expected differences in ligatures, underlay, clefs, division of note-values, etc., CS 41 has a substantive variant in the Patrem of the Credo.[42] In the Sanctus the canonic Altus and Tenor voices are reversed in CS 41, which adds a charming biblical rubric, 'Duo Seraphim clamabant alter ad alterum', missing in Petrucci.[43] Finally, in Agnus Dei III, something appears to be wrong with the CS 41 version. Sherr notes that 'one of the six voices (the second Bassus) has been left out, and there is no canon showing how it could be derived'.[44] He goes on to point out that these two voices sing alone at one point in the movement, making a performance from CS 41 impossible. There is indeed a problem here, but it is not quite the one Sherr observed. Pl. 19 shows Petrucci's Bass and Tenor *resolutiones*. As can be seen, each voice gives part of the *L'homme armé* melody; the Tenor gives its middle section straight, then in retrograde. The Bass gives the opening, or closing, of the melody in retrograde, then straight. In the CS 41 version (Pl. 20) the Tenor takes the first half of Petrucci's Tenor followed by the last half of his Bassus, thus giving the whole latter part of the cantus firmus (Agnus Dei I has already given the first half of the melody; the Tenor is silent in Agnus Dei II). If this voice is sung simultaneously in cancrizans motion, the result will be the same as Petrucci's resolutions. The canonic indication is admittedly lacking in CS 41; but it seems very possible to me that CS 41's version—if a canonic rubric were added—might be the composer's original (note that Petrucci gives only resolutions, not the canons themselves).[45]

[40] Sherr, 'The Papal Chapel', 223, 226; Dean, 'The Scribes of the Sistine Chapel', 233. To the manuscript sources for the mass given by Smijers (Leipzig, Bibliothek der Thomaskirche, MS 51 [III A a 22–23]; Milan, Archivio della Veneranda Fabbrica del Duomo, Sezione Musicale, MS 2267; CS 41; Vatican C VIII 234; Stuttgart 47; Vienna 11778) should be added Jena, Universitätsbibliothek, Cod. Mus. 31; Segovia, Catedral, Archivo Capitolar, MS s.s.; Casale Monferrato M; and Poznań, Biblioteka Uniwersytecka im. Adama Michiewicza, MS 7022; on this last see Miroslaw Perz, 'The Lvov Fragments: A Source for Works by Dufay, Josquin, Petrus de Domarto, and Petrus de Grudencz in 15th-Century Poland', *TVNM* 36 (1986), 26–51.

[41] These include the Segovia manuscript and possibly the Lvov manuscript. See above, n. 40.

[42] Altus, b. 17. The sources are split on this; the CS 41 version is found in the Chigi manuscript and in Stuttgart 47.

[43] Isa. 6: 2–3. This motto is also found in the Segovia manuscript and in Vienna 11778.

[44] Sherr, 'The Papal Chapel', 226.

[45] Unfortunately the movement is missing in two of the earliest sources for the mass, the Chigi and Segovia manuscripts. Jeremy Noble informs me that the movement as found in Casale Monferrato M, a source I had not examined, presents the Tenor as does CS 41 and supplies a verbal canon, 'ante et retro', as well.

By way of summary I shall simply say that I think a respectable body of evid-ence exists to show that the masses of Josquin were indeed known in Rome in versions independent of their printed state. Many but not all the differences I have noted are shared with other manuscript sources, although no two sources appear to be identical for any of the masses. I leave the complex problems of filiation to Josquin editors; I wanted simply to let the music speak to, or at least hint of, the composer's presence in the papal city.

10

A Virtuoso Singer at Ferrara and Rome:
The Case of Bidon

LEWIS LOCKWOOD

N O performer in early sixteenth-century Italy was more famous in his
time than the soprano singer Antonio Collebaudi, called 'Bidon'.[1]
Born around 1480, probably in Asti, Bidon carved out a career that
lasted from about 1500 to the early 1520s, when he died. His vocal virtuosity,
which deeply impressed contemporary witnesses, made him an unusually
desirable candidate for recruitment by rival patrons. As early as 1502, Bidon
was one of three singers that the Ferrarese agent Gian de Artiganova brought
back with him from a recruiting trip to Savoy; on arrival in Ferrara, Gian
informed Duke Ercole I d'Este that the singers were 'excellent in this art'.
Gian's main local rival in court politics, Girolamo de Sestola, equally assured
Ercole that these singers were 'truly perfect'; that Ercole's son, Don Alfonso
d'Este, 'cannot wait for Your Lordship to come here . . . to hear these singers';
and that Ercole 'will derive . . . enjoyment and consolation from them . . . not
only in the chapel but in the chamber as well, and in any use you like'.[2]

[1] The name 'Bidon' has a number of meanings in old French, one of which is a 'trickster'. The nickname is
comparable to those carried by many musicians and court agents of the time. His surname, Collebaudi (French
'Colebault'), is the same as that of the well-known composer Jacques Colebault or Collebaudi, known more
familiarly as Jacquet of Mantua (*c.*1483–1559). Jacquet was already active in Ferrara by about 1520, and could
have been a brother or cousin of Bidon. That Bidon came from Asti is indicated by contemporary references to
him as 'Bidon da Asti', as in one of the two poems by Girolamo Casio, of 1525 (see below). See George Nugent,
'The Jacquet Motets and their Authors' (Ph.D. diss., Princeton University, 1973), 57–60; and my 'Jean Mouton
and Jean Michel: French Music and Musicians in Italy, 1505–1520', *JAMS* 32 (1979), 191–246 at 232–3.

[2] On the singers brought back by Gian see my 'Josquin at Ferrara: New Documents and Letters', in Lowinsky
and Blackburn (eds.), *Josquin des Prez: Proceedings*, 103–37. That Bidon was in fact one of the three from Savoy
is shown by his being listed as a Savoy court singer from 1500 to 1 July 1502; see Marie-Thérèse Bouquet, 'La
cappella musicale dei duchi di Savoia dal 1504 al 1550', *Rivista italiana di musicologia*, 5 (1970), 3–36 at 35
under the name 'Collebot . . . alias *Bidon* Anthoine'. These dates fit perfectly with that of Gian's recruiting trip
to Savoy in the summer of 1502 and his letter of 7 Aug. 1502 to Ercole. It looks as if Bidon might have returned
to Savoy for a few months in 1504, since Bouquet cites a Savoy court document listing him as a member of that
chapel for the date 1 Oct. 1504, while the Ferrarese court records show him as a ducal singer continuously from
1502 to 1516 (with a hiatus in 1511; see below); but admittedly in 1504 he is paid only for seven months, suggesting a trip to Savoy and then a return to Ferrara. This is interesting, since it shows that under Ercole I d'Este,

Nine years later, in 1511, Castiglione heard Bidon at Mantua and singled him out for special comment in the *Cortegiano*. In a famous passage he compared the singing styles of Bidon and Marchetto Cara, distinguishing their different kinds of vocal expression. Cara, said Castiglione, performs 'in a manner serene and full of plaintive sweetness[;] he touches our souls, gently impressing a delightful sentiment upon them'.[3] Bidon, on the other hand, sang in a way that was 'skillful, rapid, impassioned, excited . . . varied in melody . . .', inflaming the spirits of the listeners, who are 'thus so transported that they are raised to the skies'.[4] The impression is that Bidon sang with force and brilliance, perhaps with rapid passage-work and embellishments; his style may have been a prototype of the kind of singing that strongly aroused the first opera audiences a century later.

Personal references of this kind are important in Castiglione, whose touch in cultural politics was delicate and probing. It looks as if he was deliberately advertising the two major singers of the rival courts of Ferrara and Mantua, at a time when Bidon was basically in Ferrarese service and Cara at Mantua was the long-time favourite of Isabella d'Este, Alfonso's sister and Castiglione's patron. Castiglione's deletion of this praise of Bidon in the second version of the *Cortegiano* may not mean that he changed his mind about him, but could reflect his political sensitivity to Bidon's defection in the meantime from Ferrara to Rome and the service of Pope Leo X.[5] This is the turning-point in Bidon's career that is the main topic of this chapter.

Bidon's high reputation as singer grew further throughout the earlier part of Leo's reign; in 1514, one year after Leo's election, a Ferrarese agent in Rome said about a young French soprano that, according to two experienced singers, this young man is 'a new Bidon'.[6] A well-known passage in Folengo suggests Bidon was still alive in 1521 and puts him squarely among the singers of Leo X, showing a Roman bias.[7] The same Roman tendency is found in the two satirical poems on Bidon by Girolamo Casio, in his *Cronica* published in 1525.[8] Casio's use of past tense and references to Bidon's singing among the angels makes clear that by this time Bidon was no longer alive.

his brief return to service in Savoy did not jeopardize his situation at Ferrara, where he was obviously welcomed back and where he remained.

[3] Translation from William Prizer, *New Grove*, iii. 764, article 'Cara'.

[4] Translation mine. For commentary see James Haar, 'The Courtier as Musician: Castiglione's View of the Science and Art of Music', in Ruth W. Hanning and David Rosand (eds.), *Castiglione: The Ideal and the Real in Renaissance Culture* (New Haven, 1983), 165–90; the passage on Bidon is given in the original Italian on 182 ff.

[5] The first version of the *Cortegiano* is from 1513–14; the second is from 1520–1; see the chronology in Hanning and Rosand, *Castiglione*, pp. xxi ff.

[6] See my 'Jean Mouton and Jean Michel', 218.

[7] Folengo's often-quoted reference is from his *Opus Merlini Cocai macaronicorum* (1521), fo. 196ʳ.

[8] The Casio poems, all epitaphs, are from his *Libro intitolato Cronica . . . composto per il Magnifico Casio Felsineo*

The upshot is that Bidon was not just one of a handful of famous singers of the time: he was seen as a truly exceptional one. He made his living as a singer, not in other capacities; the only effort at composition we have from him is a routine *sexta pars* for Josquin's five-voice *Miserere*, preserved in St Gall 463. Since singers of such calibre were rare and highly sought after, it is not surprising that Bidon would make an effort to manipulate his patrons, knowing that they would go to some lengths to bargain for his services. At least he hoped and assumed that they would.

So in 1502 he arrived in Ferrara as a singer of 'bewitching' quality, and from 1503 to 1510 he remained in Este service, except for four or five months in 1504 when he was apparently back in Savoy. He witnessed the last years of the ageing Duke Ercole I d'Este (d. January 1505) and worked under a succession of chapelmasters: Josquin des Prez (April 1503 to April 1504); Jacob Obrecht (September 1504 to early 1505); Antoine Brumel, for five months in 1505.[9] In the early part of Alfonso's reign, from 1505 to 1510, Bidon was a leading figure in the traditionally large Ferrarese establishment, with its average of nineteen or twenty singers. But as Alfonso's political troubles with Pope Julius II continued to mount, the chapel suffered a setback in 1511, and along with several other singers Bidon settled at Mantua for four months. When Alfonso reconstituted the chapel in 1512, but with only four singers on his regular payroll, Bidon returned to Ferrara, along with Jannes Pezenin, Zoanne Grivion, and the singer, scribe, and agent Jean Michel.[10] From 1512 to 1516 he was a steady member of Alfonso's chapel, and was apparently well treated. By the standards of the time he was as well paid as any other Ferrarese court singer, receiving 216 lire per year (by comparison, in 1513 only the main viol-player, Agostino della Viola, received more, 324 lire). But Bidon was also given a house in Ferrara—as we know from archival records showing payments to him for it, and also a payment of 1514 in which Costanzo Festa was paid for some motets that were delivered to Bidon's house by a courier.[11] This apparent con-

Cavaliero (1525), fo. 48[v]. Both are quoted by André Pirro, 'Leo X and Music', *Musical Quarterly*, 21 (1935), 1–35. The first of Casio's poems on Bidon is as follows: 'Il Musico Bidon, ch'in gorga et voce | Pari al mondo non hebbe, ito con Giove | Ove fatto ha con gli Angioli gia prove | Voce ha miglior, et Gorga piu veloce.' The second is as follows: 'Bidon da Asti, eccelso, almo cantore | Che al decimo Leon fioriva il choro | Tolto ha Giove, et hor fa nel suo foro | Sovran perfetto, basso, alto, et tenore.'

[9] See Lockwood, *Music in Renaissance Ferrara 1400–1505: The Creation of a Musical Centre in the Fifteenth Century* (Oxford, 1984), 196–210.

[10] In 1512 these were the four principal singers (thus grouped in the payment registers), to which we can add Ilario Turluron and 'Metregian Franxese Cantore' (indicated as paid in Rome), plus the instrumentalist Agostino della Viola (source = ASMo, Canc., Memoriale del Soldo, 1512).

[11] Payments to Bidon for his house in Ferrara are, e.g., in ASMo, Memoriale del Soldo, 1505, fo. 150, under date 8 Nov. In this list eight singers are paid the same amount (LM 15.0.0) for 'la provisione de la chaxa loro', including not only Bidon but Felice da Nola, Girolamo Beltrandi, Massino, Janes Pezenin, Ilario Turluron, Piedro Som de Milleville (see below), and Zoanne Michiele (= Jean Michel). For the Festa payment see my 'Jean Mouton and Jean Michel', 230. I take this opportunity to correct a misprint in the transcription: in the Italian

nection with Festa in 1514 suggests that Festa could have been a potential link to Leo X, since we know that Festa was in the pope's service himself by 1517; but this is entirely conjectural.

Thanks to a document discovered by Richard Sherr in Roman archives, in 1508 Bidon is, surprisingly, noted as being an Augustinian canon as well as singer in the Ferrarese court chapel.[12] The document concerns a dispute over the priory of S. Antonio della Mirandola of the Augustinian order, in the diocese of Reggio (certainly Reggio Emilia). Now, if Bidon was an Augustinian canon it would seem unlikely that he could also have been married, but as the date of the document is 1508 it is possible that he left the order at that time (while keeping the benefice) and married; his son Gasparino could well have been born around 1508 and would have been about 8 or 9 years old at the time of Bidon's letters of 1517 (see below).

There is no reason to doubt that Bidon could have remained in Ferrara to the end of his life. But in 1516 he accepted a payment from Leo X, thus making his first career move in fourteen years. Frey documents a payment of eighty gold ducats from the pope to Bidon and some companions on 28 August 1516, and assumes that Bidon was then temporarily at the papal court.[13] Again thanks to information supplied by Richard Sherr, it is clear that Leo's payments to Bidon between 1516 and 1519 were generous by the standards of the time. Bidon was not made a member of his *musici segreti* but was rather kept on as a favourite of Leo's, apparently on a private basis, and was not made a member of the papal chapel until 1519. It looks as if Bidon, in 1516, might have discovered on arriving in Rome that he was not to receive a fixed and secure position right away, equivalent to the one he had enjoyed in Ferrara; if so, this would help to explain his attempt to return to Ferrarese service so soon after leaving.[14]

In Rome Bidon obviously encountered a much larger and more complex musical scene. Although Ferrara for its size was a tremendously active centre, with patrons both at the ducal court and elsewhere in the city and with ample means of contact with musicians from elsewhere, especially France—still its musical life was dwarfed by that of Rome, especially after Leo became pope. Public and private life in Rome, particularly that of the church aristocracy, rose

version the amount paid is L. 18, while in the English translation the amount is wrongly given as L. 58 (the other numbers are correct). See the facsimile on p. 231.

[12] I am indebted to Richard Sherr for having communicated information on this document to me in 1981, and also for suggestions on its interpretation, i.e. concerning Bidon's apparent status as an Augustinian and the evidence of his married status at a later time.

[13] Herman-Walther Frey, 'Regesten zur päpstlichen Kapelle unter Leo X', *Musikforschung*, 9 (1956), 148.

[14] I am indebted here to Richard Sherr for his help in understanding Bidon's treatment by Leo X in 1516–19.

to new heights of flamboyance after Leo's coronation. As Peter Partner writes, even by the traditional standards of Roman festivals, the *possesso* of Leo X was 'the greatest of all these festivals . . . the *possesso* was the taking possession by the Pope of the physical control and the temporalities of the Roman bishopric'.[15] Processions trouped through the city, triumphal arches proclaimed Leo as peacemaker, as head of the Lateran Council, and as patron of arts and letters. Figures of pagan gods, including Apollo, Mercury, and Athena, adorned the arches. Elephants, imported as physically enormous, exotic, and astounding live trophies from the new worlds being explored beyond the seas, began to be used for display in 1514, when the Portuguese ambassador presented one to Leo along with horses, panthers, and leopards. We get a sense of the scene when we learn that the elephant 'halted and knelt to salute the Pope when it approached Ponte Elio, and Leo awaited the embassy in the Castel Sant'Angelo'.[16] Characteristically, many cardinals and other prelates, members of rival families, had to have their own elephants (certainly including Cardinal Ippolito d'Este) and a report from Beltrando Costabili, regular Ferrarese ambassador in 1514, gives us a sample of the elephant craze that was sweeping Rome:

per honorare la Incoronatione della gloriosa pazia del Abbate de Caijeta, quale, della insania sua, a caval dello elefante, trionferà mercore proximo.[17]

to honour the crowning of the glorious madness of the Abbot of Gaeta, who in his insanity and astride an elephant, will triumph [through Rome] next Wednesday

Leo's support of musicians is famous, and in the eyes of contemporaries as well as later historians it was coupled with carefree neglect of the critical situation of the Church in the years of the budding Lutheran revolt. A typical portrait of Leo comes from Young's *The Medici*, adopted from Roscoe:

Leo was a simple Epicurean Pagan. He was not a coarse voluptuary, but his speech on becoming Pope frankly displayed his mind—'Since God has given us the Papacy, let us enjoy it.' And he did. Hunting and hawking parties in the Campagna, pleasant gatherings at his villa of La Magliana, convivial supper parties at Rome, the delights of literature, poetry, music, and theatrical representations, a 'revelry of culture' as Gregorovius has called it—these things occupied the greater portion of his time. Unlike most scholars, or any previous Pope, Leo was greatly devoted to sport and often spent a month or more at a time . . . either fishing or pheasant shooting round the lake of Bolsena . . . taking part in grand *battues* of stags, wild boar, and every sort of game, and scandalizing the Papal master of ceremonies by appearing in hunting costume and . . . in long riding boots.[18]

[15] Peter Partner, *Renaissance Rome* (Berkeley, 1976), 193–7; the quotation is from p. 193.   [16] Ibid.
[17] ASMo, Amb., Roma, B. 21, Doc. 143-II/9, of 25 Sept. 1514.
[18] George F. Young, *The Medici* (New York, 1930), 303.

Throughout these years the Ferrarese ambassadors probably shared the current concerns of political figures all over Italy when they reported on Leo's expenditures for music and other entertainments. This is the probable point of Costabili's report in 1518, in which he tells Alfonso exactly how much Leo paid his singers for some motets sung after dinner. It is probably also the subtext of another ambassadorial dispatch, which first describes Leo's playing chess with one of the cardinals, then two days later reports on a consistory called to deal with the problem of Martin Luther, 'which appears to be a very poisonous matter'.[19]

Accordingly, we should see Leo as a pleasure-loving patrician who had risen to the topmost seat of power available to an Italian aristocrat and for whom the papacy was not a springboard for temporal political action but was a guarantee of family and self-glorification, comfort, and luxury. He had been groomed for this role ever since he had been made a cardinal at the age of 13, in 1489. The Medici exile from Florence had given him an opportunity to travel to Germany, France, and the Low Countries in the late 1490s, and it probably had given him some exposure to the high quality of northern European musicians. Later, in Rome from 1505 on, living first in the Palazzo Ottieri, and then in the Palazzo Medici (later Palazzo Madama, now the seat of the Italian senate), he spent his time amassing collections of valuable books, works of art, and antiques. His career embodies the aspirations of comparable second sons of patrician families who were also sent into the Church with little or no religious inclinations. A parallel is that of Ippolito d'Este, brother of Duke Alfonso and patron of Ariosto, a figure of much more violent and aggressive temper than Leo's, who built up wealth and power by acquiring benefices on a grand scale from southern Italy to Hungary.[20]

So for a singer like Bidon Rome offered potential contact with church and lay patrons from all over Europe, whose rivalries were heightened by the pope's own activity as music patron, by a continuous stream of state visitors, by the pilgrimages of the faithful, and by the army of agents, ambassadors, and occasional visitors from Italian and foreign courts who swarmed around the papal court. Thanks to the research of Frey and Sherr, the growth of musical life under Leo is much better documented than before: it is clear that he was one of the most musically active popes in history. His musicians in these years included, along with Bidon, Antoine Bruhier (1513–17), Andreas de Silva (1519), Hilaire Penet (1514–19), Jacotin Level (1516–19), and many

---

[19] ASMo, Amb. Roma, B. 26, dispatches of 20 May and 22 May 1520; Docs. 170-VII/11 and 170-VII/12.
[20] See my 'Adrian Willaert and Cardinal Ippolito I d'Este: New Light on Willaert's Early Career in Italy, 1515–1521', *EMH* 5 (1985), 85–112.

others.[21] That Bidon ranked high in this group is evident from Folengo's grouping of names in his reference to Leo's singers: 'Bidon, Carpentras, Silva, and Bruhier'.

And yet the case of Bidon shows that Leo was not entirely a naïve employer—rather, it shows that Bidon mistakenly thought that he was. As shown above, Bidon's first appearance in Leo's service was in the summer of 1516. Yet not more than seven months later, in May 1517, Costabili reported that Bidon wanted to leave the pope and return to Este service in Ferrara; perhaps, as I suggested earlier, because the pope seemed not to be quite ready to give him a firm and secure position. And now begins a series of letters that include two written by Bidon to Duke Alfonso, asking to be readmitted to his service. His first letter is dated 6 July 1517, the second is from 7 November 1517; both are autograph and both are preserved in the Archivio di Stato di Modena, in the miscellaneous *fondo* 'Particolari', under the name 'Bidon'. These letters shed new light on the mentality and social situation of this highly regarded singer as he attempts to bargain with his former patron, Duke Alfonso, both for himself and for his family, in an anxious bid to extricate himself from Leo's service and return to Ferrara.

I begin with the letter of 6 July 1517. Bidon thanks Duke Alfonso for a letter received from him (now lost), and is appropriately humble in thanking the duke for writing to 'a servant among your servants', while asking Alfonso to 'excuse my ignorance'. Since Alfonso had apparently demanded to know why Bidon had left his service, Bidon tries valiantly to regain Alfonso's confidence by the usual fulsome boot-licking that is standard practice in similar letters of the period. Thus Bidon professes his 'great affection and obligation' that 'I bear towards you . . . still more because I was raised and nourished in that most noble House and brought up in my youth—I cannot deny that I feel almost like an adopted son of that noble House of Este'. Now follows his apology for having defected:

It is true that in this I have repaid your Most Illustrious Lordship with the sin of ingratitude, but patience! no one is held to the impossible; it's been done, and if one could do a thing twice over men would be wiser than they often are.

Then, as if he were in the confessional, Bidon continues:

I have committed a great sin against God, who has punished me in this way: that when God wishes to punish a man the first thing he does is to take away his memory and his mind, and his intellect, and so it happened to many. I am not the first such man, and if

---

[21] See Frey, 'Regesten', *Musikforschung*, 8 (1955), *passim*, and 9 (1956), for additional material. For a contemporary view of musical life under Leo see Bonnie J. Blackburn, 'Music and Festivities at the Court of Leo X: A Venetian View', *EMH* 11 (1992), 1–37.

I have done wrong I most deeply and wholeheartedly repent of it, and if God did not have mercy and desire to pardon sinners when they repent, he would not be called [God]; his glory is not reserved for the just but for the sinners . . .

and so on in this vein.

Bidon pleads for Alfonso's mercy and then comes to his main point. What he wants is to renounce a benefice in the Ferrarese territory (that of the church of San Leonardo) in favour of his son Gasparino, and to renounce it with the right of regression. As he explains, in a colourful image, 'I want to renounce it in such a form and manner that if he were to die before I do, I would not remain with my hands full of flies. I would have to reserve the income as well as the right of regression for myself, and these are two clauses for which I would have to pay.'

Now Bidon not only wants Alfonso to approve the transfer but wants to finish the process before leaving Rome, in order to save money. 'If I do this in Rome, the pope will do it as a favour to me, and will make me a present of it as a farewell gift; therefore I would like to do it before I leave Rome.' Pleading that he would rather serve Alfonso than 'see God face to face', Bidon claims that by finishing the transfer before leaving Rome he will save two hundred ducats (a sizable sum; in fact this had been Josquin's annual salary in 1503–4 in Ferrara).

Bidding for Alfonso's sympathy, Bidon takes the risk of asking the duke to give him another letter, stipulating that he, Bidon, 'will never be deprived of my salary, neither by you or by your eldest son your successor, so long as I live'. And, hedging his bets even further, he asks Alfonso to obtain this same favour from Cardinal Ippolito, 'whom I also hold as my master, to assure me by means of a letter, signed in his own hand, that he will never in the future remind me of any injury that I might have done or incurred towards [him] in the past or up to the present time . . .'. Since Ippolito's notorious vindictiveness was well known to everyone in Italian courtly circles, this may have seemed a sensible request. Still, it may have been unwise of Bidon to speak openly of Ippolito as 'also . . . my master' in writing to the duke. There were rumours in the land that Ippolito was a serious political rival to his brother Alfonso, and Ippolito's sudden death in 1520, at a relatively young age, has never been adequately explained. It is conceivable that he was murdered.[22]

Now Bidon comes to the final point of his first letter, promising Alfonso that there will be no problem about leaving the pope. In a revealing sidelight he says:

---

[22] On Ippolito's personality a rich and colourful account is given by Riccardo Bacchelli, *La congiura di don Giulio d'Este* (Milan, 1958).

His Holiness is not a man to hold on to anyone against his will by force, but only by affection. I believe he will be sorry to lose me, even though he has several who are better than I, and nevertheless His Holiness shows me the greatest benevolence, even though he has not indicated to what end; perhaps it is not yet my time . . . And if it should be my luck or misfortune that His Holiness does not wish to give me my release, your ambassador can return the letters and money to you . . . you may be certain that I will do more than Carlo did in France to satisfy you . . .[23]

He closes with protestations that he wants nothing more than to be the 'slave and servant' of the House of Este. The implication is that Leo had not yet given Bidon all that he must have expected, whether in money or in income from benefices.

But this impassioned screed produced no results whatever. The ambassador tells the Duke on 20 September, two months later, that Bidon has been to see him and is worried about not having received a reply from Alfonso. It also seems clear from this dispatch that Bidon is working through his former colleague Jean Michel to get back into Alfonso's service. On 24 September Costabili reports that Bidon will see the pope tomorrow and ask for his release. But over the next month matters evidently stalled, as we see from Costabili's dispatches of 1, 5, and 17 October.[24] Finally, on 7 November, Bidon writes his second letter to Alfonso, now in apparent desperation:

in order to shorten the time as much as possible, it is necessary for Your Lordship to . . . have a letter written . . . to your ambassador . . . in Rome . . . that he accept . . . the renunciation of my benefice of San Leonardo . . . in favour of my son Gasparino . . . For I do not want to trust in anyone living except in Your Lordship, to whom I have given the care of my body and soul, and I want to live and die both for myself and my loved ones, with you. If this renunciation is made quickly, as rapidly as the good weather permits a rider to travel, I will send the new prior with his mother to Your Excellency, begging Your Most Illustrious Lordship to do me this favour, that you be content to see that this boy obtain some position as a servant, to serve and be raised under the shadow, first of Your Excellency, and second, of my lord Don Hercules your eldest son . . . For I am more than certain that, if it please God, he will be wiser than I have been and that he will not bring shame on his father . . . and when Your Excellency sees the boy I think he will please you greatly, for he has a very good voice and a rare intellect, but he needs to keep it a little more in bounds, for he is a very proud boy but very lovable . . .

[23] I have not yet identified the 'Carlo' to whom Bidon refers. In 1503 a wardrobe register at Ferrara mentions a certain 'Carlo de Fiandra compositore de chanti che sta con el signor don Alfonso' (ASMo, Guardaroba, 1503–4, 'Zornalle de pagni e lino e oltra', fo. 14ᵛ, dated 25 Mar. 1503. But I do not know if this can be the musician to whom Bidon refers.

[24] ASMo, Amb., Roma, B. 21 (1518).

While he is at it, Bidon asks Duke Alfonso to make provision for a certain 'Piedrossono', either as singer or in some other job. Saying that this man would be useful to fill out the sound of a full choir, Bidon claims that he has a 'very beautiful voice'. The name 'Piedrossono' (= 'Pierreson' or 'Pierre Som') is familiar from Ferrarese and papal documents as referring to the singer Pierre Som di Milleville, who was apparently brought back from France by Duke Alfonso in the summer of 1504; he may very well be the 12-year-old singer who is mentioned with respect by a chronicler, and we know that Pierre Som de Milleville, often simply called 'Pierre Som' (with the usual variant spellings) served at Ferrara from 1504 to 1511.[25] Thereafter he disappears from Ferrara but Frey has found references to him in papal documents of 1518 and 1519, in which he is mentioned as a papal singer. Bidon's letter shows that Pierre Som de Milleville was in Rome by 1516 at latest; he may very well have been there several years earlier than that.

Bidon claims that Milleville has great affection for Alfonso and for Ferrara, and that 'Piedrossono' would be perfectly content with two or three ducats per month plus bread and wine.

What did all this come to? In the end, nothing. Duke Alfonso turned out to be much more stubborn than Bidon had bargained for and would not take him back; nor did he take Pierre Som de Milleville either. All this is clear from the harsh description Alfonso gives of Bidon in a letter of 26 July 1520, three years after Bidon's attempt to return. He orders Paolucci to tell Bidon to stop annoying the Ferrarese court chamberlain, Girolamo Zilioli, about a certain benefice, 'since Bidon knows who Maestro Girolamo is, and how much we hold him in affection, he should cease and desist this attempt to litigate with him . . . we would have believed that, for love of us and of our house, which he served so long and by which he was so well treated, that he should have behaved much better . . .'.[26]

The larger background of all this is centred not only in Alfonso's pride and Bidon's miscalculation, but in the long twilight struggle between Ferrara and the papacy, which had been going on for many decades. Although Ferrara itself was formally a papal fief, Modena and Reggio had been acquired from the Empire. The duchy as a whole, in its stubborn independence, stood in the way of the traditional papal hope for a powerful stronghold in the Romagna and

[25] ASMo, Memoriale del Soldo, 1504 (Reg. 4910/97), fo. 208ʳ, under the date 31 Dec. 1504, summarizing payments for the year to each singer; the list includes 'Piedro som de milleville a L.18 el mexe per mixi 6'; thereafter he is carried in every register in this series through 1511, when he disappears. For the papal documents of 1518 and 1519 see Frey, 'Regesten', *Musikforschung*, 8 (1955), 192. That Pierre Som could have been the 12-year-old prodigy is suggested by Anthony Newcomb, article 'Milleville', *New Grove*, xii. 323. I am once again grateful to Richard Sherr for help that led to this identification, correcting my earlier reading of the text.

[26] ASMo, Amb., Roma, B. 26, Doc. 170-IX/98.

up to the Po. Its politics had been essentially pro-French for almost a century
by this time, a policy adopted in order to protect Ferrara from being swallowed
up by Venice or weakened by the various alliances that had lived and died in
the course of the later fifteenth century. Under Alexander VI the marriage of
Alfonso d'Este to Lucrezia Borgia, in 1502, had probably prevented its invasion by Cesare Borgia. Under Julius II, peace held for a short while but then
collapsed when Alfonso took the French side in the power struggle over northern Italy. In 1510 Julius excommunicated Alfonso and deprived him of his
titles.[27] Going further, Julius stripped the Ferrarese duchy of the towns and
territories of Modena and Reggio, its most important secondary cities. He
himself led the siege of Mirandola in 1511 and was probably on the point of
invading and conquering Ferrara when he was stopped by Alfonso's artillery
and later by the French and Ferrarese victory at Ravenna in 1512.[28]

Nevertheless, in 1512 Alfonso was forced to appear at Rome as a penitent,
to sue for peace. Now, in 1513, with Leo's accession, things should have
improved somewhat, but Leo made them worse immediately in April 1513
when he prolonged for four months the interdict that Julius had placed on
Alfonso, demanding that Alfonso pay his annates to the papal See. And then
Leo kept on prolonging this interdict at four-month intervals, until in 1514
Alfonso found the money to pay all that was owed. Worse still, Leo purchased
Modena from the emperor for forty thousand ducats, leaving Alfonso with no
choice but to seek French protection once again. This is the background to the
famous meeting at Bologna in 1515, when Francis I met Leo X, and at which
the French royal chapel and the papal chapel singers must have been in contact,
certainly including Mouton and the young Willaert.[29]

The political background helps to explain why even so gifted a performer as
Bidon found himself trapped in a power game that he could not manipulate.
To leave Ferrarese service after so many years and move to the great stage of
Rome was not as advantageous as he had expected. Despite his stature as performer and his apparent belief that he could come and go as he pleased, Bidon
discovered that in the harsh world of court politics he was merely a pawn. To
judge from these letters, his main reason for wanting to return was to secure
his benefice in the Ferrarese territory for himself and his son Gasparino, along
with a minor position at court for the boy, thus assuring at least a modest

[27] ASMo, Carteggio di Principi Esteri, Roma, Papi, Letters of Pope Julius II of 8 July 1510, 9 Aug. 1510;
11 June 1512.

[28] On 11 April 1512 Alfonso and his French allies defeated the papal and Spanish army at Ravenna;
Alfonso's artillery was the decisive factor in the victory. For a stirring account based on contemporary accounts
see E. G. Gardner, *The King of Court Poets: A Study of the Work, Life and Times of Lodovico Ariosto* (London, 1906),
87–9; also L. Chiappini, *Gli Estensi* (Varese, 1967), 228–9.

[29] See my 'Jean Mouton and Jean Michel', 211–14.

income and some future security for his family. Perhaps he had discovered on arriving in Rome that the pope would not give him an equivalent benefice—this is admittedly speculation, but it is plausible. Conceivably Leo may have encouraged Bidon to believe that he would eventually become a member of the papal chapel, and indeed he kept this promise in 1519, when he also bestowed some money on young Gasparino.

But the basic weakness of Bidon's situation emerges clearly from the letters of 1517. However acclaimed he might be as a performer, he could not out-manœuvre his employers when issues of pride, rank, power, and money rose beyond his control. In the social system of his time and milieu he was a highly acclaimed figure, but he could not turn his prestige to practical advantage beyond a reasonable limit; and that limit was not one that he could determine or influence decisively. The same was true of course for many other musicians across the century, as we see from volumes of evidence. Still more broadly—if we put this vignette into a much larger historical perspective, we are entitled to ask whether, despite all the vast transformations in society and in the roles of musicians in the service of institutions and patrons—is it really different now?

Appendix: Two Letters of 1517 from Antonio Collebaudi, alias Bidon, to Duke Alfonso I d'Este

Source: Archivio di Stato di Modena, Particolari, 'Bidone'
The two letters are the original autographs, both signed 'Antonio Bidon Cantore' (see Pls. 21 and 22). Since both letters suffered partial destruction at the edges, apparently from fire, words that are conjectural in the following texts are indicated by square brackets. The texts have been very conservatively modernized in spelling and punctuation but for the most part are given as in the originals. For assistance in checking these texts I am indebted to Alexandra Amati-Camperi.

1. Letter of 6 July 1517 (four pages, burnt slightly at the left side)

Illustrissimo et Excellentissimo Signor mio: io [h]o receputo una littra di Vostra Excellentia de la qual molto humilmente ne ringratio Vostra Illustrissima Signoria la qualle se sia degniata per gratia di quella vollere scrivere a uno servitore de li servitori soi et non merito tanta benignita in verso di quella. Tamen per non essere piu longo ne prolixo in verso di sua signoria daremo risposta al meglio che saperemo et che poter-emo, sino in tuto in parte, per avere inteso lo animo bono inverso di noy. Vostra Excellentia da la qualle la ringracio humilmente et la Signoria vostra excusara alquanto la Ignorancia mia etc.

In prima signore mio circa quella partita mi scrive vostra Signoria che mi [h]o scripto a Zoan Michielle Cantore di Vostra Illustrissima Signoria che averia desiderio di ritornare repatriare al servicio di quella e gli e il vero, benche luj me ne [h]a toccato qualche cossa pareschi et dispareschi giorni passati inprima che Io ne avesse parlato ne scripto a lui in conto alcuno, et per questo et maxime per lo admore [sic] [h]o portato et porto et portaro a vostra Illustrissima signoria et maxime per li beni [h]o riceputi da Vostra Signoria la qual le [h]o tenuta et tengo sempre in el core mio per signore et padre et patrone mio observandissimo et maxime per la grande affectione et obligatione io tengo da quella et tanto maius che me sono allevato et nutrito in quella Casa nobil-lissima et allevato in la mia juventute, non posso negare non sia quasi come uno figlio adoptivo di quella nobille Casa da Este. Et in molta Cortesia sia non tanto come servi-tore ma etiam coram orbis et hominibus come uno suo fratello et compagnio. Vero e che in questo ne [h]o rimunerato sua Illustrissima signoria del pecato de Ingratitudine, paciencia ad Imposibille nemo [te]netur questo si e facto, se si potesse far una cossa due volte l'homo saria [p]iu savio de quello non e molte volte. Io [h]o facto qualche gran-dissimo pecato [in] verso di dio che me [h]a voluto punire in questa sorte perche come dio volle [pu]nire uno la prima cossa che fa li tolle la memoria et il cervello et [lo] Intellecto cossi accade a molti. Io non sono il primo, se [h]o facto malle a me [ne] rin-cresse assai et molto, et se dio non avesse misericordia et quella [voglia] di perdonare a li pecatori quando vengino ad penitentia non se chiamareb[be] [Dio et la] sua gloria non se Intende per li justi, se intende per li pecatori perche [habbia]no bisogno di sua misericordia, et questo si e la sua gl[oria]. Quando il pecatore vienne de bon core da se medesimo ad penitentia dio si l'[h]a molto ad caro ma per non attediare vostra Excellentia piu in parolle benche in poche parolle non se po dire ne allegare troppo sub-stancia. La Signoria vostra me avera per excuso se li piace se sono uno pocco troppo longuetto et prolixo in lo mio scrivere perche a mi non me e noya nissuna perche me pare rasonare con Vostra Illustrissima Signoria. Per tanto parcatis per questa volta etc.

Signore mio bisogna piacendo a quella se fida in mi d'il tuto tanto che sia per questa negociatione mia, per tanto vollendo vostra Signoria et essere contento che Io renun-cia San Leonardo al mio figliolo Gasparino bisognia che se facia avanti che Io me parta da Roma per amore de la granda expese me li andaria se vollesse aspectare di farlo quando saria a Ferrara per rispecto de la compositione granda li andaria perche li voglio renunciare in forma et maniera che quando lui se morisse inanti di me che Io non remagniesse con le mane pienne di mosque. Me bisognia reservarme li fructi et lo regresso in persona mia che sono doe composicione che bisognara pagare. Et facendo questo in Roma il Papa me ne fara gratia et me ne fara uno presente per bene andata mia et per questo lo vorria fare inanti me partisse di Roma. Et se io penso di fare fraude ne Ingano nissuno prego a dio non mi dia mai allegreza di cossa che Io desidero, et prego vostra Signoria voglia dar fede a questa mia come fusse lo evangelio et sapia la Excellecto vostra che [h]o piu desiderio di servir quella che non [h]o desiderio di vedere Dio in faza.

Pertanto se la Signoria Vostra vorra che Io facia a questo [mo]do me fara respargniare ducati dozente de oro in oro, perche [altri]mente non [h]aria il modo. D'onde se Io lo facio inanti me parti da [Roma] faro per manco di cento per se fusse Dio in terra bisogna pagare [ ], ma de le compositione il Papa me ne po far gratia. Sicque in tute le altre cosse me scrive Vostra Signoria Illustrissima le accepto di farle, et maxime de non giamai habandonare Vostra Excellentia per sin che io vivero, et post mortem, et cossi ne piu ne mancho il primogenito di Vostra Illustrissima Signoria perche ora mai e tempo di maturarse il cervello o non mai piu.

La Signoria vostra faza a questo modo, che lo Imbasciatore di Vostra Signoria facia expedire le bolle quando [h]aro facto la renuncia in persona di Guasparino, et non me le dia in mane mie per fine a tanto saro a Ferrara che sono molto contento. O veramente che Vostra Signoria veda de ogni sicureza in tuti li modi piacia ad sua Excellentia che sia possibille a mi di fare al mondo che sono contento. Et ancora mi piacendo a Vostra Illustrissima Signoria voglio per cautione mia me facia sicuro per un altra littra sua de non mai mancarme de la provisione mia ne per esso ne per il primogenito successore di quella per fin che io vivero remanente mi in servicio suo tanto de l'uno como de l'altro. Benche prego Idio dona sanitade et allegrezza che possiate vivere in bono stato tanto et quando vorria per mi medesimo et cossi a tuto la Casa da Este[.]

Ulterius, Signore prego humilmente Vostra Signoria me facia quella gratia con il signore Cardinale fratello di quella lo qualle tengo ancora Sua Excellentia per mio signore me voglia sicurarme per una sua littra signata di sua propria mano, non me vollere mai per el tempo ad vegnire ricordarmi iniuria alcuna havesse facto ne incorso inverso de sua Illustrissima et Reverendissima Signoria per il tempo passato usque ad presentem diem et se io avesse fallato in qualche cossa ignoranter che alteramente non lo facea [?] sua signoria me voglia perdonare, et recedant vettera et nova sint omnia.

[Mio?] Signore circa de la licentia mia non bisogna che vostra Signoria habia paura [di] questo perche io faro in modo prima che li sara l'honore di vostra Signoria [et] ancora simillliter lo mio, et sapia Vostra Signoria che quando non me l'avesse scripto [ ] non era delliberato di partirme senza bonna licentia di Sua Santitade [non] bisogna fare cossi pocco conto de uno par suo, et sapia Vostra Signoria [che non] mi partiria senza licentia [ ] e che non tanto per mi sed etiam per amore di Vostra Excellentia. Sua Santitade non e homo di tegnere nissuno contra sua voluntade ne per forza solum per amore. Credo bene li fara malle di perderme benche lui ne habia assai di megliori di me et niente di manco Sua Santitade, mi dimostra grandissima benevolentia, benche per fine a chi non mi l'abia ancora dimonstrato, forzi non e ancora il tempo mio. Niente di mancho se la Signoria Vostra non se volle fidare de mi faza a questo modo: me manda tute le mie expeditione tanto de li danari como de le littre et lo mandi in mano de lo oratore vel Imbasciatore di vostra Excellentia cioe a lo Episcopo de Adri lo qualle me monstra a me dicte expeditione che siano chiare in modo che sia expedito in la forma che io addimando a Vostra Excellentia et le tenga in mane sue per fine a tanto che avero licentia dal Pontifice. Et subito che li faro constare de avere habiuto dicta licentia, lui me habia a dare tute le mie expeditione, et casuto che la disgratia mia o ventura mia che la Sanctitade di nostro signore non mi vollesse dare licentia, la Imbassatore di qualla rimandara indrieto le littre et dinari di vostra Signoria et sia piu che certissimo che io faro piu che non fece Carlo in Franza de satisfare la Signoria Vostra et ancora lo intento et desiderio mio perche in tute le parte del mondo onde io voglio essere o sia sempre voglio essere servitore et schiavo de la Casa di Vostra Excellentia sine autem patientia, ad impossibile nemo tenetur non mancara de tuta la possanza et poder mio de far in tuti li modi del mondo che Vostra Signoria et ancora mi sia satisfacto, et maxime che non desidero altro prima di far questo bene al figliolo mio et di contentare lo animo di Vostra Signoria et ancora il mio. Io non saperia che dire altro a la Signoria Vostra per il presente, sino che io basco [sic] humilmente tanto che so et far posso los manos et piedes de Vostra Illustrissima Signoria a la qualle [di] continuo sempre in bona gratia di sua Illustrissima et Excellentissima [Signo]ria humilmente me Ricomando. Vale. Rome die 6 Jullij 1517.

  E. D. V.

Humillis et indignus servitor
Antonius Bidon Cantor

2. Letter of 7 November 1517. Bidon to Duke Alfonso I d'Este

[Illustrissimo] et Excellentissimo Signore mio[:] Credo che la Excellentia di sua Signoria sia stata informata tanta non solum per informatione [ ] a messer Zoane Michelle. Como anchora [h]o replicato per littre mie ultime al spectabile et nobille virtuoso jovene messer Vincentio de Mosto [written 'musto'] lo intento et desiderio mio lo qualle [h]o sempre habiuto lo intento mio a servire et ritornare a li servitii de Vostra Illustrissima Signoria, et per fare in modo li sia in prima l'honore de Vostra excellentia, et da poi lo utille et ancora honore mio, me e stato forza dilactare et lassare incorrere il tempo de longo. Hora facio intendere a la excellentia di quella como per adbreviare il tempo piu curto, bisogna che la Signoria sua me facia tanta gratia [?] voglia contentarse de fare scrivere da parte sua Excellentia a lo suo Imbasciatore che e qua in Roma. Voglia aceptare in persona sua la renuntia del mio beneficio de San Leonardo juspatronatus de sua Excellentia, et da poi questo che subito litteris non confectis dicto imbassiatore, che inmediate lo habia a renunciare in persona del mio Gasparino con modo et via se potera pigliare la migliore secondo la informatione averemo qua in Roma. Perche non me voglio fidare in nissuno che viva sino in la Illustrissima Signoria Vostra a la qualle li [h]o dacto l'animo et lo corpo in preda, et voglio vivere et morire con quella mi et li mei, et facto questa renuntia subito che el tempo sia bono che se possa cavalcare io mandaro in prima il priore novo cum la matre da la Ecellentia Vostra pregando sua Illustrissima Signoria me facia tanta gratia se voglia degnare di contentarse che dicto puto habia qualche commercio et pratica di servitore, per servire et allevarse sotto l'ombra primamente di sua Excellentia et dapoi cum il signore don Herculles primogenito de la Excellentia sua, affinche essendo provisto de li beni de questo mondo per mezo di vostra Illustrissima Signoria, li habia a goldere [sic] sempre mai a li servicii del signore don Hercules et il signore don Yppolito, perche sono piu che certo se piacera a Dio sara piu savio non sono stato mi et che non fara vergogna al padre. Et la Excelentia sua como veda lo puto credo li piacera molto, perche assai bona voce et [h]a uno pellegrino intellecto ma lo bisogna tenere un pocco sotto la correctione, perche e molto fiero puto ma molto admorevolle.

Da poi che lui sara partito io restaro quindeze giorni o de piu o di mancho per far expedire le sue bolle mediante lo adiuto di vostra Excellentia perche sine ipsso factum est nichil. Bisognia [?] che sua Signoria me facia dare quelli danari a monsignore lo imbassatore per via de la littra del bancho che tiene sua Signoria, per expedire le facende, el piu breve che se potra perche non desidero altro in questo mondo sino de vedere sua Excellentia cum tuta la corte.

Signore mio vorria ancora pregare humilmente la Excellentia sua per amore mio me voglia far questa gratia de essere contento di provedere di qualche cossa pro victu de Piedrossono il qualle e molto affectionato a la Illustrissima Signoria Vostra. Lui mi [h]a dicto se la Signoria sua non se ne volle tanto servire per cantore li voglia donar qualche officio a fare o ad excercitarse che lui si e per far ogni cossa pur che facia cossa che sia grata ad sua Excellentia. Et quando se avesse di bisogno di cantare qualche cossa a piena voce lui lo fara molto volluntieri la Excellentia sua se ne potra servire, in qualche modo, et io ancora ne restaro molto obligato ad sua Excellentia, et per la fede mia ch[e] lui si [h]a una bellissima voce et altro non diro. La Excellentia sua in questo [h]a altro tanto Iudicio che mi et piu Io credo quando sua Excellentia li donasse [d]ui o tri ducati il mese et pane et vino, lui se contentaria molto piu di stare cum sua Excellentia che non sa[ria] con el Papa ne con homo del mondo. Lui se ricomanda a li piedi de sua Excellentia Signore mio Illustrissimo. [Non] saro piu longo in el scrivere mio per non fastidir la sua Illustrissima Signoria sua a la qualle di [conti]nuo con tuto il core humilmente a sua Excellentissima Signoria m'aricomando. Rome 7. novembre 1517.

[E.] D. V.

humillis et Indignus servitor
Antonius Bidon Cantor

11

Who Wrote Ninot's Chansons?

LOUISE LITTERICK

URING the late fifteenth and early sixteenth centuries, a number of
new secular styles began to appear in chanson sources. One that came
to prominence in the first years of the sixteenth century is generally
referred to as the four-part popular arrangement, a designation that reflects the
assumption that pieces in this style are built on pre-existent popular melodies
and their associated texts. The texts appear to be free combinations of various
borrowed elements. They evoke a pastoral context rather than a courtly one,
and they tend to be irreverent, sexually nuanced, and playful. The fully evolved
musical style of these secular compositions includes such traits as integrated
voice-parts, disposed frequently in balanced imitative pairs, interspersed with
fuller, often more homophonic, textures; syllabic text-setting; internal repetitions; and shifts from binary to ternary mensuration.[1] This new chanson style
helped lay the groundwork for some of the most important trends in secular
music of the next generation: the Parisian chanson of Claudin de Sermisy and
his contemporaries; the imitative Netherlandish chanson; and above all the
brilliant narrative chanson of Clément Janequin and other composers associated with him. Moreover, the shift in style signals and reflects a broader current in French musical and cultural life of the time. Whether or not such pieces
are based on actual popular melodies, their material and manner stand in sharp
contrast to the late manifestations of the courtly chanson that dominated secular production in France up to that time.

---

[1] Howard Mayer Brown appears to have been the first to use the designation 'four-part popular arrangement'
and to describe the salient traits of the genre. See Brown, 'The *Chanson rustique*: Popular Elements in the 15th-
and 16th-Century Chanson', *JAMS* 12 (1959), 16–26, and 'The Genesis of a Style: The Parisian Chanson,
1500–1530', in James Haar (ed.), *Chanson and Madrigal 1480–1530: Studies in Comparison and Contrast*
(Cambridge, Mass., 1964), 1–36 at 21–5. Lawrence Bernstein presents an excellent overview of the literature
on and treatment of the evolving chanson of the early 16th c. in 'Notes on the Origin of the Parisian Chanson',
Journal of Musicology, 1 (1982), 275–326.

Among the earliest and most numerous representatives of the new style are secular pieces transmitted under the name Ninot or Ninot le Petit or some recognizable variant of it, such as Nino or Nino le Petit, N. le Petit, or 'Minot lepetit'. Yet because the sobriquet 'Ninot' survives nowhere outside music sources, there are few clues to—and until rather recently there has been no agreement about—this composer's further identity. Two decades ago, however, Ninot le Petit was identified as Johannes Baltazar, a singer employed in the papal chapel from June 1488 presumably continuously until his death in 1501 or early 1502.[2] This identification, assumed by virtually all scholarship since that time, was based on the following evidence.

Not long after Baltazar's death, and some time between 1503 and 1507, three motets—*In illo tempore*, *Psallite noe*, and *Si oblitus fuero*—were copied into Vatican CS 42 with an ascription to Jo. le Petit.[3] The name Johannes Petit (or J. Petit) appears on a number of extant documents with the alias 'Baltazar' (or some recognizable variant of it: J. Petit alias Baltazar, Johannes Petit alias Baltazar, Baldesaris alias Petit). The name Baltazar (in one case Valtazar) appears consistently on payment rolls for the papal chapel from June 1488 through March 1494, when the lists stop. When they resume, his name reappears, although more sporadically, sometimes crossed out, and in one instance (payment for April 1501) with a cross in front of it, the usual symbol for indicating that the person named is deceased. Baltazar's name appears for the very last time in the list of payments made for November 1501.[4] In a single instance, in the payment list for January 1501, the singer is referred to not as Baltazar but as Jo. lepetit. Although the entry is crossed out, the use of the abbreviation Jo. and the definite article make this one version of Baltazar's alias indistinguishable from the attribution attached to the motets in the Vatican manuscript and would seem identify Baltazar as the composer of those motets.

More puzzling than the singularity of the use of Baltazar's alias in the payment rolls is the fact that this is the only instance in which the alias carries a

[2] Richard Sherr, 'The Papal Chapel ca. 1492–1513 and its Polyphonic Sources' (Ph.D. diss., Princeton University, 1975), 49–50, was the first to make this connection. Anthony M. Cummings, 'A Florentine Sacred Repertory from the Medici Restoration (Manuscript II. I. 232 of the Biblioteca nazionale centrale, Firenze' (Ph.D. diss., Princeton University, 1979/80), 25–8, confirmed and expanded upon the hypothesis. For Ninot's works, see Ninot le Petit, *Johanni[s] Parvi Opera Omnia*, ed. Barton Hudson (CMM 87; Neuhausen-Stuttgart, 1979).

[3] For a description and dating of this source see Sherr, 'The Papal Chapel', 227–46, and now *Papal Music Manuscripts in the Late Fifteenth and Early Sixteenth Centuries* (Renaissance Manuscript Studies, 5; Neuhausen-Stuttgart, 1996), 157–75. Unless otherwise noted, the indications of provenance and chronology derive from the *Census-Catalogue*. Call numbers and more complete citations of prints appear in App. A, in alphabetical order, with a list of the pieces they contain by Ninot and the form of the attribution to him (if any).

[4] The payment for November was made in December. Indeed in most instances the actual payment is made at the beginning of the month following that for which the musicians are being paid. In this article, if only one month is indicated, it is the month for which Baltazar was paid, whether the payment itself was made and recorded during that same month (only one instance in 1501) or the following.

definite article. Yet because the entry for Jo. lepetit appears in the same position in the payment lists as does the name Johannes Baltazar in other months,
its intention to point to the papal musician seems unquestionable. Equally
puzzling is the fact that the entry is crossed out. Perhaps Baltazar was already
ill. The cross before his name in the roll for April followed by another crossed-
out entry for May and a complete absence of any version of his name for June
could indicate that he was dead by April 1501. If that were the case, the reap-
pearance of his name three more times (for July, August, and November 1501)
might indicate that his heirs collected his wages during that time.[5] Baltazar had
unquestionably died by 17 May 1502, when the 'canonry and prebend' at
Narbonne was transferred because it had been made 'vacant by death (outside
Rome) of Jo. Baldesaris alias Petit'.[6] Since Baltazar died outside Rome, news
of his death and the transfer of his benefices may not have been as immediate
as they otherwise would have been. The cross before his name in the payment
list for April 1501 should perhaps be taken seriously.

The same three motets ascribed to 'Jo. le petit' in CS 42 appear, grouped
together, in Florence II.I.232, copied *c*.1515. Here, however, the attributions
read 'Ninot', the name that appears elsewhere primarily in association with
chansons in the newer style, sometimes with the surname 'Le petit'. As a
diminutive for the Latin Johannes, 'Ninot' is plausible. In French names of the
time 'Johannes' would be rendered 'Jehan' as often as 'Jean'. 'Jehan' would
often be transformed into either 'Jehanin' or 'Jehanot' or even 'Jehaninot'. The
suffix '-ot' as a common derivative of '-in' implies familiarity and endearment,
connoting not simply 'little Jehanin' but 'dear little Jehanin', from which
'Ninot' would represent a further diminutive.[7] (This composer must have
been very beloved, or very small, or both, or—if the nickname is an ironic
one—immense.) The interlocking evidence of the cross-attribution to 'Ninot'
and 'Jo. le petit', and the pseudonymous association of 'Baltazar' and 'Petit'—
most specifically through the single payment record in which he is represented

---

[5] Richard Sherr has kindly informed me in a private communication that occasionally the name of a dead
singer would remain on the rolls for up to six months while the heirs collected wages.

[6] The reference is to a benefice concerning Baltazar discovered by Jeremy Noble, of which he has graciously
provided me with a transcription.

[7] I am grateful to Herbert Kellman for suggesting, during discussion after presentation of this paper, the
specific derivation of Ninot from Jehan and the implication of endearment that the extra diminution suggests.
Charles vanden Borren originally suggested a similar derivation from the Italian Giovanni/Giovannino, but the
French origin of 'Petit' as well as the presence of a final 't' on 'Ninot' in some sources suggests that Ninot (le
Petit) and Johannes Petit alias Baltazar, whether they are to be identified with each other or not, both came from
French-speaking territory. This assumption is explicit in the case of Baltazar. I wish to thank Jeremy Noble for a
private communication in which he informed me that 'two of [Baltazar's benefices] describe Petit [alias Baltazar]
as a priest or cleric of the diocese of Châlons-sur-Marne . . ., and the earliest of them grants him an expectative
in the dioceses of Toul and/or Verdun, . . . both in the duchy of Lorraine. . . . It seems to me highly likely that
Petit [alias Baltazar] was either born in Lorraine or had early connections with it.'

as 'lepetit'— made virtually inescapable the conclusion that the composer of the innovative chansons is none other than the papal musician Johannes Baltazar.

The association with Baltazar does more than provide Ninot with a biography, however. It also implies something significant about the geography and chronology of the new chanson style: that it originated not in French-speaking territories but in Rome, and that it had reached its fully evolved expression already by 1501. The identification of Ninot as Baltazar thus both alters our understanding of Roman compositional activity during the last decades of the fifteenth century and revises dramatically the history of the chanson.

However neat this apparent fit of composer attribution and biographical reference, it becomes problematic when set in a larger context. 'Nynot' is one of many musicians called upon in Pierre Moulu's *Mater floreat florescat* to 'render glory to the King and Queen':[8]

Rutilet Delphicus de Longueval tamquam sol inter stellas, Lourdault, Prioris amenus. Nec absint decori fratres de Févin, Hilaire hilaris, Divitis felix. Brumel, Isaac, Nynot, Mathurin Forestier, Bruhier facundi, Mouton cum vellere aureo: date gloriam regi et reginae in cordis et organo.	May the Apollonic Longueval shine like the sun among the stars, Lourdault, the charming Prioris. Nor should we miss the agreeable brothers De Févin, Hilaire, the cheerful, and the happy Divitis. The eloquent Brumel, Isaac, *Nynot*, Mathurin Forestier, Bruhier, and Mouton with the Golden Fleece: Render glory to the King and the Queen with strings and organ.

The locus of the motet is the north, specifically France.[9] The piece dates from the early sixteenth century, although the precise time of composition has not yet been determined.[10] All the composers named spent at least large portions of their careers in the north; and none— unless we identify Ninot as Baltazar— worked exclusively in Italy. Moreover, all the musicians named in the *secunda pars* lived at least into the second decade of the sixteenth century, unless, again, one assumes Ninot to be Baltazar.

Similarly, the French court manuscript Cambridge 1760 (copied *c*.1509–14, probably in 1509) carries an attribution to 'N. Le petit'.[11]

---

[8] Text and translation taken from Edward E. Lowinsky (ed.), *The Medici Codex of 1518* (Monuments of Renaissance Music, 3; Chicago, 1968), 73.

[9] For the complete text and a discussion of this motet see ibid. 73–4. The very reference to King and Queen eliminates most European contexts; and France, rather than Naples or England, is the only one that makes sense, given the roster of musicians named.

[10] Lowinsky dates it May 1517, but it seems likely that it would have been written before 1511 or 1512, before Lourdault and Antoine de Févin had died.

[11] On the dating see the *Census-Catalogue* and Louise Litterick, 'The Manuscript Royal 20.A.XVI of the British Library' (Ph.D. diss., New York University, 1976), 51–6.

Characteristically insular in its repertory, this collection devotes more than one-third of its contents to the work of a single composer, Antoine de Févin, who served at the royal court until his death in late 1511 or early 1512 and who is not known to have gone anywhere else.[12] The other composers represented also have strong French credentials. The piece bearing the ascription to 'N. Le petit'—*J'aime bien mon amy*—is indicated in the index of the same manuscript as being by Févin ('de fevin'), whose work it is generally considered to be. Yet despite the latter composer's overwhelming presence in this source, Ninot may be the author after all. Neither the conflict nor its resolution matters here, however. Of interest for this argument is simply the fact that the French scribe of Cambridge 1760 knew of N[inot] le Petit and, furthermore, associated his name with a chanson in French style and with a repertory of early sixteenth-century exclusively French music.[13] The attribution, correct or not, places Ninot geographically and stylistically in the north, and chronologically, once again, with composers active through at least the first decade of the sixteenth century.

Ninot also keeps French company in two other indisputably French manuscripts, of slightly earlier origin than Cambridge 1760: Paris 1597 (copied *c.*1500) and Uppsala 76a (relevant section copied *c.*1495). Paris 1597 transmits anonymously his *Mon seul plaisir* as well as the elsewhere triply attributed *Lourdault, lourdault*, and Uppsala 76a gives to 'Minot lepetit' an otherwise unknown chanson, the double canon *Pourtant si mon amy*.[14] If Ninot were to

---

[12] On the tendency of manuscripts copied at the French court to favour composers active there, see Litterick, 'The Manuscript Royal 20.A.XVI', 57–69. On Févin's biography, see Howard Mayer Brown, 'Antoine de Févin', *New Grove*, vi. 515, and Edward Clinkscale, 'The Complete Works of Antoine de Févin' (Ph.D. diss., New York University, 1965), i. 1–25.

[13] Jacob Obrecht, with a mostly northern but not explicitly French career, is the apparent exception here. *Parce domine*—the single piece by which he is represented in this source—is something of an exception chronologically as well, entering circulation as early as the late 1490s (Uppsala 76a, scribe A, and Bologna Q 17). It is worth noting that a single piece by him, most often this very *Parce domine*, appears not infrequently in manuscripts of unquestionably French provenance containing otherwise entirely French repertory. *Parce domine* is the single piece by Obrecht also in the French sources Copenhagen, Det Kongelige Bibliotek, MS Ny kongelige Samling 1848, 2° and Uppsala 76a. In other French sources he is also represented by a single piece: Paris 1597 contains his *Si sumpsero*, and London, Royal College of Music, MS 1070 his *Alma redemptoris mater*. He receives similarly honoured yet similarly token representation in Italian sources (as part of the northern core of their repertories). *Parce domine* opens Bologna Q 17, his one appearance in that source as well, and the same piece is one of two by him in Bologna Q 18. A token single piece by him appears in Florence, Biblioteca Nazionale Central, Magl. XIX.178 (*Mestkin*) and in Rome, Biblioteca Casanatense, MS 2856 (*Si bien fait*).

[14] *Mon seul plaisir* appears anonymously also in two additional northern sources, Brussels, Bibliothèque Royale Albert Ier, MS 11239 (*c.*1500, Savoy) and MS IV.90/Tournai, Bibliothèque de la Ville, MS 94 (1511, Bruges). The attribution to 'Nino Le petit' appears in a fourth northern manuscript, Florence 2439. Basle F.X.1–4 (1522–4 and/or later, German) gives both *Mon seul plaisir* and *Lourdault, lourdault* to Josquin. The attributions for Franco-Netherlandish repertory in Basle F.X.1–4 are generally untrustworthy, however, while those of Florence 2439 are unusually accurate. Moreover, Florence 2439 originally both opened and closed with songs by 'Nino' (see the facsimile *Basevi Codex, Florence, Biblioteca del Conservatorio, MS 2439*, ed. Honey Meconi (Intro.) (Peer, 1990), 5, 7, and 8). *Mon seul plaisir*, the original first piece, carries a coat of arms and is the only

be identified with Baltazar, the pieces by him would be the only outsiders in these sources as well.

The most important source of Ninot's secular music, Florence 2442, is of uncertain and possibly non-French provenance, yet it too projects a biographical and chronological context at variance with that of Baltazar. All the other composers represented for whom any biographical information is known were associated with the north (whatever Italian sojourns they may have enjoyed), and two—Févin and Jean Braconnier—had ties only to France and Burgundy.[15] All but one, moreover, had careers that extended into the second decade of the sixteenth century or beyond.[16] The manuscript is organized by composer. With thirteen chansons, 'Ninot Le petit' is by far the most represented composer. He is flanked by the two next most represented, with six compositions apiece: Josquin, with pride of place in opening the collection, and Antoine Bruhier, whose music manifests a similar generic and stylistic profile to that of Ninot and who is grouped with him in the second section of the *secunda pars* of Moulu's motet.

If the evidence considered thus far strongly supports the hypothesis that Ninot's context would have been more the north through at least the first decade of the sixteenth century than Italy before and *c*.1500, the music itself only reinforces this impression. A first hint of the temporal context of his output can be derived from a chronology of first appearances of the chansons that survive in extant sources. Of the twenty attributed to Ninot in at least one source, at most six appear to have entered circulation before Baltazar's death (assuming the latest possible *terminus ante quem* for that event, May of 1502, which is probably too late by at least some months; see above). Three more chansons appeared two or three years later, and two others somewhat later still. For eight of these pieces, however, Florence 2442, copied *c*.1510–15 or later, is the earliest source. Still another, probably spurious, chanson did not enter

composition to receive elaborate decoration. It is unlikely that an ascription to the composer thus honoured would be in error.

As for *Lourdault, lourdault*, even with the elimination of the attribution in Basle F.X.1–4, a conflict remains between attributions to Ninot in Bologna Q 17 and to Compère in Regensburg, Bischöfliche Zentralbibliothek, MS C 120 (early 1520s, South German or Tirolean) and RISM 1502².

[15] On Févin, see above. Jean Braconnier, dit Lourdault, served in Nancy at the court of Duke René II of Lorraine in 1478, in the chapel of Philip the Fair of Burgundy from 1496 to 1506, and at the French royal court of Louis XII from 1507 to 1512 (Lewis Lockwood, 'Jean Braconnier ('Lourdault')', *New Grove*, iii. 150). For a summary of the careers of other composers represented in Florence 2442, cf. Bernstein, 'Notes on the Origin', 287.

[16] Of the composers for whom biographical information is available (twelve of the sixteen represented, not counting Ninot), once again Obrecht is the exception; he died in 1505. As is often his lot, he is represented by a single work, *Tant que nostre argent dura*, the penultimate piece in the collection. Given the pattern described in n. 13, this token representation could be taken as further evidence of French provenance for Florence 2442.

circulation until the 1550s.[17] (Appendix B provides a catalogue of the chansons in order of earliest extant transmission.)

An analysis of the chansons following the chronological framework constructed from the pattern of their earliest transmission reveals that some of the pieces that first enter circulation only in 1510 or later manifest stylistic traits, and combinations of traits, not present, or present only embryonically, in those already in circulation a decade earlier: lilting triple-metre sections included within an otherwise duple-metre context; groups of minims or semiminims set syllabically in a more or less declamatory manner; increased use of motifs treated in hocket fashion; more systematic employment of balanced duos coalescing into and out of four-voice textures; more pervasive manipulation of thematic material; greater use of block-like repetition, and concomitantly more articulated textures; more complex (and unpredictable) repetition schemes; and, a result of the last-mentioned aspects, greater length. Although many of these descriptions could be applied appropriately to pieces composed before the turn of the century, their combination in fully evolved guise is virtually unknown before *c*.1500. Thereafter, however, this combination of traits becomes integral to the distinctive four-voice chansons written early in the sixteenth century by northern composers such as Jean Mouton, Loyset Compère, and Bruhier.[18] At least in this general way, then, the chronology of the transmission of Ninot's chansons reflects the relative chronology of the works themselves, allowing the division of Ninot's secular output—and not simply the sources of his chansons—into earlier and later.

A brief look at two of his secular songs, *Mon seul plaisir* and *N'as tu poinct mis ton hault bonnet*, will bring this point home vividly (see Exx. 11.1 and 11.2). With one likely exception, *Mon seul plaisir*, which entered circulation by *c*.1500 at the latest, is Ninot's earliest surviving chanson.[19] All but one of its extant

---

[17] The single attribution to Ninot of *C'est donc par moy*, in the 18th-c. MS London, British Library, Add. 29381, is certainly not to be trusted. The piece appears in Heilbronn X. 2 (early 1550s) as the work of Willaert.

[18] Although Bruhier's known biography is puzzling and incomplete, he was almost certainly French. He had connections with Este Ferrara between 1505 and 1510, he was in the employ of the duke of Urbino presumably in 1508, and he worked for Pope Leo X from 1513 or 1514 until at least 1521. (See Albert Dunning, 'Antoine Bruhier', *New Grove*, iii. 374, and Richard Sherr, in the revision of *New Grove* (forthcoming).) Whatever the significance of the connection with Ferrara and Urbino, these Italian positions post-date the main evolution of the chanson under discussion. For Bruhier's known French employment, see below, n. 30.

[19] The exception is the double canon *Pourtant si* in Uppsala 76a. This is Ninot's only double canon, a subgenre that represents only one or two pieces in the output of the other composers who attempted it, and most such pieces survive in sources dating from the last decade of the 15th c. Should *Lourdault, lourdault* turn out to be by Ninot rather than by Compère—it is surely not by Josquin—that piece would date from about the same time, based on its appearance also in Paris 1597. *Nostre chamberiere, si malade elle est*, Ninot's only representation in the *Odhecaton*, 1501, would also have been written at about the same time. That only one chanson made it into the collection could be a result of Ninot's not yet having achieved sufficient fame, possibly because he had not yet written most of the other extant chansons. In any case, this publication pattern is suggestive of the chronology for the composer outlined in this chapter and in contrast to that of Baltazar. Ninot's representation

Ex. 11.1. Ninot le Petit, *Mon seul plaisir* (after *Opera Omnia*, ed. Hudson, no. 13)

in Petrucci's prints increases after 1501. He is represented by two or three chansons in *Canti B*, 1502, and three in *Canti C*, 1504, and by three motets in *Motetti C*, 1504, and one in *Motetti libro quarto*, 1505.

Ex. 11.1. *cont.*

Ex. 11.1. *cont.*

Ex. 11.2. Ninot le Petit, *N'as tu poinct mis ton hault bonnet* (after *Opera Omnia*, ed. Hudson, no. 14)

Louise Litterick

Ex. 11.2. *cont.*

Ex. 11.2. *cont.*

Ex. 11.2. *cont.*

sources are of northern provenance and originated during the first decade or so of the sixteenth century.[20] *N'as tu poinct mis ton hault bonnet* is one of the eight songs by Ninot for which the extant transmission suggests entry into circulation between 1510 and 1515 at the earliest.[21]

Mon seul plaisir is built on quasi-cantus-firmus technique in which each phrase takes off from and treats at least somewhat imitatively a main melodic line that appears to derive from a pre-existent melody. The resulting texture consists of uneven, overlapping phrases of varied and not clearly profiled motivic design, with text declamation that is somewhat melismatic and syllables set to semibreves and minims. By contrast, *N'as tu poinct mis ton hault bonnet* is patterned, built on a dramatic and formal use of repetition of musical units. Its articulations are clear, and its harmonic and voice-leading methods smooth and consistent. All its motivic material comes from the opening statement, and the particular motivic derivation of any given section recurs repeatedly. Text declamation is predominantly syllabic and occurs for the most part on minims and semiminims.

Mon seul plaisir sets the first stanza of a four-strophe poem of eight lines (two quatrains), each rhyming ababcdcd. In the best fifteenth-century manner, this well-constructed fricassée of chanson quotations coheres. Ninot disposes the text so that the setting follows a simple AAB form, despite the overrunning of articulations and the absence of repeated blocks of material internally.[22] The text of *N'as tu poinct mis ton hault bonnet*, however—apparently also a grab bag of quotations, but from the popular realm rather than from fifteenth-century courtly chansons—does not cohere. The single sentence of one and a half poetic lines that forms the textual material of more than the first half of the piece and its end—'N'as tu poinct mis ton hault bonnet, petit bonhomme'—is obscure in meaning and has no obvious connection with the flirtatious strophes and nonsensical refrain of the intervening text. Nor could that one line of text (whether or not the main melodic material setting it derives from a popular melody) in any way be considered to have predetermined the expansive, varied, and shifting texture that forms the first section (bb. 1–48) of the piece. Despite, or perhaps because of, its motivic unity and its use of repeated units of musical material, the repetition scheme of *N'as tu poinct mis ton hault bonnet* is so complex that its form is difficult to characterize. An oversimplified approximation that misrepresents its motivic coherence might appear as follows.

---

[20] See above and n. 24.

[21] All eight appear in Florence 2442. *N'as tu poinct mis ton hault bonnet* also appears, along with four other chansons by Ninot, in Florence, Biblioteca Nazionale Centrale, Magl. XIX.164–7, copied in Florence *c.*1515–22 at the earliest.

[22] Hudson provides a list of sources, including the two containing the text alone, Paris 12744 and *Le Jardin de Plaisance*. He also points out that the poem is a fricassée (*Opera Omnia*, ed. Hudson, p. xxiii).

A	A fantasy	B	C	B′	C′	B′	C′	A varied	B varied	A varied
1	10	41	49	57	67	71	78	82	89	90

Variety of thematic material in *Mon seul plaisir* is reflected in tonal multiplicity: cadences on various degrees occur in a somewhat unpredictable sequence, although the G final is firmly reclaimed by the end of the piece. They are generally of the 7–6–8 suspension type, including two instances of an archaic 'double leading-note' progression (bb. 19–20 and 43–4). In the motivically unified *N'as tu poinct mis ton hault bonnet*, a G centricity is clear throughout, with most of its many cadences on that pitch, some on D, and a few on A. At main structural points stereotypical formal suspension cadences are preceded by what would be considered today a pre-dominant—IV leading to V–I in the bass (for instance, bb. 8–9 and the ending). Gone altogether are the double leading-note cadences.

Although these differences by themselves suggest an evolution of style between the writing of the two songs, they stop short of the heart of the matter. The seventy-two bars of *Mon seul plaisir* still bespeak an essentially fifteenth-century aesthetic, while the ninety-three of *N'as tu poinct mis ton hault bonnet* point to that of the early sixteenth century. The characteristics that most strikingly distinguish the latter song from the former are the individuality of its narrative and its large architecture, which do not derive specifically from any pre-existent melody or coherent poetic text, or any specific compositional technique. Most significantly, the terms of the narrative change during the course of *N'as tu poinct mis ton hault bonnet*. After an essentially homophonic presentation of the basic material (bb. 1–9), the first section continues polyphonically, utilizing various asymmetrically disposed voice pairs. The transformation of an apparently incidental cadential counterpoint (superius, upbeat to b. 4 through downbeat of b. 5) into an independent motif that passes into and out of its original context while undergoing various rhythmic manipulations is characteristic of Ninot's developmental procedure in the later chansons (see bb. 12–13, superius; 16–17, altus; upbeat to bb. 19–21, superius; upbeat to bb. 24–5, altus; 33–5, superius; 35–6, altus; 37–9, superius; 42–3, altus; 83–4, superius; and 87–8, superius).

With these manipulations the discourse begins to shift. The texture becomes simpler and clearer, utilizing increasingly syllabic declamation and balanced, homophonic voice pairs, on the text 'petit bonhomme' (bb. 33 ff.). At first the voice pairs coalesce into and out of four-voice texture, but soon they appear as distinct small units of repetition (bb. 41 ff.), with intervening hocket punctuations on 'petit' (bb. 40 and 44–6). This development culminates in a clearly demarcated section of patter consisting of short regular phrases made up of repeated rhythmic and melodic patterns that utilize semiminims and fast syllabic declamation (on the semiminim) of a text transformed into nonsense syllables (bb. 49–56). This is far from the world of *Mon seul plaisir*.

N'as tu poinct mis ton hault bonnet is more than half over before this patter section, which reveals itself to be a refrain, appears for the first time. Once in, however, it recurs after only ten bars and then again after only seven and a half (bb. 67 and 78 ff.), at which point it leads without a break into a triple-metre abstraction of the opening (bb. 82–93), up to the point at which the refrain first appeared (bb. 82–6 = bb. 1–9; 86–8 = bb. 1–5; 'petit' in bb. 84 and 88 refers most specifically to the hocket in bb. 40 and 44–6; the upbeat to bb. 89–90 refers most specifically to the upbeat to bb. 47–8; and bb. 90– end = another variation of bb. 5–9). The piece as a whole thus accumulates formally in two dramatic moves: first, the evolution from melismatic polyphonic sub-tlety to syllabic homophonic regularity that culminates in patter, and second, the turn to triple metre for a transformed reprise. How soon and how often the refrain comes back, and the way in which it overlaps with the concluding section, are subtle heightening effects that would not come into consideration in Ninot's earlier style.

The evolutionary aspect of Ninot's work manifests itself in another way. The earlier chansons are characterized by the occasional presence of parallel fifths, mostly between the two upper voices, and by somewhat awkward dissonance treatment. In Ex. 11.3, from *Mon seul plaisir*, in b. 36, the altus, in addition to creating parallel fifths with the superius, anticipates the note of resolution of a suspension between the two lower voices. Similarly, the passage from *Et levez vous hau, Guillemette* (Ex. 11.4) demonstrates parallels between superius and altus and, on the downbeat of b. 75, another anticipation of a note of

Ex. 11.3. Ninot le Petit, *Mon seul plaisir*, bb. 35–9

Ex. 11.4. Ninot le Petit, *Et levez vous hau, Guillemette*, bb. 74–6

resolution of a suspension (the B♭ in the superius anticipates the note of resolution of the 7–6 suspension between altus and bassus). Moreover, the
cadence itself, with its descending semiminims and under-third gesture in the
superius, projects a late fifteenth-century sonority. Although Ninot's technique never achieves complete smoothness, these features of voice-leading and
cadential gesture occur far less frequently in pieces that enter circulation only
after *c.*1510.

    Ninot's Latin-texted works manifest many of the same traits as the chan-
sons. His unique extant mass, *Sine nomine*, is preserved only in Casale
Monferrato L (copied as late as *c.*1515 to 1518). The mass is stylistically con-
gruent with Ninot's apparently later chansons in its use of balanced, mostly
imitative, voice pairs moving in and out of four-voice textures, homophonic
sections characterized by syllabic declamation, and mostly smooth dissonance
treatment. It shares these textures and techniques with other masses and
motets written in France in the early sixteenth century—by Mouton, or
Josquin in his late works, for example—but it resembles nothing written in Italy,
and little if anything written even in France before the turn of the century.

    A motet not yet considered, *O bone Jesu*, published by the Italian printer
Ottaviano Petrucci in the *Motetti libro quarto* of 1505 and attributed to 'Ninot'
there, resembles more closely the chansons that circulated at about the time of
its publication than it does the later ones, particularly in its occasionally dissonant voice-leading and parallel fifths, as shown in Ex. 11.5. The first excerpt,
Ex. 11.5(*a*), shows parallels between superius and altus. In Ex. 11.5(*b*), b.
358, the 7–6 suspension of the altus against the bassus forms parallel fifths
with the superius, and the note of resolution (C) of the altus forms a dissonant
second with the rising tenor line. The duos of this motet tend to be very long,

Ex. 11.5. Ninot le Petit, *O bone Jesu*: (*a*) bb. 283–5; (*b*) bb. 358–9

unbalanced by an answering voice pair, and thematically unrelated. The extreme length of these duos and the concomitant length of the piece as a whole—365 bars in modern notation—as well as slow-moving homophonic sections, represent generic differences from the chansons. Moreover, *O bone Jesu* incorporates a section in triple metre, which the coeval chansons by Ninot do not.[23] But its other features—the characteristic voice-leading described above, a tendency towards non-matching voice pairs, little rhythmic manipulation or melodic development of thematic material—connect it clearly with them.

[23] One chanson, *Et levez vous hau, Guillemette*, contains a short passage in coloration that has the effect of a temporary shift to triple metre (*Opera Omnia*, no. 6, bb. 33–8) although no actual change in metre occurs. This practice could be interpreted as a transitional phase between the absence of triple-metre sections in the earliest chansons and the frequent change in metre in the later ones. This indication that *Et levez vous* might occupy a chronological space between the earlier and later chansons is reinforced by its sources—it appears in the last of Petrucci's three great chanson collections, *Canti C* (1504), as well as in the two latest major sources containing Ninot's secular works—and by the fact that it is somewhat longer (seventy-six bars in modern notation) than some of the earlier pieces, reflecting its somewhat more complex repetition scheme.

The publication of Ninot's *O bone Jesu* in 1505 occurred contemporane-
ously with the copying of the three motets attributed to Jo. Le Petit in CS 42
and Petrucci's own anonymous publication of two of them in 1504, and the
Vatican motets have much in common with *O bone Jesu* as well as with each
other. All four motets share with Ninot's early chansons a slightly quirky dissonance treatment, occasional parallel fifths between superius and altus, and
sometimes awkward approaches to voice-leading and cadencing. In Ex.
11.6(*a*), the first excerpt from *Si oblitus fuero* illustrates the by now familiar parallels between superius and altus in a cadential context that closely resembles
that of Ex. 11.5(*a*) (the first excerpt from *O bone Jesu*). Ex. 11.6(*b*) shows the
familiar simultaneous presence of notes of resolution with their suspensions;
the instance marked by the rectangle yields successive mirror seconds against
the moving altus.

More generally, all four motets utilize mostly unbalanced and sometimes

Ex. 11.6. Ninot le Petit, *Si oblitus fuero*: (*a*) bb. 96–8; (*b*) bb. 205–9

very long duos, sections in triple metre, and four-voice homophonic segments that move preponderantly in longer note-values. Like *O bone Jesu*, the Vatican motets are long, ranging from 247 to 274 bars in modern notation. The adoption of extensive biblical passages as motet texts, with a concomitant increase in length, is a preference that first shows up in the early sixteenth century, in the works of northern composers.[24]

Although the voice-leading irregularities shown in Exx. 11.3–6 might raise questions about Ninot's technical competence, such polyphonic solutions were not uncommon at the time. In any case, their significance here has not to do with competence or uniqueness but rather with their strong family resemblance to one another. All the examples involve the altus, generally the last voice part to be composed in the early sixteenth century, suggesting that Ninot was not yet entirely at ease writing for four voices.[25] Thus the motet attributed uniquely to 'Ninot' (*O bone Jesu*), the three Vatican motets bearing attributions both to 'Ninot' and to Jo. le Petit, and the secure early chansons ascribed to 'Nino(t) (le Petit)' all share traits not just of time and place but of apparently personal style, binding the pieces together as the work of a single composer.

It is difficult to see this composer as Baltazar, however, a difficulty that only increases when still other considerations are taken into account. One of these is Petrucci's attribution practice. The Italian printer published anonymously eight pieces that appear elsewhere with an attribution to Ninot,[26] and he published with ascriptions to 'Ninot' one chanson in 1502 (*Hélas hélas hélas*) and the motet *O bone Jesu* (discussed above) in 1505. In 1508, however, he printed the lauda *O Jesu dolce* as the work of 'Baldasar'. If the ascription of the lauda was in fact intended to identify the papal musician, then it would seem that for Petrucci, at least, 'Ninot' and 'Baldasar' were not the same composer. Certainly the music of *O Jesu dolce*, even allowing for differences in generic presuppositions, evidences little stylistic affinity with the other music under consideration. Although the motets make their slow way through lengthy texts, not always in a riveting fashion, they do not show the degree of tonal ambiguity

---

[24] In a book in progress, Richard Sherr draws a wider comparison between the motets ascribed to 'Jo. Le petit' in CS 42 and those by Mouton in that source and in another Vatican manuscript, CS 44. The similarity among the pieces goes beyond the use of long duos to the employment of closely related melodic figures and, even more revealing for the present argument, the common adoption of Psalms and other long biblical passages as texts. On the basis of the two Vatican manuscripts, the earliest sources to contain pieces of this type, Sherr places the beginning of this trend in motet texts, with the expansion of proportions and other musical stylistic features that result from it, in the early sixteenth century. The composers first writing motets of this sort in the Vatican manuscripts were, with the possible exception of Ninot (should he turn out to be Baltazar), employed in the north.

[25] In Ex. 11.6(*b*), it is the decision to make the altus imitate the superius—something that Ninot did not attempt in the other examples—that creates the problem.

[26] This count does not include *Lourdault, lourdault*, which Petrucci published in *Canti B* with an attribution to Compère.

that Baldasar achieves in a piece requiring only thirty-one bars in modern notation.

A final consideration weighs against the identification of Baltazar with Ninot. It was not uncommon at the time for composers to use an alias: Antoine Le Riche was also known as Divitis; Jean Braconnier, Lourdault; Johannes Ghiselin, Verbonnet; Antoine Colebault (Antonio Collebaudi), Bidon; and so forth. None, however, seems to have used two aliases. It is to 'Johannes Baltazar'—without an alias, and with only one exception—that payment is made in the chapel rolls. In other extant documents, the papal singer is always referred to with an alias, most often in the order 'J.' or 'Johannes Petit alias Baltazar', but in one instance 'Jo. Baldesaris alias Petit'. Never, however, is he referred to as 'Ninot'. The supposition that he is also that composer implies a superfluity of pseudonyms: Johannes Petit alias Baltazar alias Ninot.

If there is reason to be sceptical, then, about the identification of Baltazar with Ninot, there may be reason as well to be sanguine about another candidate.[27] In 1966 François Lesure suggested that the chanson composer might be identical with one Jean Lepetit who served as *maître de la psallette* from 1506 through 1510, then as canon until 1529, at St-Mammès Cathedral in Langres (in eastern France).[28] Support for this identification is provided indirectly by two mass choirbooks from Casale Monferrato. Ninot appears in Choirbook L, mentioned above, with 'Hotinet Barra' (Jean Barra, dit Hottinet), who also served at Langres cathedral during Jean Lepetit's tenure there.[29] A sister manuscript, Choirbook M, contains two unique masses by Bruhier, who frequently turns up in Ninot's company, and whose earliest documentation is in the year 1504, also in Langres.[30] Although Bruhier's stay there did not overlap with that of Lepetit and Barra, the convergence of place

[27] Gerald Montagna represents a significant exception to the general acceptance of Baltazar as the composer in question. In 'Caron, Hayne, Compère: A Transmission Reassessment', *EMH* 7 (1987), 107–57, he argues from the evidence of the sources of Ninot's music as I do, but while he also rejects the identification with Baltazar, his conclusions differ from mine in other respects.

[28] François Lesure, 'La Maîtrise de Langres au xvie siècle', *Revue de musicologie*, 52 (1966), 202–3. The position of *maître de la psallette*, which Lepetit held from 6 Mar. 1506, 'date de sa réception', until 14 Sept. 1510, was the equivalent of chapelmaster. The Master had the 'droit à l'habit de chanoine, mais dans les stalles il se tient au dernier rang'. Thereafter 'chanoine', Lepetit's position as canon would presumably no longer have been 'au dernier rang', nor would he have been responsible any longer for the training and housing of the choirboys. Cf. Bernard Populus, 'La Psallette de Langres; notes et documents sur la musique à la Cathédrale avant la Révolution', *Bulletin de la Société historique et archéologique de Langres*, 2 (1946), 205, 207, 250.

[29] Barra left the Sainte-Chapelle in Paris, where he had been since Nov. of 1510, to become *maître de la psallette* at the Langres cathedral, where he remained from 31 May 1512 until at least 22 July of 1514. (See Joshua Rifkin, 'Jehan [Jean] de Barra [Barrat; Hotinet]', *New Grove*, ii. 178; Lesure, 'La Maîtrise de Langres', 203; and Populus, 'La Psallette de Langres', 250.)

[30] Bruhier was *maître de musique*—the same position, referred to as *maître de la psallette*, held later by Lepetit and Barra—at St-Mammès Cathedral at least from 29 Apr. until 16 Aug. 1504. Bruhier 'a du quitter la psallette' in Oct. or Nov. 1504 and had already been replaced by 13 Nov. of that year (Populus, 249).

of employment with common representation in sources adds particular weight to this possible identification for Ninot.

The profile of the composer Ninot presented here, and the tentative (re)identification of him with Jean Lepetit of Langres, leaves the apparent anomaly of the attributions in CS 42 to 'Jo. le petit', attributions that would seem to have been intended by the copyist to signify Baltazar. That the scribe Johannes Orceau, who entered papal service in 1497 and copied the motets some time between 1503 and 1507, could have mistaken someone else's music for that of a musician employed with him at the Vatican for four or five years would appear to fly in the face of our most profound evidentiary beliefs.[31] Yet this seeming anomaly may be more illusory than real. Orceau may in fact have intended the formulation 'Jo. le petit' to signify not Johannes Petit alias Baltazar but an entirely different musician, Ninot le Petit. It does not seem excessively complicated to suppose that for a collection of motets intended for use at the Vatican the scribe would have used an abbreviation of the Latin, formal version of the composer's given name rather than the more familiar, informal, even affectionate, diminutive. Moreover, if Baltazar were not primarily a composer at all, or if he were a composer of laudas but not of motets, Orceau would not have foreseen that—some centuries later—an attribution to 'Jo. le Petit' could mislead.[32] The combined facts that the papal musician was referred to in the payment rolls simply as 'Johannes Baltazar' (with one exception) and that his alias, 'Petit', when used in other contexts, lacked the definite article (also with one exception), make plausible the theory that for Orceau, 'Le Petit' pointed unambiguously to the motet and chanson composer Ninot, who was not to be confused with the papal musician Johannes Baltazar. The latter, if he is not Ninot, never achieved prominence as a composer and had already been dead some two to six years by the time the three motets were ascribed to Jo. le Petit. Should this, or any other, explanation remain unconvincing, however, and the apparent anomaly remain, it should be remembered that the attribution to 'Jo. le Petit' in CS 42 for the motets given to 'Ninot' in Florence II.I.232 is the single anomaly in this re-revised history, while the identification of Ninot with Baltazar is anomalous in every aspect except, possibly, this one.[33]

---

[31] On the identification of the scribe Johannes Orceau and the dates of his service in the papal chapel, see Sherr, 'The Papal Chapel', 171–4; in *Papal Music Manuscripts*, 30, he shows that the date of Orceau's entry into the papal chapel was 1497.

[32] In the discussion following this paper, Jeffrey Dean suggested that if it had been common knowledge that the recently deceased papal musician composed nothing but laudas, never motets, the anomaly of the Vatican attributions might simply vanish.

[33] Joshua Rifkin reminded me during discussion after this paper of a strikingly parallel instance—'another case of a similarly ironclad attribution that turns out not to hold water'—in which a mis-identification was made because a musician in the musical establishment for which a work was being copied had the same name as the

Whether Ninot le Petit and Jean Lepetit are the same musician, and I believe it likely that they are, virtually all indications point to the composer Ninot's having been employed in the north throughout at least the first decade of the sixteenth century. The single piece of potentially contradictory evidence is not so potent that it must be considered incontrovertible in view of the other indications against the identification of Ninot with Baltazar. It is almost certainly not the case that the papal musician Johannes Petit alias Baltazar was the progenitor, and Rome of the 1490s the birthplace, of the new style of chanson that a decade later was to blaze brightly—if briefly—across the European musical firmament under the name Ninot le Petit.

Appendix A: Early Sources of Music by Ninot le Petit

MANUSCRIPTS:

Cambridge 1760 (French royal court, *c*.1509–14)
   'N. Le Petit' (body of MS), [Antoine] 'de Fevin' (index): *J'ayme bien mon amy*
Casale Monferrato L (Casale Monferrato; relevant portion *c*.1515–18)
   'Ninot': mass
Florence 2439 (Brussels/Mechlin, 1506–14, probably *c*.1508).
   'Nino': *Mon seul plaisir, Si bibero crathere*
Florence 2442 (Florence? France? *c*.1510–15 or later)
   'Ninot Le petit': thirteen chansons (earliest source for eight)
Florence II.I.232 (Florence, *c*.1515)
   'Ninot' (index): *In illo tempore, Psallite noe, Si oblitus fuero*
Paris 1597 (France; *c*.1500)
   Anon.: *Mon seul plaisir, Lourdault, lourdault*
Uppsala 76a (southwestern France; relevant section *c*.1495 or later)
   'Minot lepetit': *Pourtant si mon amy*
Vatican CS 42 (Rome; the scribe Johannes Orceau copied the three motets some time between 1503 and 1507)
   'Jo. le Petit': *In illo tempore, Psallite noe, Si oblitus fuero*

---

actual composer. A manuscript from the reign of Leo X—Vatican CS 16—contains a mass attributed to 'Hillaire', the composer of which was assumed to be Hilaire Daleo alias Turleron, a singer in the papal chapel at the time that the manuscript was copied (see Sidney R. Charles, 'Hillary–Hyllayre: How Many Composers?', *Music and Letters*, 55 (1974), 61–9, and Rifkin, 'Hilaire [Hylaire] Daleo [Turleron]', *New Grove*, viii. 551). Sherr argues convincingly, however, that the composer of the mass is not the musician in residence but Hilaire Bernoneau, chapelmaster at the French royal court (Richard Sherr, 'The Membership of the Chapels of Louis XII and Anne de Bretagne in the Years Preceding their Deaths', *Journal of Musicology*, 6 (1988), 60–82, esp. 61–4).

PETRUCCI PRINTS:
Canti B, 1502
  'Ninot': *Helas helas helas*
Motetti libro quarto, 1505
  'Ninot': *O bone Jesu*
Laude libro secondo, 1508
  'Baldasar': *O Jesu dolce*

Appendix B: Catalogue of Ninot's Secular Works by Earliest Extant Source

Pourtant si mon amy: *c*.1495 or later (Uppsala 76a)
Mon seul plaisir: *c*.1500 (Paris 1597; also Florence 2439)
Nostre chamberiere, si malade elle est: 1501 (*Odhecaton*)
Et la la la: 1502 (*Canti B*; also Florence 2442)
Helas helas helas: 1502 (*Canti B*)
Et levez vous hau, Guillemette: 1504 (*Canti C*; also Florence 2442)
Gentilz gallans adventureulx: 1504 (*Canti C*; also Florence 2442)
Mon amy m'avoit promis: 1504 (*Canti C*; also Florence 2442)
Si bibero crathere (*a* 3): 1505–8 or *c*.1508 (Florence 2439)
En chevauchant pres d'ung molin: 1510–15 (Florence 2442; unicum)
En l'ombre d'ung aubepin: 1510–15 (Florence 2442)
En revenant de Noyon: 1510–15 (Florence 2442; unicum)
Et levez vo gambe, Jennette: 1510–15 (Florence 2442; unicum)
Helas, helas, qui mi confortera?: 1510–15 (Florence 2442; unicum)
Je mi levay l'autre nuytee: 1510–15 (Florence 2442)
L'ort villain jaloux: 1510–15 (Florence 2442)
N'as tu poinct mis ton hault bonnet: 1510–15 (Florence 2442)

DOUBTFUL, OR WITH CONFLICTING ATTRIBUTION:
C'est donc par moy: early 1550s (Heilbronn X. 2, attr. Willaert)
J'ayme bien mon amy (*a* 3): *c*.1509 or 1509–14 (Cambridge 1760)
Lourdault, lourdault: 1490s, or before 1500 (Bologna Q 17: 'Nino petit'; also Paris
    1597: Anon.; *Canti B*: 'Compere')

12

Palestrina at Work

JESSIE ANN OWENS

I T is surprising, given Palestrina's prominence in his own time as well as
his place in history, that little attention has been paid to the question of
how he composed. The only scholar to have considered this issue at any
length was Raffaele Casimiri, who discussed some of the revisions in Rome,
San Giovanni in Laterano, Archivio musicale lateranense, Codice 59, a manuscript largely in Palestrina's hand.[1] While Casimiri's study continues to be useful, in part because of the access it offers to the manuscript,[2] the question of
Palestrina's working methods deserves further consideration. There is additional evidence not considered by Casimiri: the Mantuan correspondence concerning Palestrina's Santa Barbara masses as well as three other autograph
manuscripts. This evidence, when seen in the broader context of recent discoveries about compositional process in Renaissance music, sheds new light
on aspects of Palestrina's compositional procedures.

The Mantuan commission

The archives in Mantua preserve portions of the correspondence surrounding
the commission that Palestrina received to compose a series of masses for Santa
Barbara, the palatine basilica in Mantua.[3] The masses were commissioned by

This study is a revised and expanded version of material presented in ch. 11 of my book *Composers at Work: The
Craft of Musical Composition 1450–1600* (New York, 1997). I am grateful to Jane Bernstein, Bonnie Blackburn,
James Ladewig, Megumi Nagaoka, Robert Kendrick, and Richard Sherr for their valuable comments. Unless
otherwise specified, the translations are mine.

[1] Hereafter: Rome SG 59. Raffaele Casimiri, *Il 'Codice 59' dell'Archivio Musicale Lateranense autografo di
Giovanni Pierluigi da Palestrina* (Rome, 1919).

[2] The manuscript has been virtually inaccessible; I am grateful to Giancarlo Rostirolla for arranging for me
to see it for several hours in 1990. A facsimile edition is now in preparation by Maestro Rostirolla.

[3] Knud Jeppesen, 'Pierluigi da Palestrina, Herzog Guglielmo Gonzaga und die neugefundenen Mantovaner-
Messen Palestrina's', *Acta musicologica*, 25 (1953), 132–79; Antonio Bertolotti, *Musici alla corte dei Gonzaga in
Mantova* (Milan, 1890); Oliver Strunk, 'Guglielmo Gonzaga and Palestrina's *Missa Dominicalis*', *Musical*

Guglielmo Gonzaga, duke of Mantua, an avid amateur composer who had on at least two occasions sent his own music to Palestrina with the request that he make suggestions for improvements. Guglielmo specified that the masses were to be: (i) alternatim (that is, divided between chant and polyphony), (ii) based on the newly revised chants of the Santa Barbara liturgy, and (iii) imitative throughout. Palestrina thought that he could compose one mass every ten days. In fact, the chronology drawn from the correspondence shows that he was working at the rate of approximately one mass every three weeks between October 1578 and April 1579.[4]

The evidence about Palestrina's working methods comes from the beginning of the series of letters from 1578–9. The Duke's agent in Rome, Don Annibale Capello, reported on 18 October 1578:[5]

M. Gio. da Palestina non servendogli per l'indispositione grave havuta di fresco la testa, ne la vista, per essercitar La gran voluntà di servir in quel modo che può ha cominciato a porre sul Leuto le chirie et la Gloria della prima messa, et me le ha fatti sentire pieni veramente di gran suavità et leggiadrie.

. . . ma quando prima dalla debolezza gli sara permesso, spiegarà ciò ch' ha fatto col liuto con tutto il suo studio . . .

Having passed recently through a serious illness and being thus unable to command either his wits or his eyesight in the furtherance of his great desire to serve Your Highness in whatever way he can, M. Giovanni da Palestrina has begun to set the Kyrie and Gloria of the first mass on the lute, and when he let me hear them, I found them in truth full of great sweetness and elegance.

. . . And as soon as his infirmity permits he will work out what he has done on the lute with all possible care.[6]

Quarterly, 33 (1947), 228–39; repr. in his *Essays on Music in the Western World* (New York, 1974), 94–107. See also Iain Fenlon, *Music and Patronage in Sixteenth-Century Mantua* (Cambridge, 1980) and id., 'Patronage, Music and Liturgy in Renaissance Mantua', in Thomas F. Kelly (ed.), *Plainsong in the Age of Polyphony* (Cambridge, 1992), 209–35, esp. 216–29.

[4] (1) 18 Oct. 1578: Palestrina has set the Kyrie and Gloria to the lute.
(2) 1 Nov. 1578: Palestrina is sending the first mass; he will send one every ten days.
(3) 5 Nov. 1578: Palestrina has sent the first mass (fourth mode, cantus firmus transposed up a fifth or an octave, Missa In duplicibus minoribus I or II).
(4) 15 Nov. 1578: Capello has sent the second mass.
(5) 10 Dec. 1578: Capello has sent the fourth mass (one that Palestrina particularly liked).
(6) 17 Mar. 1579: payment (by Strozzi on behalf of the duke) of 100 scudi to Palestrina.
(7) 18 Mar. 1579: Strozzi has sent a mass.
(8) 21 Mar. 1579: Palestrina has sent three *ultime* [last? or most recent? or latest?] masses, composed according to Capello's most recent instructions ('ultimo avertimento'), i.e. with a different disposition of chant in the Sanctus.
(9) 1 April 1579: Strozzi has sent a mass.
[5] ASM, Archivio Gonzaga, Roma, E.XXV.3 b. 923 Roma-diversi 1578, fo. 439: Letter from Don Annibale Capello to Guglielmo Gonzaga, duke of Mantua, 18 Oct. 1578.
[6] Translation from Strunk, 'Guglielmo Gonzaga', 99–100.

Capello's remarks about the lute are intriguing. Does *porre sul leuto* mean that Palestrina was using the lute as a tool in composing, or was it merely a convenient way to perform the music for Capello in the absence of a choir? Was Palestrina playing the mass as it would have sounded as a choral composition, or was he simply giving Capello a taste, perhaps playing the essential sonorities, the main motifs, or a kind of reduction for lute?

Capello's reference to Palestrina's 'indispositione grave havuta la testa ne la vista' ('the serious illness that the head had in the vision or sight', to translate literally) raises other questions. Did the illness interrupt Palestrina's activities altogether, or did it simply prevent him from writing anything down? And what exactly does 'spiegarà ciò ch' ha fatto col liuto' mean? *Spiegare* can have the sense of making something clear or accessible, extending something, unfolding a map.[7] John Florio, author of an early Italian–English dictionary, defines it as 'to displaie, to explaine, to expound, to unfold, to spred abroad'.[8] Was Capello describing Palestrina's normal procedure or did the composer's illness cause him to alter his practices in some way?

The reply to this letter, discovered by Jeppesen among chancellery documents, shows that its contents were hard to understand even for its intended recipient. Written by an unknown court official, it is preserved in draft form in two slightly different versions. The first version reads:[9]

Al capello	To Capello:
S. Alt.a ordina che V.S. dica à	His Highness commands that Your
M. Giovanni di Palestina che attenda	Lordship tell Messer Giovanni di Palestina
à risanarsi, ne si affretti di porre sul	that he should take care to get well and not
leuto li chirie et la gloria con l'altre	hurry to set to the lute the Kyrie and the
compositioni, perché havendovi posto	Gloria with the other compositions, because
mano tant'altri valent'huomini non	having at hand many other talented men
bisogna compositione di leuto, ma si	there is no need for compositions for lute,
bene compositione fatta con molto	but instead for compositions made with
studio.	great care.

The second draft of the letter adds a few important details about the commission:

S. Alt.a ordina che V.S. dica à	His Highness commands that Your
M. Giovanni di Palestina che attenda	Lordship tell Messer Giovanni di Palestina
à risanarsi, ne si affretti di porre sul	that he should take care to get well and not
leuto le messe disid[erando] ella	hurry to set the masses to the lute, since he

---

[7] G. Devoto and G. C. Oli, *Dizionario della lingua italiana* (Florence, 1971).

[8] John Florio, *A Worlde of Wordes* (London, 1598; repr. New York, 1972), 389.

[9] ASM, Archivio Gonzaga, Serie F.II.7, Busta 2207: Letter (draft) from a court official to Capello, 23 Oct. 1578. Partial facsimile: Jeppesen, 'Pierluigi da Palestrina', 161.

ch'esse siano fugate continovamente
et sopra'l soggetto come hanno
fatto gl'altri, et esso istesso nel
Doppio maggiore.

desires that they employ imitation
throughout and be written on the chant as
the other composers have done and as he
himself did in the mass for Major Double
feasts.

There are ten 'Santa Barbara' masses by Palestrina extant:[10] two settings of masses 'in duplicibus minoribus', three 'in festis beate Mariae virginis', two 'in festis apostolorum', two 'in semiduplicibus maioribus', and one 'in dominicis diebus'. Paola Besutti recently discovered a document that records the copying of a 'Missa in duplicibus maioribus' by Palestrina in 1574—surely the most important for the liturgy—suggesting that the commission had begun as much as four years earlier.[11]

How do we interpret the duke's response? He may have thought that Palestrina was *transcribing* the music—the Kyrie and Gloria 'with the other compositions' (it is unclear what this other music might be—possibly the other movements of the mass ordinary?)—for lute.[12] The duke saw no need for more lute music; he valued music 'fatto con molto studio', which implies that lute music was not so carefully crafted. This may be another way of expressing his preference for the thorough-going imitative texture possible in vocal music and more difficult to achieve on the lute. The fact that Palestrina might have been using the lute for composing vocal music seems not to have occurred to him, perhaps an indication that neither he nor other composers whom he knew used the lute.

Capello's comments about Palestrina's working methods resonate with other evidence. It seems possible that Palestrina was actually composing at the

[10] Preserved in Milan, Conservatorio di Musica 'Giuseppe Verdi', Fondo Santa Barbara 164 and 166, and *Missae dominicales quinis vocibus diversorum auctorum a F. Iulio Pellino carmel. mant. collectae* (Milan: Tini, 1592¹). See Strunk, 'Guglielmo Gonzaga', 103–4. The masses are edited in Giovanni Pierluigi da Palestrina, *Le messe di Mantova, inedite dai manoscritti di S. Barbara*, ed. Knud Jeppesen (Le opere complete di Giovanni Pierluigi da Palestrina, 18–19). On the Santa Barbara liturgy see Jeppesen, 'Pierluigi da Palestrina', 158–9. On the Kyriale and chant at Santa Barbara, see Paola Besutti, 'Catalogo tematico delle monodie liturgiche della Basilica Palatina di S. Barbara in Mantova', *Le fonti musicali in Italia, studi e ricerche*, 2 (1988), 53–66 and ead., 'Giovanni Pierluigi da Palestrina e la liturgia Mantovana', in *Atti del II Convegno internazionale di studi palestriniani* (Palestrina, 1991), 157–64.
[11] And possibly as early as 1568, to judge from Palestrina's well-known letter of 2 Feb. 1568 about an unidentified mass ('. . . essendomi comandato da si Eccellente signore, et per mano di virtuoso cosi raro, come m. Giacches di far questa Messa, qui inclusa, la quale ho fatta così come m'ha instrutto m. Aniballe Cappello, se in questa prima volta non havrò sodisfatta la mente di V.ra Eccel.za se li piacerà comandarmi, come la voglia, o, breve, o, longa, o che si sentan le parole, io mi provar servirla secondo il mio potere'), cited by Jeppesen, 'Giovanni Pierluigi da Palestrina'. On the 1574 document, see Paola Besutti, 'Giovanni Pierluigi da Palestrina e la Liturgia mantovana (II)', read at the III Convegno Internazionale di Studi Palestrina e l'Europa (Palestrina, October 1994). Besutti also found a payment for a 'Missa Dominicalis', which probably refers to the mass published in 1592. It now appears that Palestrina provided settings for the first six of the ten masses in the 'Kyriale ad usum ecclesie Sancte Barbare'.
[12] I thank Prof. Richard Sherr for this interpretation.

lute, and perhaps even jotting down ideas in lute tablature.[13] There are a few references to composing at the keyboard; the lute, another 'perfect' instrument, would work as well.[14]

The notation of music for solo instruments such as the lute or keyboard had to convey the entire fabric of the polyphonic composition—both the separate lines and the resulting harmonies—in such a way as to make it possible for a single performer to play all the parts. Given the obvious advantages of this notation, it is not surprising to find evidence connecting it with composition. Wolfgang Schonsleder, writing in 1631, recommended tablature as one of the possible formats used by composers, along with the ten-line staff and score.[15] The advantages of tablature were that it was easy to see mistakes, it took little space, and it required just a scrap of paper, not a *cartella* or slate; its chief disadvantage was that the composer himself had to prepare the clean copy and could not relegate the task to a student.

Yet few examples of a composer using tablature for composing vocal music have survived. One possible instance comes from the second layer of Uppsala 76b. A hand believed by Vaccaro to be that of the French lutenist and composer Guillaume Morlaye wrote a fragmentary sketch in mensural notation of an otherwise unknown six-voice chanson, *Nul n'est* (the superius is written out in full with revisions, and the beginnings of the other voices are placed on the remaining staves (in the order AI AII TI TII B)). On the facing page, the same composition exists in two different drafts, notated in French lute tablature.[16]

---

[13] Casimiri (*Il 'Codice 59'*, 10) thought that Palestrina worked first in 'tabulatura', by which I think he meant score.

[14] Hermann Finck (*Practica musica* (Wittenberg, 1556), sig. Ooiiiᵛ) criticized would-be composers who (in Edward Lowinsky's paraphrase, 'On the Use of Scores by Sixteenth-Century Musicians', in *Music in the Culture of the Renaissance and Other Essays* (Chicago, 1989), 799 n. 15), 'torture the keyboard until they hit on some awkward piece, full of mistakes, which they later learn to transfer to paper'. Vincenzo Galilei (*Dialogo della musica antica et della moderna* (Florence, 1581), 138–9) recognized that some instrumentalists knew how to compose while playing their instrument, but could not write the music down, while others who could not play at all could write music down with a pen. There were few who could do both.

[15] Wolfgang Schonsleder, *Architectonice musices universalis ex qua melopoeam per universa et solida fundamenta musicorum, proprio marte condiscere possis* (Ingolstadt, 1631): 'Tertius modus est per litteras, hoc est, notas ipsum clavium, quae singulae suis litteris noscendae proponuntur. Modus superiori aetate usitatissimus: iam tantum non contemptus & vilis. Tamen commoda haec habet. Primum non est opus cartella, seu deletili tabula (quae ad secundum modum pertinet,) sed quaevis chartula sufficiet, cui tua cogitata illinas. Deinde quod his angusto brevique spatio scribis, ibi (in notis) tertio aut quarto tanto spatio opus erit, pluriumque loci capiendum. Praeterea vicinitas & distinctio clavium magnam lucem facilitatemque affert scribenti. Ad haec facilius citiusque videbis si quid aberraveris. Unicum incommodum est, quod puerum describendo allegare non potes (ut in secundo modo) auctorique ipsi labor ille suscipiendus. Hunc modum ad finem libri trademus. Nos in docendo iam utemur secundo modo tamquam usitatissimo, oculisque magis patente: quoniam contra torrentem niti irritus labor est. Qui tertio velit insuescere, iisdem huius tractatus praeceptis utetur & adiuvabitur.'

[16] *Uppsala, Universitetsbiblioteket, Vokalmusik i handskrift 76b*, introduction by Thomas G. MacCracken (Renaissance Music in Facsimile, 20; New York, 1986). See Guillaume Morlaye, *Œuvres pour le lut*, ed. Jean-Michel and Nathalie Vaccaro, ii: *Manuscrits d'Uppsala* (Paris, 1989). Hiroyuki Minamino, 'Sixteenth-Century Lute Treatises with Emphasis on Process and Techniques of Intabulation' (Ph.D. diss., University of Chicago, 1988) discusses the Uppsala example and provides a transcription (pp. 82–4, 307–14). I am grateful to Dr

As a general rule, however, it seems that composers used the notation and format customary for the particular kind of music they were writing during the process of composing: keyboard or open score for keyboard music, separate parts in mensural notation for vocal music, lute tablature for lute music.

Capello's comments resemble in some ways Claudio Monteverdi's own account of his process:[17]

... così visto il comandamento di S.A.S. di longa mi posi a comporre in musica il sonetto, et vi sono statto dietro sei giorni, et duoi altri tra provarlo e rescriverlo.

and so on seeing His Highness's [= Vincenzo, Fourth Duke of Mantua] commission, I straightway began setting the sonnet to music and was engaged in doing this for six days, then two more what with trying it out and rewriting it.

... l'altro sonetto lo manderò in musica composto a V.S. Ill.ma quanto prima poichè nella mente mia nella sua orditura è da me fatto, ma caso che niente dilongassi il tempo secondo il volere di S.A.S. mi farà gratia d'un minimo cenno che di longo lo manderò ...

... I shall send Your Lordship the other sonnet, set to music, as soon as possible— since it is already clearly shaped in my mind—but if I should spin out the time even a little, in His Highness's opinion, please be good enough to let me know and I shall send it at once.[18]

Monteverdi's language ('nella mente mia nella sua orditura è da me fatto') invokes the rich imagery of weaving. 'Orditura' is the pattern of warp lines laid down initially on the loom. By extension it means the essential lines of an intellectual work.[19] The implication is that the composition—at least in its essence—existed virtually complete in Monteverdi's mind: all that remained was to write it down. And then, of course, to follow the process he used for the other sonnet, namely, to try it out and to rewrite it. If we take Monteverdi's words literally—and we must remember that he could be making empty claims—then composing and writing out were quite different activities. The first piece had taken six days to compose and write down, then two more to perform, revise, and rewrite. The second piece was nearly composed, that is, Monteverdi knew its main outline, its *orditura*, despite the fact that it was not yet written down. Monteverdi's remarks seem somehow reminiscent of

Arthur Ness for drawing my attention to Morlaye's possible role in the manuscript as well as to Minamino's work.

[17] Claudio Monteverdi, *Lettere*, ed. Éva Lax (Florence, 1994), 18–19: letter to Annibale Iberti, Cremona, 28 July 1607.

[18] *The Letters of Claudio Monteverdi*, trans. Denis Stevens, rev. edn. (Oxford, 1995), 44. Stevens imagines that the two sonnets mentioned in the letter could be the two *a cappella* settings in the next book of madrigals to be published (Book VI, 1614): *Zefiro torna* and *Ohimè il bel viso* (both by Petrarch).

[19] Devoto and Oli, *Dizionario*. Florio (*A Worlde of Wordes*, 248) defines *orditura, ordimento* as 'a warping, a weaving, a devise, a complotting, a contriving'.

Capello's. Was Palestrina, like Monteverdi, composing in the mind, and simply playing the music on the lute, waiting until he was well to write it down?

While I doubt that we can arrive at a definitive interpretation of Capello's letter, it is possible to suggest a hypothesis. Given the problem with Palestrina's health, particularly his eyesight, it seems unlikely that he notated the music at all—in tablature or mensural notation—while he was sick. Nor was Palestrina one of the beginners whom Finck ridicules for needing to sound out consonances before writing them down. If Palestrina used the lute for composing, I suspect that it was to hear his ideas; he could also have been using it to show the duke's agent that he had been working on the commission. The description suggests the same two-step process to which Monteverdi alluded when he claimed that a piece was composed already in his mind, implying that all that remained was to write it down.

The Mantuan correspondence offers tantalizing hints about Palestrina's methods, but little concrete information. For a better understanding, we need to consider the documents in the light of his extant autograph manuscripts.

Palestrina autographs

Palestrina left a large number of compositions in manuscript when he died in 1594. Only forty-three of his masses were published during his lifetime, while thirty-eight appeared in print after his death, presumably taken from autograph manuscripts or manuscripts copied from his autographs. But from this legacy only four sources have survived.[20] It is interesting to note—in the light of Capello's remarks—that all are notated in mensural notation, and not in tablature.

Jeppesen identified Palestrina's hand in the choirbook Vatican, Vat. lat. 10766.[21] Palestrina added his (otherwise unknown) *falso bordone* setting of Ps. 109, *Dixit Dominus*, on a blank opening at the end of the choirbook, and corrected a mistake in the text of one of the hymns. The opening, while not containing any significant revisions, does perhaps reflect Palestrina's writing out or writing down of the piece rather than a simple copying from another source. He initially identified the four quadrants—cantus, altus, tenor,

[20] Knud Jeppesen, 'Palestrina', *MGG* x, col. 667. Unfortunately, there are no known inventories of Palestrina's estate. On Palestrina's son and heir Iginio, see Robert F. Hayburn, *Papal Legislation on Sacred Music 95 A.D. to 1977 A.D.* (Collegeville, Minn., 1979), 44–57.
[21] Hereafter Vatican 10776: choirbook, 59 fos., *c.* 390 × 270, fos. 55ᵛ–56ʳ, *Dixit Dominus* (Ps. 109). Facsimile: Knud Jeppesen, 'Palestriniana: Ein unbekanntes Autogramm und einige unveröffentlichte Falsibordoni des Giovanni Pierluigi da Palestrina', in *Miscelánea en homenaje a Monseñor Higinio Anglés* (Barcelona, 1958–1961), 417–32; Anthony Grafton (ed.), *Rome Reborn: The Vatican Library and Renaissance Culture* (Washington, DC, 1993), pl. 162.

bassus—with the part-names in the middle of the stave, but when space ran short, he crossed out 'tenor' and 'bassus' because he needed the stave. A rather sharp change in ink colour for the last two verses may indicate that he worked on the piece at two different times.

The other three manuscripts, by contrast, all contain revisions of one sort or another. Two sets of parts are now found in the library at the Conservatorio di Musica 'Santa Cecilia'; each contains the music for an eight-voice motet, copied on eight sheets of paper, front and back. *Omnis pulchritudo* is in upright format, with nine staves per side.[22] *Beata es* is in oblong format, six staves per page.[23] The motets are both responsories, set as polychoral pieces for two four-voice choirs.

We do not know much about the context for the composition of these two motets. There are a number of possibilities.[24] One is the Chiesa Nuova, the centre of Filippo Neri's activities. According to Noel O'Regan, eight-voice music by Lasso, Palestrina, Giovanni Animuccia, and Marenzio—published using a full eight-voice texture—was revised in manuscript to create true *cori spezzati* (that is, with harmonically self-sufficient choirs) for use in the Chiesa Nuova. While the two Santa Cecilia motets have not been specifically linked to the Chiesa Nuova, they conform in style to music that can be. Other possibilities, also suggested by O'Regan, are the Oratory of Santissima Trinità dei Pellegrini, where Palestrina led the music for Holy Week in 1576 and 1578, and Santo Spirito in Sassia.[25] He could also have written the music for St Peter's: *Beata es* is also preserved in a source associated with the Cappella Giulia, XIII.24, a set of partbooks containing polychoral music.

The fourth and most substantial of the manuscripts is the Lateran choirbook studied by Casimiri, Rome SG 59.[26] Quite small in size (*c.* 15.5 × 11 in.), at least in comparison with the choirbooks of the time, the manuscript contains sixty-four compositions, written on ninety-four folios: office hymns,

---

[22] Rome, Biblioteca Musicale Governativa del Conservatorio di Musica 'Santa Cecilia', G.MSS.O.232 (*olim* Riv.B.I.I; 112) (hereafter Rome SC O.232), 8 fos., 237 × 171, *Omnis pulchritudo domini*. Facsimile, fo. 1: Giovanni Pierluigi da Palestrina, *Omnis pulchritudo domini*, ed. V. Mortari (Rome, [1950]); *Manoscritti musicali rari*, no. 1 (Rome, 1949).

[23] Rome, Biblioteca Musicale Governativa del Conservatorio di Musica 'Santa Cecilia', G.MSS.O.231 (*olim* 111.I) (hereafter: Rome SC O.231), 8 fos., 170 × 233, *Beata es Virgo Maria*; 2.p. *Ave Maria*. Facsimile (complete): *Atti del II Convegno internazionale di studi palestriniani* (Palestrina, 1991), 638–45. Edition: *Werke*, xxx. 162; *Opere complete*, xxxiv. 41. Concordances: Vatican CG XIII.24 (Llorens 34); Vatican City, Barb. lat. 4184.

[24] On Roman polychoral music, see Noel O'Regan, 'The Early Polychoral Music of Orlando di Lasso: New Light from Roman Sources', *Acta musicologica*, 56 (1985), 234–51; id., 'Palestrina and the Oratory of Santissima Trinità dei Pellegrini', *Atti del II Convegno internazionale di studi palestriniani* (Palestrina, 1991), 95–121; and id., ' "Blessed with the Holy Father's Entertainment": Roman Ceremonial Music as Experienced by the Irish Earls in Rome, 1608', *Irish Musical Studies*, 2: *Music and the Church* (1991), 41–61.

[25] See Noel O'Regan, *Institutional Patronage in Post-Tridentine Rome: Music at Santissima Trinità dei Pellegrini 1550–1650* (Royal Musical Association Monographs, 7; London, 1995).

[26] 94 fos., 397 × 278 mm. Facsimiles: Casimiri, *Il 'Codice 59'*; *Werke*, xxxi; Jeppesen, 'Palestriniana', 432.

Lamentations, a few canticles, the responsory for the Dead, the Improperia, and a motet (see the Appendix). While the other three autographs served primarily for performance or, in the case of the two motets, for transmission as well as for performance, the Lateran choirbook seems to have been Palestrina's personal copy of some of his music.

We know that composers kept personal copies of their music. The title-page of the 1555 print of Ruffo's motets, for example, boasts that the music was corrected from his 'proprii originali', his own 'original' manuscript: *Cantus Motetti, a sei voci composti da Vincentio Ruffo, maestro della capella, del domo, di Verona, dedicati, al signor Luca Grimaldi, novamente posti in luce da li suoi proprii originali, corretti, & stampati* (Venice: Girolamo Scotto, 1555). 'Proprii originali' is evidently synonymous with the more common designation 'proprii essemplari', found frequently in Scotto prints.[27] *Originale* seems to mean a final version, presumably a fair copy, perhaps with revisions.[28]

I consider Rome SG 59 to be Palestrina's *originale* in part because of the revisions he made in the music and in part because of the ordering of the music in the manuscript.[29] While there has not yet been a systematic study of the paper, gathering structure, or other physical evidence that could help determine the chronology of its compilation, the ordering of its contents suggests that it was a working manuscript, not a polished or final copy. The manuscript falls into four main sections. The Lamentations for Holy Week are divided between the first and third sections. The hymns are in the second and fourth sections. The rest of the pieces in the manuscript seem to have been fitted in wherever space would permit.

Casimiri recognized that the manuscript had not been written at one time. He used the appearance of the writing to posit three main stages in the manuscript's genesis, listed in the Appendix in the column 'period/hand'.[30] The first stage was for the rather neat, small hand that entered the Lamentations on fos. 2^v–6^r and 23^v–26^r. The second stage represents the bulk of the manuscript, including almost all the hymns. The third stage, characterized by a larger, bolder script and a different kind of text-repetition mark, includes the Magnificat on fos. 77^v–80^r and *Hodie Christus natus est* on fos. 90^v–91^r. He noted two other scribal appearances, a slightly later 'calligraphic' hand for fos. 39^v–42^r and 45^v–46^r, and a hand that he thought was not necessarily Palestrina's, on fos. 33^v–34^r and 42^v–45^r. I suspect that a careful check of

[27] I am indebted to Prof. Jane Bernstein for this information. Casimiri (p. 24) cited another example: an Altaemps manuscript (no longer extant) from the early 17th c. containing a copy of Palestrina's ferial hymns marked 'ex propriis originalibus', perhaps copied from Rome SG 59.

[28] I am indebted to Joshua Rifkin for the valuable suggestion of 'fair copy' in this context.

[29] Casimiri (*Il 'Codice 59'*, 26) was the first to describe Rome SG 59 as Palestrina's *originale*.

[30] Casimiri, *Il 'Codice 59'*, 11–21.

Roman manuscripts will turn up scribal concordances for Casimiri's 'calli-graphic' hand, his 'altra mano', his 'third' stage, and possibly even the 'first' stage, leaving as Palestrina's work the hymns and some of the miscellaneous liturgical pieces of his 'second' stage. Until the manuscript truly becomes accessible, this question must obviously remain open.

Dating the manuscript has proved difficult. The presence of the year '1560' on the first page led some scholars (for example, Baini and Haberl) to assign it to Palestrina's time at San Giovanni in Laterano, from October 1555 until July 1560. Casimiri, however, realized that '1560' was a later addition to the man-uscript, and that the presence of the manuscript in the Archivio musicale of San Giovanni in Laterano was unrelated to Palestrina's service as *maestro di cap-pella*—simply an accident of history.[31] His suggestion that the manuscript belonged to Palestrina himself, and was among the manuscripts left to his son after his death, seems quite plausible.

Casimiri was intent on establishing as broad a range of dates for the creation of the manuscript as possible, between 1555, when Palestrina began to work at San Giovanni in Laterano, and 1588 or 1589, the date of publication of one of the Lamentations (1588) and most of the hymns (1589). I think it far more likely that the manuscript dates from Palestrina's second period as *maestro di cappella* in the Cappella Giulia, from 1571 until his death in 1594. The evidence actually suggests an even narrower time frame, from about the mid-1570s until the mid-1580s.

Palestrina may have stopped using the manuscript by 1587. The final piece is a draft of a *falso bordone* setting of *Benedictus Dominus* (fo. 94ᵛ) that was pub-lished in Giovanni Guidetti's *Cantus ecclesiasticus* of 1587.[32] At the early end of the temporal spectrum, two of the pieces bear the names of singers from the Cappella Giulia.[33] Matching the names against archival evidence shows that the Improperia on fos. 89ᵛ–90ʳ were sung in 1573. The Lamentation on fo. 1ʳ, however, could have been sung anywhere between 1573 and 1578. We know, however, from the Mantuan correspondence that Palestrina was busy com-posing Lamentations in 1574.[34] Documents preserved in Rome indicate that

---

[31] Casimiri (*Il 'Codice 59'*, 1, 23–6) recognized that the portion of the title bearing the date '1560' was an 18th-c. addition by Girolamo Chiti. He noted that the manuscript was not included in an inventory of the Lateran collection made in 1620–2; it first appeared in an inventory of 1748, under its present collocation.

[32] Jeppesen, 'Palestriniana', 419–20.

[33] Casimiri, *Il 'Codice 59'*, 17–18. The most recent archival work (Giancarlo Rostirolla, 'La Cappella Giulia in San Pietro negli anni del magistero di Giovanni Pierluigi da Palestrina', in *Atti del Convegno di studi palestrini-ani* (Palestrina, 1977), 99–283) confirms Casimiri's dates for the Improperia, but suggests a wider span for the Lamentation. Rostirolla (p. 117) suggested that the presence of individual singers' names indicated performance by soloists, a practice that Professor Sherr documents for Holy Week in the Sistine Chapel as well.

[34] Jeppesen, 'Pierluigi da Palestrina', 157; letter of Annibale Capello from 17 Apr. 1574, cited by Bertolotti, *Musici alla corte*, 50: 'Non sopportando il mio grandissimo desiderio d'honorarmi con servire a V. E. che la scusa della tardanza fatta in rimandarle la messa da lei giudiosissimamente composta sia portata da altri che da me

the scribe Johannes Parvus copied a set of Lamentations in 1575 (the manuscript has unfortunately not survived).[35] Jeppesen assumed, quite reasonably, that the Lamentations Palestrina was working on in 1574 were the same as this set from the Lateran choirbook; the presence of the names of the singers on fo. 1[r] seems like convincing evidence.

The hymns probably date from somewhat later. Casimiri noticed that many of them had barlines dividing the music and speculated that Rome SG 59 had been used as the source for the 1589 print; the barlines sometimes coincided with page-turns. In fact, Rome SG 59 served as the source for the Cappella Giulia manuscript XV.19, which Alessandro Pettorini copied in 1581–2 (he was paid in February 1582).[36] By a wonderful coincidence, Pettorini was the tenor from the Cappella Giulia whose name Palestrina had written in the margin of fo. 90[r] in 1573. CG XV.19 is in a very poor state of preservation and has apparently never been filmed. A comparison of several openings in good enough condition to be examined shows exact correspondence between the barlines in Rome SG 59 and page-turns in CG XV.19 as well as in the rubrics (for example, the names of feasts) in both manuscripts.[37]

It seems likely that Palestrina used Rome SG 59 for gathering the earliest known version of his hymns. It is not a neat copy, with the hymns written out in the characteristic liturgical order, but instead a rather rough working manuscript. For reasons that are not clear, the hymns for the first part of the liturgical year (*temporale*) occur in the middle of the manuscript (hymns that appear in CG XV.19 as nos. 1–23 are written out on fos. 46[v]–92[r]), while those from the middle of the *sanctorale* are at the beginning (hymns that appear in CG XV.19 as nos. 24–41 are on fos. 6[v]–23[r]).

---

stesso, sara cagione, che questa volta usi soverchio ardire con lo scrivere imediatamente a V. Ecc. La qual supplico ad attribuire a questo sol rispetto tanta licenza che mi ho preso. Et a credere insieme che l'occupationi di M. Gio. da Palestina in comporre alcune lamentationi per ordine del Papa et nelle cappelle di questi giorni santi hanno fatto tardare esso M. Gio. a fare alcune poche considerationi et avertimenti sopra la detta compositione'; Casimiri, *Il 'Codice 59'*, 19, proposed a date of 1574 for the Lamentation.

[35] Jeppesen, 'Palestrina', col. 699. On Parvus, see Mitchell Brauner, 'The Parvus Manuscripts: A Study of Vatican Polyphony, ca. 1535 to 1580' (Ph.D. diss., Brandeis University, 1982); Rostirolla, 'La Cappella Giulia', 252–3.

[36] Jeppesen, 'Palestrina', col. 699; Jose M. Llorens, *Le opere musicali della Cappella Giulia*, i: *Manoscritti e edizioni fino al '700* (Studi e testi, 265; Vatican City, 1971), no. 31 (with a list of contents). It contains all the hymns from Rome SG 59 except for a rejected version of *Tibi Christe splendor patris*, an incomplete setting of *Conditor alme siderum*, and the (extra) even strophes of several hymns. On Pettorini, see Rostirolla, 'La Cappella Giulia', 140–2, 256. On Palestrina's hymns, see Daniel Zager, 'The Polyphonic Latin Hymns of Orlando di Lasso: A Liturgical and Repertorial Study' (Ph.D. diss., University of Minnesota, 1985), 167–78. Zager (p. 173) speculated that Rome SG 59 'may well be the earliest complete source of Palestrina's hymns and the exemplar from which Cappella Giulia XV 19 was copied in 1582. Certainly the identical content of these two manuscript sources strongly suggests that the one is linked to the other very closely, with both predating the 1589 print'.

[37] A careful study of the sources of Palestrina's hymns that takes into consideration both contemporary settings and changes in the liturgy is badly needed.

The physical placement of the hymns in Rome SG 59 may help determine the chronology of Palestrina's work on the cycle. It is curious, for example, that he fit two hymns, *Tristes erant apostoli* and *Deus tuorum militum*, onto blank staves on pages already occupied by other hymns. Was he just being parsimonious, or should we conclude that this was the last available space and he needed to fit the whole cycle into this manuscript? He rejected the version of *Tibi Christe splendor* that he had written on fos. 9^v–10^r (no. 10), and added the final version on fos. 22^v–23^r at the end of a group of sixteen hymns, presumably on the next available space.

Perhaps as an aid to the scribe using the disordered contents of Rome SG 59 for preparing a formal choirbook, Palestrina put in a series of cross-references. For example, he wrote on the rejected version of *Tibi Christe splendor patris* a reference to the location of the final version: 'For [the hymn for the feast of] St Michael Archangel, turn thirteen folios' ('In S.ti Michaelis Archangeli voltate tredici carte'). Another is the reference on fo. 39^v to the first Lamentation for Holy Saturday at the beginning of the book. The presence of such references among both the hymns and the Lamentations suggests that the manuscript could have served as the source not only for the hymns but also for the Lamentations.

The choirbook, in short, seems to have functioned like a notebook for preserving compositions, for writing them out so that they could be performed and then revised if necessary, and also for providing scribes or typesetters with an authoritative source from which to make copies for public transmission.

Compositional procedures

While the autographs—especially Rome SG 59—need more thorough study, it is possible to offer some preliminary conclusions about Palestrina's compositional procedures, particularly by considering the sources in the broader context of autograph composing manuscripts of the period. I have been able to identify over 100 extant manuscripts used by some thirty composers for various stages of composition. These stages divide into three main categories: sketches, drafts, and fair copies with revisions.[38]

For Palestrina, unfortunately, no sketches or rough drafts have survived. The only possible examples of working drafts are the two *falso bordone* settings in Rome SG 59, both in 'quasi-score' ('pseudo-score'); they occur, significantly, on the first and the last page of the manuscript. The one on fo. 1^r has no text; the one on fo. 94^v is texted and has a slight revision. These two

---

[38] See *Composers at Work*, chs. 6 and 7.

examples may indicate that Palestrina, like many of his contemporaries, used quasi-score for sketching or drafting. We cannot be certain, however, since both the chordal style of the settings and the fact that he was working in both cases with just a single page rather than a full opening make quasi-score the logical choice of format. It is certainly possible that these pages do reflect his first written version of the material.

The rest of Palestrina's surviving autographs are fair copies. Three of the four sources contain revisions that reflect either the correction of copying mistakes or substantive musical changes, the kind of polishing that took place at the final stage of composition, perhaps following a performance.

Casimiri listed many of the revisions he found in Rome SG 59, some among the hymns, but many in the two Lamentations he thought belonged to the earliest period of work on the manuscript.[39] Some of them were subtle changes in voice-leading or text placement, just a note or two, perhaps a rest.[40] One brief example not cited by Casimiri illustrates the changes. In the fifth strophe of the hymn *Christe redemptor* Palestrina rewrote altus and bassus, eliminating the more pungent passing sixth chord on the last beat of b. 29 as well as the *d* in the bass and the *f′* in the altus that worked against the cadence on A between the cantus and tenor in b. 30 (see Ex. 12.1). But there were also more extensive revisions.[41] In one place Palestrina thought a canon would work, but when it did not he crossed out the rubric indicating canon and added the fifth voice on a hand-drawn stave at the bottom of the page. In another instance, mentioned above, he crossed out an entire setting of *Tibi Christe splendor*, and added another one.

The changes in *Omnis pulchritudo* seem to reflect the kind of polishing and refining found frequently in Rome SG 59. *Omnis pulchritudo* is a respond, with the overall form ABCB′; it is homophonic in texture, employing alternating choirs of high and low voices. The manuscript parts have a number of small-scale corrections, all of which occur in the two B sections (see Table 12.1). The second B (really a B′) is not an exact repeat: Palestrina switched voices within the choirs (lines 2 and 3 are exchanged in the lower choir, lines 1 and 2 in the upper choir) and wrote some of the details differently (while keeping the same sonorities). Some of the mistakes in the first B section do not recur in the second (nos. 1–5, 9 in Table 12.1); others needed to be changed in both (nos.

---

[39] Casimiri, *Il 'Codice 59'*, 27–45. Ch. 4 is entitled 'Il codice-autografo, documento d'autocritica del Palestrina'.

[40] Fos. 6r, 34r, 51v, 54r, 61r, 62v, 63r.

[41] The revisions included: fos. 5v–6r, Lamentation, rewriting cantus at 'novi diluculo' and rewriting two voices at 'convertere'; fo. 23v, rewriting 'et respice', condensing three bars into two and eliminating a repeat at 'lassis'; fos. 26v–27r, changing the harmonies in *Ecce nunc*; fos. 57v–58r, shortening a phrase at 'sustulit'; fo. 15v, changing a canon into a notated fifth voice.

Ex. 12.1. Corrections in Palestrina, *Christe redemptor . . . conserva*, fifth strophe: (*a*) first version; (*b*) second version

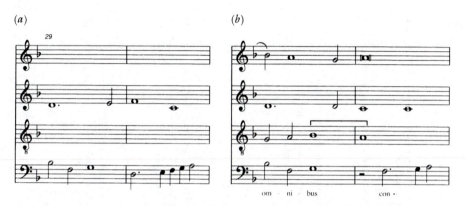

(*a*)   (*b*)

6–7/11–12); and the second B does have one error not found in the first (no. 10). It seems as though he was working from a kind of chordal grid—whether written or 'in the mind'—that he realized twice, in slightly different ways, and then polished. The fact that the corrections are all in the same ink suggests that there was little or no delay between writing and correcting.[42]

The lack of any examples of the earliest written stages—apart from the two *falso bordone* settings mentioned above—means that the evidence about Palestrina's techniques for sketching and drafting must be gleaned from the fair copies themselves. It is no simple task to envisage what format he may have been using. The evidence from the autograph manuscripts of other composers suggests a number of possibilities: a haphazard arrangement of lines fit into the available space; quasi-score with the lines written out one above the other; choirbook format with the lines in separate quadrants; and even separate parts notated on individual pieces of paper.

One of the errors in Rome SG 59 may indicate a possible format. Palestrina wrote out the first verse of the four-voice hymn *Plasmator hominis* in the usual choirbook format: cantus/tenor facing altus/bassus (see Fig. 12.1). The first strophe calls for CATB, while the third (the next one to be set polyphonically) calls for ATTB. He made the mistake at the beginning of the third strophe, beginning to write music for the top voice, in this instance the altus, in the customary place for the cantus, that is, the upper left of the opening, and with the cantus (g2) clef. The notes are in the correct place on the stave but the incorrect clef (g2 instead of c2) means that the pitches are wrong (first note is C and

---

[42] My thanks to Prof. James Ladewig for verifying the ink colours. These remarks are based on notes taken from seeing the manuscript only once, and could very well need to be revised.

TABLE 12.1. Provisional list of changes in *Omnis pulchritudo*

Text (with repetitions; abbreviations are expanded without comment; original spelling is retained)

A Omnis pulchritudo domini Omnis pulchritudo domini exaltata est super sydera exaltata est super sydera

B species eius in nubibus caeli et nomen eius [1] et nomen eius in eternum permanet [2].
   species [3] eius in nubibus caeli [4] in nubibus caeli et nomen [5] eius et nomen eius et nomen eius in eternum permanet in eternum [6] permanet.
   Alleluia Alleluia Alleluia [7] Alleluia [8, 9]

C A summo caelo egressio eius a summo caelo egressio eius
   Et occursus eius et occursus eius usque ad summum eius usque ad summum eius

B' species eius species eius in nubibus caeli in nubibus caeli et nomen eius et nomen [10] eius et nomen eius in eternum permanet.
    species eius in nubibus caeli et nomen eius et nomen eius et nomen eius in eternum permanet in eternum [11] permanet.
    Alleluia Alleluia Alleluia Alleluia [12, 13]

no.	bar	choir/voice	text; description[a]
1	36	II A	*-ius*; B changed to D [no change in b. 113]
2	39	II T1	*permanet*; custos erased, staff extended by hand into the margin, original reading not visible [no change in b. 116]
3	42	I C2	*e-*; B dotted minim, C semiminim, D semibreve changed to G semibreve, A minim, B minim [no change in b. 119]
4	46	II T2	*-li*; F minim or semibreve erased? semibreve rest is splotchy [no change in b. 123]
5	50	II A, T1	*-men*; A: F minim changed to A; T1: C minim changed to F [no change in b. 127]
6	56	II T1	*e-*; F minim changed to D [see no. 11]
7	69	I A	[*-ja*]; breve D changed to semibreve [see no. 12]
8	70	II T1	[*lu-*]; B A semiminims original reading uncertain) changed to B minim [related to no. 13?]
9	71	II T1	[*lu-*]; D dotted minim, D semiminim, D semibreve changed to D semibreve, D semibreve [no change in b. 148]
10	112	II A	*-men*; C minim changed to G minim [no change in b. 35]
11	133	II T2	[see no. 6]
12	146	I A	[*-ja*]; breve D changed to semibreve [see no. 7]
13	147	II T2	[*lu-*]; B semiminim changed to minim [slip of the pen? cf. no. 8]

[a] Differences in repeated passage are indicated in square brackets.

69ᵛ CANTUS Strophe 1 [g2 clef] Strophe 3 stave 4:	70ʳ ALTUS Strophe 1 [c2 clef] Strophe 3 [c2 clef] stave 4:
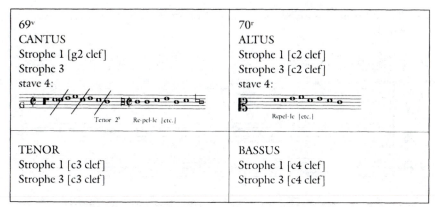	
TENOR Strophe 1 [c3 clef] Strophe 3 [c3 clef]	BASSUS Strophe 1 [c4 clef] Strophe 3 [c4 clef]

FIG. 12.1. Layout of *Plasmator hominis* in Rome SG 59, fos. 69ᵛ–70ʳ

should be F). Realizing his mistake, he crossed out the music (rests and eight notes, seven bars in all) and added the rubrics 'Cantus tacet' and 'Tenor 2.s'. The next stage presumably included writing the music he had crossed out in its correct place (fo. 70ʳ, stave 4) and adding the music for the tenor secundus in the space after the crossed-out notes (fo. 69ᵛ, stave 4). It seems that he instinctively tried to write the top line where it is usually found. He may have been working from a version notated in quasi-score like the *falso bordone* examples, with the top line at the top of a page, or from one in choirbook format with the altus as the top voice in the upper left-hand corner.

The corrections on the fair copy of *Ave Maria*, the second part of the eight-voice motet *Beata es*, reveal how difficult it is to use this sort of evidence with any degree of certainty. The motet employs separate four-voice choirs, the first consisting of cantus I, cantus II, altus, and bassus (with the cleffing g2, g2, c2, c4), and the second consisting of cantus, altus, tenor, and bassus (with the cleffing g2, c2, c3, c4). The music divides into segments defined partly by the alternation of the choirs and partly by the text (see Ex. 12.2):

Segment 1: Choir II
bb. 1–16
    (*a*) Ave Maria (bb. 1–9)
    (*b*) gratia plena (bb. 9–12)
    (*c*) gratia plena (bb. 12–16, original text: Dominus tecum)

Segment 2: Choir I
b. 15–30
    (*a*) Ave Maria (bb. 15–22)
    (*b*) gratia plena (bb. 22–5)
    (*c*) Dominus tecum (bb. 25–30)

Ex. 12.2. Palestrina, *Ave Maria*, bb. 1–41. After Palestrina, *Opere complete*, xxxiv (based on CG XIII. 24)

Ex. 12.2. *cont.*

Ex. 12.2. *cont.*

Segment 3: Choir II
bb. 30–7

    Dominus tecum

Segment 4: Choir I
m. 37–9

    Genuisti qui te fecit

Segment 5: Choir II
m. 39–41

    Genuisti qui te fecit

    There are three major mistakes, all of which involve writing the wrong music into one of the voices. In each one Palestrina noticed the mistake after writing a stave or two, crossed out the wrong notes, and wrote the correct music. In the first case, he wrote the music for the cantus, Choir II, of Segment 1(*a*) (bb. 1–9) into the cantus II, Choir I, of Segment 2(*a*) (bb. 15–22). He wrote the notes for an entire stave and started adding the text, getting as far as 'Ave Maria' before stopping (see Ex. 12.3). This would have been an easy mistake to make because apart from the presence of rests, both parts are identical for the first fourteen notes. Segment 2(*a*) is in fact a reworking of the material

Ex. 12.3. Mistaken and correct versions of Choir I, cantus II, in *Ave Maria*, Segment 2(*a*)

with which Choir II begins the second part of the motet. The cantus (Choir II) in Segment 1(*a*) becomes the cantus II (Choir I) in Segment 2(*a*), decorated with a newly composed upper voice. The point of imitation is altered by eliminating the third entry on C (b. 5) and bringing the final entry on F in earlier (see Ex. 12.2). Palestrina's mistake was to write out the original version of the primary motif (cantus, Choir II) rather than the new version (cantus II, Choir I).

The second mistake also involves reworked material. He wrote one and a half staves of music without any text from the altus of Choir II (bb. 13–39) onto the top two staves of the verso of the altus of Choir I.[43] The mistake occurred at the break between recto and verso (b. 25); Palestrina used the original version of the upper line of the two-part module of Segment 1(*b*) (altus, Choir II, bb. 9–12) instead of the revised version in Segment 2(*b*) (altus, Choir I, bb. 22–5). Ex. 12.4 shows the two-voice module as it occurs in the two segments; Segment 2(*b*) has both the wrong and the right version of the altus.

There is an additional factor beyond melodic similarity in this instance. The location of this mistake is associated with a revision of the text. Palestrina originally concluded the opening section of the piece (Segment 1(*c*)) with the words 'Dominus tecum', but during his work on the fair copy he crossed them out and substituted 'gratia plena' in the cantus and altus. The two phrases were

---

[43] The facsimile mixes up these pages, presenting fo. 3ᵛ (Altus, Choir I) as fo. 6ᵛ (Altus, Choir II) and fo. 6ᵛ as fo. 3ᵛ; see *Atti del II Convegno*, 640, 643.

Ex. 12.4. Comparison of the two-voice module in *Ave Maria*, Segments 1(*b*) and 2(*b*)

identical in both number of syllables and the pattern of accentuation, making
the substitution easy. The mistaken copying of music for the altus of Choir II
into the altus of Choir I may well have been triggered by the text. He wrote
out a line that originally had the text 'Dominus tecum' in the place where those
words occurred.

The third mistake, unlike the first two, is not between choirs but instead
between voices in Choir II; like the second, it takes place at the break between
recto and verso of the tenor of Choir II. Palestrina wrote out one and a half
staves (but none of the text) before realizing his mistake (see Ex. 12.5(*a*)). The
first third of the stave had the correct notes. Then, perhaps fooled by a series
of rests, he copied the rests and notes from the bassus (shown in Ex. 12.5(*b*))
into the tenor (Ex. 12.5(*a*)). He wrote a c3 clef, the correct clef for the begin-

Ex. 12.5. Palestrina, *Ave Maria*: (*a*) Tenor, Choir II (mistaken notes, crossed out); (*b*) Bassus, Choir II; (*c*) Tenor, Choir II (correct version)

ning of the stave and for the tenor part; the music of the bassus that he copied by mistake, however, employed a c4 clef. He wrote the pitches as though the clef were a c4 (an improbable A♯ indicates that he was thinking F♯ in the imagined c4 clef); at the beginning of the next stave he wrote c4 over c3. Ex. 12.5(*c*) shows the correct version of the tenor.

What can we learn from these errors? First, we can speculate about the appearance of the written material from which Palestrina was working. It seems unlikely that he was copying from a score; the mistakes would be too far apart on the page. For the same reason, it is also hard to imagine the lines grouped by choir, for example, in quasi-score. Nor does choirbook seem likely, particularly given the fact that this is true polychoral music. None of the standard arrangements of voices in choirbook format (choirs divided between recto and verso, voices grouped in pairs according to function, etc.) can explain the mistakes. That leaves two possibilities. He may have been working from eight separate sheets that were similar to the final fair copy. If these sheets had had part-names only on the front, that would explain the mistakes that began on the verso. The other—and to my mind more plausible explanation—is that the parts were jumbled up in close proximity on a page, fully worked out but not clearly labelled. When Palestrina went to make the fair copy, perhaps after a break in his work, he copied the wrong line in two places, fooled by the similar music in reworked passages, and by the rests in the third instance.

We know from the recently discovered sketches and drafts of Francesco Corteccia just how messy a composer could be in scribbling his ideas.[44] Another instance is Antonio Goretti's account of working with Monteverdi's drafts. On 27 November 1627 he wrote to Marquis Enzo Bentivoglio: 'The parts still must be copied, and I have already written a good part of Signor Claudio's composition, which, as it comes from under his hands, is so entangled and mixed up and confused that I protest to Your Highness that he makes me guess.' He continued:

Signor Claudio composes only in the morning and in the evening, and after lunch he does not want to do anything; I urge him on and relieve him from work, that is I take away the compositions from under his hands after we have discussed them and played them through, and they are so entangled and mixed up that I—I assure Your Excellency—have more work than if I were to compose them all myself.[45]

The difficulty in deciphering the messy drafts is evident.

Apart from the issue of the appearance of the sketches and drafts, the mistakes and changes in the *Ave Maria* are a window into Palestrina's process. In composing the polychoral motet, he took as his point of departure both the text and the potential for repetition and alternation that this style afforded. His initial thought was to have opening segments for each choir, linked through shared musical material; each would present the first three phrases of the text: 'Ave Maria', 'gratia plena', 'Dominus tecum'. Later he made the subtle change of substituting 'gratia plena' for 'Dominus tecum' in the opening segment. The repetition of 'gratia plena' and the deferral of 'Dominus tecum' until Segment 2 heightens rhetorical structure and helps to set up the ensuing series of alternating units of the text.

It is surely worth noting that the mistakes all happened within the first third of the second part, as though by the time he had finished the rest of the piece and begun preparing the fair copy he had forgotten what he was doing and could no longer tell by simply looking at what he had jotted down. His mistakes are interesting in that they reveal aspects of the musical structure. As he turned the page of his fair copy, it was easy to shift to the wrong part. The process of preparing the fair copy required significant effort; it also allowed for

[44] Florence, Biblioteca Nazionale Centrale, Magl. XIX.117. See Owens, *Composers at Work*, ch. 8.

[45] I cite these passages from Silke Leopold, *Monteverdi: Music in Transition*, trans. Anne Smith (Oxford, 1991), 25. Monteverdi was composing music for the wedding festivities in Parma in 1628.

revisions (for example, the change in text) that continued to improve the piece.

To summarize briefly, the evidence is fragmentary but we can make a few observations. The most important is that Palestrina was clearly not using a score for composing. That may be a surprising conclusion, given the well-known fact that he prepared a score of the music Duke Guglielmo had sent for his comments so that he could study it ('per meglio contemplarlo'), but it fits the evidence of all other known manuscripts of vocal music.[46] Most examples of composition in score come not from vocal but from keyboard music.[47] It seems likely that he may have used several other arrangements instead, including quasi-score, choirbook format, a haphazard arrangement of parts on a page, and possibly even separate sheets of paper. Secondly, he continued to revise and polish his music both while he prepared fair copies and afterwards. Thirdly, he may have used the lute in composing, probably as a way of sounding out the music and possibly as a way of notating it. For now, I believe that that is all the evidence will allow us to say.

Postscript: The long-awaited facsimile edition of Rome SG 59 (*Il Codice 59 dell' Archivio Musicale della Basilica di San Giovanni in Laterano autografo di Giovanni Pierluigi da Palestrina*, edizione anastatica a cura di Giancarlo Rostirolla, Palestrina: Fondazione Giovanni Pierluigi da Palestrina, 1996) appeared while this article was in press, too late to be taken into consideration.

[46] A translation of Palestrina's letter of 3 March 1570 can be found in Palestrina, *Pope Marcellus Mass*, ed. Lewis Lockwood (New York, 1975), 25. See Knud Jeppesen, 'Über einen Brief Palestrinas', in K. Weinmann (ed.), *Festschrift Peter Wagner zum 60. Geburtstag* (Leipzig, 1926), 100–7.

[47] For example, Bergamo, Biblioteca Civica, Misericordia Maggiore 1143 and Florence, Biblioteca Nazionale Centrale, MS II.I.295. One exception is a draft of an eight-voice Magnificat found in Coimbra, Biblioteca Geral da Universidade, MS 48; it is significant that this manuscript, a large anthology in score, was copied by an organist. These examples are discussed in *Composers at Work*.

Appendix: Inventory of Rome, San Giovanni in Laterano, Codex 59

No.	Folio	Title/incipit	Liturgical function	Clefs	Period/hand (Casimiri)	Rubric/comments	CG 31	1589
Section 1: Lamentations								
1	1r	De lamentatione	Lam III/1 (sections 1, 6, 7)	g2g2g2c3	second	singers: 1573–8		
2	1r	[Miserere mei] textless	psalm, *falso bordone*	c1c2c3c4F4	second			
3	1v–2r	Incipit lamentatio	Lam 1/1	c1c1c2c3	first	1588/1		
4	2v–3r	De lamentatione	Lam II/1, beginning	c1c1c2c3	first			
5	2v–3r	Heth. Peccatum	Lam 1/2, fragment	c1c1c2c3	first			
	3v–5r	continuation of 4	Lam II/1	c1c1c2c3	first			
	5v–6r	continuation of 1	Lam III/1 (sections 2–5, 8–9)		first	5v: 3.a sera lectio p.a il principio in capo del libro		
Section 2: Hymns								
6	6v–7r	Aurea luce *Et decore rosco	SS Peter and Paul	c1c3c4F4	second		24	19
7	7v–8r	Lauda mater ecclesia *Lauda christi	St Mary Magdalene	g2c2c3F3	second		25	20
8	8v–9r	Petrus beatus catenarum laqueos *Catenarum	St Peter in Chains	g2c1c3F4	second		26	21
9	8v–10r	Quicumque Christum quaeritis *Oculos	Transfiguration	c1c3c4F4	second		27	22

No.	Folios	Incipit	Occasion	Clefs	Position	Notes		
10	9v–10r	Tibi Christe splendor patris *Vita virtus	St Michael Archangel	c1c3c4F4	second	crossed out; 9v: In S.ti Michaelis Archangeli voltate tredici carte	29	24
11	10v–12r	Christe redemptor omnium *Conserva	All Saints	g2c2c3F3	second		30	25
12	11v–13r	Exultet coelum laudibus *Resultet	Apostles	c1c3c4F3	second		36	27
13	13v–14r	Deus tuorum militum *Sors et corona	One martyr	c1c3c4F4	second		37	29
14	14v–15r	Sanctorum meritis *Inclita gaudia	Many martyrs	c1c3c4F4	second		38	31
15	15v–16r	Iste Confessor *Domini sacratus	Confessors	c1c3c4F4	second		39	32
16	16v–17r	Iesu corona virginum *Quem mater	Virgins	g2c2c3F3	second		40	34
17	17v–18r	Huius obtentu *Deus alme	Martyrs	c1c3c4F4	second		41	35
18	17v–19r	Urbs beata *Dicta pacis	Dedication of a church	c1c3c4F4	second		34	30
19	19v–20r	Rex gloriose martirum *Corona	Many martyrs (Paschal Time)	g2c2c3F3	second			
20	20v–21r	Iesu corona virginum *Quem	Virgins (Paschal Time)	g2c2c3F3	second		35	33
21	21v–22r	Vexilla regis prodeunt *Quo vulneratus	Invention of the Holy Cross	g2c2c3F3	second		32	17
22	22v–23r	Tibi Christe splendor patris *Vita	St Michael Archangel	c1c3c4F4	second		28	23

Section 3: Lamentations

No.	Folios	Incipit	Occasion	Clefs	Position
23	23v–26r	Incipit oratio	Lam III/3	c1c2c3c4F3F4	first
24	26v–27r	Ecce nunc benedicite Dominum	psalm	g2c2c3c4	second
25	27v–28r	Nunc dimittis	canticle	g2c2c3c3	second

No.	Folio	Title/incipit	Liturgical function	Clefs	Period/hand (Casimiri)	Rubric/comments	CG 31	1589
26	28ᵛ–30ʳ	Incipit lamentatio	Lam I/1	c2c3c3c4	second			
27	29ᵛ–31ʳ	Vau	Lam I/2	c3c3c4F3	second			
28	31ᵛ–33ʳ	Iod	Lam I/3	c4c4c4F3F4	second			
29	33ᵛ–34ʳ	Lamed	Lam II/2	c4c4c4F4	'altra mano?'	33ᵛ: lectio prima de lamentatione cogitavit dominus in principio del librro a .3. carte overo inanti [crossed out] dopo questa 34ᵛ: Magna est tre fogli voltate		
30	34ᵛ–36ʳ 36ᵛ–37ʳ	De lamentatione continuation of 29	Lam II/1	c3c4c4F4	second 'altra mano?'			
31	37ᵛ–39ʳ	Aleph	Lam II/3	c3c3c4c4F3	second			
32	39ᵛ–42ʳ	Aleph. Quomodo	Lam III/2	c4c4c4F3F4	'calligraphic'	39ʳ: Sabbato Sancto Lectio prima de lamentatione in capite libbri 3. sera		
33	42ᵛ–45ʳ	Incipit oratio	Lam III/3	c3c3c4c4F3F4	'altra mano?'			
Section 4: hymns								
34	45ᵛ–46ʳ	Conditor alme siderum* Eterna lux	Advent	g2c2c3F3	'calligraphic?/second'	chant incipit	–	–

35	46ᵛ–49ʳ	Conditor alme siderum *Eterna lux	Advent		second	c1c3c4F4	1	1
36	49ᵛ–53ʳ	Christe redemptor omnium* Ex patre	Christmas		second	g2c2c3F3	2	2
37	53ᵛ–55ʳ	A solis ortus *Ad usque terre	Christmas, lauds		second	g2c2c3c4	3	3
38	55ᵛ–56ʳ	Salvete flores martyrum *Quos lucis	Holy Innocents		second	g2c2c3F3	4	4
39	56ᵛ–59ʳ	Hostis Herodes impie *Christum	Epiphany		second	g2c2c3F3	5	5
40	59ᵛ–61ʳ	Lucis creator optime *Lucem	Sundays		second	g2c2c3F3	6	6
41	61ᵛ–63ʳ	Immense celi	Feria II		second	g2c2c3F3	7	–
42	62ᵛ–63ʳ	Tristes erant apostoli *De nece	Apostles (Paschal Time)	added	second	g2c2c3F3	31	26
43	63ᵛ–65ʳ	Telluris ingens / 42 continued	Feria III		second	g2c2c3F3	8	–
44	65ᵛ–66ʳ	Coeli deus santissime / 42 continued	Feria IIII		second	g2c2c3F3	9	–
45	66ᵛ–67ʳ	Magne deus	Feria V		second	g2c2c3c4	10	–
46	67ᵛ–69ʳ	Deus tuorum militum *Sors et corona	Martyr (Paschal Time)	added	second	g2c2c3F3	33	28
47	69ᵛ–71ʳ, 70ᵛ–71ʳ	Plasmator hominis / continuation of 46	Feria VI		second	g2c2c3c4	11	–
48	71ᵛ–72ʳ	O lux beata trinitas *Et principalis	Saturdays		second	c1c3c4F4	12	7
49	72ᵛ–73ʳ	Audi benigne conditor *Nostras preces	Saturdays, Lent		second	g2c2c3F3	13	–
50	73ᵛ–75ʳ	Ad preces nostras *Deitatis aures	Sundays, Lent		second	g2c2c3F3	14	8
51	75ᵛ–77ʳ	Vexilla regis prodeunt *Fulget crucis	Passion Sunday		second	g2c2c3F3	15	9

BIBLIOGRAPHY

ADAMI, ANDREA, *Osservazioni per ben regolare il coro de i cantori della Cappella Pontificia* (Rome, 1711; facs. edn., Musurgiana, 1; Lucca, 1988).

ALBERIGO, GIUSEPPE, *Chiesa conciliare: identità e significato del conciliarismo* (Testi e ricerche di scienze religiose, 19; Brescia, 1981).

ALLSEN, JON MICHAEL, 'Style and Intertextuality in the Isorhythmic Motet 1400–1440' (Ph.D. diss., University of Wisconsin-Madison, 1992).

AMBROS, AUGUST WILHELM, *Geschichte der Musik* (2nd edn., Leipzig, 1881).

AMIET, ROBERT, 'La Messe pour l'unité des chrétiens', *Revue des sciences religieuses*, 28 (1954), 1–35; revised as 'La Messe "pro unitate ecclesiae" ', *Ephemerides liturgicae*, 76 (1962), 296–334.

ANTONOWYTSCH, MYROSLAW, 'Renaissance-Tendenzen in den Fortuna-desperata-Messen von Josquin und Obrecht', *Musikforschung*, 9 (1956), 1–26.

APEL, WILLI (ed.), *French Secular Compositions of the Fourteenth Century* (CMM 53; American Institute of Musicology, 1970).

ATLAS, ALLAN W., *Music at the Aragonese Court of Naples* (Cambridge, 1985).

AUBERY, ANTOINE, *Histoire générale des cardinaux*, 5 vols. (Paris, 1642–9).

BACCHELLI, RICCARDO, *La congiura di don Giulio d'Este* (Milan, 1958).

BAINI, GIUSEPPE, *Memorie storico-critiche della vita e delle opere di Giovanni Pierluigi da Palestrina*, 2 vols. (Rome, 1828; repr. Hildesheim, 1966).

BANNISTER, HENRY MARRIOTT (ed.), *Sequentiae Ineditae: Liturgische Prosen des Mittelalters aus Handschriften und Frühdrucken* (Analecta Hymnica, 40; Leipzig, 1902, repr. New York, 1962).

BARBLAN, GUGLIELMO, 'Vita musicale alla corte sforzesca', in *Storia di Milano*, ix: *L'epoca di Carlo V. (1536–1559)* (Milan, 1961), 787–852.

Basevi Codex, Florence, Biblioteca del Conservatorio, MS 2439, ed. Honey Meconi (Peer, 1990).

BENT, MARGARET, 'A Contemporary Perception of Early Fifteenth-Century Style: Bologna Q15 as a Document of Scribal Editorial Initiative', *MD* 41 (1987), 183–201.

—— 'Fauvel and Marigny: Which Came First?' in Margaret Bent and Andrew Wathey (eds.), *Fauvel Studies: Allegory, Chronicle, Music, and Image in Paris, Bibliothèque Nationale, MS fr. 146* (Oxford, 1997).

—— 'The Fourteenth-Century Italian Motet', *L'Ars nova italiana del Trecento*, 6 (Certaldo, 1992), 85–125.

—— 'Humanists and Music, Music and Humanities', in Raffaele Pozzi (ed.), *Tendenze e metodi nella ricerca musicologica. Atti del Convegno internazionale (Latina 27–29 Settembre 1990)* (Florence, 1995), 29–38.

—— 'New Sacred Polyphonic Fragments of the Early Quattrocento', *Studi musicali*, 9 (1980), 175–9.

BENT, MARGARET, 'A Note on the Dating of the Trémoïlle Manuscript', in Brian Gillingham and Paul Merkley (eds.), *Beyond the Moon: Festschrift Luther Dittmer* (Ottawa, 1990), 217–42.

—— 'Pietro Emiliani's Chaplain Bartolomeo Rossi da Carpi and the Lamentations of Johannes de Quadris in Vicenza', *Saggiatore musicale*, 2 (1995), 5–16.

—— 'A Preliminary Assessment of the Independence of English Trecento Notations', *L'Ars nova italiana del Trecento*, 4 (1978), 65–82.

—— (ed.) *The Fountains Fragments* (Musical Sources, 26; Clarabricken, 1987).

—— with Howlett, David, '*Subtiliter alternare*: The Yoxford Motet *O amicus/ Precursoris*', in Peter M. Lefferts and Brian Seirup (eds.), *Studies in Medieval Music: Festschrift for Ernest Sanders* (New York, 1990) = *Current Musicology*, 45–7 (1990), 43–84.

BERNSTEIN, LAWRENCE F., 'Notes on the Origin of the Parisian Chanson', *Journal of Musicology*, 1 (1982), 275–326.

BERTOLOTTI, ANTONIO, *Musici alla corte dei Gonzaga in Mantova* (Milan, 1890).

BESSELER, HEINRICH, 'Dufay in Rom', *AfMw* 15 (1958), 1–19; repr. with additions in *Miscelánea en homenaje a monseñor Higinio Anglés*, 2 vols. (Barcelona, 1958–61), i. 111–34.

—— 'Hat Matheus de Perusio Epoche gemacht?', *Musikforschung*, 8 (1955), 19–23.

—— 'Studien zur Musik des Mittelalters I: Neue Quellen des 14. und beginnenden 15. Jahrhunderts', *AfMw* 7 (1925).

—— 'Studien zur Musik des Mittelalters II: Die Motette von Franko von Köln bis Philipp von Vitry', *AfMw* 8 (1926), 137–258.

BESUTTI, PAOLA, 'Catalogo tematico delle monodie liturgiche della Basilica Palatina di S. Barbara in Mantova', *Le fonti musicali in Italia, studi e ricerche*, 2 (1988), 53–66.

—— 'Giovanni Pierluigi da Palestrina e la liturgia Mantovana', in *Atti del II Convegno internazionale di studi palestriniani* (Palestrina, 1991), 157–64.

BIZZOCHI, ROBERTO, *Chiesa e potere nella Toscana del Quattrocento* (Annali dell'Istituto Storico Italo-Germanico, 6; Bologna, 1987).

BLIEMETZRIEDER, F., *Literarische Polemik zu Beginn des grossen abendländischen Schismas* (Vienna, 1909).

BLUME, CLEMENS, and BANNISTER, HENRY MARRIOTT (eds.), *Liturgische Prosen des Übergangsstiles und der zweiten Epoche* (Analecta Hymnica, 54; Leipzig, 1915, repr. New York, 1961).

BOCKHOLDT, RUDOLF, 'Die Hymnen der Handschrift Cambrai 6: Zwei unbekannte Vertonungen von Dufay?', *TVNM* 29 (1979), 75–91.

BOONE, GRAEME MACDONALD, 'Dufay's Early Chansons: Chronology and Style in the Manuscript Oxford, Bodleian Library, Canonici Misc. 213' (Ph.D. diss., Harvard University, 1987).

BORREN, CHARLES VAN DEN (ed.), *Polyphonia Sacra* (Burnham, 1928).

BOUQUET, MARIE-THÉRÈSE, 'La cappella musicale dei duchi di Savoia dal 1450 al 1500', *Rivista italiana di musicologia*, 3 (1968), 233–85.

—— 'La cappella musicale dei duchi di Savoia dal 1504 al 1550', *Rivista italiana di musicologia*, 5 (1970), 3–36.

BOURSY, RICHARD, 'The Mystique of the Sistine Chapel Choir in the Romantic Era', *Journal of Musicology*, 11 (1993), 277–329.

BOWERS, ROGER, 'Fixed Points in the Chronology of English Fourteenth-Century Polyphony' *Music and Letters*, 71 (1990), 313–35.

BOYLE, LEONARD A., *A Survey of the Vatican Archives and of its Medieval Holdings* (Subsidia Medievalia, 1; Toronto, 1972).

BRASSART, JOHANNES, *Opera omnia*, ed. Keith Mixter, ii (CMM 35; American Institute of Musicology, 1971).

BRAUNER, MITCHELL P., 'The Catalogue of Raffaele Panuzzi and the Repertory of the Papal Chapel in the 15th and 16th Centuries', *Journal of Musicology*, 8 (1990), 427–43.

—— 'Jean du Conseil (Johannes Consilium): His Life and Motets' (M.F.A. thesis, Brandeis University, 1978).

—— 'Music from the Cappella Sistina at the Cappella Giulia', *Journal of Musicology*, 3 (1984), 287–311.

—— 'The Parvus Manuscripts: A Study of Vatican Polyphony, ca. 1535 to 1580' (Ph.D. diss., Brandeis University, 1982).

BREWER, CHARLES, 'The Introduction of the "Ars Nova" into East Central Europe: A Study of Late Medieval Polish Sources' (Ph.D. diss., City University of New York, 1984).

BROWN, HOWARD MAYER, 'The *Chanson rustique*: Popular Elements in the 15th- and 16th-Century Chanson', *JAMS* 12 (1959), 16–26.

—— 'The Genesis of a Style: The Parisian Chanson, 1500–1530', in James Haar (ed.), *Chanson and Madrigal 1480–1530: Studies in Comparison and Contrast* (Cambridge, MASS., 1964), 1–36.

BULAEUS, CAESAR EGASSIUS [César Du Boulay], *Historia Universitatis Parisiensis, collegiorum plus quam triginta fundationes, statuta, privilegia, reformationes. . . aliarum universitatum erectiones. . . aliaque id genus ex autographis desumpta manuscriptis codicibus et membranis*, 4 vols. (Paris, 1668; repr. 1966).

Bullarium privilegiorum ac diplomatum romanorum pontificum amplissima collectio (Rome, 1740); repr. as *Magnum bullarium romanum* (Graz, 1964).

BURCKARD, JOHANNES, *Liber Notarum ab anno MCCCCLXXXIII usque ad annum MDVI*, ed. Enrich Celani, 2 vols. (Rerum italicarum scriptores, 32; Città di Castello, 1906–13).

BURNEY, CHARLES, *The Present State of Music in France and Italy*, in P. A. Scholes (ed.), *Dr. Burney's Musical Tours of Europe*, vol. i: *An Eighteenth-Century Musical Tour in France and Italy* (London, 1959).

BURNS, CHARLES, *Golden Rose and Blessed Sword: Papal Gifts to Scottish Monarchs* (Glasgow, 1970).

BUSNOYS, ANTOINE, *Collected Works*, Part 2: *The Latin-Texted Works*, ed. Richard Taruskin (New York, 1990).

CAMERON, JAMES KERR, 'Henry of Langenstein: A Letter on Behalf of a Council of Peace', in Matthew Spinka (ed.), *Advocates of Reform: From Wyclif to Erasmus* (Philadelphia, 1963), 106–39.

CARDELLA, LORENZO, *Memorie storiche de' Cardinali della santa romana chiesa*, 9 vols. (Rome, 1792–7).

CARON, PIER GIOVANNI, *La Rinuncia all'ufficio ecclesiastico* (Milan, 1946).

CARTECHINI, PIO, 'La Miscellanea Notarile dell'Archivio di Stato di Macerata', in *Atti del III Convegno di Studi Maceratesi, Camerino 26 Novembre 1967* (Macerata, 1968), 3–22.

CASIMIRI, RAFFAELE, *Il 'Codice 59' dell'Archivio Musicale Lateranense autografo di Giovanni Pierluigi da Palestrina* (Rome, 1919).

—— (ed.), *I Diarii Sistini: I primi 25 anni (1535–1559)* (Rome, 1939; originally published in *Note d'archivio per la storia musicale*, 1924–39).

CATTA, DOMINIQUE, 'Aux origines du Kyriale', *Revue Grégorienne*, 34 (1955), 175–82.

CATTIN, GIULIO, 'Ricerche sulla musica a S. Giustina di Padova all'inizio del Quattrocento (I): Il copista Rolando da Casale. Nuovi frammenti musicali nell'Archivio di Stato', *Annales musicologiques*, 7 (1978), 17–41.

—— and FACCHIN, FRANCESCO (eds.), *French Sacred Music* (PMFC 23A/B; Monaco, 1989).

CÉLIER, LÉON, *Les Dataires du XVᵉ siècle et les origines de la Daterie apostolique* (Bibliothèque des Écoles Françaises d'Athènes et de Rome, 103; Paris, 1910).

CHAILLEY, JACQUES, *40,000 Years of Music: Man in Search of Music*, trans. R. Myers (New York, 1964).

CHARLES, SYDNEY R., 'Hillary–Hyllayre: How Many Composers?', *Music and Letters*, 55 (1974), 61–9.

—— (ed.), *The Music of the Pepys Ms. 1236* (CMM 40; American Institute of Musicology, 1967).

CHIAPPINI, L., *Gli Estensi* (Varese, 1967).

Chronicum siculum incertis auctoris ab anno 340 ad annum 1396, ed. Jo. de Blasiis (Naples, 1887).

CICONIA, JOHANNES, *The Works*, ed. Margaret Bent and Anne Hallmark (PMFC 24; Monaco, 1985).

CLARK, ALICE V., 'Concordare cum Materia: The Tenor in the Fourteenth-Century Motet' (Ph.D. diss., Princeton University, 1996).

CLERCX, SUZANNE, 'Ancora su Johannes Ciconia (1335–1411)', *Nuova rivista musicale italiana*, 11 (1977), 573–90.

—— *Johannes Ciconia: Un musicien liégeois et son temps (vers 1335–1411)*, 2 vols. (Classe des Beaux-Arts, Mémoires, ser. 2, vol. 10, fasc. 1a/1b; Brussels, 1960).

CLINKSCALE, EDWARD, 'The Complete Works of Antoine de Févin' (Ph.D. diss., New York University, 1965).

COBIN, MARIAN, 'The Aosta Manuscript: A Central Source of Early Fifteenth-Century Sacred Music' (Ph.D. diss., New York University, 1978).

COHEN, JUDITH, *The Six L'homme armé Masses in Naples, Biblioteca Nazionale, MS VI E 40* (American Institute of Musicology, 1968).

Colloques de Wégimont II, 1955: L'Ars nova. Recueil d'études sur la musique du XIVᵉ siècle (Paris, 1959).

Corpus Iuris Canonici, pars secunda, Decretalium Collectiones; Decretalium Gregorii pape IX [et al.] (Leipzig, 1879; repr. Graz, 1955).

CORSI, GIUSEPPE, *Poesie musicali del Trecento* (Bologna, 1970).

COURTEL, ANNE-LISE, 'Les Clientèles des cardinaux limousins en 1378', *Mélanges de l'École Française de Rome. Moyen Age – Temps Modernes*, 89 (1977), 889–944.

—— *See also* Rey-Courtel

COVILLE, A., 'Philippe de Vitri: notes biographiques', *Romania*, 59 (1933), 520–47.

CRAWFORD, DAVID, 'Guillaume Dufay, Hellenism, and Humanism', in Carmelo P. Comberiati and Matthew C. Steel (eds.), *Music from the Middle Ages through the Twentieth Century: Essays in Honor of Gwynn S. McPeek* (New York, 1988), 81–93.

CREIGHTON, G., 'When Did a Man in the Renaissance Grow Old?', *Studies in the Renaissance*, 14 (1967), 7–32.

CROWDER, C. M. D., *Unity, Heresy, and Reform, 1378–1460: The Conciliar Response to the Great Schism* (New York, 1977).

CUMMING, JULIE EMELYN, 'Concord out of Discord: Occasional Motets of the Early Quattrocento' (Ph.D. diss., Unviersity of California, Berkeley, 1987).

CUMMINGS, ANTHONY M., 'A Florentine Sacred Repertory from the Medici Restoration (Manuscript II. I. 232 of the Biblioteca nazionale centrale, Firenze' (Ph.D. diss., Princeton University, 1979/80).

—— 'Toward an Interpretation of the Sixteenth-Century Motet', *JAMS* 34 (1981), 43–59.

D'ACCONE, FRANK A., 'Music and Musicians at Santa Maria del Fiore in the Early Quattrocento', in *Scritti in onore di Luigi Ronga* (Milan and Naples, 1973), 99–126.

—— 'Una nuova fonte dell'Ars Nova italiana: il codice di S. Lorenzo 2211', *Studi musicali*, 13 (1984), 3–31.

—— 'The Singers of San Giovanni in Florence during the 15th Century', *JAMS* 14 (1961), 307–58.

D'ALESSI, GIOVANNI, *La Cappella musicale del duomo di Treviso* (Treviso, 1954).

DEAN, JEFFREY, 'The Repertory of the Cappella Giulia in the 1560s', *JAMS* 41 (1988), 465–90.

—— 'The Scribes of the Sistine Chapel 1501–1527' (Ph.D. diss., University of Chicago, 1984).

—— (ed.), *Vatican City, Biblioteca Apostolica Vaticana, Cappella Sistina MS 46* (Renaissance Music in Facsimile, 21; New York and London, 1986).

DELARUELLE, ÉTIENNE, *et al.*, *L'Église au temps du Grand Schisme et de crise conciliare (1378–1449)* (Paris, 1962).

DE LUCA, ATTILIO, 'Frammenti di codici in beneventana nelle Marche', in *Miscellanea in memoria di Giorgio Cencetti* (Turin, 1973), 101–40.

DENIFLE, HEINRICH, *Chartularium Universitatis Parisiensis*, 4 vols. (Paris, 1894; repr. Brussels, 1964).

DES PREZ, JOSQUIN, *Werken*, ed. Albert Smijers *et al.* (Amsterdam, 1921–69).

DESPY, G., 'Notes sur les offices de la curie d'Avignon: les fonctions du "magister capelle pape" ', *Bulletin de l'Institut historique belge de Rome*, 28 (1953), 21–30.

DE WEESE, MALCOLM L., 'A Study of Decision-Making in France During the Reign of Charles VI (The Rejection of the Avignon Papacy 1395)' (Ph.D. diss., University of Washington, 1973).

DI BACCO, GIULIANO, and NÁDAS, JOHN, 'Verso uno "stile internazionale" della musica nelle cappelle papali e cardinalizie durante il Grande Scisma (1378–1417): il caso di Johannes Ciconia da Liège', *Collectanea I*, 7–74.

DONELLA, VALENTINO, 'La Costituzione "Docta Sanctorum Patrum" di Giovanni XXII (1324–25): una persistente attualità', *Rivista internazionale di musica sacra*, 4 (1983), 353–77.

DROZ, E., and THIBAULT, G., 'Un chansonnier de Philippe le Bon', *Revue de musicologie*, 7 (1926), 1–8.

DUFAY, GUILLAUME, *Opera omnia*, ed. Heinrich Besseler, 6 vols. (CMM 1; Rome, 1950–96).

DYKMANS, MARC, *L'Œuvre d'Agostino Patrizi Piccolomini ou le cérémonial papal de la première Renaissance*, 2 vols. (Studi e testi, 293–4; Vatican City, 1980–2).

EGIDI, FRANCESCO, 'Un frammento di codice musicale del secolo XIV', in *Nozze Bonmartini–Tracagni XIX Novembre MCMXXV* (Rome, 1925).

EHRLE, FRANZ, and EGGER, HERMANN, *Der vatikanische Palast in seiner Entwicklung bis zur Mitte des XV. Jahrhunderts* (Studi e testi per la storia del Palazzo Apostolico Vaticano, 2; Vatican City, 1935).

ESCH, ARNOLD, 'Über den Zusammenhang von Kunst und Wirtschaft in der italienischen Renaissance: Ein Forschungsbericht', *Zeitschrift für historische Forschung*, 8 (1981), 179–222.

ESPOSITO, ANNA, ' "Magistro Zaccara" e l'antifonario dell'Ospedale di S. Spirito in Sassia', in Paolo Cherubini, Anna Esposito, *et al.*, 'Il costo del libro', in Massimo Miglio *et al.* (eds.), *Scrittura, biblioteche e stampa a Roma nel Quattrocento, Atti del 2. seminario* (Littera Antiqua, 3; Vatican City, 1983), 334–42, 446–9.

EUBEL, KONRAD, *Hierarchia Catholica medii aevii sive summorum pontificum, S.R.E. cardinalium, ecclesiarum antistitum series ab anno 1198 usque ad annum 1431 perducta* (2nd edn., Münster and Regensburg, 1913–14).

FACCHIN, FRANCO, 'Una nuova fonte musicale trecentesca nell'Archivio di Stato di Padova', in Giulio Cattin and Antonio Lovato (eds.), *Contributi per la storia della musica sacra a Padova* (Fonti e ricerche di storia ecclesiastica padovana, 24; Padua, 1993), 115–39.

FALLOWS, DAVID, 'Ciconia padre e figlio', *Rivista italiana di musicologia*, 11 (1976), 171–7.

—— *Dufay* (London, 1982; rev. edn., 1987).

—— 'Two Equal Voices: A French Song Repertory with Music for Two More Works of Oswald von Wolkenstein' *EMH*, 7 (1987), 227–41.

—— (ed.), *Oxford, Bodleian Library MS. Canon. Misc. 213* (Late Medieval and Early Renaissance Music in Facsimile, 1; Chicago and London, 1995).

FENLON, IAIN, *Music and Patronage in Sixteenth-Century Mantua* (Cambridge, 1980).

—— Patronage, Music and Liturgy in Renaissance Mantua', in Thomas F. Kelly (ed.), *Plainsong in the Age of Polyphony* (Cambridge, 1992), 209–35.

FESTA, COSTANZO, *Opera Omnia*, ed. Alexander Main and Albert Seay, 8 vols. (CMM 25; American Institute of Musicology, 1962–79).

FINK, KARL AUGUST, *Repertorium Germanicum*, iv (Berlin, 1958).

FISCHER, KURT VON, 'Bemerkungen zur Trecento-Motette: Überlegungen zu einem Aufsatz von Margaret Bent', in *Die Motette: Beiträge zu ihrer Gattungsgeschichte* (Neue Studien zur Musikwissenschaft, 5; Mainz, 1991), 19–28.

—— 'Bemerkungen zur Überlieferung und zum Stil der geistlichen Werke des Antonius dictus Zacharias de Teramo', *MD* 41 (1987), 161–82.

—— 'Neue Quellen zur Musik des 13., 14. und 15. Jahrhunderts', *Acta musicologica*, 36 (1964), 79–97.

—— *Studien zur italienischen Musik des Trecento und frühen Quattrocento* (Publikationen der Schweizerischen musikforschenden Gesellschaft, 2/5; Berne, 1956).

FLORIO, JOHN, *A Worlde of Wordes* (London, 1598; repr. New York, 1972).

FOREVILLE, RAYMONDE, 'L'Idée de Jubilé, chez les théologiens et les canonistes (XIIᵉ–XIIIᵉ s.) avant l'institution du Jubilé romain (1300)', in *Thomas Becket dans la tradition historique et hagiographique* (London, 1981), essay no. XIV.

—— *Le Jubilé de Saint Thomas Becket: du XIIIᵉ au XVᵉ siècle (1220–1470)* (Paris, 1958).

FRANSEN, G., *Les Décrétales et les collections de décrétales* (Tournhout, 1972).

FRATI, LUIGI (ed.), *Le due spedizioni militari di Giulio II* (Bologna, 1886).

FRENZ, THOMAS, *Die Kanzlei der Päpste der Hochrenaissance (1471–1527)* (Bibliothek des Deutschen Historischen Instituts in Rom, 63; Tübingen, 1986).

FREY, HERMAN-WALTHER (ed.), *Die Diarien der Sixtinischen Kapelle in Rom der Jahre 1560 und 1561* (Düsseldorf, 1959).

—— 'Das Diarium der Sixtinischen Sängerkapelle in Rom für das Jahr 1594 (Nr. 19)', *Analecta musicologica*, 14 (1974), 445–505.

—— 'Das Diarium der Sixtinischen Sängerkapelle in Rom für das Jahr 1596 (Nr. 21)', *Analecta musicologica*, 23 (1985), 129–204.

—— 'Die Gesänge der Sixtinischen Kapelle an den Sonntagen und hohen Kirchenfesten des Jahres 1616', in *Mélanges Eugène Tisserant*, 7 vols. (Studi e testi, 231–7; Vatican City, 1964), vi. 395–437.

—— 'Regesten zur päpstlichen Kapelle unter Leo X. und zu seiner Privatkapelle', *Musikforschung*, 8 (1955), 58–73, 178–99, 412–37; 9 (1956), 46–57, 139–57, 411–19.

FULLER, SARAH, 'A Phantom Treatise of the Fourteenth Century? The *Ars Nova*', *Journal of Musicology*, 4 (1986), 23–50.

GALLO, F. ALBERTO, 'Da un codice italiano di mottetti del primo Trecento', *Quadrivium*, 9 (1968), 25–36.

—— (ed.), *Il codice Squarcialupi* (Lucca and Florence, 1993).

—— and VON FISCHER, KURT (eds.), *Italian Sacred and Ceremonial Music* (PMFC 13; Monaco, 1987).

—— —— (eds.), *Italian Sacred Music* (PMFC 12; Monaco, 1976).

GARDNER, E. G., *The King's Court Poets: A Study of the Life and Times of Lodovico Ariosto* (London, 1906).

GASTOUT, MARGUERITE (ed.), *Suppliques et lettres d'Urbain VI (1378–1389) et de Boniface IX (cinq premières années: 1389–1394)* (Analecta Vaticano-Belgica, 29: Documents relatifs au Grand Schisme, vii; Rome, 1976).

GENET, ELZÉAR (CARPENTRAS), *Opera omnia*, iii, ed. Albert Seay (CMM 58; American Institute of Musicology, 1972).

GERBER, RUDOLF, 'Römische Hymnenzyklen des späten 15. Jahrhunderts', *AfMw* 12 (1955), 50–73.

GHERARDI, JACOPO, *Il Diario romano di Jacopo Gherardi da Volterra dal vii settembre MCCCCLXXIX al xii agosto MCCCCLXXXIV*, ed. Evaristo Carusi (Rerum Italicarum Scriptores, 23/3; Città di Castello, 1904–6).

GHISI, FEDERICO, 'Inno lauda polifonica all'Assunta ritrovato nell'Archivio Comunale di Cortona', *Quadrivium*, 15 (1974), 105–11.

GILLMANN, F., 'Die Resignation der Benefizien', *Archiv für Katholischen Kirchenrecht*, 80 (1900), 50–79, 346–78, 523–69, 665–788; 81 (1901), 223–42, 433–60.

GIRGENSOHN, DIETER, 'Il testamento di Pietro Miani ('Emilianus') vescovo di Vicenza (†1433)', *Archivio veneto*, ser. 5, vol. 132 (1989), 5–60.

GLAREANUS, HENRICUS, *Dodekachordon* (Basle, 1547; facs. edn., Monuments of Music and Music Literature in Facsimile, 2/65; New York, 1967).

GRAFTON, ANTHONY, 'The Ancient City Restored: Archaeology, Ecclesiastical History, and Egyptology', in Grafton, *Rome Reborn*, 87–123.

—— (ed.), *Rome Reborn: The Vatican Library and Renaissance Culture* (Washington, DC, 1993).

GREENE, GORDON (ed.), *French Secular Music* (PMFC 18–19; Monaco, 1981–2).

GREGOROVIUS, FERDINAND, *History of the City of Rome in the Middle Ages*, 7 vols., trans. from the 4th German edn. by Annie Hamilton (London, 1900).

GUILLEMAIN, BERNARD, 'Cardinaux et société curiale aux origines de la double élection de 1378', in *Genèse et débuts du grand schisme d'occident, 1362–1394*, Proceedings of the Conference held in Avignon, 1978, ed. Jean Favier (Colloques Internationaux du Centre National de la Recherche Scientifique, 586; Paris, 1980), 19–30.

—— *La Cour pontificale d'Avignon (1309–1376): Étude d'une société* (Bibliothèque des Écoles Françaises d'Athènes et de Rome, 201; Paris, 1962).

GÜNTHER, URSULA, 'The 14th-Century Motet and its Development', *MD* 12 (1958), 27–58.

—— 'Problems of Dating in Ars nova and Ars subtilior', *L'Ars nova italiana del Trecento*, 4 (1978), 289–301.

—— 'Quelques remarques sur des feuillets récemment découverts à Grottaferrata', *L'Ars nova italiana del Trecento*, 3 (1970), 315–97.

—— 'Unusual Phenomena in the Transmission of Late Fourteenth-Century Polyphonic Music', *MD* 38 (1984), 87–118.

—— 'Zur Biographie einiger Komponisten der Ars subtilior', *AfMw* 21 (1964), 172–99.

—— (ed.), *The Motets of the Manuscripts Chantilly, Musée Condé, 564 (olim 1047) and Modena, Biblioteca Estense, α.M.5.24 (olim lat. 568)* (CMM 39; American Institute of Musicology, 1965).

GUSHEE, LAWRENCE, 'New Sources for the Biography of Johannes de Muris', *JAMS* 22 (1969), 3–26.

HAAR, JAMES, 'The Courtier as Musician: Castiglione's View of the Science and Art of Music', in Ruth W. Hanning and David Rosand (eds.), *Castiglione: The Ideal and the Real in Renaissance Culture* (New Haven, 1983), 165–90.

— 'Palestrina as Historicist: The Two *L'homme armé* Masses', *Journal of the Royal Musical Association*, 121 (1996), 191–205.

— 'Some Remarks on the "Missa La sol fa re mi" ', in Lowinsky and Blackburn (eds.), *Josquin des Prez: Proceedings*, 564–88.

HABERL, FR. X., *Die römische 'schola cantorum' und die päpstlichen Kapellsänger bis zur Mitte des 16. Jahrhunderts* (Bausteine für Musikgeschichte, 3; Leipzig, 1888).

— *Wilhelm Du Fay* (Bausteine für Musikgeschichte, 1; Leipzig, 1885).

HAGGH, BARBARA, 'Itinerancy to Residency: Professional Careers and Performance Practices in 15th Century Sacred Music', *EM* 17 (1989), 359–67.

— 'Music, Liturgy, and Ceremony in Brussels, 1350–1500' (Ph.D. diss., University of Illinois, 1988).

HALLMAN, BARBARA McCLUNG, *Italian Cardinals, Reform, and the Church as Property* (Berkeley, 1985).

HALLMARK, ANNE, 'Gratiosus, Ciconia, and Other Musicians at Padua Cathedral: Some Footnotes to Present Knowledge', *L'Ars nova italiana del Trecento*, 6 (1992), 69–84.

HAMM, CHARLES, *A Chronology of the Works of Guillaume Dufay, Based on a Study of Mensural Practice* (Princeton Studies in Music, 1; Princeton, 1964).

— 'Dating a Group of Dufay Works', *JAMS* 15 (1962), 65–71.

— and SCOTT, ANN BESSER, 'A Study and Inventory of the Manuscript Modena, Biblioteca Estense Alpha X.1.11', *MD* 26 (1972), 101–43.

HANNAS, RUTH, 'Concerning Deletions in the Polyphonic Mass Credo', *JAMS* 5 (1952), 155–86.

HARRISON, FRANK LL., *Music in Medieval Britain*, 2nd edn. (London, 1963).

— (ed.), *Motets of French Provenance* (PMFC 5; Monaco, 1965).

HARVEY, MARGARET, 'The Household of Cardinal Langham', *Journal of Ecclesiastical History*, 47 (1996), 18–44.

— *Solutions to the Schism* (Sankt Ottilien, 1983).

HAY, DENYS, *The Church in Italy in the Fifteenth Century* (Cambridge, 1977).

HAYBURN, ROBERT F., *Papal Legislation on Sacred Music 95 A.D. to 1977 A.D.* (Collegeville, Minn., 1979).

HIGGINS, PAULA, 'Music and Musicians at the Sainte-Chapelle of the Bourges Palace, 1405–1415', in Angelo Pompilio *et al.* (eds.), *International Musicological Society, Report of the Fourteenth Congress, Bologna, 1987: Trasmissione e recezione delle forme di cultura musicale*, 3 vols. (Turin, 1990), iii. 689–701.

— 'Parisian Nobles, a Scottish Princess, and the Woman's Voice in Late Medieval Song', *EMH* 10 (1991), 145–200.

Histoire de l'Église depuis les origines jusqu'à nos jours, ed. F. Delaruelle, P. Ourliac, and

E.-R. Labande, xiv/1: *L'Église au temps du Grand Schisme et de la crise conciliaire* (Paris, 1962).

HOUDOY, JULES, *Histoire artistique de la cathédrale de Cambrai, ancienne église métropolitaine Notre-Dame* (Paris, 1880).

HUBER, RAPHAEL M., *A Documented History of the Franciscan Order: From the Birth of St. Francis to the Division of the Order under Leo X, 1182–1517* (Milwaukee, Wis., 1944).

HUCKE, HELMUT, 'Das Dekret "Docta Sanctorum Patrum" Papst Johannes' XXII', *MD* 38 (1984), 119–31.

HUDSON, BARTON, 'A Neglected Source of Renaissance Polyphony: Rome, Santa Maria Maggiore JJ.III.4', *Acta musicologica*, 48 (1976), 166–80.

— 'Two Ferrarese Masses by Jacob Obrecht', *Journal of Musicology*, 4 (1985–6), 276–302.

HUGHES, ANDREW, *Late Medieval Liturgical Offices: Resources for Electronic Research* (Toronto, 1994).

— and BENT, MARGARET (eds.), *The Old Hall Manuscript*, 3 vols. (CMM 46; American Institute of Musicology, 1969–73).

JEDIN, HUBERT (ed.), *Handbuch der Kirchengeschichte*, iii/2 (Freiburg i. Br., 1968).

JEPPESEN, KNUD, 'Palestriniana: Ein unbekanntes Autogramm und einige unveröffentlichte Falsibordoni des Giovanni Pierluigi da Palestrina', in *Miscelánea en homenaje a Monseñor Higinio Anglés* (Barcelona, 1958–1961), 417–32.

— 'Pierluigi da Palestrina, Herzog Guglielmo Gonzaga und die neugefundenen Mantovaner-Messen Palestrina's', *Acta musicologica*, 25 (1953), 132–79.

— 'Über einen Brief Palestrinas', in K. Weinmann (ed.), *Festschrift Peter Wagner zum 60. Geburtstag* (Leipzig, 1926), 100–7.

JOSEPHSON, NORS, 'The *Missa de Beata Virgine* of the Sixteenth Century' (Ph.D. diss., University of California at Berkeley, 1970).

JUSSIEU, ALEXIS DE, *La Sainte-Chapelle du Château du Chambéry* (Chambéry, 1868).

KAMINSKY, HOWARD, 'The Politics of France's Subtraction of Obedience from Pope Benedict XIII, 27 July, 1398', *Proceedings of the American Philosophical Society*, 115 (1971), 366–97.

— *Simon de Cramaud and the Great Schism* (New Brunswick, NJ, 1983).

KENDALL, P. M., *Louis XI* (New York, 1971).

KIANG, DAWSON, 'Josquin Desprez and a Possible Portrait of the Ottoman Prince Jem in Cappella Sistina Ms 41', *Bibliothèque d'humanisme et Renaissance*, 54 (1990), 411–26.

KÜGLE, KARL, 'Codex Ivrea, Bibl. cap. 115: A French Source "Made in Italy" ', *Revista de Musicología*, 13 (1990), 527–61.

— 'The Manuscript Ivrea, Biblioteca Capitolare 115: Studies in the Transmission and Composition of Ars Nova Polyphony' (Ph.D. diss., New York University, 1993).

LANDOW, GEORGE P., *Hypertext: The Convergence of Contemporary Critical Theory and Technology* (Parallax: Re-Visions of Culture and Society; Baltimore and London, 1992).

LANDWEHR-MELNICKI, MARGARETA, and STÄBLEIN, BRUNO (eds.), *Die Gesänge des altrömischen Graduale Vat. lat. 5319* (Monumenta monodica medii aevi, 2; Kassel, 1970).

LAOR, LIA, 'Concerning the Liturgical Usage of Dufay's Fragmentary Masses', *Current Musicology*, 37–8 (1984), 49–58.

LECCISOTTI, TOMMASO, 'La Congregazione benedettina di S. Giustina e la riforma della chiesa al secolo XV', *Deputazione Romana di Storia Patria Archivo*, 67 (1944), 461.

LEECH-WILKINSON, DANIEL, 'The Emergence of *ars nova*', *Journal of Musicology*, 13 (1995), 285–317.

LEFFERTS, PETER M., *The Motet in England in the Fourteenth Century* (Ann Arbor, 1986).

LE PETIT, NINOT, *Johanni[s] Parvi Opera Omnia*, ed. Barton Hudson (CMM 87; Neuhausen-Stuttgart, 1979).

LESURE, FRANÇOIS, 'La Maîtrise de Langres au XVIᵉ siècle', *Revue de musicologie*, 52 (1966).

LIONNET, JEAN, 'Palestrina e la Cappella Pontificia', in Lino Bianchi and Giancarlo Rostirolla (eds.), *Atti del Convegno internazionale di studi palestriniani: Palestrina e la sua presenza nella musica e nella cultura europea da suo tempo ad oggi, Anno Europeo della Musica 3–5 maggio 1986* (Palestrina, 1991), 127–35.

— 'Performance Practice in the Papal Chapel during the 17th Century', *EM* 15 (1987), 3–15.

— 'Una svolta nella storia del collegio dei cantori pontifici: il decreto del 22 giugno 1665 contro Orazio Benevolo, origine e conseguenze', *Nuova rivista musicale italiana*, 17 (1983), 72–103.

LITTERICK, LOUISE, 'The Manuscript Royal 20.A.XVI of the British Library' (Ph.D. diss., New York University, 1976).

LLORENS, JOSÉ M., *Capellae Sixtinae Codices musicis notis instructi sive manu scripti sive praelo excussi* (Studi e testi, 202; Vatican City, 1960).

— 'Cristóbal de Morales, cantor en la Capilla Pontificia de Paulo III (1535–1545)', *Anuario Musical*, 8 (1953), 39–69.

— 'Los Maestros de la Capilla Apostólica hasta el Pontificado de Sixto V (1585–1590)', *Anuario Musical*, 43 (1988), 35–66.

— 'The Musical Codexes of the Sistine Chapel Written through the Generosity of the Pauline Popes' in James W. Pruett (ed.), *Studies in Musicology: Essays in the History, Style, and Bibliography of Music in Memory of Glen Haydon* (Chapel Hill, NC, 1969), 18–50.

— *Le opere musicali della Cappella Giulia*, i: *Manoscritti e edizioni fino al '700* (Studi e testi, 265; Vatican City, 1971).

— 'Reglamentación del Colegio de Cantores Pontificios: las *Constitutiones Apostolicae* y el *Liber Punctorum Capellae*', *Anuario Musical*, 30 (1975), 97–107.

LOCKWOOD, LEWIS, 'Adrian Willaert and Cardinal Ippolito I d'Este: New Light on Willaert's Early Career in Italy, 1515–1521', *EMH* 5 (1985), 85–112.

— 'Jean Mouton and Jean Michel: French Music and Musicians in Italy, 1505–1520', *JAMS* 32 (1979), 191–246.

— 'Josquin at Ferrara: New Documents and Letters', in Lowinsky and Blackburn (eds.), *Josquin des Prez: Proceedings*, 103–36.

LOCKWOOD, LEWIS, 'Music at Ferrara in the Period of Ercole I d'Este', *Studi musicali*, 1 (1972), 101–31.

—— *Music in Renaissance Ferrara 1400–1505: The Creation of a Musical Centre in the Fifteenth Century* (Oxford, 1984).

LOWINSKY, EDWARD E., 'Ascanio Sforza's Life: A Key to Josquin's Biography and an Aid to the Chronology of his Works', in Lowinsky and Blackburn (eds.), *Josquin des Prez: Proceedings*, 31–75.

—— 'On the Use of Scores by Sixteenth-Century Musicians', in *Music in the Culture of the Renaissance and Other Essays*, ed. Bonnie J. Blackburn (Chicago, 1989), 797–800.

—— (ed.), *The Medici Codex of 1518* (Monuments of Renaissance Music, 3–5; Chicago, 1968).

—— and BLACKBURN, BONNIE J. (eds.), *Josquin des Prez: Proceedings of the International Josquin Festival-Conference* (London, 1976).

LÜTOLF, MAX (ed.), *Das Graduale von Santa Cecilia in Trastevere (cod. Bodmer 74)*, 2 vols. (Cologny-Geneva, 1987).

LÜTTEKEN, LAURENZ, *Guillaume Dufay und die isorhythmische Motette: Gattungstradition und Werkcharacter an der Schwelle zur Neuzeit* (Schriften zur Musikwissenschaft aus Münster, 4; Hamburg, 1993).

MAIANI, BRAD, 'Notes on Matteo da Perugia: Adapting the Ambrosian Liturgy in Polyphony for the Pisan Council', *Studi musicali*, 24 (1995), 3–28.

MARTÈNE, E., and DURAND, E. (eds.), *Thesaurus novus Anecdotorum*, ii (Paris, 1717).

MELVILLE, JOANNA, 'A Study in Coherence in Four Motets by Philippe de Vitry' (MA thesis, University of Wales, Bangor, 1994).

MEUTHEN, ERICH, *Das 15. Jahrhundert* (Oldenbourg Grundriß der Geschichte, 9; Munich, 1984).

MINAMINO, HIROYUKI, 'Sixteenth-Century Lute Treatises with Emphasis on Process and Techniques of Intabulation' (Ph.D. diss., University of Chicago, 1988).

MIXTER, KEITH, 'Johannes Brassart: A Biographical and Bibliographical Study', *MD* 18 (1964), 37–62, and 19 (1965), 99–108.

MÖLLER, HARTMUTH, 'Motetten nach den Offertorium im 17. und 18. Jahrhundert', in *Collectanea II*, 289–331.

MONSON, CRAIG, 'Stylistic Inconsistencies in a Kyrie Attributed to Dufay', *JAMS* 28 (1975), 245–67.

MONTAGNA, GERALD, 'Caron, Hayne, Compère: A Transmission Reassessment', *EMH* 7 (1987), 107–57.

MONTEVERDI, CLAUDIO, *Lettere*, ed. Éva Lax (Florence, 1994).

—— *The Letters of Claudio Monteverdi*, trans. Denis Stevens (rev. edn., Oxford, 1995).

MORLAYE, GUILLAUME, *Œuvres pour le lut*, ed. Jean-Michel and Nathalie Vaccaro, ii: *Manuscrits d'Uppsala* (Paris, 1989).

MUSIELAK, HENRI, 'W poszukiwaniu materiałów do biografii Mikolaja z Radomia', *Muzyka*, 18 (1973), 82–9.

NÁDAS, JOHN, 'Further Notes on Magister Antonius dictus Zacharias de Teramo', *Studi musicali*, 15 (1986), 167–82; 16 (1987), 175–6.

—— 'Manuscript San Lorenzo 2211: Some Further Observations', *L'Ars nova italiana del Trecento*, 6 (1992), 145–68.

—— 'The Transmission of Trecento Secular Polyphony: Manuscript Production and Scribal Practices in Italy at the End of the Middle Ages' (Ph.D. diss., New York University, 1985).

—— and ZIINO, AGOSTINO (eds.), *The Lucca Codex (Codice Mancini). Introductory Study and Facsimile Edition* (Ars Nova, 1; Lucca, 1990).

NOBLE, JEREMY, 'New Light on Josquin's Benefices', in Lowinsky and Blackburn (eds.), *Josquin des Prez: Proceedings*, 76–102.

NOSOW, ROBERT, 'The Florid and Equal-Discantus Motet Styles of Fifteenth-Century Italy' (Ph.D. diss., University of North Carolina, Chapel Hill, 1992).

NUGENT, GEORGE, 'The Jacquet Motets and their Authors' (Ph.D. diss., Princeton University, 1973).

O'REGAN, NOEL, ' "Blessed with the Holy Father's Entertainment": Roman Ceremonial Music as Experienced by the Irish Earls in Rome, 1608', *Irish Musical Studies*, 2: *Music and the Church* (1991), 41–61.

—— 'The Early Polychoral Music of Orlando di Lasso: New Light from Roman Sources', *Acta musicologica*, 56 (1985), 234–51.

—— *Institutional Patronage in Post-Tridentine Rome: Music at Santissima Trinità dei Pellegrini 1550–1650* (Royal Musical Association Monographs, 7; London, 1995).

—— 'Palestrina and the Oratory of Santissima Trinità dei Pellegrini', in *Atti del II Convegno internazionale di studi palestriniani* (Palestrina, 1991), 95–121.

OSTHOFF, HELMUTH, *Josquin Desprez*, 2 vols. (Tutzing, 1962–5).

OWENS, JESSIE ANN, 'Music Historiography and the Definition of "Renaissance" ', *Notes*, 47 (1990), 205–30.

PALESTRINA, GIOVANNI PIERLUIGI DA, *Omnis pulchritudo domini*, ed. V. Mortari (Rome, [1950]).

—— *Pope Marcellus Mass*, ed. Lewis Lockwood (New York, 1975).

—— *Werke*, ed. Fr. X. Haberl *et al.* (Leipzig, 1862–1903).

PALUMBO, JANET, 'The Foligno Fragment: A Reassessment of Three Polyphonic Glorias, ca. 1400', *JAMS* 40 (1987), 169–209.

PARTNER, PETER, 'The "Budget" of the Roman Church in the Renaissance Period', in Ernest F. Jacob (ed.), *Italian Renaissance Studies: A Tribute to the Late Cecilia M. Ady* (London, 1960), 256–77.

—— *The Pope's Men* (Oxford, 1990).

—— *Renaissance Rome* (Berkeley, 1976).

PASTOR, LUDWIG VON, *Geschichte der Päpste seit dem Ausgang des Mittelalters*, iii: *Geschichte der Päpste im Zeitalter der Renaissance von der Wahl Innozenz VIII. bis zum Tode Julius II. Erste Abteilung: Innozenz VIII. und Alexander VI.* (Freiburg i. Br., 1924).

[PATRIZI, AGOSTINO], *Rituum ecclesiasticorum sive sacrarum cerimoniarum .S.S. romanae ecclesiae libri tres*, ed. Cristoforo Marcello (Venice, 1516; facs. edn. Ridgewood, NJ, 1965).

PERKINS, LEEMAN, 'Notes bibliographiques au sujet de l'ancien fond musical de L'Église de Saint Louis des Français à Rome', *Fontes Artis Musicae*, 16 (1969), 57–71.

PERZ, MIROSLAW, 'Il carattere internazionale delle opere di Mikolaj Radomski', *MD* 41 (1987), 153–9.

—— 'The Lvov Fragments: A Source for Works by Dufay, Josquin, Petrus de Domarto, and Petrus de Grudencz in 15th-Century Poland', *TVNM* 36 (1986), 26–51.

—— 'Polish Contributions to the Problem of Polyphonic Repertories in the 14th and 15th Centuries', in *Atti del XIV Congresso della Società Internazionale di Musicologia (Bologna 1987)*, i: *Round Tables* (Turin, 1990), 175–81.

—— 'The Structure of the Lost Manuscript from the National Library in Warsaw, No. 378 (WarN 378)', in Albert Clement and Eric Jas (eds.), *From Ciconia to Sweelinck: Donum Natalicium Willem Elders* (Chloe: Beihefte zum Daphnis, 21; Amsterdam, 1995), 1–11.

—— (ed.), *Sources of Polyphony up to c. 1500: Facsimiles* (Antiquitates Musicae in Polonia, 13; Graz and Warsaw, 1973).

—— (ed.), *Sources of Polyphony up to c. 1500: Transcriptions* (Antiquitates Musicae in Polonia, 14; Graz and Warsaw, 1976).

PETROBELLI, PIERLUIGI, 'La musica nelle cattedrali e nella città', *Storia della cultura veneta*, 5 vols. (Vicenza, 1976–), ii, pt. 2.

PFEIFFER, RUDOLF, *History of Classical Scholarship from the Beginnings to the End of the Hellenistic Age* (Oxford, 1968).

PICKER, MARTIN, 'The Career of Marbrianus de Orto (ca. 1450–1529)', in *Collectanea II*, 1994), 529–57.

PIRRO, ANDRÉ, 'Leo X and Music', *Musical Quarterly*, 21 (1935), 1–35.

PIRROTTA, NINO, 'Church Polyphony apropos of a New Fragment at Foligno', in Harold Powers (ed.), *Studies in Music History: Essays for Oliver Strunk* (Princeton, 1968), 113–26; Italian reprint with a 'post scriptum', 'Polifonia da chiesa: a proposito di un frammento a Foligno', in *Musica tra medioevo e rinascimento* (Turin, 1984), 115–29.

—— 'Music and Cultural Tendencies in 15th-Century Italy', *JAMS* 19 (1966), 127–61 (Italian edn., 'Musica e orientamenti culturali nell'Italia del Quattrocento', in *Musica tra medioevo e rinascimento* (Turin, 1984), 213–49).

—— 'Zacarus Musicus', *Quadrivium*, 12 (1971), 153–75.

PLANCHART, ALEJANDRO ENRIQUE, 'The Early Career of Guillaume Du Fay', *JAMS* 46 (1993), 341–68.

—— 'Guillaume Du Fay's Benefices and his Relationship to the Court of Burgundy', *EMH* 8 (1988), 117–71.

—— 'Parts with Words and without Words: The Evidence for Multiple Texts in Fifteenth-Century Masses', in Stanley Boorman (ed.), *Studies in the Performance of Late Medieval Music* (Cambridge, 1983), 237–42.

—— 'What's in a Name? Reflections on Some Works of Guillaume Du Fay', *EM* 16 (1988), 165–75.

PLÖCHEL, WILLIBALD, *Geschichte der Kirchenrecht* (Vienna, 1953–4).

POLC, JAROSLAV, *De origine festi visitationis B.M.V.* (Corona Lateranensis, 9A; Rome, 1967).

POPULUS, BERNARD, 'La Psallette de Langres; notes et documents sur la musique à la Cathédrale avant la Révolution', *Bulletin de la Société historique et archéologique de Langres*, 2 (1946).

PRIZER, WILLIAM F., 'Music at the Court of the Sforza: The Birth and Death of a Musical Center', *MD* 43 (1989), 141–94.

RASMUSSEN, NEILS KROGH, '*Maiestas Pontificia*: A Liturgical Reading of Étienne Dupérac's Engraving of the *Capella Sixtina* from 1578', *Analecta Romana Instituti Danici*, 12 (1983), 109–48.

REANEY, GILBERT (ed.), *Early Fifteenth Century Music*, vi (CMM 11; American Institute of Musicology, Stuttgart, 1977).

REES, OWEN, 'Guerrero's *L'homme armé* Masses and their Models', *EMH* 12 (1993), 19–54.

REGIS, JOHANNES, *Opera Omnia*, ed. Cornelius Lindenburg (CMM 9; American Institute of Musicology, 1956).

REY-COURTEL, ANNE-LISE, 'L'Entourage d'Anglic Grimoard, Cardinal d'Albano (1366–1388)', in *Genèse et débuts du grand schisme d'occident, 1362–1394*, Proceedings of the Conference held in Avignon, 1978, ed. Jean Favier (Colloques Internationaux du Centre National de la Recherche Scientifique, 586; Paris, 1980), 59–64.

REYNOLDS, CHRISTOPHER A., The Origins of San Pietro B 80 and the Development of a Roman Sacred Repertory', *EMH* 1 (1981), 257–304.

—— *Papal Patronage and the Music of St. Peter's, 1380–1513* (Berkeley, 1995).

Le Roman de Fauvel in the edition of Mesire Chaillou de Pesstain: A Reproduction in Facsimile of the Complete Manuscript Paris, Bibliothèque Nationale, Fonds Français 146. Introduction by Edward H. Roesner, François Avril, and Nancy Freeman Regalado (New York, 1990).

ROSTIROLLA, GIANCARLO, 'La Cappella Giulia in San Pietro negli anni del magistero di Giovanni Pierluigi da Palestrina', in *Atti del Convegno di studi palestriniani* (Palestrina, 1977), 99–283.

ROTH, ADALBERT, 'Die Entstehung des ältesten Chorbuches mit polyphoner Musik der päpstlichen Kapelle: Città del Vaticano, Biblioteca Apostolica Vaticana, Fondo Cappella Sistina, Ms. 35', paper read at the conference *Die Entstehung einer musikalischen Quelle im 15. und im 16. Jahrhundert*, Herzog August Bibliothek, Wolfenbüttel, 13–17 Sept. 1992 (in press).

—— 'L'homme armé, le doubté turcq, L'ordre de la toison d'or: Zur "Begleitmusik" der letzten grossen Kreuzzugsbewegung nach den Fall von Konstantinopel', in Detlev von Altenberg, Jörg Jarmut, and Hans-Hugo Steinhoff (eds.), *Festen und Feiern im Mittelalter* (Sigmaringen, 1991), 469–79.

—— 'Napoli o Firenze? Dove sono stati compilati i manoscritti CS 14 e CS 51?', in Piero Gargiulo (ed.), *La musica a Firenze al tempo di Lorenzo il Magnifico: Congresso Internazionale di Studi, Firenze 15–17 giugno 1992* (Florence, 1993), 69–100.

ROTH, ADALBERT, ' "Primus in Petri aede Sixtus perpetuae harmoniae cantores introduxit": alcune osservazioni sul patronato musicale di Sisto IV', in Massimo Miglio *et al.* (eds.), *Un pontificato ed una città: Sisto IV (1471–1484). Atti del convegno Roma 3–7 dicembre 1984* (Istituto storico italiano per il Medio Evo, Studi storici, fasc. 154–62; Rome, 1986), 217–41.

— 'La storia della Cappella Pontificia nel Quattrocento rispecchiata nel Fondo Camerale I dell'Archivio di Stato di Roma', in Bianca Maria Antolini, Arnaldo Morelli, and Vera Vita Spagnuolo (eds.), *La musica a Roma attraverso le fonti d'archivio. Atti del Convegno internazionale Roma 4–7 giugno 1992* (Lucca, 1994), 446–51.

— *Studien zum frühen Repertoire der päpstlichen Kapelle unter dem Pontifikat Sixtus' IV. (1471-1484): Die Chorbücher 14 und 51 des Fondo Cappella Sistina der Biblioteca Apostolica Vaticana* (Capellae Apostolicae Sixtinaeque Collectanea Acta Monumenta, 1; Vatican City, 1991).

— 'Zur Datierung der frühen Chorbücher der päpstlichen Kapelle', in Ludwig Finscher (ed.), *Quellenstudien zur Musik der Renaissance*, 2: *Datierung und Filiation von Musikhandschriften der Josquin-Zeit* (Wolfenbütteler Forschungen, 26; Wolfenbüttel, 1983), 239–68.

— 'Zur "Reform" der päpstlichen Kapelle unter dem Pontifikat Sixtus' IV. (1471-1484)', in Jorg O. Fichte, Karl-Heinz Göller, and Bernhard Schimmelpfennig (eds.), *Zusammenhänge, Einflüsse, Wirkungen: Kongreßakten zum ersten Symposion der Mediävisten in Tübingen, 1984* (Berlin and New York, 1986), 168–95.

SALAVILLE, S., 'L'Origine avignonnaise de la messe "ad tollendum schisma" ', *L'Année théologique*, 3 (1942), 117–22.

SANDERS, ERNEST, and LEFFERTS, PETER (eds.), *English Music for Mass and Office* (I) (PMFC 16; Monaco, 1983).

SASAKI, TSUTOMU, 'The Dating of the Aosta Manuscript from Watermarks', *Acta musicologica*, 64 (1992), 1–16.

SAVINI, F., *Septem dioecesis aprutinensis* (Rome, 1912).

SCHERING, ARNOLD, 'Musikalisches aus Joh. Burkhards Liber Notarum', in *Festschrift Johannes Wolf* (Berlin, 1929), 171–5.

SCHIMMELPFENNIG, BERNHARD, 'Die Funktion der Cappella Sistina im Zeremoniell der Renaissancepäpste', in *Collectanea II*, 123–74.

— 'Der Papst als Territorialherr im 15. Jahrhundert', in Ferdinand Seibt and Winfried Eberhardt (eds.), *Europa 1500. Integrationsprozesse im Widerstreit. Staaten, Regionen, Personen-Verbände, Christenheit* (Stuttgart, 1986), 84–95.

— *Die Zeremonienbücher der römischen Kurie im Mittelalter* (Bibliothek des deutschen historischen Instituts in Rom, 10; Tübingen, 1973).

SCHMITT, C., 'La Position du card. Leonard de Giffoni OFM dans le conflict du Grand Schisme d'Occident', *Archivium franciscanum historicum*, 50 (1957), 273–331; 51 (1958), 25–72, 410–72.

SCHRADE, LEO, 'The Cycle of the Ordinarium Missae', in Higinio Anglés *et al.* (eds.), *In Memoriam Jacques Handschin* (Strasburg, 1962), 87–96.

SCHULER, MANFRED, 'Die Musik in Konstanz während des Konzils, 1414–1418', *Acta musicologica*, 38 (1966), 150–68.

—— 'Zur Geschichte der Kapelle Papst Eugens IV', *Acta musicologica*, 40 (1968), 220–7.

—— 'Zur Geschichte der Kapelle Papst Martins V', *AfMw* 25 (1968), 30–45.

SEAY, ALBERT, 'An "Ave maris stella" by Johannes Stochem', *Revue belge de musicologie*, 11 (1957), 93–108.

—— 'Ugolino of Orvieto, Theorist and Composer', *MD* 9 (1955), 111–66.

SETTON, KENNETH M., *The Papacy and the Levant (1204–1571)*, ii: *The Fifteenth Century* (Memoirs of the American Philosophical Society, 127; Philadelphia, 1978).

SHEARMAN, JOHN, 'La costruzione della cappella e la prima decorazione al tempo di Sisto IV', in *La Cappella Sistina: I primi restauri, la scoperta del colore* (Novara, 1986).

SHERR, RICHARD, 'A Biographical Miscellany: Josquin, Tinctoris, Obrecht, Brumel', in Siegfied Gmeinwieser *et al.* (eds.), *Musicologia Humana: Studies in Honor of Warren and Ursula Kirkendale* (Florence, 1994), 65–72.

—— 'Competence and Incompetence in the Papal Chapel in the Age of Palestrina', *EM* 22 (1994), 606–30.

—— 'The Diary of the Papal Singer Giovanni Antonio Merlo', *Analecta musicologica*, 23 (1985), 75–128.

—— 'From the Diary of a 16th-Century Papal Singer', *Current Musicology*, 25 (1978), 83–98 at 91–4.

—— '*Illibata Dei Virgo nutrix* and Josquin's Roman Style', *JAMS* 41 (1988), 434–64.

—— 'The Membership of the Chapels of Louis XII and Anne de Bretagne in the Years Preceding their Deaths', *Journal of Musicology*, 6 (1988), 60–82.

—— 'Music and the Renaissance Papacy: The Papal Choir and the Fondo Capella Sistina', in Grafton (ed.), *Rome Reborn*, 199–223.

—— 'Notes on Some Papal Documents in Paris', *Studi musicali*, 12 (1983), 5–16.

—— 'The Papal Chapel ca. 1492–1513 and its Polyphonic Sources' (Ph.D. diss., Princeton University, 1975).

—— *Papal Music Manuscripts in the Late Fifteenth and Early Sixteenth Centuries* (Renaissance Manuscript Studies, 5; Neuhausen-Stuttgart, 1996).

—— 'The Performance of Josquin's *L'homme armé* Masses', *EM* 19 (1991), 261–8.

—— 'The Singers of the Papal Chapel and Liturgical Ceremonies in the Early Sixteenth Century: Some Documentary Evidence', in Paul A. Ramsey (ed.), *Rome in the Renaissance: The City and the Myth* (Medieval and Renaissance Texts and Studies 18; Binghamton, NY, 1982), 249–64.

—— 'The "Spanish Nation" in the Papal Chapel, 1492–1521', *EM* 20 (1992), 601–9.

STÄBLEIN, BRUNO (ed.), *Hymnen I. Die mittelalterlichen Hymnenmelodien des Abendlandes* (MMMA 1; Kassel, 1956).

—— and LANDWEHR-MELNICKI, MARGARETA (eds.), *Die Gesänge des altrömischen Graduale Vat. lat. 5319* (MMMA 2; Kassel, 1970).

STÄBLEIN-HARDER, HANNA (ed.), *Fourteenth-Century Mass Music in France* (CMM 29; American Institute of Musicology, 1962).

STAEHELIN, MARTIN, 'Zum Schicksal des alten Musikalien-Fonds von San Luigi dei Francesi in Rom', *Fontes Artis Musicae*, 17 (1970), 120–7.

STARR, PAMELA F., 'Communication', *Plainsong and Medieval Music*, 2 (1993), 215–16.

—— 'Josquin, Rome, and a Case of Mistaken Identity', *Journal of Musicology*, 15 (1997), 43–65.

—— 'Music and Music Patronage at the Papal Court, 1447–1464' (Ph.D. diss., Yale University, 1987).

—— 'Rome as the Centre of the Universe: Papal Grace and Music Patronage', *EMH* 11 (1992), 223–62.

—— *Storia della Cappella Pontificia, dal Concilio di Costanza al pontificato di Giulio II* (forthcoming).

—— 'Towards the Cappella Sistina: A Profile of the *Cappella Pontificia* during the Pontificates of Nicolas V, Calixtus III, Pius II, and Paul II (1447–1471)', in *Collectanea II*, 451–75.

STEVENSON, ROBERT, 'European Music in 16th-Century Guatemala', *Musical Quarterly*, 50 (1964), 341–52.

—— *Renaissance and Baroque Musical Sources in the Americas* (Washington, DC, 1970).

—— *Spanish Cathedral Music in the Golden Age* (Berkeley, 1961).

STONE, ANNE, 'Writing Rhythm in Late Medieval Italy: Notation and Musical Style in the Manuscript Modena, Biblioteca Estense, Alpha.M.5.24' (Ph.D. diss., Harvard University, 1994).

STROHM, REINHARD, 'Centre and Periphery: Mainstream and Provincial Music', in Tess Knighton and David Fallows (eds.), *Companion to Medieval and Renaissance Music* (New York, 1992), 55–9.

—— 'Ein englischer Ordinariumssatz des 14. Jahrhunderts in Italien', *Musikforschung*, 18 (1965), 178–81.

—— 'Filippotto da Caserta, ovvero i francesi in Lombardia', in Fabrizio Della Seta and Franco Piperno (eds.), *In cantu et in sermone: A Nino Pirrotta nel suo 80° compleanno* (Florence, 1989), 65–74.

—— 'Magister Egardus and Other Italo-Flemish Contacts', *L'Ars nova italiana del Trecento*, 6 (1992), 41–68.

—— *Music in Late Medieval Bruges* (Oxford, 1985).

—— 'Neue Quellen zur liturgischen Mehrstimmigkeit des Mittelalters in Italien', *Rivista italiana di musicologia*, 1 (1966), 77–87.

—— *The Rise of European Music* (Cambridge, 1993).

—— 'Vom Internationalen Stil zur Ars Nova? Probleme einer Analogie', *MD* 41 (1987), 5–13.

STRUNK, OLIVER, 'Church Polyphony apropos of a New Fragment at Grottaferrata', *L'Ars nova italiana del Trecento*, 3 (1970), 305–13.

—— 'Guglielmo Gonzaga and Palestrina's *Missa Dominicalis*', *Musical Quarterly*, 33 (1947), 228–39; repr. in id., *Essays on Music in the Western World* (New York, 1974), 94–107.

—— *Source Readings in Music History* (New York, 1950; repr., 5 vols., New York, 1965).

SUMMERS, WILLIAM, 'Fourteenth-Century English Music: A Review of Three Recent Publications', *Journal of Musicology*, 8 (1990), 118–39.

— 'Medieval Polyphonic Music in the Dartmouth College Library: An Introductory Study of Ms. 002387', in Bernd Edelmann and Manfred Hermann Schmid (eds.), *Alte im Neuen: Festschrift Theodor Göllner zum 65. Geburtstag* (Tutzing, 1995), 113–30.

— (ed.), *English Fourteenth-Century Polyphony: Facsimile Edition of Sources Notated in Score* (Tutzing, 1983).

SWANSON, R. N., *Universities, Academics and the Great Schism* (Cambridge Studies in Medieval Life and Thought, 12; Cambridge, 1979).

TINCTORIS, JOHANNES, *Liber de arte contrapuncti*, in his *Opera theoretica*, ed. Albert Seay, 2 vols. (CSM 22; American Insitute of Musicology, 1975–8), ii. 11–157.

TOMASELLO, ANDREW, *Music and Ritual at Papal Avignon 1309–1403* (Ann Arbor, 1983).

UGOLINO OF ORVIETO, *Declaratio musicae disciplinae*, ed. Albert Seay (CSM 7; Rome, 1959–62).

Uppsala, Universitetsbiblioteket, Vokalmusik i handskrift 76b, introduction by Thomas G. MacCracken (Renaissance Music in Facsimile, 20; New York, 1986).

VAN, GUILLAUME DE, 'An Inventory of the Manuscript Bologna, Liceo Musicale, Q 15 (*olim* 37)', *MD* 2 (1948), 231–57.

VAN DIJK, STEPHEN J. P., *The Sources of the Modern Roman Liturgy*, 2 vols. (Leiden, 1963).

— and WALKER, JOAN HAZELDEN (eds.), *The Ordinal of the Papal Court from Innocent III to Boniface VIII and Related Documents* (Spicilegium Friburgense, 22; Fribourg, 1975).

VERGER, JACQUES, 'L'Entourage du cardinal Pierre de Monteruc (1356–1385)', *Mélanges de l'École Française de Rome. Moyen Age – Temps Modernes*, 85 (1973), 515–46.

VINCENET, *The Collected Works*, ed. Bertran E. Davis (RRMMA 9–10; Madison, 1978).

VITRY, PHILIPPE DE, *Ars nova*, ed. G. Reaney, A. Gilles, J. Maillard (CSM 8; American Institute of Musicology, 1964).

VOCI, ANNA MARIA, *Nord o sud? Note per la storia del medioevale Palatium Apostolicum apud sanctum Petrum e delle sue capelle* (Capellae Apostolicae Sixtinaeque Collectanea Acta Monumenta, 2; Vatican City, 1992).

— and ROTH, ADALBERT, 'Anmerkungen zur Baugeschichte der alten und der neuen *capella magna* des apostolischen Palastes bei Sankt Peter', in *Collectanea II*, 13–102.

WARD, TOM R., 'The Polyphonic Office Hymn and the Liturgy of Fifteenth-Century Italy', *MD* 26 (1972), 161–88.

— *The Polyphonic Office Hymn, 1400–1520: A Descriptive Catalogue* (Renaissance Manuscript Studies 3; Neuhausen, 1980).

WARMINGTON, FLYNN, '*Abeo semper Fortuna regressum*: Evidence for the Venetian Origin of the Manuscripts Cappella Sistina 14 and 51', unpublished paper presented at the 22nd Conference on Medieval and Renaissance Music, Glasgow, 10 July 1994.

WATHEY, ANDREW, 'The Motets of Philippe de Vitry and the Fourteenth-Century Renaissance', *EMH* 12 (1993), 119–50.

—— 'The Peace of 1360–1369 and Anglo-French Musical Relations', *EMH* 9 (1990), 129–74.

WEBER, WILLIAM, *The Rise of Musical Classics in Eighteenth-Century England: A Study in Canon, Ritual, and Ideology* (Oxford, 1992).

WELKER, LORENZ, *Musik am Oberrhein im späten Mittelalter: Die Handschrift Strasbourg, olim Bibliothèque de la ville, C.22* (Habilitationsschrift, Basle, 1993).

WELTSCH, RUBEN, *Archbishop John of Jenstein (1348–1400): Papalism, Humanism and Reform in Pre-Hussite Prague* (The Hague and Paris, 1968).

WESTFALL, CARROLL W., *In this Most Perfect Paradise: Alberti, Nicholas V and the Invention of Conscious Urban Planning in Rome 1447–55* (London, 1974).

WOOD, DIANA, *Clement VI: The Pontificate and Ideas of an Avignon Pope* (Cambridge, 1989).

WRIGHT, CRAIG, 'Dufay at Cambrai: Discoveries and Revisions', *JAMS* 28 (1975), 175–229.

—— 'Du Fay's *Nuper rosarum flores* and King Solomon's Temple', *JAMS* 47 (1994), 395–441.

—— *Music at the Court of Burgundy 1364–1419* (Henryville, Ottawa, and Binningen, 1979).

YOUNG, GEORGE F., *The Medici* (New York, 1930).

ZACOUR, NORMAN P., 'Papal Regulation of Cardinals' Households in the Fourteenth Century', *Speculum*, 50 (1975), 434–55.

ZAGER, DANIEL, 'The Polyphonic Latin Hymns of Orlando di Lasso: A Liturgical and Repertorial Study' (Ph.D. diss., University of Minnesota, 1985).

ZIINO, AGOSTINO, ' "Magister Antonius dictus Zacharias de Teramo": alcuni date e molte ipotesi', *Rivista italiana di musicologia*, 14 (1979), 311–48.

—— 'Precisazioni su un frammento di musica francese trecentesca conservato nell'Archivio Comunale di Cortona', in I. Deug-su and E. Menestò (eds.), *Università e beni culturali: il contributo degli studi medievali e umanistici* (Florence, 1981), 351–8.

—— (ed.), *Il Codice T. III.2 (The Codex T.III.2), Torino, Biblioteca Nazionale Universitaria, Studio introduttivo ed edizione in facsimile a cura di Agostino Ziino (Introductory Study and Facsimile Edition by Agostino Ziino)* (Ars Nova, 3; Lucca, 1994).

ZUTSHI, PATRICK N. R., *Original Papal Letters in England (1305–1415)* (Vatican City, 1990).

INDEX

Index compiled by Frank Pert